MUSIC'S MONISMS

MUSIC'S MONISMS

Disarticulating Modernism

DANIEL ALBRIGHT

With a foreword by Alexander Rehding

THE UNIVERSITY OF CHICAGO PRESS
Chicago & London

The University of Chicago Press, Chicago 60637
The University of Chicago Press, Ltd., London

Published 2021
Printed in the United States of America

30 29 28 27 26 25 24 23 22 21 1 2 3 4 5

ISBN-13: 978-0-226-79122-7 (cloth)
ISBN-13: 978-0-226-79136-4 (e-book)
DOI: https://doi.org/10.7208/chicago/9780226791364.001.0001

Library of Congress Cataloging-in-Publication Data

Names: Albright, Daniel, 1945–2015, author. | Rehding, Alexander, writer of foreword.
Title: Music's monisms : disarticulating modernism / Daniel Albright ; with a foreword by Alexander Rehding.
Description: Chicago : University of Chicago Press, 2021. | Includes bibliographical references and index.
Identifiers: LCCN 2021012765 | ISBN 9780226791227 (cloth) | ISBN 9780226791364 (ebook)
Subjects: LCSH: Music—Philosophy and aesthetics. | Monism.
Classification: LCC ML3845 .A42 2021 | DDC 781.1—dc23
LC record available at https://lccn.loc.gov/2021012765

♾ This paper meets the requirements of ANSI/NISO Z39.48-1992 (Permanence of Paper).

CONTENTS

MUSICAL EXAMPLES

FOREWORD

Daniel Albright

Collector, Critic, Fancier

Alexander Rehding
Fanny Peabody Professor of Music, Harvard University

DANIEL ALBRIGHT HAD REMARKABLE HANDS. ONE DOES NOT have to believe in the pseudoscience of physiognomy to be fascinated by their expressivity. Anyone who met him will remember them: long, slender fingers, nails always immaculately manicured. These exquisite—and exquisitely maintained—hands stood out because they contrasted oddly with the rest of his appearance, about which he did not seem to care a great deal. His hair was rarely cut. His glasses were perfunctory. His dress sense was best described as academic shabby chic, consisting usually of a blue blazer over a t-shirt paired with blue jeans. But it seems that he rarely missed a session with his manicurist.

Those meticulously filed and polished fingernails were nothing short of mesmerizing. In conversation he made excellent use of them to underscore his points. He would use his fingers to punctuate a well-made argument with great dramatic flourish. In seminars he would place his elbows on the table, hands at a ninety-degree angle, and point the fingers of both hands toward the person or persons whose points he was picking up, often rotating his wrists from one person to the other in the process. No one would have been the least bit surprised if laser beams had shot out of those fingers.

Small wonder, then, that a rhetoric of deixis features strongly in Albright's arguments. He did not live to hold this printed book in his hands, but his unique brand of deixis, the art of showing and of pointing out, is the hallmark of *Music's Monisms*. Ostensibly, this book is about nothing: namelessness, nonaction, nobody, nonrepresentation, nonexpressiveness. We are, of course, talking about the Great Nothing here, the favored topic of Modernism. But Albright's arguments never deal with big philosophical issues in the abstract. Instead, he beckons us to think about them in the most concrete terms, by pointing us from artwork to artwork, referring us from author to author, indicating poem after poem, until he finally puts his finger—or rather, guides us to put our finger—on exactly what these nothings are about.

Albright cites Claude Lévi-Strauss's observation that abstract art is never truly abstract, and he concurs: "I know what he means." Of course he does. There is never an abstract thought in Albright's work. Even when dealing with the most cerebral issues, he constantly points us back to the boundless ground of concreteness.

He could do this because of his encyclopedic knowledge of literature and music. I mean this almost literally. I first met Daniel Albright around 2004, shortly after we both joined the faculty at Harvard University, and first had the opportunity to talk to him during an interdisciplinary seminar titled Music and Experience. It was impossible not to be fascinated by what he had to say. Over the years it became clear to me that Albright had read and listened to everything. In fact, I remember only a single occasion when I mentioned a literary work that he had not read, and it was a fairly obscure title: Hans Henny Jahnn's *Fluß ohne Ufer* (1949–50). This sprawling, two-thousand-page monster of a novel, only excerpts of which have been translated into English, is probably the best of the B list of German Modernist novels. With its abrupt scene changes, its focus on music, and its specially composed musical examples firmly embedded in the text, I am sure Albright would have found much in it to enjoy. But in a sense, this lone gap in his knowledge served merely to highlight the comprehensiveness of his grasp of literature, in the same way that advertisers sometimes admit to tiny flaws in their product in order to underscore how impeccable everything else is.

Testing the limits of Albright's knowledge became something of a parlor game. I never managed to come up with a piece of music that Albright did not know. He would lovingly speak about the widest range of music, effortlessly moving from Josquin's *Missa Pange lingua* to Percy Grainger's *Free Music for Four Theremins* and to Schoenberg's *Dance of the Butchers*. In this book, too, he gives us a little flavor of his catholic musical tastes. We flit between Mozart's little-known early opera *Betulia liberata* (1771) and Pauline Oliveros's sonic meditations, between Giacomo Carissimi's mid-seventeenth-century oratorio *Vanitas vanitatum* and Poulenc's opera *Les mamelles de Tirésias* (1947), between Georg Benda's melodrama *Pygmalion* (1779) and Benjamin Britten's big-band number *The Spider and the Fly* (1939), between Emmanuel Chabrier's opera *L'étoile* (1877) and György Ligeti's orchestral work *Clocks and Clouds* (1972). This selection, a dazzling array of compositions by anyone's standards, conveys a good sense of what a conversation with him was like. Many more examples could be cited here, and this list is paralleled by a similarly improbable list of literary titles. There was never a moment in which he would not find the perfect example from music or literature to elegantly sum up a given situation.

It would be easy to be pretentious about this impressive range of references at his fingertips, but Albright never was. He was driven by the love and the passion—in a word, by the obsession—that is at the core of the psychological makeup of the collector. The collector, not unlike the character of the cross-dressing Baba from *The Rake's Progress*, about whom Albright writes eloquently in his Stravinsky chapter, likes to talk about the things he has gathered, hold them up, admire them. But he is never a snapper-up of unconsidered trifles. As Susan Stewart reminds us, what is characteristic about the collector is the act of curation, in which objects are not amassed ad infinitum but deliberately filled out with a view toward achieving completion of a finite collection, such as is necessary to document a particular narrative and tell a particular story. In this sense, Albright displays his collection of literature and music lovingly in front of us in order to weave a dense web of references to which he can point. Armed with these techniques, which he learned from T. S. Eliot and Ezra Pound, he takes us by the hand to guide us confidently from one object to the next, charting paths that the rest of us would never have found on our own.

The references often come fast and furious. Within a few sentences we traverse the space from Brecht to Rossini, to Nietzsche and Socrates, to Smetana. Or from Villier de l'Isle-Adam to Piranesi, to Borges, to Perrault, to Nabokov, to Beckett and Auden. Albright cherished these fast-paced connections, which can almost appear like an endless, goalless, shapeless web of Renaissance correspondences. But they are never without purpose. Just as the bumbling hero of Joseph von Eichendorff's novella *From the Life of a Good-for-Nothing* (1826) realizes upon returning from Italy that nothing that happened to him on his meandering trip south was ever an accident or a coincidence, so everything in Albright's casual and chatty prose appears scrupulously planned and laid out. For instance, when he heaps lavish but seemingly unnecessary praise on Ashbery's translation of Rimbaud, this is in fact a carefully calculated legerdemain, which allows him to transition to the next section. Nothing is ever arbitrary in Albright's deictic web of references. Is it a surprise, though, that he is deeply attracted to Maeterlinck's "random inevitable"? To W. H. Auden's celebration of the arbitrary?

Oftentimes Albright encourages us to imagine what might have been. Had *The Rake's Progress* been written ten years later, in the 1960s, Albright conjectures, Baba's part might have been written as aleatoric music. In a similar vein, he may offer some imaginative suggestions as to how the works he describes for us came about in the first place by reminding us what their poets and composers remembered. Stravinsky may indeed have "remembered" Monteverdi's "Possente spirto" while composing parts of *The Rake's Progress*. In his *Serres chaudes*, Maeterlinck may indeed have had a line in mind from Tristan l'Hermite's poem *La grotte*. Debussy's *Sirènes* may well have remembered a line from Poe's *The Fall of the House of Usher*, and Auden may be remembering an allusion to Goddeck's *Das Buch vom Es*. We will never know for sure. But these remembrances, connections, allusions that make up Albright's amicable and less angst-ridden version of the "anxiety of influence" are always razor-sharp and convincing. They have to be, because they exist in Albright's own vivid imagination; they form an inextricable part of his web of correspondences.

Sometimes, in these imaginary games, it seems that Albright enters into friendly competition with the authors he is discussing. Are the adjectives he uses when he describes Wagner's music—"viscid," "gloppy"—a little more extravagant because they occur in the direct vicinity of Baudelaire? Is he not gently arm-wrestling with Rimbaud when he tops the poet's "Chinese, Hottentots, Gypsies, nincompoops, hyenas" with his own "cheerleaders, tax accountants, werewolves, tattooed men"? Who can find terms that are more outlandish, more absurd, more freakish?

It is perhaps in his witty summaries where this urge toward one-upmanship comes to the fore most clearly, a desire to pile up descriptions that become ever more drastic, ever more pithy, ever more polished—until he can hold them up and they beam with the shiny succinctness of the aphorism. Not only are Wagnerian leitmotifs a nametag that reads "Enforced Anonymity," but he feels compelled to take this bon mot one step further and act it out: "Hi, I'm—don't ask, no matter what."

Albright had an unfailing sense of the grotesque, and he never took himself too seriously. It seems safe to say that only in Albright's work would we encounter Moses at the burning bush as slapstick. Only here would Mr. Potato Head be placed right next to Greek tragedy. Albright's magically funny world is full of bearded Aphrodites, smashed Kabuki, and zeppelins lifting knights up to Empyrion. Here we learn about the world beginning and ending in clucks and farts, and about Gilbert and Sullivan in hell. Albright clearly relished the absurdity of such irreverent juxtapositions. He liked, in his more dramatic moments, to raise a manicured middle finger to academic decorum.

He was a master of the metaphor. The literal meaning of this word—"transfer," "carrying across"—describes precisely the definition of criticism that he offers in this book: the effort, or rather the struggle, to remove an object of art from the context in which it exists and deposit it in another. This can be the transfer of a piece of music from the concert hall to a set of theoretical principles. But the transfer can also indicate its placement within his carefully curated collection of related art objects, which allows us to follow his indications along the path he has chosen for us.

His pronounced love of the drastic, in every sense, means that he thinks of musical works not as silent scores, but as sounding objects. Whenever he talks about a piece of music, he considers aspects of its imaginary performance. He conjures up the acoustics of the newly built Coventry Cathedral during the premiere of Britten's *War Requiem* in 1962. He reads Mélisande's lines in contrasting interpretations (and he would doubtless have acted them out in a spoken version of this chapter). He mentally dresses and outfits a scintillating Kundry in his ideal staging of *Parsifal*. He considers Stravinsky's *Symphony of Psalms* from the perspective of its breath marks. Music is never an abstract pattern of notes; it is always something that we sing with our inner voice or hear at least with our inner ear.

While I greatly admire Albright's hands, it was really his ears that were the most fascinating part of his anatomy. So many of his fresh observations are so to the point that it is hard to ever disentangle our hearings from his. Yes, I believe he is spot-on in his speculation that the initial chords of Mendelssohn's *A Midsummer Night's Dream* spell out the opening incantation of all fairy tales: "Es war einmal." I will probably never listen to this beautifully scored plagal cadence with the same ears again. Similarly, I find it entirely plausible that Albright really got his understanding of the song of a nightingale from the iconic field recording that forms part of Ottorino Respighi's symphonic poem *The Pines of Rome*. (I doubt, however, that many other people did, as he politely surmises.) And I will at least try to hear water, certainly French water, as speaking a language of irregular rhythms across major seconds, as he wittily concludes from his analyses of Debussy's and Dukas's watery musics.

What Albright demonstrates so effortlessly and expertly is nothing other than what Coleridge's *Biographia literaria* called *fancy*, a term that Albright invokes in his Britten chapter. Coleridge is conflicted about this quality: dealing with fixities and definites, fancy is a much more basic faculty than the imagination—it is tied more closely to the external world; it does not spread its wings to lift off but must observe the law of associations. It is, however, emancipated from time and space, and as such it is capable of reorganizing the elements of experience. We can see where this is going: the Modernists begin to value fancy over imagination, and it quickly advanced to become the major aesthetic mode of Modernism.

The collector, the critic, the fancier: these are probably not the worst ways to describe Daniel Albright's physiognomy as a writer. In each instance, invisible hands place—or rearrange—objects within a new imaginary space, to let them tell their story. We merely need to be shown the starting point and turned in the right direction. Is it a coincidence that deixis has recently been highlighted as a model of good writing style? One of Albright's colleagues, the psychologist Steven Pinker, makes a recommendation to writers: point to objects and don't stand in the way. It is hard to imagine a more expert pair of hands doing just that.

ONE

Thesis

MONISM IS THE PHILOSOPHICAL CONVICTION THAT THINGS that appear to be two are actually one. The large bifurcations by which we make sense of reality (matter versus spirit, concrete versus abstract, body versus soul) are somehow superseded by the monist. This does not mean that all monists agree. Bishop Berkeley was a monist who considered the physical world to be purely ideal, unsolid. As the poet William Butler Yeats put it:

> And God-appointed Berkeley that proved all things a dream,
> That this pragmatical, preposterous pig of a world, its farrow that so
> solid seem,
> Must vanish on the instant if the mind but change its theme

Karl Marx, however, was a monist of exactly the opposite character: a materialist, he believed that only the physical world existed. But there is a kind of convergence of these opposites: for Marx and Berkeley alike, all that is solid must melt into air.

The term *monism* has been widely used in literary criticism in recent years. John Milton, for example, has been called a monist because he posited a continuum between the spiritual and physical worlds: for example, in *Paradise Lost* (1674) the angel Raphael explains that his celestial digestive processes can incorporate regular human food into his ethereal self, "corporeal into incorporeal turn" (book 5, line 413). In this sense the monist Milton was the exact opposite of his contemporary, the dualist René Descartes, who taught that spirit and matter were immiscible, hermetically sealed domains, except for one tiny point of contact in the pineal gland of the brain.

But Milton was also a dualist of sorts, in that he regarded the spiritual and physical worlds as distinct from one another: he was a monist only in that he believed that a continuum existed between them. When I use *monism* in this book, I use it in a more Modernist sense: the philosophy that insists on the interchangeability, even the identicality, of the basic dichotomies that govern our thinking, our modes of organizing the universe. For the Modernist monist, the physical world isn't subsumed into the spiritual (as it was for Berkeley), and the spiritual world isn't subsumed into the physical (as it was for Marx): instead, the two worlds are the somehow same thing, regarded from different points of view. When T. S. Eliot writes, "Soul is to body as cutting is to the axe,"[1] he is monistic in a fashion far more extreme than Milton.

As I've often had occasion to state, I think of Modernism as a movement, or heap of movements, devoted to aesthetic extremism. Modernism is a *testing of the limits of aesthetic construction*. According to this perspective, the Modernists tried to find the ultimate bounds of certain artistic possibilities: volatility of emotion (Expressionism); stability and inexpressiveness (the New Objectivity); accuracy of representation (Hyperrealism); absence of representation (Abstractionism); purity of form (Neoclassicism); formless energy (Neobarbarism); cultivation of the technological present (Futurism); cultivation of the prehistoric past (the Mythic Method). These extremes, of course, have been arranged in pairs, because aesthetic heresies, like theological ones, come in binary sets: each limit point presupposes an opposite limit point, a counterextreme toward which the artist can push. Much of the strangeness, the stridency, the exhilaration of Modernist art can be explained by this strong thrust toward the verges of the aesthetic experience: after the nineteenth century had established a remarkably safe, intimate center where the artist and the audience could dwell, the Modernist age reaches out to art's freakish circumferences. The extremes of the aesthetic experience tend to converge: in the Modernist movement, the most barbaric art tends to be the most up-to-date and sophisticated. In these convergences Modernism shows its radically monistic character.

Of all artistic media, music is perhaps most at ease in demonstrating the collapse of dualities. In opera and in much instrumental music, the composer sets forth sharply contrasting binaries, only to erase them. This practice comes more easily to music drama than to the spoken variety, because, while music is infinitely rich in binaries (diatonic versus chromatic, staccato versus legato, major versus minor, tonic versus dominant, tonal versus atonal, and so forth), there is always some larger system of musical reference that comprehends, reconciles, abnegates, sublates, or otherwise does away with these binaries. A language like music, in which every element (pitch, rhythm, harmony) is overtly relative and contingent, in which no absolute can be found, is Jacques Derrida's dream language: the binaries that undergird any organization of reality, such as nature and culture, undo themselves effortlessly.[2] Black is just white understood in a different modality; the word *black* has sometimes been thought to have a common origin with the French *blanc*, that is, *white*.

All composers in all ages have availed themselves of these possibilities for reconciling opposites; the sonata form itself can be understood as institutionalized reconciliation. But among the Modernists—and I think a good case can be made that Richard Wagner, Charles Baudelaire, and Friedrich Nietzsche were among the first Modernists—there is a special effort not simply to reconcile opposites but to annihilate them, to deny that they ever existed in the first place. The composers I study in this book are notable for both their intelligence and their sensitivity to the intellectual ethos of the age: Wagner, Claude Debussy, Benjamin Britten, Arnold Schoenberg, and Igor Stravinsky. The chapters are independent, and they can be read in any order; what draws them together into a book is their formal congruence, the similar shape of their internal workings.

The study of musical semantics fascinates because of the ways in which the meanings of musical gestures tend to reverse themselves over time. In spoken drama, the rhetoric of comedy and the rhetoric of tragedy are often hard to distinguish: *Romeo and Juliet* and the galumphingly hilarious Pyramus and Thisbe skit in *A Midsummer Night's Dream* are the same play, even down to certain details in the handling of oxymorons and other tropes. But the situation is far worse in the case of music drama. Hector Berlioz once noted that you could listen to a certain chorus in Christoph Willibald Gluck's *Alceste* and not know whether it meant rejoicing or lamentation, and this is quite a usual circumstance—composers are sometimes exasperated by the faintness, the uncertainty, of musical representations of affect, but this semi-impotence can be, paradoxically, a source of power. When Gluck decided to write Orpheus's tragic aria about Eurydice's second death, "Che farò senza Euridice," in the untragical key of C major, he was at once extending the semantic range of C major and proving the Orwellian musical axiom that wrong is often righter than right itself. Much of the most intense music I know derives its intensity by hovering between two opposing constructions of its meaning. Tragic ecstasy is a form of imaginary joy, vitiated only by the fact that it does not actually come to pass. Puccini's "Un bel dì" would be the most joyous aria in the repertoire if Pinkerton were to show up and kneel before Butterfly with a wedding ring in hand.

The very first significant opera, Claudio Monteverdi's *L'Orfeo* (1607), is a comic version of the Orpheus myth, but its libretto was published separately with a suggestion of a tragic resolution, as the maenads dance threateningly around Orpheus. When Carl Orff adapted Monteverdi's opera for the modern stage in a German translation (*Orpheus*; 1923, rev. 1940), he preferred the tragic ending, which he obtained convincingly and without much trouble by moving Monteverdi's joyous conclusion back to the first act. But with a little more imagination he could have made the happy moresca that ends the original opera into something angry and biting, its snap rhythms potentially as useful in depicting Furies as wedding guests. Why did Wagner and Franz Liszt labor so hard at their craft, if not to prove that any emotional content could be extracted from any sequence of notes?

TWO

Wagner's Names

I GREW UP IN AN UNMUSICAL HOUSEHOLD: MY PARENTS WERE content to go about the business of their lives in silence broken only by quiet discussion. But at the age of fourteen I had, for the only time in my life, a Saul-on-the-road-to-Damascus experience: I turned on the radio and chanced upon a broadcast from the Bayreuth Festival of *Das Rheingold*. At first I listened with only half an ear and paid no attention to the announcer's plot summary (if there was one); but three hours later I felt that something had just happened that was worth devoting my life to studying. In a sense I have done exactly that. Except for a piece on ballad structure in *Der fliegende Holländer* (*The Flying Dutchman*; composed 1840–41, premièred 1843), I have written nothing about Wagner, but only out of a sense that I had first to learn about the pre- and post-Wagnerian universe.

I promptly told my father that we needed, right now, to buy a lot of serious high-fidelity sound equipment, and, to my amazement, he said all right. Soon the silence of the house was broken by endless hours of Valkyries and vassals, minnesingers and mastersingers, Norwegian maidens and Rhine maidens and flower maidens and heavy emoters of every sort. (My parents seemed relaxed about living inside this mini-Bayreuth; maybe they were glad that I'd at last found something commensurate with my gift for—what? intensity?) My high school offered good German instruction, and I spent my nights writing my own private translation of *Der Ring des Nibelungen*, improving Wagner's text wherever possible: because I didn't like horses, I eliminated Grane; and I made Sieglinde offer Siegmund a glass of wine, because I thought he deserved something better than a mere sip of water or mead. I read everything on Wagner I could get my hands on: I almost memorized Ernest Newman's books and pored over tabulations of Wagner's musical motifs—it seemed strange to me that one commentator referred to a certain modulatory wrench in *Die Walküre* (*The Valkyrie*) as the Fate motif, while another called it the Death motif. In a moment of triumph I found a motif that No One Had Ever Found Before: the Raven motif (on the basis of a certain vague resemblance in patterned semitones between Wotan's "Er floh dir zu seinem Heil!" in *Siegfried* and Hagen's "Erräth'st du auch dieser Raben Geraun'?" in *Götterdämmerung*—in act 3, scene 2 of their respective works). I suppose I imagined that I would spend my life discerning the correct names of all the Wagnerian motifs and finding many occult ones that had escaped previous detection.

I found, however, other things worth loving. By the age of sixteen I was as wrapped up, rapt up, in Richard Strauss's *Die Frau ohne Schatten* (*The Woman without a Shadow*) as I had ever been in *Das Rheingold*; then in college there came Schoenberg's *Erwartung* (*Expectation*) and Stravinsky's *The Rake's Progress*, and Verdi's *Otello*, and Mozart's *Don Giovanni*, and Puccini's *Tosca*, and the whole flood. But I always felt that I could learn new composers only by forbidding myself to listen to Wagner: Wagner could too easily seize control of my mind and sensorium. To this day tears come to my eyes when I hear the opening scene of *Das Rheingold*: when the Rhinemaidens, too elated to mock, invite Alberich to laugh with them in the light of the gold, they seem to forgive him for being an ugly greedy dwarf, and I am a teenager once again, wondering whether any girl would ever see through my ugliness and greed, would ever want to kiss me. The name Alberich is disturbingly like my last name.

Over the years I noticed a strange thing: I felt that most of the composers that I studied I knew better and better; but Wagner I knew worse and worse. When I was young I felt that the whole structure of Wagner-world was luminous and articulate in my head; now it seems viscid, gloppy, not (I think) through my own failure of memory but through its own internal processes of evolution. I believe that Wagner means for his semantic systems first to ramify and grow clear, then to sink into unmeaning. He first names, then he unnames. Wagner said that the great project of his life, his series of music dramas *Der Ring des Nibelungen* (*The Ring of the Nibelung*), concerned a god who willed his own destruction:[1] the music dramas also will their own destruction.

In Wagner's works there are two problems of naming: figuring out the names of characters and figuring out the names of musical motifs. I believe that these are two aspects of the same problem.

Samuel Beckett, a more Wagnerian writer than he at first appears, always gave the most intense scrutiny to the names of his characters: some are mere puns (Miss Fitt, Miss Carriage); some are based on arcane allusions (the characters in *Endgame* are named after hammer—Hamm—or nails—Nell, Nagg from the German *Nagel*, Clov from the French *clou*); some are arbitrary babblings (Bam, Bem, Bom, Krim, Kram); and finally, there is the unnamed narrator of *The Unnamable*. A similar range of naming play can be found in Wagner: characters with no names (the Flying Dutchman), characters who don't know their names (Siegmund, Parsifal), characters whose names get all twisted up (Tristan, who calls himself Tantris so that the hostile witch Isolde, nursing him to health, won't recognize him as the man who killed her betrothed), characters who can't keep a steady purchase on their names (in their ecstasy Tristan calls Isolde Tristan, and Isolde calls Tristan Isolde), characters whose names are jokes or puns (Pontio Pilato in *Das Liebesverbot*—and in an 1861 draft of *Die Meistersinger von Nürnberg* the absurd critic Veit Beckmesser was called Veit Hanslich, after Eduard Hanslick, a Viennese critic not fond of Wagner's music)—and finally a character addressed as Namenlose (Nameless One), though she is known by many names, including Kundry. Names seem to be like sacred talismans: the name is the source of character's power, and to be master of someone's name is to be master of the person. This is why, at the beginning of act 2 of *Parsifal*, the sorcerer Klingsor casts his spell over Kundry by calling her Nameless One, then summoning her with the full roster of her names, epithets, or avatars: Rose of Hell, Herodias, Gundryggia, Kundry. Similarly, in act 2, scene 2 of *Tristan und Isolde*, the lovers cry that they are "namenlos in Lieb' umfangen"—without names, caught up in love. As we will see, Wagner's names, like Beckett's, also tend to be nothing at all.

In Plato's dialogue *Cratylus* (fourth century BCE), Socrates referees an argument between Hermogenes, who believes that words are just arbitrary labels pasted onto things, and Cratylus, who argues that things may be rightly or wrongly named—and, of course, a right name is ideal, metaphysically prestigious, in a sense sacred. Socrates seems somewhat inclined to disapprove of Cratylus's line of speculation: he scoffs at the idea that a word can be equivalent to an object:

> How ridiculous would be the effect of names on things, if they were exactly the same with them! For they would be doubles of them, and no one would be able to determine which were the names and which were the realities.[2]

Any real name, Socrates suggests, is a more or less faulty representation of its correspondent thing. He asks himself if the original "legislator"—the fellow who invented names and attached them to things—was extraordinarily wise or knowledgeable; no, Socrates answers, the legislator was more ignorant than we are today—so there is no special glory in the origins of Greek words or those of any other language. We see, then, that Socrates was bemused by the notion of an ideal language but seems ultimately to have rejected it. Wagner was deeply attracted to a Cratylian model of names, in which some mana, essence, or phlogiston is hidden in etymological roots; but the more closely he looks at these magic syllables, the more their dark power dispels. Naming and unnaming are part of the rhythm of his imagination.

Lohengrin (composed 1846–48, premièred 1850) is an opera *about* naming. Two villains, Ortrud and Telramund, have falsely accused Elsa of Brabant of murdering her brother; in desperate need of a champion to fight for her honor, Elsa recounts to the court her dream of a noble knight who will come rescue her; at the last second the unknown knight arrives in a boat drawn by a swan, defeats Telramund in an ordeal by combat, and agrees to marry Elsa, under the single stipulation that she must never ask him his name or his country of origin. (This repeats a plot point from Wagner's first opera, *Die Feen* [*The Fairies*; composed 1833, premièred 1888], in which Arindal's half-fairy lover Ada commands him, "Vor allem magst acht Jahre lang du nimmer fragen, wer ich sei!" [Above all you must, for eight years, never ask who I am].) But Ortrud preys on Elsa's mind, sowing doubts about the wisdom of marrying a man about whom she knows nothing; and on their wedding day she asks him the fatal question, and he sorrowfully, eloquently, tells her and the court that he is Lohengrin, son of the king of the Grail knights Parzifal—and now, having exposed his identity, the terms of his service to humanity compel him to return home, for the Grail's light must never be revealed too explicitly to the profane. The swan boat returns, but the swan itself is disenchanted and turns into a boy, Elsa's long-lost brother.

This is the sort of opera plot that a composer devises when he is coming to hate the notion of opera. The witchy Ortrud and her heroic but easily manipulated consort Telramund (a new version of the Macbeths), the romantic Elsa, the conscientious King Heinrich der Vogler—these are all familiar operatic types and are given familiar (though unusually incisive and memorable) operatic music, from heraldic fanfares to Ortrud's black chromatic writhing to Telramund's unsteady, dotted-rhythm stalking about. In the midst of these easily named characters and easily named musical figures, there flashes forth the nameless knight, suddenly the object of everyone's attention—at once center of the action and yet only weakly involved in the physical world. Wagner wrote to Hermann Franck:

> Als Symbol der Fabel kann ich nur festhalten: die Berührung eine übersinnlichen Erscheinung mit der menschlichen Natur und die Unmöglichkeit einer Dauer derselben.[3]

> I can only hold fast to this as the fable's symbol: the contact of a suprasensuous apparition with human nature, and the impossibility of its lasting.

Wagner further explained that he hoped to imply, without actually saying so, that the bonds of human love were unbecoming to this "passive" Grail knight. Pure and passionless, except for his hardwired needs to right all wrongs and to obey his oath of service, he has no immune system to ward off the passions of earthly beings: Elsa seems to infect him with something of her own erotic desires. He is neither chaste nor unchaste, just a tabula nearly rasa on which others can inscribe any traits that don't conflict with his prime directive. This is what it means to try to live without a name. In this same letter Wagner compared Lohengrin to Zeus descending to Semele—Semele too was tricked into asking her lover to reveal his unfeigned self—but Lohengrin is a considerate, pale and recessive, etiquette-bound Zeus. A hollow image of Elsa's desire, a reflection trembling on the surface of a river, he vanishes when forced apart from her.

Just as Elsa and Ortrud and Telramund want to assign a name to Lohengrin, so does the music. But the music does not succeed. The opera begins with a beautiful prelude depicting (as Wagner put it in a program note of May 1853) a host of angels descending from heaven to earth, bearing the Grail—the cup that caught the blood flowing from Christ's side—the "sensuous representation of this suprasensuous thing" (sinnlichen Vorstellung dieses Übersinnlichen)—and then re-ascending, smiling, taking back the Grail—"In the brightest light of heaven's blue ether the sublime host vanishes" (im hellsten Lichte des blauen Himmeläthers verschwindet die hehre Schaar).[4] In the quiet opening the Grail theme appears in the highest instruments, a shimmer at the edge of hearing—the timbres and rhythms are elusive, hard to grasp. The first harmonic movement is from tonic to relative minor and back to tonic (I–vi–I, in A major); and, as the music slowly descends to earth, wafting in the modulatory breeze, that progression remains audible. This is not the sort of music that one expects to find in an opera, or indeed anywhere at all, even in church—it's an image of a religious rite, not an accompaniment for one.

Some of its earlier listeners described it as extraterrestrial in aspect: Charles Baudelaire, in his essay "Richard Wagner et Tannhäuser à Paris" (1861), quoted Franz Liszt's rapturously synesthetic description of the *Lohengrin* prelude (Liszt saw in Wagner's music "golden" doors, "asbestos" joists, "opal" columns, walls of "chrysoberyl") and then, after quoting his own sonnet *Correspondances* in praise of synesthesia, he continued with his rhapsody:

> Je me sentis délivré *des liens de la pesanteur*, et je retrouvai par le souvenir l'extraordinaire *volupté* qui circule dans *les lieux hauts*. . . . Ensuite je me peignis involontairement l'état délicieux d'un homme en proie à une grande rêverie dans une solitude absolue, mais une solitude avec *un immense horizon* et une *large lumière diffuse*; *l'immensité* sans autre décor qu'elle-même. Bientôt j'éprouvai la sensation d'une *clarté* plus vive, *d'une intensité de lumière* croissant avec une telle rapidité, que les nuances fournies par le dictionnaire ne suffiraient pas à exprimer *ce surcroît toujours renaissant d'ardeur et de blancheur*. Alors je conçus pleinement l'idée d'une âme se mouvant dans un milieu lumineux, d'une extase *faite de volupté et de connaissance*, et planant au-dessus et bien loin du monde naturel.[5]

> I felt myself delivered *from the bonds of gravity*, and through memory I recaptured the extraordinary voluptuousness that circulates in *high places*. . . . Finally I imagined involuntarily the delightful state of a man rapt in a great reverie in absolute solitude, but a solitude with *an immense horizon* and a *wide diffuse light*; *immensity* without any décor other than itself. Soon I felt the sensation of a most vivid *clarity, with an intensity of light* growing with such speed that the nuances provided by the dictionary would not suffice to express *this ever-renascent surplus of ardor and whiteness*. Then I plainly conceived the idea of a soul moving in a luminous midst, with an ecstasy *made of voluptuousness and awareness*, and gliding above and very far from the natural world.

For Baudelaire, the *Lohengrin* prelude was not only extramundane but, in a sense, extramusical, transsensuous: synesthesia is a means of imaging the beauty beyond the realm of the senses by appealing to the wrong sense organ. I believe that Wagner means the prelude as an evocation of pure music,

music snatched back into the sky before it can be corrupted by contact with the earth.

But Wagner despises opera precisely because it is dominated by purely musical considerations rather than dramatic ones. One of Wagner's major projects in the year of *Lohengrin*'s premiere was the writing of his longest piece of critical prose, *Oper und Drama* (written 1850–51, published 1851), in which he complains that operatic music tries to twist itself into a monstrous surrogate of drama, instead of remaining drama's obedient handmaiden:

> Die Musik, die als eine Kunst des *Ausdruckes*, bei höchster Fülle in diesem Ausdrucke nur wahr sein kann, hat hierin naturgemäß sich immer nur auf das zu beziehen, *was* sie ausdrücken soll: in der Oper ist dies ganz entschieden die Empfindung des Redenden und Darstellenden, und eine Musik, die dies mit überzeugendster Wirkung tut, ist gerade das, was sie irgend sein kann. Eine Musik, die aber mehr sein, sich nicht auf einen auszudrückenden Gegenstand beziehen, sondern ihn selbst erfüllen, d. h. dieser Gegenstand zugleich sein will, ist im Grunde gar keine Musik mehr, sondern ein von Musik und Dichtkunst phantastisch abstrahiertes Unding, das sich in Wahrheit nur als Karikatur verwirklichen kann.[6]

> Music, which as an art of *expression* can be true only in the highest abundance of this expression, has therefore, according to its nature, to concern itself only with *what* it is to express: in opera this is definitely the feelings of those who speak and play their roles, and a music that does this with most convincing effect is just that, a music that does what it can. A music, however, that would be more than this, that would concern itself not with any object to express but with its fulfillment in itself—a music that would at the same time constitute its own object—is fundamentally not music any more, but a fantastically abstracted un-thing made of music and poetry, that in truth can only realize itself as a caricature.

> Sehr wichtig ist es, zu beachten, daß alles, was auf die Gestaltung der Oper bis in die neuesten Zeiten einen wirklichen und entscheidenden Einfluß ausübte, *lediglich aus dem Gebiete der absoluten Musik*, keineswegs aber aus dem der Dichtkunst, oder aus einem gesunden Zusammenwirken beider Künste, sich herleitete.[7]

> It is very important to observe that, down to the most recent times, everything that has exercised a real and decisive influence on the shaping of

> opera has derived *strictly from the realm of absolute music*, in no way from poetry or from a healthy interaction of both arts.

Now it's easy to defend the prelude to *Lohengrin* as an expression of feeling. But Wagner himself used the word *suprasensuous* in describing his music, and whatever feeling-content the music possesses cannot easily be attached to any of the characters, except to Lohengrin himself in his precarnal, "metaphysical" mode of being, standing at Parzifal's side in the Castle of the Grail, both heroes more like mosaic images on a frieze than like human beings. So: Wagner has not abolished absolute music from the domain of opera, as he claims he wishes to do; instead, he has relegated it to a crystalline domain of inaction, blue-translucent, far from the fibrillations and aneurysms and night sweats of the rest of the music. In traditional opera, according to Wagner, music busies itself with a hopeless attempt to supply the missing drama; *Lohengrin*, by contrast, is carefully calculated to show the inability of Music-with-a-capital-M to engage itself with actual theatrical events, except in special and limited ways.

In the aria known as "Elsa's Dream" the music world of the Grail first obtrudes on human affairs. Up until this point, the chief event of act 1 has been Telramund's accusation of Elsa, an effective piece of musical declamation—Telramund doesn't have a leitmotif so much as a gestural profile and a sort of speech prefix: as he opens his mouth to begin, the orchestra plays a few notes of what we soon come to know as Telramundiana. Elsa has even less of a personal music motif: instead she has a dream theme, heroic, delicately scored, dreamily modulating. The dream theme's harmonic structure is tonic to relative minor to dominant (I–vi–V), related to the I–vi–I at the beginning of the Grail motif and marked with the same double-dotted rhythm. Elsa has found a motif for her nameless-rescuer-to-come by forcing the elusively shaped Grail motif into a conventional knightly pattern, thereby allowing the hero to enter the world of opera. This is teleological music, music with a mission, not Grail music that goes nowhere, simply circles back whence it came. Elsa's Dream is in A♭ major, as opposed to the A major of the act 1 prelude; and in a sense we have dropped into a flatter, more matter-of-fact world.

It would be easy to refer to the dream theme as the Lohengrin motif: it is even possible to think of the vast expansion of the dream theme in the excited chorus "Seht! Welch ein seltsam Wunder!" (Look! What a strange wonder!) as a sort of enormous speech prefix to Lohengrin's first words (though the two measures immediately preceding his first words play the

Grail motif). On the other hand, in the course of the opera Lohengrin himself doesn't seem strongly engaged with the dream theme: he is engaged directly with the Grail, not with its distillate through Elsa's imagination. Toward the end of act 3, the climactic "In fernem Land" (In a far-off land), in which Lohengrin reveals his identity, is (more or less) the Grail music from the act 1 prelude recast as an aria, but it succeeds less in hauling absolute music down to earth than in constructing a zeppelin that will lift Lohengrin back into the empyrean. The Grail motif never appears in the opera except as a shard of sky; it is the dream theme that has to do the heavy work of heroic action.

But the dream theme belongs, I think, more to Elsa than to Lohengrin: it is the theme of a fantasy of rescue so desperate and precise that it manages to bring a rescuer into being; it is, as Shelley puts it, the hope that creates from its own wreck the thing it contemplates. Lohengrin's own most characteristic music is found in an epigram, "Nie sollst du mich befragen" (You are never to ask me), in which he forbids Elsa to ask his name or origin. I call it an epigram rather than a motif, because Wagner meant the tune always to be associated with the words to which it is first sung—in fact twice over, in order to gash the words firmly into Elsa's mind. An epigram lacks a motif's power of symphonic development: it is less an element for imaginative play than a static placard, music as *écriture*, though in places Wagner subjects "Nie sollst du mich befragen" to certain transformations.

In his later works he found ways of making his epigrams dissolve into motifs, then harden back into epigrams at his pleasure: an example from *Der Ring des Nibelungen* is Alberich's Curse, "Wie durch Fluch er mir gerieth, verflucht sei dieser Ring!" (As through a curse it came to me, accursed be this ring!; *Das Rheingold*, act 1, scene 4), in which the melody, ending with a major triad that weirdly unresolves into a diminished chord, can thread its way through the musical events as a half-perceptible sense of doom, or grow conspicuous during a murder, or even wordlessly state its entire burden of words, as in the prelude to act 2 of *Siegfried* (composed 1856–57 and 1869, premièred 1876) when the orchestra quotes not only the music for the words of the curse itself, but also the music just after the curse, to which Alberich expanded his warning to future owners of the ring. Lohengrin's "Nie sollst du mich befragen" is treated more inflexibly; and, like all inflexible musical events in Wagner's mature work, it develops a stable meaning and a verifiable name: the Prohibition. It is therefore that odd thing, a name that insists on a character's refusal to name himself. It is a name tag that clearly reads "Enforced Anonymity"—Hi, I'm—don't ask, no matter what! Until he sings "In fernem Land" at the opera's end, Lohengrin is best known musically through this antiname.

"Nie sollst du mich befragen," then, is a placeholder for the absent name Lohengrin; it pries open empty spaces in the drama that can be filled only with music that doesn't belong to the drama at all—that is, with the music of the Grail. The plot development is motivated by the search for something that exists outside the plot, outside all plots. As we shall see, this is generally true of names in Wagner's work: even when we are confident that we have correctly named a motif or other musical event (and the music comprises much that is completely unnameable), the name is at best a temporary placeholder, a moment in a chain of deferring. Wagner's music is about freedom, and anything that has a name is unfree.

After Debussy visited Bayreuth and heard *Der Ring des Nibelungen*, he mocked Wagner for his habit of making his characters sing their *cartes de visite* as soon as they stepped onstage.[8] And it is certainly true that many a character drags his musical motif wherever he goes, as if it were a lead ball fastened to his foot with a chain. Hunding—Sieglinde's coarse, hateful husband in *Die Walküre* (composed 1854–56, premièred 1870)—is so cramped by his little tune that he lacks any possibility for development, any scope for free play. Siegmund and Sieglinde themselves, however, have no strongly particularized motifs: in the tissue of music they sing, together or apart, the listener can find certain tendencies that aggregate toward the man, and others toward the woman, but these tendencies are only half extricated from the general musical mass. What there *is*, is a Wälsung motif, a melody clearly identified with the children of Wälse, Wotan in disguise—a musical entity that means Siegmund and Sieglinde together and eventually includes the son, Siegfried, born of the incestuous love of these twins. (Similarly, Tristan and Isolde are, musically speaking, a composite being: it is hard to be certain that there's a specific Tristan motif or Isolde motif.) The absence of a determinate Siegmund motif is at first a sign that he is a man who doesn't know his name; then a sign of his freedom of action as he defies Hunding, defies the taboo against adultery (and therefore Fricka, Wotan's wife, the goddess of holy wedlock), defies fate.

And yet Siegfried, far stronger than Siegmund, seemingly gifted with the greatest possible range for free expansion of his will, does have a determinate musical motif—prophesied to the pregnant Sieglinde in act 3, scene 1 of *Die Walküre*, present everywhere, it seems, in *Siegfried* and *Götterdämmerung*, unforgotten, unforgettable. As he explains in *Eine Mittheilung an meine Freunde* (A Communication to My Friends, 1851), Siegfried is, for Wagner, freedom incarnate:

> Ich war mit der Konzeption des "Siegfried" bis dahin vorgedrungen, wo ich den Menschen in der natürlichsten, heitersten Fülle seiner sinnlich belebten Kundgebung vor mir sah; kein historisches Gewand engte ihn mehr ein; kein außer ihm entstandenes Verhältnis hemmte ihn irgendwie in seiner Bewegung, die aus dem innersten Quelle seiner Lebenslust jeder Begegnung gegenüber sich so bestimmte, daß Irrthum und Verwirrung, aus dem wildesten Spiele der Leidenschaften genährt, rings um ihn bis zu seinem offenbaren Verderben sich häufen konnten, ohne daß der Held einen Augenblick, selbst dem Tode gegenüber, den inneren Quell in seinem wellenden Ergusse nach Außen gehemmt, oder je etwas Anderes für berechtigt über sich und seine Bewegung gehalten hätte, als eben die nothwendige Ausströmung des rastlos quillenden inneren Lebensbrunnens. Mich hatte "Elsa" diesen Mann finden gelehrt: er war mir der männlich verkörperte Geist der ewig und einzig zeugenden Unwillkür, des Wirkers wirklicher Thaten, *des Menschen* in der Fülle höchster, unmittelbarster Kraft und zweifellosester Liebenswürdigkeit.[9]
>
> With the conception of "Siegfried" I had advanced to the point that I saw before me man manifest, sensuously animate in his most natural, most cheerful fullness of being; no historical garment cramped him; nothing from outside hemmed his movement—movement so determined by the innermost wellspring of his life-lust, in the face of every encounter, that error and confusion, fed from the wildest play of passion, could heap themselves around him to the point of apparent ruin, without making the hero block the inner spring in its welling outflow for one moment, even in the face of death, and without making the hero accept any authority over him and his movement, except the authority of the necessary outstreaming of the ceaselessly surging fountain of life. "Elsa" taught me how to find this man: he was, to me, the male-incarnate spirit of the sole and eternal involuntary impulse, the effector of effective deeds, *the man* in the fullness of his highest, most immediate force and most certain loveworthiness.

And yet the puzzling reference to Elsa suggests, perhaps, something of the limits of Siegfried's freedom. Elsewhere Wagner describes Elsa as a creature of the unconscious, the instinctive, the involuntary (*Unwillkürliche*), as opposed to the completely conscious Lohengrin. A fully conscious, awake person has the faculty of making choices; a creature governed by involuntary impulses is the prisoner of his own spontaneity. If Lohengrin is Elsa's dream of a rescuer, then Siegfried is Sieglinde's dream of a successor to her dead lover Siegmund, and Wotan's dream of an agent not bound by the constraints of oaths, and Mime's dream of a hero to kill the dragon Fafner and regain the ring—and ultimately Brünnhilde's dream of a rescuer.

Siegfried has no particular purpose of his own: he is a weapon or stick of dynamite waiting for someone to assign a purpose to him. In his autobiography Wagner congratulated himself for writing a Schopenhauerian drama before he had read Schopenhauer[10]—and, in true Schopenhauerian fashion, Siegfried represents the will-lessness of absolute will, blind and endlessly self-entangled, all "error and confusion." In his later writings Wagner tended to emphasize the absence of freedom that marks the behavior of this supremely free hero; as he wrote in 1871, in the epilogue to *Der Ring des Nibelungen*:

> Die völlige Gleichheit dieser besteht aber darin, daß Tristan wie Siegfried das ihm nach dem Urgesetze bestimmte Weib, im Zwange einer Täuschung, welche diese seine That zu einer unfreien macht, für einen Anderen freit, und aus dem hieraus entstehenden Misverhältnisse seinen Untergang findet.[11]

> The complete likeness of these two consists in this: Tristan, like Siegfried, in thrall to a deception that makes his deed unfree, woos for another man a woman destined for him by primal law, and from the consequent false relation finds his downfall.

Unfree. Like all unconscious and instinctive beings, Siegfried is an easy gull to the calculations of others; despite the immense burden of family myth he carries on his shoulders, he lives in the present instant and effortlessly shrugs off his own past: Hagen's drug of oblivion (which makes Siegfried forget Brünnhilde and woo Gutrune) is only an overt sign of the general *lethe* of his life, for any memory of the past would constrain his behavior in the present, and he will brook no constraint. He is the slave of his own freedom.

Wagner did not encourage the production of a nomenclature—a table of musical motifs drawn from his work. In the act of composing he would sometimes label short melodies ("Fafner" or "Waldvogel"). When discussing his finished works, he would on occasion refer to his themes by name, but often in somewhat odd ways: for instance, he described to his wife, Cosima, what he called the Norns' theme in the prelude to act 3 of *Siegfried* as follows:

> R. lacht: "Ja, es klingt kindlich und kreischend: wie das Jungfräuliche, das nie geliebt hat . . . etwas dämonisch kindlich Kreischendes . . . man kann sich eine Hexenstimme nur hoch und kindlich denken; der bebende Ton des Herzens klingt nicht darin."[12]

> R. laughs: "Yes, it sounds childish and shrieking: like some virginal presence that has never loved . . . some demonic childish shrieking thing. You think of a witch's voice only as high and childish; the heart's quaking tone can't be heard in it."

But commentators don't usually speak of a "Norns' theme" here, because the Norns (the Norse version of the Greek Parcae, the spinners of destiny), when they actually appear for the first time, in the prologue to *Götterdämmerung* (The Twilight of the Gods; composed 1869–71, premièred 1876), are characterized by a sedate and elusive interweave of chromatic arpeggios, altogether different; and nothing in the text or dramatic action of act 3, scene 1 of *Siegfried*, in which Wotan tries to learn deep truth from Erda (Earth personified, the mother of the Norns), would lead a critic to think of cackling witches; Wagner is caught up in a private response to his own music, and assigning a name and a description almost through whim. The whole matter of the Norn music shows the exasperations of naming themes: in the 1850 composition sketch "Siegfrieds Tod" (Siegfried's Death), an early version of the prologue to *Götterdämmerung*, the Norns' motif is what we now call the Valkyrie motif, its electric swerve to the mediant (I–III) retarded and softened into quiet contemplation. It is fascinating to trace the evolution of this prophetic melody from Wagner's beautiful and somber song *Der Tannenbaum* (1838; text by Georg Scheurlin), in which a pine tree prophesies its future as a coffin, to "Siegfrieds Tod," in which the Norns prophesy (or devise) the main events of the whole cycle of music dramas, to *Die Walküre*, in which the Valkyrie Brünnhilde, a sort of elated vulture, prophesies to Siegmund that he will soon die.

But many of the names we assign to motifs are clearly, in some sense, correct. The Giants motif, with its ponderous clomp-about; the Nibelung motif, a fast, rhythmic hammering suitable for this race of smiths; the Spear motif, an authoritative scalar descent; the Sword motif, a fanfare brandish; the motif of Siegfried's sword Nothung, an octave drop and lop; the shape-shifting Tarnhelm motif, mysteriously evolving chords (i–vi–i–vi–i–vi–III) that pivot around the middle note of the initial minor triad; and so on—no one, I think, would dispute these names. (Though I might prefer to call some of these units of motility by gerunds, not nouns: Smiting instead of Spear, Brandishing instead of Sword, Transshifting instead of Tarnhelm.) There is one clear case where Wagner confesses, implicitly, that he is thinking of a theme according to its name, not according to its place in the drama: in scene 3 of *Das Rheingold* (The Rhinegold; composed 1853–54, premièred 1869), Alberich whispers a magic spell to the Tarnhelm and transforms himself into a dragon; much later, in act 3, scene 2 of *Siegfried*, Siegfried finds the lair of Fafner—formerly a giant, now a dragon—who is given the same tune as the temporary dragon Alberich, even though these two dragons have nothing in common except the fact of dragonhood.

Many of Wagner's most easily named themes have this in common: they refer to tools. Swords and spears are implements of war; the Nibelungs bang anvils; the Giants are plodding laborers, the construction crew for the building of Valhalla. If you are a hammer, or a weapon, or a device for moving large rocks, you get a named motif. Names work well for inanimate objects, or for somewhat faceless laborers. The extreme namedness of Siegfried (musically speaking) is, I believe, a secret sign that Siegfried is himself a tool: wielded unsuccessfully by Mime and Brünnhilde, more successfully by Hagen and even in a sense by Wotan, insofar as Wotan makes good use of Siegfried in the course of willing his own destruction. Siegfried is conscious of his own pure instrumentality: as he tells Brünnhilde in the prologue to *Götterdämmerung*,

> nicht Siegfried acht' ich mich mehr,
> ich bin nur Brünnhilde's Arm.
>
> Siegfried is nothing to me now,
> I am only Brünnhilde's arm.

A tool, of course, is never an end in itself, only a means toward an end: and the easily named motifs all come to be superseded in time by pure combinatorial play—dissection and *Durchführung* of named motifs, strong presentation of unnamed motifs. It is possible to find a name (such as

Redemption by Love) for the final motif we hear in *Der Ring des Nibelungen*, as Valhalla and all the gods burn up and the Rhine overflows its banks, but such a name isn't really a name but an index useful for pointing at *shantih*, the peace that passeth understanding, the calm at world's end.

Some of Wagner's tools (such as Nothung) are proper nouns, others (such as Sword) are common nouns; but whether or not they have achieved official personification, they all have a deep backstory in myth. The Sword isn't just any stray blade, but the sword that Wotan thrust so deeply into the tree in Hunding's hut that only the mighty Siegmund could pull it out; the Spear isn't any pointed stick, but the spear cut out of the World Ash Tree, into which are carved the runes that give Wotan dominion so long as he obeys the laws that they enounce. There is a certain sense that these implements have existed since the beginning of the world, or shortly thereafter; they can be destroyed (as Siegmund's sword is shattered by the angry Wotan), but sometimes only temporarily: Siegfried reforges the splinters of his father's sword and names it Nothung—either inventing a new name or finding the unknown name it always had. These tools are, in a sense, attributes of the universe itself.

Often it seems that names as well as tools have existed since the beginning of things. A fascination with etymology, with the deep roots of names, can be found everywhere in Wagner's writings, but it is especially prominent in his remarkable essay *Die Wibelungen* (1848). Wagner said, quite justly, that his entire life's work was in place by the time he was thirty-six years old (that is, 1849);[13] and between1848 and 1850 he conceived his mature musicodramatic rhetoric and made the fateful decision to turn away from historical drama (his minutely planned project on Friedrich Barbarossa) to the Nibelung myth. (This is why, in *Oper und Drama*, he says of Siegfried, "No historical garment cramped him.") *Die Wibelungen* is Wagner's most ambitious attempt to understand history according to its foundations in the prehistorical, the realm of deep myth, and the essay reveals the frustrations that attend such research. On one level the essay is simply an attempt to reconstruct the source of the authority of kings; on another level it is a dark meditation on the wretchedness of modern life, where no authority can exist.

Wagner begins by imagining a prehistoric patriarchy in which the head of the clan—the stem father, Wagner calls him—was a god himself, or a god's avatar, after the Great Flood had isolated all human beings onto a few mountaintops in the Caucasus. But as these Caucasian tribes migrated west and organized themselves into larger political units administered by kings, those kings' authority was challenged by those who cared more about worldly property than about divine things. Thus began the defining dialectic of the human race, between the sacred and the profane.

At this point Wagner shifts his attention to German history, to show that the Frankish rulers were the true descendants of the archaic god-men:

> [. . .] hier vor allem in dem alten Königsgeschlechte der Franken, in welchem sich unter dem Namen der "Wibelingen" oder "Gibelinen" ein uralter Königsanspruch bis zum Anspruch der Weltherrschaft steigerte. Das fränkische Königsgeschlecht tritt in der Geschichte zunächst unter dem Namen der "Merwingen" auf: uns ist bekannt, wie bei der tiefsten Entartung dieses Geschlechtes doch nie den Franken es einfiel, aus einem andern als diesem sich Könige zu wählen [. . .]
>
> Unbestritten ist die Sage von den Nibelungen das Erbeigenthum des fränkischen Stammes. Dem Forscher ist erwiesen, daß der Urgrund auch dieser Sage religiös-mythischer Natur ist: ihre tiefste Bedeutung war das Urbewußtsein des fränkischen Stammes, die Seele seines Königsgeschlechtes, unter welchem Namen es auch jenes urheimathliche Hochgebirge Asiens zuerst erwachsen gesehen haben möge.—Von der ältesten Bedeutung des Mythus, in welcher wir Siegfried als Licht- oder Sonnengott zu erkennen haben, wollen wir für jetzt absehen [. . .]
>
> [. . .] alles Streben und alles Ringen geht nach diesem Horte der Nibelungen, als dem Inbegriffe aller irdischen Macht, und wer ihn besitzt, wer durch ihn gebietet, ist oder wird Nibelung.
>
> Die Franken, welche wir in der Geschichte zuerst in der Gegend des Niederrheins kennen lernen, haben nun ein königliches Geschlecht, in welchem der Name "Nibelung" vorkommt, und namentlich unter den ächtesten Gliedern dieses Geschlechtes, welche noch vor Chlodwig von einem Verwandten, Merwig, verdrängt wurden, später als Pipingen oder Karlingen die königliche Gewalt aber wieder gewannen. Dieß genüge für jetzt, um auf die, wenn nicht genealogische, doch gewiß mythische Identität des fränkischen Königsgeschlechtes mit jenen Nibelungen der Sage hinzuweisen [. . .]
>
> Mochte nun der Heldenglanz Karls des Großen, in dessen Macht der Keim des Nibelungenhortes zu vollster Kraft zu gelangen schien, eine Zeit lang den tiefen Unmuth der deutschen Stämme zertheilen, und namentlich den Glanz der eigenen Königsgeschlechter sie allmählich vergessen machen, nie doch verschwand die Abneigung gänzlich [. . .][14]

> [. . .] here above all in the old royal race of the Franks, in which under the name of the "Wibelings" or "Gibelins" an *ur*-ancient claim of kingship intensified into a claim of world dominion. The Frankish royal race first stepped forth into history under the name of "Merwings": it is known that, even during the deepest degeneration of this race, it never occurred to the Franks to choose their kings out of any other [. . .]
>
> The saga of the Nibelungs is indisputably the ancestral property of the Frankish stem. Research has proved that the *ur*-ground of this saga is also religious-mythical in nature: its deepest meaning was the *ur*-consciousness of Frankish stem, the soul of its race of kings, under whatever name it may have first been seen maturing in its *ur*-home in the high country of Asia. For now we will not speak of the oldest meaning of the myth, in which we have recognized Siegfried as a god of the light or the sun [. . .]
>
> [. . .] all striving and all struggling [in the Nibelung saga] goes after this hoard of the Nibelungs, as the apex of all earthly might, and who possesses it, who rules through it, is or becomes Nibelung.
>
> Now the Franks, whom we meet in history first in the region of the lower Rhine, have a royal race, in which the name *Nibelung* appears, and particularly among the purest branches of this race—even before Chlodwig was ousted by his kinsman Merwig, later when Pipings or Karlings won back the royal sway. This suffices for now, to indicate the mythical, if not genealogical, identity of the Frankish royal race with those Nibelungs of the saga [. . .]
>
> If now the heroic gleam of Karl the Great [Charlemagne], in whose might the germinative force of the Nibelungs' hoard seemed to reach full development, dissipated for a long time the German stems' deep resentment [the resentment of the Bavarians and Saxons and the other tribes defeated by the Franks], and the gleam of their own royal races was gradually forgotten, yet the old aversion never vanished.

So: Charlemagne was, among his other titles, the greatest of the historical Nibelungs. But the might of the Wibelungs/Nibelungs/Ghibellines started to decline not long after Charlemagne was crowned Holy Roman Emperor in 800 CE. The great crusader Frederick Barbarossa managed to restore some of its glory, but by 1268 it was gone:

> Erst mit der Enthauptung des jungen Konrad in Neapel ist das uralte Königsgeschlecht der "Wibelingen" als gänzlich erloschen zu betrachten.

> Only with the beheading of young Konrad at Naples are we to consider the *ur*-old royal race of the "Wibelings" completely extinct.

Wagner then turns his attention to Italy and the great rivalry between the Ghibellines, the imperial party, and the Guelphs, the papal party. Wagner's distaste for the Guelphs is strong:

> [. . .] wichtig, die unmittelbare Gegenpartei der Wibelingen, die der Welfen, näher zu bezeichnen. Auch dieser Name ist bedeutungsvoll. In der deutschen Sprache heißen "Welfe" in gesteigerter Anwendung: Säuglinge, nämlich zunächst der Hunde, dann vierfüßiger Thiere überhaupt. [. . .]
>
> Alles, was hierauf Bezug hat, können wir aber das (einer Stammsage gänzlich bare) "welfische" Prinzip nennen, dem gegenüber das der Wibelungen zu nichts Geringerem, als einem Anspruch auf die Weltherrschaft heranwuchs.[15]

> [. . .] it is important to designate more closely the party directly opposed to the Wibelings, the Welfs. Even the name is significant. In the German language "Welfe," in cumulative practice, means: sucklings, first of dogs, then of quadrupeds in general. [. . .]
>
> Everything related so far [the struggles of defeated Germanic tribes against the central royal authority of the Wibelungs] we can name as the *Welfic* principle (completely lacking any stem saga), which, counter to the Wibelungs' principle, evolved into nothing less than a claim to world dominion.

The Guelphs are a people without a saga: profane, grasping, "modern"; in the absence of a controlling myth, they concern themselves simply with the acquisition of material goods.

In order to explain the distinction between Ghibelline and Guelph, Wagner turns to an analysis of the Nibelung saga. He proposes two different ways of understanding the hoard, the massed treasure of the Nibelung: a healthy solar reading, in which the hoard is simply

> die Erde mit all' ihrer Herrlichkeit selbst, die wir beim Anbruche des Tages, beim frohen Leuchten der Sonne als unser Eigenthum erkennen und genießen, nachdem die Nacht verjagt, die ihre düsteren Drachenflügel über die reichen Schätze der Welt gespenstisch grauenhaft ausgebreitet hielt.

> the earth itself with all its glory, that at dawn, in the sun's glad light, we recognize and enjoy as our own possession, after night is driven away, the night that holds its dreary dragon wings outspread ghostly-ghastly over the world's rich treasures.

versus a sick nocturnal reading, in which the hoard is simply empty gold, empty power, amassed by a dragon or a pope:

> die Beherrschung der Welt, die Knechtung der Völker, nicht mehr die Beherrschung des inneren Menschen, die Bezwingung der egoistisch thierischen Leidenschaft im Menschen, war fortan die Religion Rom's. [. . .]
>
> Mit dem Untergange der Wibelungen war die Menschheit von der letzten Faser losgerissen worden, mit der sie gewissermaßen an ihrer geschlechtlich-natürlichen Herkunft gehangen hatte. Der Hort der Nibelungen hatte sich in das Reich der Dichtung und der Idee verflüchtigt; nur ein erdiger Niederschlag war als Bodensatz von ihm zurückgeblieben: *der reale Besitz.*[16]

> dominion over the world, enslavement of its peoples, no longer dominion over the inner man, conquest of his egoistic animal passion, was, from now on, Rome's religion. [. . .]
>
> With the downfall of the Wibelungs, one might say that mankind had been cut loose from the last dangling thread that connected it to its racial-natural origin. The hoard of the Nibelungs had volatilized into the realm of poetry and idea; an earthy precipitate was all that remained as the dregs: *real property.*

We live today, then, as sad Guelphs lost in a post-Ghibelline world.

What is the source of value? Why is gold anything more than a metal unusual for its weight, its scarcity, its color, and its resistance to rust? One answer lies in the fact the poets tell pretty stories about it—poetry not demoted to some idle fantasy world but instinctive in human constructs of reality. In William Butler Yeats's *The King's Threshold* (1904), a poet starves himself in a hunger strike to protest the loss of his old prerogatives; he tells the king's chamberlain,

> Cry out that the King's money would not buy,
> Nor the high circle consecrate his head,

> If poets had never christened gold, and even
> The moon's poor daughter, that most whey-faced metal,
> Precious

But after the death of the sixteen-year-old Conradin in 1268, it seemed that the light of myth had been quenched; the power to authorize value had vanished. To some extent Wagner conceived *Der Ring des Nibelungen* to bring the dead gods back to life, but it is not clear whether this project can succeed when, wherever Wagner stares, he can see only Guelphs and Guelphicity. Perhaps he can only devise an impressive fake, like the spooky procession of the old gods in Heinrich Heine's *Atta Troll* (1847), gods somewhat the worse for wear.

It is possible that we have also lost the true names of things. Wibelung, Wibeling, Nibelung, Gibelin—these may be mangled syllables, the remnants of missing names. For a dramatist obsessed with names, Wagner has a hard time keeping the names of his characters in order. There is Wotan. But in *Siegfried* he is known only as "der Wanderer," even in the cast of characters—he is a dispossessed god, even dispossessed of his name. In the riddle scene (*Siegfried*, act 1, scene 2), as the Wanderer explains cosmic demography to Mime, he refers to the ruler of the gods as "Licht-Alberich," as if Wotan were best understood as Alberich's less evil twin. When he sojourns with human beings, around the time of the childhood of his son Siegmund, he is known as Wälse. Or, if not Wälse, Wolfe. In *Lohengrin*, Ortrud sings a vehement prayer to her desecrated god Wodan. Sometimes Wotan even seems as much a place as an organic being. There is a moving moment in act 1, scene 2 of *Die Walküre*, after Siegmund remembers how he once came home to find that marauders had laid everything waste and his father was gone: Sieglinde asks Siegmund where his father is now, and Siegmund replies, "Den Vater fand ich nicht" (I did not find my father), as the orchestra whispers the Valhalla motif, telling us what neither Sieglinde nor Siegmund knows, that his—their—father is Wotan. The motif is a metonymy: the building does the work of identifying the architect. Wotan is never assigned a clear musical motif of his own until he becomes the Wanderer, at which point most of his plasticity of being, his scope for play, has gone: if his verbal name has become typal and enigmatic, his musical name has become rigid.

Wotan's name is also an issue in *Die Wibelungen*:

> Der Inbegriff dieser ewigen Bewegung, also des Lebens, fand endlich selbst im "Wuotan" (Zeus), als dem obersten Gotte, dem Vater und

> Durchdringer des All's, seinen Ausdruck, und mußte er seinem Wesen nach als höchster Gott gelten, als solcher auch die Stellung eines Vaters zu den übrigen Gottheiten einnehmen, so war er doch keinesweges wirklich ein geschichtlich älterer Gott, sondern einem neueren, erhöhteren Bewußtsein der Menschen von sich selbst entsprang erst sein Dasein; er ist somit abstrakter als der alte Naturgott, dieser dagegen körperlicher und den Menschen gleichsam persönlich angeborener.[17]
>
> The climax of this eternal motion, and so of life, finally found its expression in *Wuotan* (Zeus), as the highest god, the father and interpenetrator of the All; and if, according to his being, he had to be classified as the highest god, and therefore to take his place as a father to the other deities, still he was in no way a historically older god, for his existence sprang first from man's newer, heightened consciousness of himself; therefore he is more abstract than the old nature god—the old nature god is by contrast more corporeal, as if personally inborn in man.

Watching *Der Ring des Nibelungen*, we might reasonably have thought that in Wotan we had found the absolute, aboriginal, *uralt* godhead, subject to nothing but Dike and Anangke. But no, Wotan himself is an upstart; it seems that the whole race of gods—Fricka, Freia, Froh, Donner, Loge—are parvenu deities, shadowed darkly by some unspeakable, unnameable god, too corporeal to have a body. The Valhalla pantheon consists of improvised gods: the starry cosmos does not rest on their shoulders. Their very lack of solidity provides Wagner with room to create his own system of myth, room to be a deifactor.

In Percy Bysshe Shelley's *Prometheus Unbound* (1820), we hear the voice of Demogorgon, the Ground of all Being, who announces, "The deep truth is imageless." Does Wagner provide any images of the nature god, the stem god? I can argue that, in *Der Ring des Nibelungen*, the stem god, absent from the dramatis personae, is present in the orchestra: during the prelude to *Das Rheingold*, the harmonically invariant but ever-iridescing, ever-phosphorescing chord, at once a fleeting shimmer and the stablest thing imaginable, seems an immanence of an inexplicable god. The prelude represents the Rhine, and that river, passingly personified in the Rhinemaidens, passingly embodied in the Rhinegold, is the closest thing to a stem god we are likely to find here. In his autobiography Wagner used the language of mysticism to explain how he composed it, in Genoa after attacks of seasickness and dysentery:

> dafür versank ich in eine Art von somnambulem Zustand, in welchem ich plötzlich die Empfindung, als ob ich in ein stark fließendes Wasser versänke, erhielt. Das Rauschen desselben stellte sich mir bald im musikalischen Klange des Es-dur-Akkordes dar, welcher unaufhaltsam in figurirter Brechung dahin wogte; diese Brechungen zeigten sich als melodische Figurationen von zunehmender Bewegung, nie aber veränderte sich der reine Dreiklang von Es-dur, welcher durch seine Andauer dem Elemente, darin ich versank, eine unendliche Bedeutung geben zu wollen schien. Mit der Empfindung als ob die Wogen jetzt hoch über mich dahinbrausten, erwachte ich in jähem Schreck aus meinem Halbschlaf.[18]

> I sank into a kind of somnambulistic condition, in which I suddenly felt as if I were sinking into strongly flowing water. The rushing soon presented itself to me in musical sound, an E♭ major chord, restlessly surging in embellished arpeggios; these arpeggios arose in melodic figurations of increasing movement, but the pure triad of E♭ major never changed, and seemed by its persistence to intend to give an infinite significance to the element in which I sank. Feeling as if the waves were roaring high over me, I woke out of my half-sleep in sudden terror.

The stem god may simply be the concept of a cosmic tonic note. On the other hand, music is a system of relations and contingencies: neither E♭ nor any other note can pretend to be the universe's own fundamental. Wagner fully accepted the notion that keys have no character of their own: as he wrote to Theodor Uhlig,

> Hing man sich also an die "individualität" der tonarten, so hing man sich an eine chimäre[19]

> If you were relying on the "individuality" of tonalities, you were relying on a chimera.

There is no individuality, no personality, no god, to be found anywhere in the scale.

Sometimes art is capable of providing a strong semblance of what art can never actually provide: the E♭ in *Das Rheingold*; the thunder-word "DA" in Eliot's *The Waste Land* (1922), the primal syllable of the divine voice; the sound of certain echoes—I think especially of the improvisations of Pauline Oliveros, Stuart Dempster, and Panaiotis inside a two-million-gallon water tank, a concrete underground cistern near Seattle built to withstand bombing, with a reverberation time of forty-five seconds—the reverberations are almost as loud as the original noise, the literal speech of the abyss. But, as Theodor Adorno remarks, the more art tries to overcome its illusoriness, the more clearly it calls attention to its own illusory character.[20]

Wagner may shadow forth the sounds of the stem god's presence not only in *Der Ring des Nibelungen* but elsewhere as well. In *Die Wibelungen* Wagner speculates that Jesus Christ was a late avatar of the stem god:

> Die elementaren oder lokalen Naturgötter hat das Christenthum aber bis auf den heutigen Tag unter uns nicht auszurotten vermocht: jüngste Volkssagen und üppig bestehender Volksaberglaube bezeugen uns dieß im neunzehnten Jahrhunderte.
>
> Jener eine, heimische Stammgott, von dem die einzelnen Geschlechter ihr irdisches Dasein unmittelbar ableiteten, ist aber gewiß am allerwenigsten aufgegeben worden: denn an ihm fand sich mit Christus, Gottes Sohne, selbst die entscheidende Ähnlichkeit vor, daß auch er gestorben war, beklagt und gerächt wurde,—wie wir noch heute an den Juden Christus rächen. Alle Treue und Anhänglichkeit ging um so leichter auf Christus über, als man in ihm den Stammgott wieder erkannte, und war Christus, als Gottes Sohn, der Vater (mindestens der geistige) *aller* Menschen, so stimmte dieß nur um so erhebender und anspruchsrechtfertigender zu dem göttlichen Stammvater der Franken, die sich ja als das älteste Geschlecht dachten, von dem alle übrigen Völker ausgegangen.[21]

> Up to the present day Christianity has not been able to exterminate the elemental or local nature gods among us: very recent folk tales and a profusion of still-existing folk superstitions attest this to us in the nineteenth century.
>
> The one native stem god, from whom the individual races directly derived their earthly being, certainly became the least easily surrendered of all: for between him and Christ, the son of God, a decisive similarity was found, that he too died, was lamented and avenged—just as we still today avenge Christ upon the Jews. All faithfulness and dependency so easily changed over to Christus, as people recognized the stem god again in him; and if Christ, as God's son, was the father (at least the spiritual father) of *all* men, this accorded (so impressively, in a manner so conducive to justifying the claim) with the divine stem father of the Franks,

> who indeed thought themselves the oldest race, the race from which all others proceeded.

In the same year as *Die Wibelungen* (1848), Wagner wrote a detailed sketch for a project called *Jesus von Nazareth*, based on the Gospels. Christ, of course, never appears as a character in any of Wagner's music dramas, but it is possible that the Grail music of *Lohengrin* and the Love Feast music of *Parsifal*—these antidramatic or predramatic or supradramatic sound images of something beyond human comprehension—are secret presentations of the stem god's own voice, in Christian form, as best as Wagner can hear it. But any attempt to realize it in a material medium threatens to render it as a parody of itself, for the frequency of its true sound is either above the threshold of hearing, as the opening of *Lohengrin* suggests, or below, as the first note of *Das Rheingold* suggests.

To wield the stem god's power on earth is difficult or impossible. When Alberich tries to ball up the force of the stem god—that is, the Rhine, as coagulated in the Rhinegold—by renouncing love and forging the gold into a ring, he becomes master of the universe. Or so all the characters seem to believe. But what can the ring actually do? It seems to make Alberich a crueler and more efficient manager of the Nibelung Mining Enterprise, but it seems that he is already the king of the Nibelungs—his very name means "elf-king." The ring is unable to help him escape when Wotan and Loge tie him up. Wotan covets it and steals it from Alberich, but why? He is already the head god; it is far from clear what he could do with more power than he has already has. He has to surrender the ring to the giants Fasolt and Fafner in order to pay them for building Valhalla, but Fafner kills Fasolt—the first victim of Alberich's Curse—and then Fafner, turned dragon, sits on it in his cave for two generations as first Siegmund and then Siegfried grow to maturity. The ring is simply an item in a safe-deposit box. None of the later evolutions of the plot ever suggests that owning the ring has any practical benefit—it cannot save Brünnhilde from being overmastered by Siegfried (when disguised as Gunther in act 1, scene 3 of *Götterdämmerung*). The ring is a tool without a use, a zero, a stage prop. It is so much a nothing that it is not even cursed, only an object so deeply, so vainly coveted that many are willing to kill to get it. Its unctuous, unstable, cycloidal motif hints at its evasive promise of a meaning it can never deliver. Created by an act of desecration and representing the vanity of treasure, the ring, and the Ring motif, may have been connected in Wagner's mind to Jewishness.

In 1881, in a remarkable meditation on Mephistopheles' invention of paper money, as Goethe imagined it in the second part of *Faust*, Wagner writes:

> Der verhängnissvolle Ring des Nibelungen als Börsen-Portefeuille dürfte das schauerliche Bild des gespenstischen Weltbeherrschers zur Vollendung bringen. Wirklich wird diese Herrschaft von den Vertretern unserer fortschrittlichen Zivilisation als eine geistige, ja moralische Macht angesehen, da nun der geschwundene Glaube durch den "Kredit," diese durch die strengsten und raffinirtesten Sicherstellungen gegen Betrug oder Verlust unterhaltene Fiktion unserer gegenseitigen Redlichkeit, ersetzt sei. Was nun unter den Segnungen dieses Kredits bei uns zu Tage kommt, erleben wir jetzt, und scheinen nicht übel Lust zu haben, den Juden lediglich die Schuld hieran beizumessen.[22]

> We might be allowed to complete the shivery picture of the ghostly world ruler by imagining the Nibelung's fateful ring turned into a pocketbook. Truly this domination is regarded by the representatives of our progressive civilization as a spiritual, even a moral force, for vanished faith is now replaced by "credit," this fiction of our mutual honesty supported by the strictest and most elaborate safeguards against betrayal or loss. We are now experiencing what comes to light under the benedictions of this credit, and appear, not with ill will, to have a certain desire to lay the blame upon the Jews alone.

But the Nibelung's ring never was anything but a fictitious entry in an account book, concocted by a sinister usurer. Alberich is the god of the modern world: as Wagner told Liszt,

> Beachten wir die Welt nicht anders, als durch Verachtung . . . Sie gehört *Alberich*: Niemand anders!! Fort mit ihr![23]

> Let us not heed the world, except with contempt . . . It belongs to *Alberich*: no one else!! Away with it!

Whether Alberich is a Jew (as Adorno and others have argued) is not perfectly clear, but Wagner certainly seems to regard him as the ancestor stereotypical of Jewish economic practices. A certain sense of such Jewishness clings to many of Wagner's villains. According to Paul Heise, there is a note of uncertain origin that suggests that Wagner intended Klingsor's magic garden to be an image of Jewish art.

Wagner's music dramas seem to be about power, authority, and archaic wellsprings of meaning. But I think it is more correct to say that they are about weakness, inauthenticity, and the loss of meaning. Wagner is an atheist of his own imagination. The stem god himself is dead—"he too died, was lamented," as Wagner says in *Die Wibelungen*—though he seems to enjoy a frenetic, somewhat doubtful afterlife in folk myth and Christian legend. And in the music dramas of Wagner.

Every locus of value that Wagner finds or tries to erect is menaced on all sides. In *Die Meistersinger von Nürnberg* (composed 1862–67, premièred 1868) he proposes Germanness—"heilige deutsche Kunst" (holy German art), as Hans Sachs puts it—as a supreme value; after all, the pure-German Franks preserved as long as possible the genetic strain of the god-kings from the Caucasus. But Wagner considered German blood weak, as Cosima reported when a friend of Wagner's suggested that the Jewish question might be resolved by assimilation through intermarriage:

> R. behauptet: Dann würde es keine Deutschen mehr geben, das deutsche blonde Blut sei nicht kräftig genug, um dieser 'Lauge' zu widerstehen.[24]

> R. asserts: Then there would no longer be any Germans, the blond German blood would not be strong enough to withstand this 'lye.'

Extinction, implosion, is Wagner's great theme, from the collapse of Valhalla to the crumbling of Klingsor's castle. At the end of Wagner's draft libretto *Wieland der Schmied* (Wieland the Smith, written 1849–50; he tried to persuade Liszt to write music for it), the entire smithy crashes down and buries Wieland's enemies in the ruins.

Wagner's reluctance to complete the *Jesus von Nazareth* project shows another aspect of his inability to find any stable ground for value—as in the Gospels, as in Germanic myth. Possibly the most interesting theme in Wagner's notes for *Jesus* is the invective against oaths and laws:

> "Ihr sollt nicht schwören"; in dem Eide lag das bindende Gesetz einer Welt, welche noch nicht die Liebe kannte. Jeder Mensch sei frei, in jedem Augenblicke nach der Liebe und nach Vermögen zu handeln: durch einen Eid gebunden bin ich unfrei: thue ich in seiner Erfüllung Gutes, so verliert dies seinen Werth (wie jede gezwungene Tugend) und das Gute

verliert den Werth der Überzeugung; führt er mich zu Üblem, so sündige ich dann aber mit Überzeugung. Der Eid bringt jedes Laster hervor: bindet er mich gegen meinen Vortheil, so werde ich ihn zu umgehen suchen (wie jedes Gesetz umgangen wird), und so wird das, was ich ganz nach Recht thäte, indem ich meinem Gedeihen nachgehe, durch den Eid zum Verbrechen; finde ich aber in ihm meinen Vortheil, (ohne meinem Gegner dadurch Nachtheil zuzufügen,) so beraube ich mich des sittlichen Genusses, jeden Augenblick nach richtigem Ermessen das Rechte frei zu thun.[25]

"You shall not swear": in the oath lay the binding law of a world that did not yet know love. Let every human being be free at every moment according to love and to his ability to act: bound by an oath I am unfree: if I do good in fulfilling it, the good deed loses its value (like any enforced virtue) and the good deed loses the value of conviction. The oath brings forth every vice: if it binds me to my disadvantage, I will try to circumvent it (as every law is circumvented), and so by what I did rightly, in pursuit of happiness, the oath turns into a crime; if, however, I find advantage in it (without causing harm to my adversary), I rob myself of the ethical pleasure of doing right at every moment freely, according to my own discretion.

Hiergegen suchte die menschliche Gesellschaft Rettung durch das Gesetz: sie band den Begriff des Guten am Gesetze, als einem uns allen verständlichen und wahrnehmbaren, fest: das am Gesetz fest gebundene war aber nur ein Moment des Guten, und wie Gott ewig zeugend, flüssig und beweglich ist, wandte sich das Gesetz daher gegen Gott selbst; denn, indem der Mensch nicht anders als nach dem Urgesetze der Bewegung selbst leben und wandeln kann, muss er, seiner Natur folgend, gegen das Gesetz, d.i. das bindende, stehende,—verstössen, somit sündig werden. Dies ist das menschliche Leiden, das Leiden Gottes selbst, der sich in den Menschen noch nicht zum Bewusstsein gekommen ist.[26]

Human society sought salvation through the law; it bound the concept of the good to the law, as to a thing comprehensible and perceptible by us all: but what was bound fast to the law was only a moment of the good, and as god is eternally procreative, flowing, and mobile, the law turned against god himself; then, as man can live and change only according to the *ur*-law of motion, he must therefore, following his nature, become guilty of transgressing against the law, the binding, standing law, and so

> becoming sinful. This is human suffering, the suffering of God himself, who has not yet come to consciousness in man.

The strange mutability of names—Wagner continually respells them, reworks them, replaces them—is only a special case of the general shiftiness of words. A word that stands still petrifies into a kind of pumice, hard and abrasive, but insubstantial, slowly becoming pulverized. The Ten Commandments, the exhortations of Krishna to Arjuna, any proposition that attempts to limit behavior is finally intolerable. Even if I swear of my own free will to behave in such-and-such a manner, this oath is a wretched shackle, because I am always turning into someone else, someone for whom the oath will not be an expression of freedom—I am "procreative, flowing, and mobile," and my language must respect the indeterminacy of all things human.

The *Jesus von Nazareth* project may have failed precisely because it is difficult to make art when meaning starts to leak out of every proposition at the moment it is uttered. Even the value of the commandment against promulgating commandments presumably has a limited duration. The music dramas of Wagner propose names, rules, meanings, but then keep twisting out of them, wringing, ringing changes, doing, undoing, continually permuting the material into strange new shapes; if this sounds a bit like Beckett's *The Unnamable* (1953), I think that Wagner and Beckett are both masters of aporia. Many of the musical motifs in Wagner's work seem to have a prime form (often when they first appear), but literal repetition is rare, and those motifs that deviate little from their prime form slowly grow bland and insignificant, even when loudly stated. Epigrams are especially susceptible to such deterioration: because they carry the burden of a fixed verbal message, they are in effect laws of the sort that Jesus condemns. But those musical motifs that are like recombinant DNA, those that exuberate into music that we can scarcely recognize as related to the original—these are pure specimens of creativity. A motif is a temporary resting point on a journey into motiflessness. Wagner considered that his music was all about transition, and as he grows older his music increasingly evolves into states of transition so continuous that it is difficult to fix either the thing transited from or the destination at which it arrives. Thirty years after Wagner's death, Ferruccio Busoni, in *Entwurf einer neuen Ästhetik der Tonkunst* (Sketch of a New Aesthetic of Tonal Art, 1916), defined this state as the ideal condition of all music.

Wagner said that none of his gifts—as composer, dramatist, or poet—was especially great in itself; what was striking was his ability to focus them all on a single point. I think that under the light from this burning glass, the object of his concentration first shines brightly, then is consumed.

As a poet, Wagner had an unusual talent for *Stabreim*—the alliterative verse of all the old Germanic languages, including English. Poets tend to corporealize language, but Wagner went to remarkable extremes in this direction. Because the alliterative pattern of *Stabreim* depends only on the initial consonant of accented syllables, Wagner (in *Oper und Drama*) scrutinized initial consonants with a bizarre intimacy of response:

> Verstehen wir unter dem Angesichte der Wurzel die ganze physiognomische Außenseite des Menschen, die uns dieser beim Begegnen zuwendet, so gewinnen wir eine genau entsprechende Bezeichnung für die entscheidende Wichtigkeit des konsonierenden Anlautes. [. . .]
>
> Wir bezeichneten die umgebenden Konsonanten als das Gewand des Vokales, oder bestimmter, als seine physiognomische Außenseite. Bezeichnen wir sie nun, und zumal um ihrer erkannten Wirkung nach innen willen, noch genauer als das organisch mit dem Innern des menschlichen Leibes verwachsene Fleischfell desselben [. . .][27]

> If we understand by the root's face a man's whole physiognomic exterior, what he turns to us when we meet, we gain an exactly corresponding designation for the decisive importance of the initial consonant. [. . .]
>
> We designated the surrounding consonants as the vowel's clothes, or, more definitively, as its physiognomic exterior. Now, for the sake of their recognized effect on our inner life, we designate them still more exactly as the skin of flesh that develops organically together with the inside of the human body. [. . .]

Words, then, have human faces, similar to what Wagner calls here the "'eye' of hearing."

But the special virtue of *Stabreim*, according to Wagner, is its capacity for yoking together words of wildly disparate meaning, especially opposites—as if the excellence of a line of poetry lay in its power to force a rough marriage between unequal partners:

> Eine gemischte Empfindung dem bereits bestimmten Gefühle schnell verständlich zu machen, hat die dichterische Sprache wiederum im *Stabreime* ein unendlich vermögendes Mittel [. . .][28]

> In *Stabreim* poetic speech has an endlessly enabling means to make a mixed emotion . . . quickly understandable [. . .]

> Setzen wir dagegen einen Vers von gemischter Empfindung, wie: "die Liebe bringt Lust und Leid," so würde hier, wie der Stabreim zwei entgegengesetzte Empfindungen verbindet, der Musiker auch aus der angeschlagenen, der ersten Empfindung entsprechenden Tonart in eine andere, der zweiten Empfindung, nach ihrem Verhältnisse zu der in der ersten Tonart bestimmten, entsprechende überzugehen sich veranlaßt fühlen.[29]

> If we consider a verse of mixed emotion, such as "die Liebe bringt Lust and Leid" (Love brings delight and sorrow), in which the *Stabreim* binds together two opposing emotions, the composer would feel disposed to cross over from the key struck first, corresponding to the first emotion, to another key, corresponding to the second emotion, determined according its relation to the emotion in the first key.

"Die Liebe bringt Lust and Leid"—again and again Wagner appeals to this line as a perfect specimen of *Stabreim*. (Wagner's Isolde will remark, "Leben und Tod sind untertan ihr, die sie webt aus Lust und Leid" [Life and death are subject to the goddess of love, for she weaves them out of delight and sorrow].) Such a line has a built-in modulation, even before the composer applies his gift to musicalizing it. To hold contraries in a tense coincidence is Wagner's mission, I believe, as poet and composer: wherever we look, we see something that looks definite start to grow vague, twinkle into its opposite.

Wagner once said to Cosima,

> Ach! Wo ist aber bei uns eine Kultur möglich, wo die Wurzel der Religion so schadhaft ist und selbst die Terminologie so wenig geregelt ist, daß man noch von Geist und Naturals Antithese spricht.[30]

> Ach! But where is culture possible among us, where religion's root is so damaged and even the terminology is so little regulated, that one still speaks of spirit and nature as antitheses.

This is a casual remark, familiar in European Romantic thought; Coleridge, for example, formulates what he calls the Law of Polarity as follows: "The

Identity of *Thesis* and *Antithesis* is the substance of all Being; their *Opposition* the condition of all *Existence*, or Being manifested."[31] I think that this sense of a radical monism underlying all dualism generates much of the oddly constructed designs of Wagner's work. He will build a drama around a clear dialectic of spirit and nature and then show that there is no dialectic at all: the two terms aren't resolved, aren't sublated, but simply turn out never to have constituted an opposition in the first place. (Wagner told Liszt that Hegel was a "Charlatan,"[32] and Wagner is indeed the least Hegelian of dramatists.)

Two of his first five operas, *Das Liebesverbot* (The Ban on Love; composed 1834, premièred 1836) and *Tannhäuser* (composed 1843–45, premièred 1845), concern the opposition between spirit and nature in the form of the conflict between chastity and sex. But the more closely we look at these operas, especially *Tannhäuser*, the less confident we become that any conflict exists at all. The *Minnesinger* Tannhäuser has spent a long time underground, in a grotto in the Venusberg, as the lover of the goddess of love; but he tires of this artificial *volupté* and wishes to return to the court of Wartburg and to Elisabeth, his human beloved. He complains that he lives in a state of complete unnature:

Die Zeit, die hier ich verweil',
ich kann sie nicht ermessen:
Tage, Monde gibt's für mich nicht mehr;
denn nicht mehr sehe ich die Sonne,
nicht mehr des Himmels freundliche Gestirne;
den Halm seh' ich nicht mehr, der frisch ergrünend
den neuen Sommer bringt;
die Nachtigall hör' ich nicht mehr,
die mir den Lenz verkünde.
Hör' ich sie nie, seh' ich sie niemals mehr?

The time I spend here with you
I cannot rightly measure:
Days and months no longer count for me;
For never can I see the sun;
The starry sky no longer gives me greeting;
No blade of grass grows fresh and green again
As the new summer comes;
I never hear the nightingale

That ever heralds spring.
Will I never hear or see them more? (*Tannhäuser*, act 1, scene 2)

Trapped in this hellish paradise of sex, Tannhäuser begs for release.

But what is the force that makes the grass take on new green, that puts the gurgle and whir in the voice of the nightingale? It is, of course, Venus—the shepherd, in his charming song that dispels the urgencies and languors of the Venusberg and returns us to the delights of nature, calls her Frau Holda, but this can only be an epithet for Venus: as the goddess of sexual love she is the universal source of generation. Part of the overture to the opera (I speak of the 1845 version, not the 1861 revision) is devoted to the trudge of pious pilgrims—chaste and chaste and chaste—and part to Venus's orgy of nymphs and satyrs, erratic, jerky, hectic, full of spurts and gusts. But both sections are in the same key, E major; and when the pilgrims' processional music appears in the recapitulation, it is decorated with a little throbbing figure that Wagner identified as the Pulse of Life—we hear it again when the pilgrims sing in the opera's final measures:

> Es ist der Jubel des aus dem Fluche der Unheiligkeit erlösten Venusberg selbst, den wir zu dem Gotteslìede vernehmen. So wallen und springen alle Pulse des Leben zu dem Gesange der Erlösung; und beide getrennten Elemente, Geist und Sinne, Gott und Natur, umschlingen sich zum heilig einenden Kusse der Liebe.[33]

> It is the elation of the Venusberg itself, redeemed from the curse of unholiness, that we hear in the hymn to god. So all the pulses of life seethe and flow in the song of redemption; and the two severed elements, spirit and senses, god and nature, entwine themselves in the holy uniting kiss of love.

The opera is a great *Stabreim* that holds together in a single tense term sexual and spiritual devotion, *geil und geistlich*, and shows how they interpenetrate one another.

This same dissolving of antitheses can be found everywhere. In act 1, scene 3 of *Die Walküre* there is a puzzling moment when Siegmund sings of his ardor for Sieglinde ("Heiligster Minne höchste Noth" [Highest need of holy love]) to the tune of the Renunciation epigram from scene 1 of *Das Rheingold* ("Nur wer der Minne Macht entsagt" [Only he who renounces love]): Wagner assigns identical music to Alberich, forswearing love in order to fulfill the conditions for making a ring out of the Rhinegold, and to Siegmund, blazing forth with love for Sieglinde. Extreme love and extreme lovelessness turn out to be the same thing. A second example: in act 1, scene 1 of *Siegfried*, the plot concerns Siegfried's attempts to free himself from the only parent he's ever known, the disgusting dwarf Mime, who has raised the boy from infancy in order to create a hero mighty enough to kill the dragon Fafner and win Alberich's ring for himself; to fulfill this hope Mime must make a hero-worthy weapon by reforging the fragments of Siegmund's sword, but he can't figure out how to do this, even though he's the master smith of all the Nibelungs; Siegfried, however, through sheer instinct succeeds, by filing down the fragments and then heating the filings in a mighty fire. Siegfried's ultra-exultant flamenco of a forging song, which occupies a great deal of space in this long scene, begins with two descending tetrachords, the second of which begins one whole step lower than the first. But we have heard this same melodic pattern before, at the opening of Mime's wheedling song "Als zullendes Kind" (As suckling child), a vile appeal to Siegfried's loyalty to his parody father. To mock Mime, Siegfried sings it back to him—and since both are tenors, for a moment they are hard to tell apart, as if Wagner were secretly experimenting with a composite being, at once the bravest of heroes and the most sniveling of villains. Opposites are twins.

In Wagner's last music drama, *Parsifal* (composed 1877–82, premièred 1882), opposites are so intimately conjoined that we seem to enter a hall of mirrors. The seductress/penitent Kundry combines so many opposites in her own person that she's a hall of mirrors all by herself: she has aspects of Mary Magdalene, the Wandering Jew (in that she mocked Christ on the cross and was condemned to endless error), Herodias (in that she erotically murders Christian virtue), a Valkyrie (in her role as the Valkyrie Gundryggia[34]—and, Valkyrie-style, she rides horses furiously across impossible distances), and a humble slave of the Grail, willing to go to Arabia to find medicine to relieve Amfortas's wound. In the abandoned Buddhist project *Die Sieger* (The Victors, 1856–58), Wagner intended to create a woman who lived a chaste life to atone for rejecting love in a previous incarnation; and Kundry, in the course of one interminable lifetime has in effect lived through every possible avatar of the feminine. She is every heroine of every opera; Cosima Wagner remembered her husband as saying:

> Man könnte sagen, den Liebestod Isolden's hat Kundry bereits hundertfach in ihren verschiedenen Wiedergeburten durchgemacht.[35]

One could say that Kundry has already undergone Isolde's Liebestod a hundred times in her various rebirths.

Parsifal's gestation was long, and as early as 1860 Wagner wrote excitedly to Mathilde Wesendonck that he had synthesized the character of Kundry out of two different characters, by combining the fabulously wild Grail messenger ("fabelhaft wilde Gralsbotin") in act 1 with the seductive woman of the second act ("mit dem verführerischen Weibe des zweiten Aktes").[36] If I were devising costumes, I would clothe Kundry in the transparent gold skink-slink ravish that Gustav Klimt devised in *Judith I* (1901); Klimt outfits the Old Testament's pious Judith (the widow of a great Israelite warrior, who sneaks into the tent of the Assyrian commander Holofernes and revels with him in order to get him so drunk that she can cut off his head) with a costume and orgasmic facial expression more suitable for that other great biblical beheader, Salome. For Klimt, as for Wagner, all women are one woman.

There are still more radical coadunations of character. The Parsifal motif is a sort of hunting call, one of those memorable nature themes that came so easily to Wagner for representing naïve heroes; it ends with three notes ascending stepwise in a dotted rhythm. If this staggered ascent were prolonged, it would turn into the very figure that represents Kundry in full gallop. Wagner, it seems, has cut a melody in two and given half to Parsifal and half to Kundry. Hans-Jürgen Syberberg's 1983 film version is wonderfully sensitive both to Parsifal's epicene nature (Parsifal is cast in some scenes as a girl, in others as a boy) and to the strange hints of incest in the seduction scene, as Kundry vamps Parsifal while recounting his mother's frantic love and death (the actress who plays Kundry offers Parsifal her breast as if to suckle). But in any production Parsifal and Kundry will seem like strangely intervolved beings, the last in the long series of lovers (beginning, maybe, with Rienzi and Irene in *Rienzi* [composed 1837–40, premièred 1842]) who are (or are like) brother and sister and mother and son. In some versions of the Tristan and Isolde legend, a tree grows from each of their graves, and the two trees start to grow together inextricably; that sense of love's power to overentangle, to re-enwomb, to consubstantialize, seems deep in Wagner's erotic imagination.

When Parsifal first enters, Gurnemanz asks Parsifal his name; Parsifal says, "Ich hatte viele, doch weiss ich ihrer keinen mehr" (I had many, but I don't know a single one any more). In one sense Parsifal is nameless; in another sense he has all the names. Parsifal and Kundry share a vast diffuseness of being. When in the second act Kundry cries out the name "Parsifal" across the magic garden, he remembers his mother pronounced it in a dream; Kundry explains that in Arabia, where his father died, it means "Pure Fool." Wagner's music removes any sting from this etymology, and in 1877 Wagner wrote a note to Judith Gautier further glorifying the deep Arabic roots of the name:

> Ce nom est arabe. Les anciens trouvères ne l'ont plus compris. "Parsi fal" signifie: "parsi"—pensez aux Parses adoreurs du feu—"pur"; "fal" dit "fou," dans un sens élevé, c'est-à-dire homme sans érudition, mais de génie. ("Fellow," en anglais, paraît être en rapport avec ce racine orientale.)[37]

> This name is Arabian. The old troubadours no longer understood it. "Parsi fal" means: "parsi"—think of the Parsees, fire-worshipers—"pure"; "fal" means "fool," in an elevated sense, that is, a man without erudition, but a man of genius. ("Fellow," in English, is related to this oriental root.)

But the fact remains that the star of the show is named Folly. Parsifal's name, like Parsifal himself, is an empty surface on which anything can be written.

In 1881 Cosima remarked in her diary,

> Wie beim Kaffee das Gespräch auf Eros und Anteros, verschmähte Liebe, kommt, sagt R., Anteros ist Parsifal.[38]

> Over coffee, conversation comes up concerning Eros and Anteros, unrequited love, R. says that Anteros is Parsifal.

Anteros is a curious god: the name comes from *Anti-Eros*, but *anti-* in the sense of counterpart—Anteros is the god of *requited* love. Wagner, however, evidently thought of Anteros in the sense of antierotic, the opponent of sexual attraction, saltpeter as deity. In this sense the entwining together of Kundry's and Parsifal's musical names becomes another version of the end of *Tannhäuser*, in which chastity and voluptuousness are somehow the same thing.

The most important intellectual influence on Wagner's later work was Arthur Schopenhauer's *Die Welt as Wille und Vorstellung* (The World as Will and Representation, 1819). Schopenhauer begins by telling us that we live our foolish lives thinking ourselves private individuals, cherishing our uniqueness, our little body of private preferences—nobody else likes cinnamon and bitter chocolate and carpet slippers and grayish-green paint and wintry landscapes with rows of leafless poplar trees in quite the same way I do. But to Schopenhauer, individuality is a delusion: there is only one desiring agent in the universe—you desire, and I desire, and the hungry squirrel on the lawn desires, but these desires are only local expressions of a single great desire that gropes its way through you and me and lambs and tigers and amoebas and blades of grass that yearn for the sun. This master desire Schopenhauer calls the will. In Thomas Mann's summary, the will is sheer-sinful, sheer-stupid, a blind reaching out:

> Indem nämlich die Weltwerdung des Willens sich nach dem principium individuationis, durch seine Zersplitterung in die Vielheit vollzieht, vergißt er seine ursprüngliche Einheit und wird, obgleich in aller Zerstückelung der Eine, zu einem millionenfach mit sich selbst entzweiten, gegen sich selbst streitenden Willen . . . und so beständig die Zähne in sein eigenes Fleisch schlägt, jenem Tartaros-Insassen gleich, der gierig sein eigenes Fleisch verzehrte.[39]

> As the will's world-forming fulfills itself according to the principle of individuation, through its shattering into multiplicity, it forgets its original unity and, although in all its dismemberments it is one, it becomes a will a million times divided against itself, striving against itself . . . and so constantly drives its teeth into its own flesh, like that resident of Tartarus who greedily ate his own flesh.

Only through chaste intellection, through choosing a dispassionate life of ideas—what Schopenhauer calls representation, *Vorstellung*—can we hope to save ourselves from will. As Wagner told Liszt, Schopenhauer's

> Hauptgedanke, die endliche Verneinung des Willens zum Leben, ist von furchbarem Ernste, aber einzig erlösend.[40]

> principal thought, the negation of the will to live, is fearfully serious, but the only thing that can save us.

In his essay "Beethoven" (1870)—his most impressive achievement as a prose writer, I think—Wagner uses Schopenhauer's philosophy to distinguish a light world, the world as given to the eye, minutely discriminated, wide awake, from a sound world, the world as given to the ear, dreamy, unconscious or half-conscious, undone. Music immerses us in this uncategoried world, indistinct and undistinguishing, where time and space no longer exist, and the names of things no longer obtain. Even the passions themselves blur, become variants of a single passion:

> Wollen wir nun den Schrei, in allen Abschwächungen seiner Heftigkeit bis zur zartesten Klage des Verlangens und als das Grundelement jeder menschlichen Kundgebung an das Gehör denken . . . die allerunmittelbarste Äußerung des Willens.[41]

> We consider the scream, in all the attenuations of its vehemence, down to the tenderest lament of longing, to be the fundamental element of every human declaration to the ear . . . the will's most immediate utterance of all.

A lullaby is a weakened scream; a tender declaration of love, a sob, a spasm, a cry of "Oh" at the buzzing of a mosquito—all are varieties of scream. Here, at last, we find the right name for any and every musical motif: Scream. In a world of vain desire, all that the desirer can do is to try to arrest the object of desire by shouting at it.

Tristan und Isolde (composed 1857–59, premièred 1865) recasts the Buddhist material from *Die Sieger* as a phantasmagoria about desire and the hope of escaping from it, less by renouncing it in the manner recommended by Schopenhauer or Buddha than by exhausting desire through surrender to it. In 1858 Wagner wrote to Mathilde Wesendonck—the closest thing to an Isolde in his personal life—that Ananda (the hero of *Die Sieger*) had persuaded Buddha to admit women to the community of saints, on the grounds that they were not so sex driven as Buddha thought; and further that Schopenhauer's scheme for salvation was wrong:

> Es handelt sich nämlich darum, den von keinem Philosophen, namentlich auch von Sch. nicht, erkannten Heilsweg zur vollkommenen Beruhigung des Willens durch die Liebe, und zwar nicht einer abstracten Menschenliebe, sondern der wirklich, aus dem Grunde der Geschlechtsliebe, d. h. der Neigung zwischen Mann und Weib keimenden Liebe, nachzuweisen.[42]

> It is a question of this, to show the way to salvation, not recognized by any philosopher, especially not by Schopenhauer: by the perfect quieting of the will through love, not indeed through abstract human love, but

> through some actually germinating love, based on sexual love, that is, on the affinity between man and woman.

Schopenhauer's eyes would have grown wide at the thought that you could dismiss the will, not by immersing yourself in the chill of abstract intellection, but by sexual intercourse. In act 1, Tristan and Isolde are individuals: Isolde raging at Tristan, first for his shallow attempt to trick her into healing him, then for (in effect) selling her off to be the bride of his liege, King Marke, as part of a peace treaty between Ireland and Cornwall; Tristan formal, decorous, faintly sneering until Isolde's hatred compels him, as an honorable knight, to offer to let her kill him. In act 2, Tristan un-Tristans and Isolde un-Isoldes: their individualities fall away as they abandon their daylight selves and enter a lightless region where orgasm and the death shudder are one—the dark side of their private moon:

> *Tristan.* Tristan du,
> ich Isolde,
> nicht mehr Tristan!
>
> *Isolde.* Du Isolde,
> Tristan ich,
> nicht mehr Isolde!
>
> *Beide.* Ohne Nennen,
> ohne Trennen,
> neu' Erkennen,
> neu' Entbrennen;
> ewig endlos,
> ein-bewußt:
> heiß erglühter Brust
> höchste Liebeslust! (act 2, scene 2)
>
> *Tristan.* You are Tristan,
> I am Isolde
> Tristan no more!
>
> *Isolde.* You are Isolde,
> I am Tristan,
> Isolde no more!

Both. Without naming,
unseparating,
new forms of knowing,
now outbreaking;
eternal-endless,
in-awareness:
hot-glowing breast
highest love-lust!

But King Marke discovers them in the midst of this dizzying duetting and, wretched, grieved, asks Tristan to account for himself; Tristan can only explain that he can't explain:

Dem Land, das Tristan meint,
der Sonne Licht nicht scheint:
es ist das dunkel
nächt'ge Land,
daraus die Mutter
mich entsandt (act 2, scene 3)

In the land that Tristan means
the sun's light never shines:
the dark land
of always-night
from which my mother
sent me out

But Tristan, a knight standing humiliated before his king, can't figure out how to get himself unborn on the spot: so he fights with Melot, the false friend who betrayed him, and lets Melot strike him with his sword.

Most of act 3 is devoted to Tristan's fever ravings in Brittany, where he waits for Isolde to come and, for the second time, cure him. But he is so excited at her arrival that he tears off his bandages and dies, just as she enters the stage; and the opera ends as she transfigures herself and her lover in a great aria, a paean to the unconscious: "unbewußt—höchste Lust!" (unconscious—highest bliss!). The climax of *Die Geburt der Tragödie* (The Birth of Tragedy, 1872), by the young Friedrich Nietzsche, asserts that here Wagner succeeds in reviving the spirit of Dionysus in the "mythless," pallid world of modern Europe:

> An diese ächten Musiker richte ich die Frage, ob sie sich einen Menschen denken können, der den dritten Act von "Tristan und Isolde" ohne alle Beihülfe von Wort und Bild rein als ungeheuren symphonischen Satz zu percipiren im Stande wäre, ohne unter einem krampfartigen Ausspannen aller Seelenflügel zu verathmen? Ein Mensch, der wie hier das Ohr gleichsam an die Herzkammer des Weltwillens gelegt hat, der das rasende Begehren zum Dasein als donnernden Strom oder als zartesten zerstäubten Bach von hier aus in alle Adern der Welt sich ergiessen fühlt, er sollte nicht jählings zerbrechen?[43]

> To true musicians I direct the question, if they can imagine a man capable of perceiving the third act of *Tristan und Isolde* with no help from word and image, purely as a monstrous symphonic movement, without expiring in a convulsion of the soul's wings, loosed from every restraint? A man like this, who has put his ear to the heart-chamber of the world-will, who feels the raging hunger for being as a thundering stream or as a brook dispersed to the sweetest mist, gushing from this source through all the world's veins—shouldn't he suddenly break to pieces?

Nietzsche's rhetoric here is almost exactly that of Wagner's own essay "Beethoven," written two years earlier: Wagner speaks of all human utterances, even the tenderest cry of longing, as attenuated forms of a scream; Nietzsche speaks of the world-will—Schopenhauer's will—as audible in the music as a thundering stream or a mildly misting brook. Elsewhere in his book Nietzsche alleges that mankind *is* dissonance—and Nietzsche may have conceived mankind's dissonance as the famous half-diminished *Tristan* chord (F–B–D♯–G♯), indeterminate, irresolute because so many resolutions are possible. In the same year that *Die Geburt der Tragödie* was published, Nietzsche composed a *Manfred-Meditation* for piano four hands, which in several places threatens to break out into the opening love-potion theme of *Tristan und Isolde* but never quite manages to get there—as if Nietzsche wanted his music to be even more incapable of resolution than Wagner's, even more will-ful.

The name of any Wagner character is finally Outis, Nobody. And all his music dramas finally take place in one setting, Nirvana. *Nirvana*, in Sanskrit, refers to the snuffing out of a candle; and Tristan und Isolde seem determined to snuff out the sun. But *Tristan und Isolde* is different from some of Wagner's other music dramas, in that it doesn't posit a particular place that is, in effect, Nowhere; instead Nirvana seems simply to be a way of construing our usual world in some manner independent of the categories of time and space, light and darkness—as if Nirvana and the world of experience exist side by side, and you can move from one to the other by willing or unwilling yourself there. Wagner wrote to Mathilde Wesendonck:

> Alles ist mir fremd, und sehnsüchtig blicke ich oft nach dem Land Nirwana. Doch Nirwana wird mir schnell wieder Tristan.[44]

> Everything is strange to me, and often with yearning I glance at the land of Nirvana. But Nirvana quickly becomes Tristan again.

The character and the state of unbeing are mysteriously hybrid.

But elsewhere it is easy to find specific Nirvana locales. In *Tannhäuser* the Venusberg is just such a place, as Wagner explained in an 1852 program note to a performance of the overture:

> Wie auf seinem Zauberruf thut sich nun das Wunder des Venusberges in hellster Fülle vor ihm auf; ungestümes Jauchzen und wilder Wonneruf erheben sich von allen Seiten; im trunkenem Jubel brausen die Bacchantinnen daher und reißen in ihrem wüthenden Tanze Tannhäuser fort bis in die heißen Liebesarme der Göttin selbst, die ihn, den in Wonne Ertrunkenen, mit rasender Gluth umschlingt, und in unnahbare Fernen, bis in das Reich des Nichtmehrseins, mit sich fortzieht.[45]

> As at his magic cry the wonders of the Venusberg present themselves in brightest fullness before him; vehement shouts and wild cries of joy rise up on all sides; in drunken elation the Bacchantes roar and in their raging dance snatch Tannhäuser into the goddess's hot arms of love, and with frenzied ardor she embraces the joy-drowned man and pulls him away into a place far off and inaccessible, the kingdom of being-no-more.

And the Castle of the Grail, in *Lohengrin*, is outside time and space, beyond the realm of stageable: it exists only as a construct of music, fully present in the Prelude, alluded to elsewhere. In *Parsifal*, however, the Castle of the Grail is both outside time and space and inside them: Wagner wants to present it as an extradimensional artifact, in that Gurnemanz and Parsifal reach it by standing still and letting the castle travel to them (on a rotating stage, one of the theatrical marvels of the new Bayreuth opera house):

Parsifal. Ich schreite kaum,
doch wähn' ich mich schon weit.
Gurnemanz. Du siehst, mein Sohn,
zum Raum wird hier die Zeit.

Parsifal. I scarcely walk,
and yet I seem to race.
Gurnemanz. You see, my son,
here time turns into space.

And yet, when we arrive at the castle, it seems in some ways a fairly normal operatic-gothic place, with an old king who is a singing corpse, a new king tortured by his wounds—the venue is too fallen to allow any uncovering of the Grail.

When Parsifal redeems himself and the Grail knights and the castle, at the end of act 3, Wagner pulls out all his immense resources of sound dazzles and tingles to hoist it out of the mundane into the wild celeste of poesy. But I suspect that the true Nirvana lies elsewhere.

In *Tannhäuser* the world of *Nichtmehrsein*, Being-no-more, was the Venusberg, a world of desire and desire's end. In Parsifal there is also a Venusberg, Klingsor's castle, and it makes a better Nirvana than the Castle of the Grail—the fact that it crumbles into nothing makes it all the more Nirvana-esque. The other place, the good castle, is, except for Amfortas, whom Klingsor wounded and tried to castrate as he embraced Kundry,[46] a domain without sex—just as Jesus, according to Wagner, was sexless, as Cosima recalled:

> Er spielt darauf für sich das erste Thema von Parsifal und kommt zurück und teilt mit, wie er durch einen Chor die Worte habe aussprechen lassen, um daß es weder weiblich noch männlich erscheine, ganz ungenerell müßte Christus sein, weder Frau noch Mann, so habe auch Leonardo in der Cena es versucht, einen beinahe weiblichen Kopf mit Bart zu geben. Weder alt noch jung dürfe er erscheinen, der Gott im Menschen.[47]

> He plays to himself the first theme of *Parsifal* and comes back and speaks of how he let a chorus utter the words, so that it would seem neither female nor male, Christ had to be completely general, neither woman nor man, thus Leonardo also, in his *Last Supper*, attempted that, showing

an almost feminine head with a beard. He must appear neither old nor young, the god in man.

But for Wagner you reach Schopenhauer's state of sanctity, release from desire, "quieting of the will," not by lacking sex organs but by having them and (over)using them. The magician Klingsor was expelled from the band of the Grail knights for castrating himself, for in effect becoming a parody of the sexless Christ. A eunuch himself—Kundry taunts him by calling out, "Haha!—Bist du keusch?" (Are you chaste?)—Klingsor, a sort of anti-Venus, presides over a garden of venereal delights, in the form of the flower maidens who tempt the Grail knights from their sacred mission. Klingsor's magic castle represents the entire round of human sexuality, from hatred of sexual desire to prostitution to (if Kundry is telling Parsifal the truth when she describes the charms of her body as redemptive, salvific) orgasmic transfiguration:

> *Parsifal.* . . . Verderberin! Weiche von mir!
> Ewig—ewig—von mir!
> *Kundry. (in höchster Leidenschaft)*
> Grausamer!
> Fühlst du im Herzen
> nur and'rer Schmerzen,
> so fühle jetzt auch die meinen!
> Bist du Erlöser,
> was bannt dich, Böser,
> nicht mir auch zum Heil dich zu einen?
> Seit Ewigkeiten—harre ich deine . . .
> So war es mein Kuß,
> der welthellsichtig dich machte?
> Mein volles Liebesumfangen
> So war es mein Kuß,
> der welthellsichtig dich machte?
> Mein volles Liebesumfangen
> schuf dich zum Gott die Stunde
>
> *Parsifal.* . . . Corrupter! Relent!
> leave me forever—forever!
> *Kundry. (in highest passion)*

You are cruel!
If you feel in your heart
only the pains of others,
now feel mine as well!
If you are redeemer,
What stops you, vile man,
from uniting with me to save me?
I wait for you for eternities . . .
Was it my kiss
that made you world-clairvoyant?
My full embrace of love
would make you a god for an hour

Kundry's desperate rhetoric could be dismissed as a seduction ploy—on the other hand, the reliable narrator Gurnemanz has told us that Kundry never lies: "nie lügt Kundry." I might argue that Parsifal's true escape from desire is here, in Klingsor's chromatic hell, and that Tannhäuser's lies in the Venusberg. The opera wavers between its Christian construction (what we see onstage), and an alternate construction, in tune with the Wagner of the 1850s—the Wagner who reads Schopenhauer and writes *Tristan und Isolde*—in which Kundry, instead of subsiding meekly, mutely, into the role of slave, undergoes her hundred-and-first "Liebestod" as she successfully seduces Parsifal and redeems herself and him.

Parsifal and *Tristan und Isolde* are twin dramas, experimenting with two different resolutions to the problem of superseding desire. Tristan and Amfortas are the same man in two different stories, as Wagner noted as he was considering an alternate construction of the third act of the earlier music drama:

> Im letzten Akte flocht ich hierbei eine, jedoch später nicht ausgeführte, Episode ein: nämlich einen Besuch des nach dem Gral umherirrenden Parzival an Tristan's Siechbette. Dieser an der empfangenen Wunde siechende und nicht sterben könnende Tristan, identifizirte sich in mir nämlich mit dem Amfortas im Gral-Roman.[48]

> Into the last act [of *Tristan und Isolde*] I wove an episode not later put on stage, namely a visit by Parsifal, wandering around in search of the Grail, to Tristan's sickbed. This Tristan, languishing from his wound and unable to die, I identified with Amfortas in the Grail romance.

Wagner's characters have certain points of differentiation, but ultimately they are all indistinct modalities of the one will, the one willnessless. You can get to the land of desire's end by renouncing all lust, as Parsifal does—although not completely, for he will become Lohengrin's father. Or you can fuck your way to Nirvana.

THREE

Maeterlinck's Modernisms

Debussy and Dukas

1. Maeterlinck's Subtractions

PELLÉAS AND MÉLISANDE TALK INTENTLY ABOUT THE FOUNTAIN that no longer restores the sight of the blind. He notes that Mélisande's hair is so long that it has fallen into the water; he warns her not to keep tossing her wedding ring high in the air, because it might fall into the water. But Mélisande cries, "Oh!":

Pelléas. Il est tombé!
Mélisande. Il est tombé dans l'eau!
Pelléas. Où est-il? où est-il?
Mélisande. Je ne le vois pas descendre!
Pelléas. Je crois la voir briller!
Mélisande. Ma bague?
Pelléas. Oui, oui; là-bas . . .
Mélisande. Oh! oh! Elle est si loin de nous! Non, non, ce n'est pas elle . . . ce n'est plus elle. Elle est perdue . . . perdue! Il n'y a plus qu'un grand cercle sur l'eau . . .[1]

Pelléas. It fell!
Mélisande. It fell in the water!
Pelléas. Where is it? where is it?
Mélisande. I didn't see it go down.
Pelléas. I think I see it shining!
Mélisande. My ring?
Pelléas. Yes, yes; down there . . .

> *Mélisande.* Oh! oh! It's so far from us! No, no, that's not it . . . That's not it any more . . . It's lost . . . lost! Nothing left but a big circle of water . . .

But during this scene the singers aren't sitting on the edge of a fountain: they're talking to each other quietly in a luxurious high-ceilinged room, wearing expensive, more or less modern clothes—Mélisande, half-sitting in a studded leather armchair, pantomimes a ring toss, while Pelléas kneels near her. They seem to be improvising an operatic scene to amuse themselves—they are too well bred, too reticent to talk directly about their affection for one another, so they make up a pseudo-medieval play-world in which they can obliquely describe their emotional landscape. "Pelléas" and "Mélisande" are simply names of characters in a role-playing game—a sort of Dungeons and Dragons for the listlessly rich, but almost completely improvised. When two people engage in this sort of feigning-together, one party proposes an event: then the second party either agrees ("It fell"; "It fell in the water!"), thereby affirming the event's existence, or corrects ("I see it shining!"; "That's not it"), thereby retracting the proposed event and substituting a new one.

I'm describing here the 1987 Lyons production of the Debussy opera, in which the director, Pierre Strosser, found a brilliant solution to a problem that had long vexed Maurice Maeterlinck himself: the inadequacy of human actors. Maeterlinck liked to write marionette plays and noted that he did not intend to write for ordinary actors:

> N'est-il pas évident que le Macbeth ou l'Hamlet que nous voyons sur la scène ne ressemble pas au Macbeth ou à l'Hamlet du livre? Qu'il a visiblement rétrogradé dans le sublime? Qu'une grande partie des efforts du poète qui voulait créer avant tout une vie supérieure, une vie plus proche de notre âme, a été annulée par une force ennemie qui ne peut se manifester qu'en ramenant cette vie supérieure au niveau de la vie ordinaire? [. . .]
>
> Je me souviens de cette mort de l'Hamlet de mes rêves. Un soir j'ouvris la porte à l'usurpateur du poème. L'acteur était illustre. Il entra. Un seul de ses regards me montra qu'il n'était pas Hamlet. Il ne le fut pas un seul instant pour moi. Je le vis s'agiter durant trois heures dans le mensonge. Je voyais clairement qu'il avait ses propres destinées; et celles qu'il voulait représenter m'étaient indiciblement indifferentes à côté des siennes. Je voyais sa santé et ses habitudes, ses passions et ses tristesses, ses pensées

> et ses oeuvres, et il essayait vainement de m'intéresser à une vie qui n'était pas la sienne et que sa seule présence avait rendue factice.[2]

> Isn't it evident that the Macbeth or the Hamlet we see on the stage bears no resemblance to the Macbeth or the Hamlet we read in the book? That his sublimity has visibly regressed? That a great part of the poet's effort to create, above all, a higher life, a life closer to our soul, has been canceled out by a hostile force that can only show itself by bringing this higher life down to the level of ordinary life? [. . .]
>
> In my dreams I remember Hamlet's death. One evening I opened the door to the poem's usurper. The actor was illustrious. He entered. It took only one glance to show me that he wasn't Hamlet. Not for one instant, as far as I was concerned. For three hours I saw him stomp around in a lie. I was clearly seeing that he had his own destiny; and the destiny he wanted to represent meant nothing at all to me when placed next to his. I was seeing his health and his habits, his passions and his miseries, his thoughts and his deeds, and he was trying in vain to interest me in a life that wasn't his own and that his very presence had made a sham.

But if Hamlet were sitting with Laertes on a sofa, talking through a pretend fencing match, then Maeterlinck wouldn't have to worry about the actor's inadequacy to the role: the actor would be, in effect, reading a book out loud from memory and inviting the audience to read along with him. If he shouted, if he sobbed, the audience would see it not as enacting a role but as illustrating it, giving voice-color, voice-shape, to some fleeting personage nowhere in the playhouse, nowhere in the world. The communal experience of the theater, and the intimacy of reading, are almost perfectly integrated in Strosser's production.

The search for a soul theater, a *théâtre pur*, uncontaminated by the vain dreck of the commonplace, anticipates many aspects of Modernist drama. The characters in Maeterlinck's plays often seem initially to be under the illusion that they're human beings but come to understand their puppetlike or transhuman status as the play comes to its end. Maeterlinck was born in 1862 and had enormous influence on the dramaturgy of slightly younger writers, such as William Butler Yeats (born 1865), John Millington Synge (born 1871), and Edward Gordon Craig (born 1872)—playwrights and directors working their way past Realism toward a harder, sparer, more abstract theater. Craig advocated that the stage was better conceived as a space for idols—what he called *Übermarionetten*—than as a space for actors; he argued that acting would be a fine thing if it were possible, but nobody has enough control over face and body actually to do it. Synge not only wrote plays in the parabolic fashion of Maeterlinck, but was also attracted, like Maeterlinck, to radical gestures of resignation, self-abandon. For example, Synge's *Riders to the Sea* (1904), set in the bleak Aran Islands, concerns a mother of six fishermen, five of whom have already died; during the course of the brief play the sixth is also swept away by the sea. Near the end, the women begin to keen in a kind of chorus, and the mother says, as if in a trance:

> They're all gone now, and there isn't anything more the sea can do to me. . . . I'll have no call now to be up crying and praying when the wind breaks from the south, and you can hear the surf is in the east, and the surf is in the west, making a great stir with the two noises, and they hitting one on the other. I'll have no call now to be going down and getting Holy Water in the dark nights after Samhain, and I won't care what way the sea is when the other women will be keening.

The declamation is a little more pointed, focused, than Maeterlinck's, but the sense of helplessness before iron necessity is similar.

Yeats's short plays also sometimes have Maeterlinckian moments of intimate relinquishment, as in *The Only Jealousy of Emer* (1919): here the wife and the mistress of the great hero Cuchulain stand over his comatose body, and the wife begs the mistress to try to waken him:

> *Emer.* Bend over him.
> Call out dear secrets till you have touched his heart
> If he lies there; and if he is not there
> Till you have made him jealous.
>
> *Eithne Inguba.* Cuchulain, listen.
>
> *Emer.* You speak too timidly; to be afraid
> Because his wife is but three paces off
> When there is so great a need were but to prove
> The man that chose you made but a poor choice.
> We're but two women struggling with the sea.

Yeats's fascination with the violently heroic—with Cuchulain, who wades into the ocean so that he can fight the waves—is foreign to Maeterlinck's somewhat quiet temperament; but Yeats's notion of a passage into abstraction works well with Maeterlinck's theater. In Yeats's last play, *The Death of Cuchulain* (1939), a beggar cuts off Cuchulain's head, which appears onstage as a black parallelogram on a stick; I think Maeterlinck might have enjoyed that effect.

Both *The Only Jealousy of Emer* and *The Death of Cuchulain* are imitations of Japanese Noh dramas—dramas about the interaction of the human and supernatural, culminating in a reconciling dance. Maeterlinck's plays don't end in ballet—unless you could imagine a dance consisting only of a few small flutters of intensely understated renunciation. But there is something musical in Maeterlinck's art, though the music lies mostly in the rhythm of event—just as the music in Samuel Beckett's (born 1906) plays lies mostly in the rhythm of event. And through Beckett's plays we can understand what Maeterlinck had to offer for the future of the theater.

Maeterlinck is a Modernist in that his plays concern characters on the threshold of nonentity, losing the power of speech, dwelling in a self-discrediting theatrical space. Despite his love for extravagant special effects, Maeterlinck is a minimalist:

Arkël. Comment te trouves-tu, Mélisande?
Mélisande. Bien, bien.—Pourquoi demandez-vous cela? Je n'ai jamais été mieux portante.—Il me semble cependant que je sais quelque chose . . .
Arkël. Que dis-tu?—Je ne comprends pas . . .
Mélisande. Je ne comprends non plus tout ce que je dis, voyez-vous . . . Je ne sais pas ce que je dis . . . Je ne sais pas ce que je sais . . . Je ne dis plus ce que je veux . . .
Arkël. Mais si, mais si . . .[3]

Arkël. How are you, Mélisande?
Mélisande. Fine, fine—Why are you asking me that? I've never been better.—It seems to me, however, that I know something.
Arkël. What are you saying?—I don't understand you . . .
Mélisande. I no longer understand all that I'm saying, you see . . . I don't know what I say . . . I don't know what I know . . . I'm no longer saying what I want to say . . .
Arkël. But you are, you are . . .
Clov. I use the words you taught me. If they don't mean anything any more, teach me others. [. . .]

> Then one day, suddenly, it ends, it changes, I don't understand, it dies, or it's me, I don't understand that either. I ask the words that remain—sleeping, waking, morning, evening. They have nothing to say.[4]

These echoey, nearly contentless exchanges—speech that keeps calling itself into question, tatters of language flapping or flagging on the stage—show how Maeterlinck opened some of the paths on which Beckett was to go further. Sometimes Maeterlinck's anticipations of Beckett are striking. In his trenchant play *Intérieur* (composed 1894, premièred 1895), written soon after *Pelléas et Mélisande* (composed 1892, premièred 1893), the Old Man and the Stranger are standing outside a house, staring through a window at a happy domestic scene in which a family is putting the baby to sleep; the spectators know that in a moment the family will receive news of the death of a young daughter of the house. The two men at the window note that the family members have ceased all movement so as not to make any noise—a skein of silk drops amid the hush—everyone is looking at the baby:

> *L'Étranger.* Ils ne savent pas que d'autres les regardent . . .
> *Le Vieillard.* On nous regarde aussi . . .[5]

> *The Stranger.* They don't know that others are looking at them . . .
> *The Old Man.* Someone is looking at us, too . . .

This moment has something of the shiver of the famous speech in *Waiting for Godot* (1953) when Vladimir says, as Estragon dozes:

> He'll know nothing. [. . .] At me too someone is looking, of me too someone is saying, He is sleeping, he knows nothing, let him sleep on.

There is a sudden sense of dilation of the reference frame, in which looking and being looked at, knowing and not knowing, are absorbed into some rhythm beyond all horizons.

The oxymoron-riddle, the leaving-off at the far verges of language, the sense of a rickety theater inset within the larger, still more rickety theater of the earth itself—these are Modernist themes, but also themes that Maeterlinck learned from Shakespeare. I am not what I am. The rest is silence, O O O O. We are such stuff as dreams are made on. Nothing, nothing,

nothing, nothing, nothing. But the idea of reassimilating the Shakespearean aesthetic (as opposed to adapting the plots of Shakespeare's plays) is itself a Modernist notion, and Maeterlinck is quite forward-looking in the way he folds into his plays the whole theatrical tradition, from Aeschylus to the mystery play to Shakespeare and beyond. There is something both minimalist and totalizing in Maeterlinck's dramaturgy, just as in Beckett's.

Maeterlinck's best-known works are dramas with such severe restrictions of language and incident that it is easy to forget that he was both a versatile playwright and a man of learning and intellectual curiosity—he read Schopenhauer, Emerson, and Darwin with care, translated into French Novalis's *Fragments* and Ford's *'Tis Pity She's a Whore*, and took Marcus Aurelius as his hero. We remember his fairy-tale plays—abstractions and evacuations of the normal theater of his age—but Maeterlinck also wrote a worthy satirical drama (*Le miracle de Saint Antoine*, 1904, in which St. Anthony of Padua visits a bourgeois household holding a wake and resurrects the matriarch from her coffin, to the consternation of most of the family, who would prefer her dead) and a topical play about the Great War (*Le bourgmestre de Stilmonde*, 1918, in which the mayor of a newly invaded Belgian town has to decide whether to offer his own life in place of the life of his old servant, wrongly accused of shooting a German officer).

Maeterlinck learned from the Symbolist theater of his time, especially from the works of Villiers de l'Isle-Adam, but he learned more from Shakespeare. Maeterlinck's first play, *La princesse Maleine* (1889), is a bizarre combination of motifs from *King Lear*, *Macbeth*, *Othello*, and other plays. It is, for a Maeterlinck play, unusually eventful: the princess escapes from a locked tower and disguises herself as a servant in order to be near her beloved, the son of a weak and dithery king; but she learns that her beloved is now engaged to be married to the daughter of an evil queen, who has seduced the weak king, the prince's father. The play ends in general havoc as the evil queen and the weak king strangle Princess Maleine and the prince stabs the evil queen to death, then kills himself with the same dagger. It is as if Lady Macbeth whispered hateful counsel to King Lear, and then, transforming herself into a female Iago, managed to destroy the life of a green and guileless Othello.

Maeterlinck returned to Shakespeare in an even more overt but much more spare and intent manner in *Joyzelle* (1903). This is, in effect, *The Tempest*, stripped of all characters except Prospero, Miranda, Ferdinand, and Ariel, with the difference that Prospero's child is now a son, and the test of fitness to marry is now given to a woman, Joyzelle, newly arrived on the island: Prospero (named Merlin in this play) plots with his familiar, Arielle (a female spirit), devising various schemes to ensure that Joyzelle's love for his son is unconditional, absolute; in the most interesting twist, Merlin makes Joyzelle think that he himself is trying to seduce her, so that father and son seem rivals. This is as close as fin-de-siècle theater can approach to the modality of Tom Stoppard's *Rosencrantz and Guildenstern Are Dead* (1966), a stripped-down metatheatrical spectacle, in which the playwright fools around on the margins of a Shakespearean text, with characters transported to some bare nebular space where they can investigate at leisure certain potentialities not quite activated in Shakespeare's drama.

Maeterlinck lived a long life and spent a great deal of time pondering Shakespeare. He was profoundly suspicious of Shakespeare's taste for the grandiose—for all those bloody blameful blades that bravely broach those boiling bloody breasts. *Othello* in particular struck Maeterlinck as overwrought, excessive. As he says in his essay "Le tragique quotidien" (from *Le trésor des humbles*, 1896):

> Est-il donc hasardeux d'affirmer que le véritable tragique de la vie, le tragique normal, profond et général, ne commence qu'au moment où ce qu'on appelle les aventures, les douleurs et les dangers sont passés? [. . .] Faut-il absolument hurler comme les Atrides pour qu'un Dieu éternel se montre en notre vie, et ne vient-il jamais s'asseoir sous l'immobilité de notre lampe? N'est-ce pas la tranquillité qui est terrible lorsqu'on y réfléchit et que les astres la surveillent; et le sens de la vie se développe-t-il dans le tumulte ou le silence? [. . .] Est-ce tandis que je fuis devant une épée nue que mon existence atteint son point le plus intéressant? [. . .]
>
> Mais nos auteurs tragiques [. . .] placent tout l'intérêt de leurs oeuvres dans la violence de l'anecdote qu'ils reproduisent. [. . .]
>
> J'admire Othello, mais il ne me paraît pas vivre de l'auguste vie quotidienne d'un Hamlet qui a le temps de vivre parce qu'il n'agit pas. Othello est admirablement jaloux. Mais n'est-ce peut-être pas une vieille erreur de penser que c'est aux moments où une telle passion et d'autres d'une égale violence nous possèdent que nous vivons véritablement? Il m'est arrivé de croire qu'un vieillard assis dans son fauteuil attendant simplement sous la lampe, écoutant sans le savoir toutes les lois éternelles qui régner autour de sa maison, interprétant sans le comprendre ce qu'il y a dans le silence des portes et des fenêtres [. . .]—il m'est arrivé de croire que ce vieillard immobile vivait, en réalité, d'une vie plus profonde, plus humaine et plus générale que l'amant qui étrangle sa maîtresse [. . .][6]

> Then is it risky to claim that the tragic aspect of life—real, normal, profound, and general—only begins at the moment when the things we call adventures, sufferings, and dangers are past? [. . .] Is it absolutely necessary to howl like the Atreides, in order to make an eternal god show himself in our life—doesn't he ever just sit down in the stillness of our lamp? Isn't it tranquility itself that is terrible, when you stop to think, a tranquility that the stars watch over; does the meaning of life develop in tumult or in silence? [. . .] Is it while I faced a naked sword that my existence reaches its real point? [. . .]
>
> But the authors of our tragedies [. . .] stash all the interest of their plays in the violence of the anecdote that they reproduce. [. . .]
>
> I admire Othello, but it doesn't seem to me that he lives the distinguished daily life of a Hamlet, who has time to live just because he doesn't act. Othello is admirably jealous. But isn't it maybe an old error to think that it's in moments when we're possessed by such a passion, and of other equally violent passions, that we truly live? I've come to believe that an old man sitting in his armchair, remaining still under the lamp, listening without knowing it to all the eternal laws that reign around his home, interpreting without understanding it what is in the silence of the doors and windows [. . .]—I've come to believe that this motionless old man lived, in reality, a life more profound, more human, more universal, than the lover who strangles his mistress [. . .]

Maeterlinck never wrote a play in which a man sits in a chair and does nothing at all—no playwright did until (perhaps) Samuel Beckett's *Nacht und Träume* (published 1982, premièred 1983). Maeterlinck came fairly close to this sort of stage entropy in his late dramaticule *Le vieux qui ne veut pas mourir*,[7] a dialogue between an old man and a shadow. But during his whole career Maeterlinck was engaged in a theater of kenosis, emptying: behind one of his plays there's often a conventional melodramatic plot, such as a love triangle, but Maeterlinck systematically dismantles most of the intrigue, either by moving it offstage or by omitting large pieces of it. This taste for eventlessness would spread widely through the Modernist age: Gertrude Stein's plays, such as *Four Saints in Three Acts* (published 1927–28, premièred 1934), display actors who stand still or noodle around the stage speaking almost contentless dialogue—indeed, Stein thought that all successful plays were plays in which

> nothing was happening . . . after all Hamlet Shakespeare's most interesting play has really nothing happening except that they live and die [. . .]

> an interesting thing is when there is nothing happening. I said that the moon excited dogs because it did nothing, lights coming and going do not excite them.[8]

Maeterlinck too was more interested in what he could subtract than what he could add, more interested in what he could paralyze than what he could set in motion.

Possibly Maeterlinck reached his limit in the domain of subtraction and paralysis quite early in his career, when he wrote *Les aveugles* (published 1890, premièred 1891) and *Les sept princesses* (published 1890, premièred 1891). *Les aveugles* concerns a group of blind men and women lost in a forest—their guide, a priest, seems to have abandoned them, and they debate what to do; at last they find the priest, dead, and it begins to snow. *Les sept princesses* is an eerier play: arriving on a warship sailing through a narrow canal, a prince enters a castle to see his grandparents (the king and queen) and his cousins, the seven princesses; but he can see the girls only vaguely, from a distance, on the other side of a locked door, as if through a misted window or a mirror—at one point the queen remarks, You'd think the hall were full of cotton. The prince calls them white shadows; he peers intently but can't make out whether he's seeing their hair or another shadow. The queen knocks on the window to try to awaken the sleepers, softly, because they are ill and mustn't be disturbed; but they remain imperturbable, blank. The king tells the prince about a corridor that goes under the princesses' cell: he makes his difficult way, pushes up the flagstone, and enters; six of the princesses begin to stir, but the seventh, Ursula, the one he loves, cannot be awakened, is not asleep, though the hysterical queen keeps crying that the servants must wake her. The play seems to concern the inaccessibility of the imagination's treasures—"Nothing that we love over-much / Is ponderable to our touch," as Yeats put it. But it also seems to concern the playwright's difficulty in putting on stage a nothing-thing, an emotionally charged stasis. Like *Intérieur*, *Les sept princesses* is a dumb show framed by an interpretive dialogue; but unlike *Intérieur*, *Les sept princesses* gives the audience something between a *tableau vivant* and a *tableau mort*, a tantalizing glimpse at a gesture so restrained that it scarcely constitutes as a gesture at all. In Beckett's prose piece "Imagination Dead Imagine" (1965), a man and a woman are folded together, two white images in a white rotunda, almost completely still except for an "infinitesimal shudder instantaneously suppressed." Something of this liveliness of dead imagination is anticipated in *Les sept princesses*.

2. *Le hasard et la nécessité*

Maeterlinck's predilection for an abstract theater affected the design of his fables. Because he had little interest in subplots, his plays can be quite linear: when he took some elements of a play by Paul Heyse to create his *Marie-Magdeleine* (1910), he simplified the plot to the point where he called Heyse's original incomparably richer than his own; and we've already seen how he seized one minor theme in *The Tempest* to make *Joyzelle*. On the other hand, the linear design of a Maeterlinck play usually has yawning gaps: the catastrophe is often at once inexorable and improbable, unmotivated. In *Pelléas et Mélisande*, Golaud is a gigantic, powerful, desperately jealous man, but he's a floundering Othello, without glory, without even a handkerchief. In the course of the play this noble prince gets lost in a forest and is injured after being thrown from his startled horse—he seems as inept as Lewis Carroll's White Knight. He tries to gather evidence of Mélisande's infidelity by bribing his little son to spy, but the son reports nothing more sinister than that Pelléas and Mélisande keep staring steadily at the light. Golaud will finally kill Pelléas, but Mélisande dies too, even though she's suffered only the smallest of wounds. In Maeterlinck's plays, you die not so much because a train of events has been set in motion that culminates in your dying, but simply because you have an air of death about you. At one point Pelléas's father (we hear) tells his son that he has the grave and friendly look of someone who won't live long; elsewhere Mélisande tells Golaud that she feels that she won't live long; and early in the play Pelléas reads a letter urging him quickly to visit his friend Marcellus, who knows the exact day he's going to die. Things you ought to know you don't know, such as (in Mélisande's case) who you are and where you come from; things you ought not to know you do know, such as the day of your death. Causality works sideways—synchronically not diachronically: at the exact moment when Mélisande's wedding ring plops into the fountain, Golaud's horse starts and topples onto Golaud. The design of the plot is linear, but the line is zigzag and full of holes.

Maeterlinck understood this quite well. In his important essay "L'évolution du mystère" (from *Le temple enseveli*, 1902), Maeterlinck speaks of rereading two or three of his plays—he doesn't say which, but *Pelléas et Mélisande* might be among them—and noticing how fate worked in them:

> Le ressort des ces petits drames était l'effroi de l'inconnu qui nous entoure. On y avait foi [. . .] à des puissances énormes, invisibles, et fatales, dont nul ne devinait les intentions, mais que l'âme du drame supposait

> malveillantes, attentives à toutes nos actions, ennemies du sourire, de la vie, de la paix, de l'amour. Peut-être étaient-elles justes, au fond, mais seulement dans la colère, et elles exerçaient la justice d'une manière si souterraine et, si tortueuse, si lente, si lointaine, que leurs châtiments,—car elles ne récompensaient jamais—prenaient l'apparence d'actes arbitraires et inexplicables du destin. En ce mot, c'était l'idée du Dieu des chrétiens mêlée à celle de la fatalité antique, refoulée dans la nuit impénétrable de la nature, et, de là, se plaisant à guetter, à déjouer, à déconcerter, à assombrir le projets, et le bonheur des hommes.[9]

> The mainspring of these little dramas was terror of the unknown that surrounds us. People trusted in powers enormous, invisible, and fatal, whose intentions no one could guess, but powers that the soul of the drama imagined as spiteful, attentive to all our actions, hostile to smiles, to life, to peace, to love. Maybe these powers were at bottom just, but just only in rage, and they exercised their justice in a manner so subterranean, so tortuous, so slow, so remote, that their punishments—for they never gave rewards—took on the appearance of arbitrary and inexplicable acts of destiny. In a word, it was the idea of the Christian God combined with the idea of the fatality of the ancients, thrust back into nature's impenetrable night, and, from there, taking pleasure in studying, thwarting, disconcerting, darkening the plans and the happiness of men.

Maeterlinck seems almost amused by the darkness of his own dramatic imagination, but he took the notion of fatality seriously, and indeed most of his writing on drama can be seen as a long meditation on the theme of fate. He thought that all great drama depended on a sense of fatedness—a sense of some implacable process that generates the plot and ennobles the struggles of those who succumb to it. Dramatists, he believed, made use of several kinds of fatalities—one is the fatality of passion itself:

> Mais pour qu'une passion soit réellement fatale dans une âme consciente, [. . .] il faut l'intervention d'un Dieu, ou de tout autre force infinie et irrésistible. Ainsi Wagner a eu recours au philtre dans *Tristan et Yseult*, Shakespeare aux sorcières dans *Macbeth* [. . .] Nous nous retrouvons, après un circuit, au coeur même de la nécessité d'autrefois. Ce circuit est plus ou moins admissible dans un drame archaïque ou légendaire, où toute fantaisie poétique est permise; mais dans un drame qui voudrait serrer de plus près la vérité actuelle, il faudrait trouver une autre

> intervention, qui nous parût réellement irrésistible, pour revêtir les crimes de Macbeth [. . .] d'une excuse fatidique, et leur donner ainsi la grandeur et la noblesse sombres qu'ils n'ont pas eux-mêmes. Ôtez de Macbeth la prédestination maudite, l'intervention de l'enfer, la lutte héroïque contre une justice occulte qui, à tout moment, devient visible par les mille fissures d'une nature révoltée, et le personnage principal n'est plus qu'un assassin odieux et forcené.[10]

> But in order for a passion to be truly fatal in a conscious soul [. . .] it requires the intervention of a God, or of some other infinite and irresistible force. Therefore Wagner had recourse to the love potion in *Tristan und Isolde*, Shakespeare to the witches in *Macbeth* [. . .] We find that we've gone in a circle, back to the very heart of what the ancients called necessity. This circling-back is more or less admissible in a drama set in archaic or legendary times, when every sort of poetical fantasy is permitted; but in a drama that would like to press closer to the truth of the present day, it would be necessary to find another sort of intervention, that would appear to us truly irresistible, in order to dress up the crimes of a Macbeth [. . .] with the excuse of fatal compulsion, and so to impart to those crimes the dark grandeur, the dark nobility that they don't have in themselves. Take away from Macbeth the predestining curse, the intervention of hell, the heroic struggle against an occluded justice that, at every moment, becomes visible through the thousand fissures of an outraged nature, and the principal character is no more than a mad and hateful assassin.

You see Maeterlinck's problem. He hungers to present in the theater contemporary problems, contemporary science, the whole intellectual and social milieu of his age. But he also thinks that a good play requires some iron slab looming in the background, secretly moving to the foreground, falling when ripeness is all. Macbeth is just a commonplace murderer unless his act has some dark aureole flickering around it. So Maeterlinck is almost always willing to sacrifice contemporaneity in order to regain the fatedness available only in legend.

Maeterlinck never succeeded in his quest to find some contemporary equivalent of destiny. He looked with great interest at Ibsen's experiment in finding a modern surrogate for fate:

> Ainsi Ibsen, en quête d'une forme nouvelle et pour ainsi dire scientifique de fatalité, a placé au milieu du meilleur de ses drames la figure voilée,

> grandiose, et tyrannique de l'hérédité. Mais au fond, dans ses oeuvres, ce n'est pas le mystère scientifique de l'hérédité qui remue en nous certaines craintes humaines plus profondes que nos craintes animales. [. . .] Non; ce qui y suscite une terreur d'un autre genre que celle d'un danger imminent, mais naturel, c'est l'obscure idée d'une justice qu'y représente l'hérédité, c'est l'affirmation audacieuse que les fautes du père retombent sur les enfants, c'est l'insinuation qu'un Juge souverain, une sorte de Maître de la race, veille sur nos actions, les inscrit au livre de bronze, et pèses-en ses mains éternelles des récompenses longtemps différées et des châtiments infinis.[11]
>
> Thus Ibsen, in quest of a new and so to speak scientific form of fatality, placed in the middle of his best dramas the veiled, grandiose, tyrannical figure of Heredity. But at bottom, in his works, it is not the scientific mystery of heredity that stirs in us certain human fears, deeper than our animal fears. [. . .] No; what excites a terror of a different kind from the terror of imminent but natural danger, is the obscure idea of a justice that heredity manifests—the bold affirmation that the sins of the father fall on the children, the insinuation that a sovereign Judge, a sort of Master of the human race, watches over our actions, inscribes them in a bronze book, and weighs in his eternal hands long deferred rewards and endless punishments.

Maeterlinck is thinking of Ibsen plays such as *Ghosts* (published 1881, premièred 1882), in which the legacy of the vile Captain Alving is the hereditary syphilis that destroys the mind of his son. But, as Susan Sontag pointed out, it's dangerous to take illness as a metaphor for anything at all, let alone for the patient working-out of justice; the spirochete is a contrived and artificial nemesis, compared to (say) the Furies of the *Oresteia*. Maeterlinck, therefore, thought that Ibsen, like all other contemporary dramatists, had not gone far enough in the quest to find new and credible Parcae:

> On peut affirmer que le poète qui trouverait aujourd'hui, dans les sciences matérielles, dans l'inconnu qui nous environne, ou dans notre propre coeur, l'équivalent de la fatalité antique, c'est-à-dire une force de prédestination aussi irrésistible, aussi universellement admise, écrirait à coup sûr un chef-d'oeuvre.[12]
>
> We can affirm that the poet who would find today, in the material sciences, in the unknown that surrounds us, or in our own heart, the equivalent of

> the fatality of the ancients, that is to say a predestining force as irresistible, as universally acknowledged, would for certain write a masterpiece.

Instead of Fatality we have today only the usual wretchedness of human life:

> Ce n'est pas exactement la Fatalité antique, il est vrai, la déesse ou plutôt le dieu bien déterminé (du moins dans l'esprit de la foule), volontaire, inflexible, implacable, aveugle mais attentif, c'est une fatalité plus vague, plus informe, distraite, indifférente, inhumaine, impersonnelle, universelle. En somme, ce n'est qu'une appellation provisoire accordée, en attendant mieux, à la misère générale et inexplicable des hommes.[13]

> It is true that it's not exactly the fatality of the ancients, the goddess or rather the well-defined god (at least in the mind of the masses), willful, inflexible, implacable, blind but attentive—instead it's a fatality more vague, more formless, absent-minded, indifferent, inhuman, impersonal, universal. In short, it's only a provisional name accorded (while waiting for a better name) to the general and inexplicable misery of men.

Maeterlinck feels that he needs fate in his dramas, in order to provide a teleology, an importance, even in some sense a sanctity to the deeds of his characters; but he has little confidence in any fate that makes larger claims than the simple statement, *You are often unhappy and you are certainly going to die*. One reason for the celebrated wispiness of Maeterlinck's plays is that destiny, design, is asserted but asserted in bad faith, amidst a regression into fairy tale. When Arkël says, in *Pelléas et Mélisande*, that we see only the back side of fate, it sounds as if someone or something, somewhere, sees the front side; but in fact Maeterlinck has the gravest doubts about the existence of an obverse. Maeterlinck wanted something he couldn't have: a vindication of the validity of design in human affairs; because he couldn't have that, but only various arty surrogates of it, his works prefigure the existential crises of a much later theater.

All through his plays Maeterlinck discredits the fatality that he so aggressively courts. In *Joyzelle*, for example, Merlin and Arielle are discussing the forthcoming test of Joyzelle's fitness to be the wife of Merlin's son:

> *Merlin.* Pourquoi tenter l'épreuve si elle est incertaine?
> *Arielle.* Si nous ne l'offrons pas, le destin l'offrira; elle est inévitable mais livrée au hasard; et c'est pourquoi j'essaie d'en diriger le cours . . .[14]

Merlin. Why do the test if the results are doubtful?
Arielle. If we don't offer it, destiny will offer it; it is inevitable but delivered at random; and that's why I'm trying to direct its course . . .

There is probably no better description of the role of fate in Maeterlinck's plays than this: the random inevitable. He returned to this theme throughout his career:

> Au problème de l'existence il n'est répondu que par l'énigme de son anéantissement. Du reste, c'est une morte indifférente et inexorable, aveugle, tâtonnant à peu près au hasard, emportant de préférence les plus jeunes et les moins malheureux[15]
>
> Inexplicables erreurs de la nature ou d'un univers où tout est prédéterminé.[16]

> There is no answer to the problem of existence except the enigma of its annihilation. Moreover, it's a death indifferent and inexorable, blind, groping nearly at random, preferring to carry off the youngest and the least unhappy
>
> Inexplicable errors of nature or of a universe where all is predetermined.

A fascinating idea: predetermined error. According to Calvinist theology, God predestined the fall of man into sin; but Maeterlinck seems to posit a God who predestines his own mistakes. Maeterlinck was obsessed with the notion that the history of the universe was pre-engraved in unalterable bronze, but that this general inexorability was the result of errors, blotches, random thrusts. He tended to look at human life under the aspect of eternity, as if time were an unrolled filmstrip in which everything was visible at the same time:

> Dans l'éternel present qui est la seule réalité du temps, on pourrait parfaitement se voir mourir avant de naître. [. . .]
>
> Qu'importe ce qui m'advient, puisque tout ce qui m'advient était déjà avant que je fusse né?[17]

> In the eternal present that is the sole reality of time, you would be perfectly able to see yourself die before you were born. [. . .]
>
> What does it matter what happens to me, since everything that happens to me was already there before I was born?

All time has, in a sense, already happened; as Eliot says, the future is a faded song. But there is no true continuity in the great story, for events come to pass through blind spasms. Beneath the utter determinedness of events, there lies sheer indeterminacy. Maeterlinck wasn't entirely comfortable with Darwin's theory of natural selection by means of random variation, but he was willing to accept it as a sort of provisional truth.[18] And Maeterlinck's plays are gardens full of odd sports.

The architecture of Maeterlinck's castles reifies fate's own architecture. His plays are full of underground tunnels, occult connections between distant things, like the corridor in *Les sept princesses* that bypasses the locked door. Opening doors and gates requires a great deal of effort, if it is possible at all: *Pelléas et Mélisande* begins with a scene, omitted in Debussy's opera, in which the servants struggle with all their strength to push open the castle's great portal. Doors threaten in other ways too: Mélisande tears her dress when it snags on a door. Maeterlinck tends to understand fate as an endless series of closings-off, intermitted by painful accessions to your future life.

Not only is your path hemmed in and full of obstacles, but the ground beneath your feet is at any moment likely to give way. Often the castle is constructed precariously over some dank grotto: in *Pelléas et Mélisande*, Golaud and Pelléas grope their way down a slippery subterranean path, full of the smell of death, and try not to fall into the stagnant water below. In the preface to the 1908 collection of his plays, Maeterlinck develops this architectural motif in Nietzschean terms—he refers to the characters of his plays as

> petits êtres fragiles, grelottants, passivement pensifs, et les paroles prononcées, les larmes répandues ne prennent d'importance que de ce qu'elles tombent dans le gouffre au bord duquel se joue le drame, et y retentissent d'une certaine façon qui donne à croire que l'abîme est très vaste parce que tout ce qui s'y va perdre y fait un bruit confus et assourdi.[19]

> fragile little beings, shivering, passively pensive—the words they utter, the tears they shed, take on importance only by falling into the chasm that edges around the drama at every turn, and by reverberating in a way that makes you believe that the abyss is very vast, because everything that gets lost in it makes a confused and muffled noise.

Maeterlinck enjoyed reading German philosophers, and he surely knew Nietzsche's famous aphorism that if you stare too long into the abyss, the abyss stares back at you.[20] Maeterlinck's stage is a labyrinth of trapdoors, and the characters always walk across it at their peril. The abyss takes an active interest in their footsteps.

The first play that Maeterlinck wrote after *Pelléas et Mélisande* was *Alladine et Palomides* (1894), in which he develops at length the theme of the grotto beneath the castle—indeed, the castle of this play is Maeterlinck's most elaborate architectural fantasy. Alladine's pet lamb falls in the castle moat and is swept away; later the desperate Alladine and Palomides find themselves in the castle's dark foundation space and embrace in desperate wonder. The lovers imagine that they are in a heaven of roses and smiling jewels, surrounded by water so blue that it seems a distillate of sky. But when the sunlight at last streams in, they see that the grotto is actually all fungus and rock and rot; the decomposed body of the lamb is there, too. (The whole scene owes much to Auguste Villiers de l'Isle-Adam's play *Axël* [written 1872–89, premièred 1890], in which two lovers find a vast treasure of jewels in the crypt beneath the castle, but scorn the expensive trash of the sensible world, choose the ecstasy of death by drinking poison. In the earlier play the real jewels are dismissed; in *Alladine et Palomides* the real dreck is promoted into imaginary splendor.) This refocusing of the theater's eye from love's delirium to death's squalor is one of Maeterlinck's simplest but most effective presentations of fate's undergirding, fate's stamina.

The castle is perched over an abyss; but it also incorporates the abyss, so to speak, into the design of the superstructure:

> *Alladine.* Je ne puis m'empêcher d'être inquiète quand je rentre au palais . . . Il est si grand et je suis si petite, et je m'y perds encore . . . Et puis toutes ces fenêtres sur la mer . . . On ne peut les compter . . . Et les corridors qui tournent sans raison; et d'autres qui ne tournent pas et qui se perdent entre les murs . . . Et les salles où je n'ose pas entrer . . .
>
> *Palomides.* Nous entrerons partout . . .
>
> *Alladine.* On dirait que je n'ai pas été faite pour l'habiter ou qu'il n'a pas été bâti pour moi . . . Une fois, je m'y suis égarée . . . J'ai poussé trente portes avant de retrouver la lumière du jour . . . Et je ne pouvais pas sortir; la dernière porte s'ouvrait sur un étang . . . Et les voûtes qui ont froid tout l'été; et les galeries qui se replient sans cesse sur elles-mêmes . . . Il y a des escaliers qui ne mènent nulle part et des terrasses d'où l'on n'aperçoit rien . . .[21]

> *Alladine.* I can't help being uneasy when I come back to the palace . . . It is so big and I'm so little, and I still get lost in it . . . And then all those

windows on the sea . . . You can't count them . . . And corridors that keep turning for no reason; and others that don't turn and lose themselves between the walls . . . And halls where I dare not go in . . .

Palomides. We'll go everywhere . . .

Alladine. You could say that I wasn't made to live in it, or that it wasn't built for me . . . Once, I wandered off . . . I pushed open thirty doors before finding daylight . . . And I couldn't get out; the last door opened on a pool . . . And vaults that are cold all summer long; and galleries that fold back endlessly on themselves . . . There are staircases that lead nowhere and terraces from which you can't see anything . . .

Where did Maeterlinck find the inspiration for this extraordinary castle? The *carceri d'invenzione* (1750) engraved by Giovanni Battista Piranesi—phantasmagorical prisons seemingly designed for lunatics by lunatics—are one possibility. Another possibility is apiculture, for Maeterlinck was a remarkably keen student of bees and wrote an erudite account of the dynamics of the hive (*La vie des abeilles*, 1901) based on his own curious experiments in bee navigational systems and on the best science of his time. Note, for example, his account of how bees begin hive construction:

> Enfin, lorsque la substance malaxée de la sorte lui paraît avoir les dimensions et la consistance voulues, elle l'applique au sommet du dôme, posant ainsi la première pierre ou plutôt la clef de voûte de la cité nouvelle, car il s'agit ici d'une ville à l'envers qui descend du ciel et ne s'élève pas du sein de la terre comme une ville humaine.[22]

> At last, when she has worked the substance until it appears to have the desired dimensions and consistency, she applies it to the high point of the dome, thus putting in position the first stone or rather the keystone of the vault of the new city, for we have here an upside-down city that descends from the sky and doesn't arise from the earth's breast in the way that a human city does.

As far as Maeterlinck is concerned, a beehive is a miracle of complex architectural thrift, just as bee society is a miracle of unanimous intent cooperative to the good of the whole. But Maeterlinck makes no claim to understand all its internal workings and is deeply puzzled by the telepathic coordination of all the individual drones, workers, and queens; here fate works perfectly, but incomprehensibly. In human society fate is not only incomprehensible but scattered, distracted, haphazard, just a name for the usual misery of things; a drama, any drama, is a poor thing next to the annual mystery play of the hive. Still, the palace of *Alladine et Palomides* looks more like a hive than like a normal palace: if not completely upside down, it contains many inverted elements, and the galleries folded back on themselves, confusingly symmetrical, are like the hexagonal cells of the honeycomb.

Jorge Luis Borges liked to imagine buildings along these Maeterlinckian lines. In "The Library of Babel" (1941), the universe has been reconstituted as a single library, consisting of hexagonal cells organized into galleries and manned by a staff of disconsolate librarians. But a still more striking echo of Maeterlinck's infinite palace-prison can be found in the city of the Immortals in Borges's "El inmortal" (1949):

> *Este palacio es fábrica de los dioses*, pensé primeramente. Exploré los inhabitados recintos y corregí: *Los dioses que lo edificaron han muerto.* Noté sus peculiaridades y dije: *Los dioses que lo edificaron estaban locos.* [. . .] Yo había cruzado un laberinto, pero la nítida Ciudad de los Inmortales me atemorizó y repugnó. Un laberinto es una casa labrada para confundir a los hombres; su arquitectura, pródiga en simetrías, está subordinada a ese fin. En el palacio que imperfectamente exploré, la arquitectura carecía de fin. Abundaban el corredor sin salida, la alta ventana inalcanzable, la aparatosa puerta que daba a una celda o a un pozo, las increíbles escaleras inversas, con los peldaños y balaustrada hacia abajo. Otras, adheridas aéreamente al costado de un muro monumental, morían sin llegar a ninguna parte, al cabo de dos o tres giros, en la tiniebla superior de las cúpulas.

> *This palace is a fabrication of the gods*, I thought at first. I explored the uninhabited enclosures and corrected the thought: *The gods that built it have died.* I noted its peculiarities and said, *The gods that built it were mad.* [. . .] I had crossed a labyrinth, but the shining City of the Immortals terrified and disgusted me. A labyrinth is a house elaborated for the sake of confusing those within it; its architecture, extravagant in symmetries, is subordinated to that end. In the palace that I imperfectly explored, the architecture lacked any end at all. The place abounded in atrocity: the exitless corridor, the window too high to reach, the ostentatious door that gave on a cell or an empty shaft, incredible inverted stairways, with steps and balustrades pointing down. Other stairways, attached airily to the

> side of a monumental wall, died leading nowhere, petering out after two or three turnings, in the highest darkness of the cupolas.

Maeterlinck's absurd palace spatializes the way that fate works in time: full of dead ends, sudden useless illuminations, vain repetitions—the replicated galleries are like the sideslips in the plot, such as (in *Pelléas et Mélisande*) the horse that rears at the instant that Mélisande's ring drops in the fountain. The elaboration of the delicate pathos of the lost has a fin-de-siècle tint; but the sheer misconstructedness of the stage set (virtual or actual) and of the fable feels Modernist. The atmosphere is refined, sober, eerily empty—Maeterlinck's kingdoms are nearly depopulated, except for the royal family and the occasional blind or sleeping beggar; but there is an odd Looney Tunes aspect to the plays, in that the scenario consists of one damned thing after another, until the Acme safe, long suspended in air, squashes the characters flat.

Maybe Maeterlinck's most telling dramatization of fate can be found in one of his most curious projects, *Les fiançailles* (1922). This is a sequel to his most successful play (in box-office terms), *L'oiseau bleu* (1908), a probable factor in his winning the Nobel Prize in 1911. I'm not sure that I've ever read a play that I dislike more than *L'oiseau bleu*—but its very repulsiveness fascinates me. It's a childish, sentimental, heavy-handed *féerie* à la Perrault in which two impoverished children discover that their skimpy little cottage isn't so bad after all, after the Fairy takes them on a tour of a panpsychic world full of talking dogs, talking trees, talking bread, talking sugar, talking light, and other special tickles so cartoonish that they may have influenced some of the early creators of animated shorts. I suspect that when, in *Lolita* (1955), Vladimir Nabokov damned the evil playwright Clare Quilty by calling him a new Maeterlinck, Nabokov had this play in mind—Nabokov also said in a 1970 interview that "Beckett is the author of lovely novellas and wretched plays in the Maeterlinck tradition."[23] And I also suspect that when W. H. Auden, in *The Sea and the Mirror* (1944), describes a fiasco of a play in which everything conceivable goes wrong, "even the huge stuffed bird of happiness,"[24] he's thinking of Maeterlinck's Blue Bird of Happiness.

In *Les fiançailles*, Tyltyl, the boy protagonist of *L'oiseau bleu*, has passed puberty with flying colors, and the Fairy asks him to ponder possible brides from among the girls of his acquaintance. I won't trouble you with any further summary of the plot, except to note that there is a character named Destiny, the enemy of Light:

> Ici s'ouvre une trappe, au milieu de la scène; et il s'en élève lentement, semblable à une tour, une gigantesque forme deux fois plus haute qu'un homme. Elle est carrée, énorme, imposante, écrasante et donne l'impression d'une masse de granit et d'une puissance aveugle et inflexible. On ne voit pas son visage. Elle est vêtue de draperies grisâtres et rigides comme des arêtes de rocher.[25]
>
> Here a trapdoor opens, in the middle of the stage; and there slowly rises, like a tower, a gigantic form twice as high as a man. It is square, enormous, imposing, crushing, and gives the impression of a granite mass and of a blind and inflexible power. You can't see its face. It is covered in rigid grayish draperies like a mountain ridge.

But Destiny shrinks: by the middle of the play Destiny is stumbling, limping; and by the end (when Tyltyl's unborn children are trying to pick their proper mother) Destiny is no bigger than a small child and lisps like a baby when he talks. At the end of the play, Light comments that necessity in human affairs comes not from fate but from a kind of general racial will:

> *La Lumière*. . . . ce n'est pas le destin, comme disent les hommes, mais la volonté de ceux qui savent tout et ne meurent jamais . . .[26]
>
> *Light*. . . . it's not destiny, as human beings say, but the will of those who know all and never die . . .

Just as the motions of bees are guided not by fate's decree but by an instinct arising from the pressure of all beekind being brought to bear on the performance of individual bees, so human Destiny recasts itself: it is no longer some exterior godhead, monumental and implacable, but a sort of collective plastic force that issues from the abiding presences of the dead, the living, the unborn. *Les fiançailles* is a cutesy-pie, uningratiating piece of work, but it suggests that, as Maeterlinck grew older and more determined to be cheerful, he made his peace, to some degree, with his old enemy fate: fate's self-discrediting is now explicit, and if the alternative to Destiny is still unconvincing, at least Maeterlinck propounds it only in the course of an obviously contrived and preposterous fable.

Maeterlinck is usually regarded as a Symbolist, but those who would identify him as such should ponder *L'oiseau bleu* and its sodden array of truly clunky symbols, from the bluebird of happiness on down. He was often remarkably not at all adept at handling overt symbols and was indeed disinclined to regard symbols as particularly important or useful literary devices. In “L’évolution du mystère,” Maeterlinck declares that the poet should be honest—should not attribute the wretchedness of human life to causes (God, heredity, and so forth) in which he doesn’t personally believe:

> Sinon, il verra dans l’enfer, dans la colère de Dieu, dans les décrets d’airain, qu’une ostentation de symboles qui ne le satisfont plus. Il est temps que les poètes le reconnaissent: le symbole suffit à représenter provisoirement une vérité admise ou une vérité qu’on ne peut ou qu’on ne veut pas encore regarder; mais quand vient le moment où l’on veut voir la vérité même, il est bon que le symbole disparaisse.[27]

> Otherwise, he will see in hell, in God’s wrath, in decrees written in bronze, only an ostentatious show of symbols that won’t satisfy him anymore. It’s time for poets to recognize this: the symbol is sufficient to represent provisionally an accepted truth or a truth that we as yet can’t or won’t confront; but when the moment comes when we want to see truth itself, it’s right for the symbol to disappear.

Not only do Maeterlinck’s plot designs work to undesign themselves, but his symbols work to unsymbol themselves. Few writers offer such a spectacle of continual discomfort with the tools of their craft.

3. Blank Souls

In his great plays of the 1890s, Maeterlinck’s plots are both overdetermined and underdetermined: overdetermined in that murder or enervation or some other doom is felt at every moment; underdetermined in that the doom isn’t the culmination of some casual chain but an arbitrary infliction. (This is another way of stating the principle of the random inexorable.) The characters are also overdetermined and underdetermined: overdetermined in that they are marionettes with carved faces, traditional roles (the jealous husband, the ingénue, the wise grandfather); underdetermined in that the characters are far more incoherent, unpredictable, chance driven, than their masks would suggest. The masks are deceptive, for Maeterlinck is far more concerned with some substrate of human being far beneath character traits or personality types. You think that Maeterlinck cares about the puppet’s face; but his real interest is wood.

In *Pelléas et Mélisande*, the heroine often seems a figure of helpless pathos, a forlorn child in a world of adult sexual complexities, a fairy whose thin wings tremble helplessly. On the other hand, it's perfectly possible for an actress to play the role in a much cannier, more self-consciously histrionic way. After she confesses her love to Pelléas, her enraptured lover exclaims that her voice is like a breath over the springtime sea, that she speaks with an angel's candor; but a slightly darker thought strikes him:

> *Pelléas.* Tu ne me trompes pas?—Tu ne mens pas un peu, pour me faire sourire? . . .
> *Mélisande.* Non; je ne mens jamais; je ne mens qu'à ton frère . . .[28]

> *Pelléas.* You aren't deceiving me?—You aren't lying just a little, to make me smile? . . .
> *Mélisande.* No; I never lie; I only lie to your brother . . .

This line can be read in a hushed voice, as another proof of angelic candor; or it can be read slightly rushed, overeager in the fashion of a seductress, smiling at her lover but smiling more to herself. Mélisande is always a kind of doll: when her hair falls like Rapunzel's from the tower, Pelléas ties it to a willow branch; later, Golaud seizes her by her hair and madly swings her from right to left, left to right—in both cases she seems more a plaything than a person. But in her perfectly submissive state she is nevertheless exercising power: both Golaud and Pelléas are in some sense lost in the coils of her hair. It's complicated—the question of who is the snarer, who the ensnared.

The play's main theme is love, but for Maeterlinck love is everything and nothing. His canon is a long and intense investigation of love from every possible angle, but love is a passion bizarrely detachable from those who suffer it. In *Aglavaine et Sélysette* (1896)—a play that, like *Pelléas et Mélisande*, concerns a love triangle, though in this case one involving two women and a man—the title characters discuss the differing qualities of their love for Méléandre. Sélysette is a reticent lover, hiding the depth of her affection:

> *Sélysette.* Il me semble que je voudrais qu'il m'aimât si je n'existais pas . . . Et alors je cachais, je cachais . . . Je voudrais cacher tout . . . Ce n'est pas de sa faute . . . Et c'est pourquoi j'étais heureuse quand il m'embrassait en haussant les épaules et en hochant la tête . . . Bien plus heureuse que

lorsqu'il m'embrassait en m'admirant . . . Mais ce n'est pas ainsi qu'il faut qu'on aime, je suppose? . . .

Aglavaine. On ne sait pas comment il faut qu'on aime . . . les uns aiment ainsi et les autres ainsi; et l'amour fait ceci, ou l'amour fait cela; et c'est toujours très bien puisque c'est l'amour . . . On le regarde au fond de soi, comme un vautour ou comme un aigle étrange dans une cage . . . La cage vous appartient, mais l'oiseau n'appartient à personne . . . on le regarde avec inquiétude, on le réchauffe, on le nourrit, mais on ne sait ce qu'il va faire, s'il va voler, se meurtrir aux barreaux ou chanter . . . Il n'y a rien au monde qui soit plus loin de nous que notre amour, ma pauvre Sélysette . . . Il faut bien qu'on attende et l'on ne peut qu'apprendre à le comprendre . . .[29]

Sélysette. It seems to me that I'd like for him to love me as though I didn't exist . . . And then I hid, I hid . . . I'd like to hide everything . . . It isn't his fault . . . And that's why I was happy when he kissed me while shrugging his shoulders and shaking his head . . . Much happier than when he kissed me while admiring me . . . But that's not how you're supposed to love, I guess? . . .

Aglavaine. No one knows how you're supposed to love . . . some love this way and others that way; and love does this, or love does that; and it's always just right because it's love . . . You look at love in the bottom of your being, like a vulture or a strange eagle in a cage . . . The cage belongs to you, but the bird doesn't belong to anybody . . . you look at him anxiously, you warm him, you feed him, but you don't know what he's going to do, if he's going to fly away, or hurt himself against the bars, or sing . . . There's nothing in the world that's so far away from us as our love, my poor Sélysette . . . You just have to wait, and learn to understand . . .

We are almost in a pagan world where the passion to kiss, or to kill, is utterly extrinsic to the person who feels it—where love is credited to Aphrodite, belligerence to Ares, not to the motions of our own soul. In a Maeterlinck play, love may be all-consuming, but it's always a visitor, not a native. There is a part of you that love leaves untouched, an absolute calm far below the tumult of the middle regions.

At around the time of *Aglavaine et Sélysette*, Maeterlinck wrote the essay "La morale mystique" (1896), which elaborates considerably on this theme:

Qu'arriverait-il, par exemple, si notre âme devenait visible tout à coup et qu'elle dût s'avancer au milieu de ses sœurs assemblées, dépouillée de ses voiles, mais chargée de ses pensées les plus secrètes et traînant à sa suite les actes les plus mystérieux de sa vie que rien ne pouvait exprimer? De quoi rougirait-elle? Que voudrait-elle cacher? Irait-elle, comme une femme pudique, jeter le long manteau de ses cheveux sur les péchés sans nombre de la chair? Elle les a ignorés, et ces péchés ne l'ont jamais atteinte. Ils ont été commis à mille lieues de son trône; et l'âme du Sodomite même passerait au milieu de la foule sans se douter de rien, et portant dans ses yeux le sourire transparent de l'enfant. Elle n'est pas intervenue, elle poursuivait sa vie du côté des lumières, et c'est de cette vie seule qu'elle se souviendra.

Quels péchés et quels crimes ordinaires aura-t-elle pu commettre? A-t-elle trahi, a-t-elle trompé, a-t-elle menti? A-t-elle fait souffrir et a-t-elle fait pleurer? Où était-elle tandis que: celui-ci livrait son frère aux ennemis? Elle sanglotait peut-être loin de lui, et, à partir de ce moment, elle sera devenue plus profonde et plus belle. Elle n'aura point honte de ce qu'elle n'a pas fait; et elle peut rester pure au centre d'un grand meurtre. Souvent, elle transforme en clartés intérieures tout le mal auquel il faut bien qu'elle assiste. Tout dépend d'un principe invisible et de là naît sans doute l'inexplicable indulgence des dieux. [. . .] Y a-t-il une morale mystérieuse qui règne en des régions plus lointaines que celles de nos pensées; et un astre central que nous ne voyons pas et dont nos plus secrets désirs ne sont que tes planètes impuissantes? Existe-t-il, au centre de notre être un arbre transparent dont toutes nos actions et toutes nos vertus ne sont que les fleurs et les feuilles éphémères?[30]

What would happen, for example, if our soul suddenly became visible and she had to move forward into the midst of a gathering of her sisters, stripped of her veils, but laden with her most secret thoughts and dragging behind her the most mysterious acts of her life—acts that nothing could explain? What would make her blush? What would she want to hide? Would she start to throw, like a modest women, the long mantle of her hair over the numberless sins of the flesh? She did not know them, and these sins have never reached her. They were committed a thousand leagues from her throne; and even the Sodomite's soul would pass in the midst of the throng without suspecting anything, and bearing in her eyes a child's transparent smile. She hasn't intervened, she spent her life close to the light, and this is the only life she will remember.

> What sins and what common crimes will she have been able to commit? Has she betrayed, has she deceived, has she lied? Has she made others suffer and has she made them weep? Where was she while this man delivered his brother into the hands of enemies? She was perhaps sobbing far away from him, and from this moment on, she will become deeper and more beautiful. She will have no shame at all over what she didn't do; and she can remain pure at the center of a great murder. Often she transforms into inner brightness all the evil at which she's had to be present. Everything depends on an invisible principle, and from there the inexplicable indulgence of the gods is doubtless born. [. . .] Is there a mysterious morality that reigns in regions more distant than those of our thoughts? is there a central star that we don't see—a star around which our most secret desires are merely powerless planets? Does there exist, at the center of our being, a transparent tree whose ephemeral flowers and leaves are all our actions and all our virtues?

Maeterlinck thought that many great plays of the past were lacking in soul—he even considered Racine's *Phèdre*, though a work of the greatest psychological acuity, to be talky and soulless.[31] Maeterlinck intended his plays to be, above all, intimate—stage presentations of that precious wraith the human soul. But if the actions and virtues and feelings of the personages are all pretty much irrelevant to their souls, then Maeterlinck has in effect predismissed the entire apparatus of the theater even before the curtain rises for act 1.

This is perhaps the most Modernist aspect of Maeterlinck: the abiding sense that despite agony and bloodshed and birth and death, nothing at all is really happening. It's all a sort of melodramatic claptrap that dimly bodies forth the soul, a luminous blank, a remote tenderness that remains immune from love, hate, talk, deed. The characters are in some sense serious, but they can't take seriously any event, even any predicate attributed to themselves. You are not what you do, no matter how violent the deed. Rage, sorrow, lovingkindness, naïveté, whorishness, intelligence, lethargy, genius, obtuseness—these traits stamp us as determinate beings, but finally they all belong to the outer husk. Beneath the husk we're all exactly alike.

Oscar Wilde once wrote:

> It is a humiliating confession, but we are all of us made out of the same stuff. In Falstaff there is something of Hamlet, in Hamlet there is not a little of Falstaff. The fat knight has his moods of melancholy, and the

> young prince his moments of coarse humour. Where we differ from each other is purely in accidentals: in dress, manner, tone of voice, religious opinions, personal appearance, tricks of habit, and the like.[32]

In a late essay, published in 1936, Maeterlinck repeated, with more circumstantial detail, the idea that the heroes of Shakespeare are more or less idle variants of the same person:

> Coriolan c'est l'Hamlet méridional, l'Hamlet monté de deux ou trois crans, ne marchant plus à pas feutrés dans le silence dangereux, dans l'obscurité suspecte et la sourde bienséance d'Elseneur, mais gesticulant au soleil, sous l'aveuglante lumière du Forum; exubérant, sanguin, méprisant, vociférant, toujours indigné, toujours en colère, déchaîné contre la stupidité et les mauvaises odeurs de la foule et les basses intrigues de ses meneurs. Au fond le même homme, la même âme, le même caractère, dans un milieu, dans des circonstances, sous des cieux et des vêtements dissemblables. Coriolan éclate déjà dans Hamlet, par exemple dans les scènes avec Polonius, avec Ophélie, avec les comédiens, comme toute la tristesse d'Hamlet transparaît dans le Coriolan des dernières scènes avec Volumnie et la silencieuse Virgilie.
>
> Mais Coriolan c'est aussi Macbeth, comme Macbeth est Hamlet qui ose parce qu'il est dédoublé et que sa volonté s'est extériorisée dans sa femme. Au fond, Macbeth est un velléitaire, un sentimental bardé de fer, qui n'a osé qu'après de longues méditations et trop tard, ce que Coriolan a risqué tout de suite et trop tôt.
>
> Mais Coriolan c'est surtout le roi Léar. Un Léar encore gonflé du sang furieux de la jeunesse. Portez Coriolan vieilli dans les noirs châteaux et les sombres bruyères de l'Écosse, parmi les crises parricides où se débat le père de Régane et de Goneril, il parlera ou plutôt hurlera comme celui-ci; de même que Lear, à trente ans au milieu des Romains et des Volsques, aurait poussé les mêmes cris d'horreur et de rage que Coriolan. Ils sont interchangeables parce qu'ils sont, dans des aventures et des lieux différents, trois frères sur la même tige, trois grappes sur le même cep, trois aspects, trois épreuves du même individu, parce qu'ils sont toujours et partout, invariablement, quant au fond, quant à l'âme, quant au moi essentiel, quant à l'axe vital, Shakespeare en personne, c'est-à-dire le même homme de génie, le même poète universel plongé dans un bain gris, rouge ou noir, le créateur en apparence multiforme et inépuisable, mais qui puise tout en lui-même, le surhomme mille fois

homme, orgueilleux, capricieux, éloquent, contradictoire, hermaphrodite, qui portait en soi, comme nous tous, des êtres innombrables, mais en qui tous ces êtres s'agitaient dans un seul archétype qui les dominait, les absorbait, les incarnait, savait parler et agir en leur nom et se révélait un grand mélancolique, un grand sceptique, un grand désésperé, en un mot l'homme qui a le mieux senti, le plus profondément compris ce qu'est la vie humaine: *"A tale told by an idiot full of sound and fury, signifying nothing."* "Une histoire contée par un idiot, pleine de fureur et de bruit et qui ne veut rien dire," ce qui, en attendant des révélations ou des découvertes sur l'humanité et l'univers, est sans doute le dernier mot de notre vérité.[33]

Coriolanus is the Hamlet of the South, a Hamlet pulled up two or three notches, no longer walking with muffled step in the dangerous silence, in the suspect darkness, in the muted decorum of Elsinore, but gesticulating in the sun, under the blinding light of the Forum; exuberant, hot-blooded, scornful, vociferous, always indignant, always full of rage, let loose against the crowd's stupidity and bad smell, and against the base intrigues of its leaders. At bottom the same man, the same soul, the same character, in a different milieu, in different circumstances, under different skies, and wearing different clothes. Coriolanus already bursts out in Hamlet, for example in the scenes with Polonius, with Ophelia, with the actors, just as all of Hamlet's sadness shows through in the Coriolanus of the final scenes with Volumnia and the silent Virgilia.

But Coriolanus is also Macbeth, just as Macbeth is a Hamlet who dares to act because he is split in two: his will is exteriorized in the figure of his wife. At bottom, Macbeth is an irresolute man, a man of feeling beneath his iron armor, who dared to commit only after long meditation, and too late, the very act that Coriolanus ventured immediately, and too soon.

But above all, Coriolanus is King Lear. A Lear as yet swollen with the furious blood of youth. Transport Coriolanus, grown old, to the black castles and somber heath of Scotland, let his parricidal daughters Regan and Goneril make him flail, and he will speak or rather howl like Lear; just as Lear, at the age of thirty among the Romans and Volscians, would have uttered Coriolanus's cries of horror and rage. They are interchangeable because they are, though differing in their adventures and their locales, three brothers from the same stock, three clusters of grapes on the same vine, three aspects, three trial versions of the same individual, because they are always and everywhere, at their core, at their soul, at their essential *I*, at their axis of vitality, Shakespeare in person, that is to say the same man

> of genius, the same universal poet dipped in a gray, or red, or black bath, the creator in his multiform and inexhaustible appearance, who draws out of himself everything, the superman a thousand times man, proud, capricious, eloquent, contradictory, hermaphrodite, who carried in himself, as we all do, numberless beings, but in Shakespeare all these beings were set in motion within a single archetype that dominated them, absorbed them, incarnated them, knew how to speak and act in their name, and revealed himself as a great melancholic, a great skeptic, a greatly desperate man, in a word the man who best felt, most profoundly understood what human life is: "A tale told by an idiot, full of sound and fury, signifying nothing." Which, until there are new revelations or discoveries about mankind and the universe, is doubtless the last word in the truth of our state.

It is part of old Romantic bardolatry, this notion of Maeterlinck's that Shakespeare was an androgynous chameleon in whom the whole human race was latent. But there is another notion a little less familiar: that Shakespeare's protagonists are also chameleons, who will effortlessly metamorphose into one another if placed in different circumstances, dipped into a different vat of dyestuff. Northrop Frye argued, in *Fools of Time* (1967), that Shakespeare's plays were to some extent fragments of a single overplay that literary criticism could hope to reconstruct; and Maeterlinck is working along similar lines. Lady Macbeth turns out to be not an independent character but a psychological contingency, a projection of her husband's will; the boundaries between one character and another, one play and another, are fluid, transshifting. There is a single impredicable soul at the heart of Shakespeare's tragedies: Shakespeare's own.

There is a single soul at the heart of Maeterlinck's plays, too. Golaud's soul is interchangeable with Mélisande's, since Golaud finally has nothing to do with his jealousy, just as Mélisande has nothing to do with her pathos. All souls are equally fragile, equally ethereal. When the dying Mélisande asks to hold her baby, we usually see the baby in the form of an immobile something that might be a doll or a bundle of rags; and this uninflected thing might be her soul, or the soul of any of the characters in the play. Maybe the moment when Maeterlinck comes closest to confessing the eerie interchangeability of his personages occurs in *Joyzelle*, when Merlin's son, speaking to Joyzelle, remembers a time when

> toutes mes pensées entouraient tes pensées, comme une eau transparente entoure une eau plus claire . . .[34]

> all my thoughts surrounded your thoughts, as a transparent water surrounds a clearer water . . .

The difference between any two of Maeterlinck's characters, then, is the difference between transparent water and clear water.

And now we look at Claude-Achille Debussy's opera *Pelléas et Mélisande*, written mostly from 1892 to 1896, though not performed until 1902. Debussy was uncannily sympathetic to Maeterlinck's aesthetic—in fact, in the entire history of Western opera I know of no case where a composer was better equipped to handle the special difficulties of a challenging text, with the possible exception of Alban Berg's response to Georg Büchner's *Woyzeck*. In fact, even before Maeterlinck wrote *Pelléas et Mélisande*, Debussy was (so to speak) in search of that very text, as we know from a transcription of a conversation of 1890 between Debussy and his old teacher, Ernest Guiraud:

> *Debussy.* Je [n']imite pas. Autre forme dramatique à mon sens: musique où finit la parole. Musique pour inexprimable. Elle doit sortir de l'ombre. Être discrète.
>
> *Guiraud.* Mais alors où est votre poète?
>
> *Debussy.* Celui des choses dites à demi. Deux rêves associés: voilà l'idéal. Pas de pays, ni de date. Pas de scène à faire. Aucune pression sur le musicien qui parachève. Musique prédomine insolemment au théâtre lyrique. On chante trop. Habillage musical trop lourd. Chanter quand ça vaut la peine. Camaïeu. Grisaille. Pas de développements musicaux pour "développer." Fautes! Un développement prolongé ne colle pas, ne peut pas coller avec les mots. Je rêve poèmes courts: scènes mobiles. Me f . . . des 3 unités! Scènes diverses par lieux et caractère; personnages ne discutant pas; subissant vie, sort, etc.[35]

> *Debussy.* I don't imitate. Other dramatic form to my way of thinking: music where the word leaves off. Music for inexpressible. It must come out of shadow. Be discreet.
>
> *Guiraud.* But then, where's your poet?
>
> *Debussy.* The poet of things half said. Two linked dreams: there's the ideal. No country, no date. No big dramatic scene. No pressure on the musician who perfects. Music insolently predominates in the lyric theater. They sing too much. Musical dressing up too heavy. Sing when it's worth the trouble. Monochrome. Grisaille. No musical developments for the sake of "developing." Mistakes! A prolonged development

> doesn't stick with the words, can't stick. I dream of short poems: mobile scenes. Fuck the 3 unities [of time, of place, and of action]! Scenes varied both in their locale and in their natures; characters not talking to one another—acquiescing to life, fate, etc.

Pelléas et Mélisande fits this recipe so exactly that it's as if Debussy had commissioned it: a play of disjointed umbral vignettes, in which half-formed characters half-speak half-thoughts in nowhere, nowhen.

After Debussy got permission from Maeterlinck to write the opera—he was surprised by the playwright's deference to him—he confronted the extraordinary difficulties of writing something like a speech-opera, in which the speakers were indistinct or unreal presences, and the plot was attenuated to near nonexistence.

Debussy's solution to the problem of the plot was to return to the aesthetic of the early opera: that is, to stick to the most local phenomena and ignore most matters of continuity and large-scale form. In 1627 Claudio Monteverdi wrote to Alessandro Striggio that musical expression should be concentrated "sopra alla parola et non sopra al senso de la clausula" (on the word and not on the meaning of the sentence); and Debussy was equally determined to register minute responses to the text. As he wrote in 1909 to Edwin Evans,

> Il vaut peut-être mieux que, par des moyens simples,—un accord? une courbe?—la musique s'essaie à rendre les états d'ambiance et d'âme successifs, cela à mesure qu'ils se produisent, sans s'astreindre à suivre, péniblement, une trame symphonique prévue et *toujours arbitre*, à laquelle on sera nécessairement tenté de sacrifier la trâme [*sic*] sentimentale; mais on aura réussi un beau développement symphonique . . . ! encore une fois ça n'a rien à faire dans le drame lyrique; au surplus, c'est esquiver une difficulté à trop bon marché. C'est pourquoi il n'y a pas de "fil conducteur" dans Pelléas et que les personnages n'y subissent pas l'esclavage du "leitmotive," comme un aveugle l'est de son caniche, ou de sa clarinette![36]

> Maybe it's better for music to try to render by simple means—a chord? a curve?—the successive states of the atmosphere, of the soul, better for music to adjust itself to everything that happens, without painfully forcing itself to follow a pre-existing and *always arbitrary* symphonic plot line, which will necessarily tempt you to sacrifice the plot line of the emotions; but you'll have succeeded in making a beautiful symphonic development . . . ! once again, that has no place in lyric drama; moreover,

> it's too cheap a way of evading a difficulty. That's why there's no "guiding thread" in *Pelléas*, and why the characters in the opera don't submit to the slavery of the leitmotif, as a blind man is slave to his poodle or his clarinet!

A leitmotif, as the name suggests, leads and moves: its recurrent forms, altered, recolored, reworked in light of the changing dramatic situation, provide an Ariadne's thread through the opera's labyrinth. But Debussy craves a musical rhetoric discontinuous and uninstructive, in which the labyrinth is left labyrinthine, unsolved. He wants to impose no arbitrary form on the near-formlessness—the random inexorable—of Maeterlinck's play. Debussy tries to provide the single perfect chord, or a curve a few bars long, to make a musical dream double for a single instant of Maeterlinck's word dream; as for large form, he is content to let the music sag into whatever sort of odd form that the play can provide.

The comment to Evans is part of a general attack on the Wagnerian leitmotif:

> Quelles scies, ces leitmotif! Quelles sempiternelles catapultes! Les *Niebelungen* où il y a des pages qui me renversent, sont une machine à trucs. Même ils déteignent sur mon cher *Tristan* et c'est un chagrin pour moi de sentir que je m'en détache . . .[37]

> What old saws, these leitmotifs! What eternal catapults! The *Ring of the Nibelung*, in which there are pages of staggering force, is a set of mechanical tricks. They even disfigure my beloved *Tristan*, and I grieve to feel myself severed from it . . .

> Le drame de MM. Zola et Bruneau [*L'ouragan*] se recommande de nombreux symboles, et j'avoue ne pas comprendre ce besoin excessif de symboles. On semble avoir oublié que le plus beau, c'est encore la musique. Naturellement, le symbole appelle le "leitmotiv": et voilà encore la musique obligée de s'encombrer de petites phrases obstinées et qui veulent être entendues malgré tout. En somme, prétendre que telle succession d'accords représentera tel sentiment, telle phrase un quelconque personnage est un jeu d'anthropométrie assez inattendu.[38]

> The drama by M. Zola and M. Bruneau [*The Hurricane*] is noted for its numerous symbols, and I admit I don't understand this excessive need

for symbols. They seem to have forgotten that the most beautiful thing is still the music. Naturally, the symbol summons forth the leitmotif; and there it is, the music is still obliged to encumber itself with little obstinate phrases that insist on being heard in spite of everything. In sum, to claim that such a succession of chords will represent such a feeling, or such a phrase some sort of personage—this is a rather unexpected anthropometrical game.

> Ah! mylord! que ces gens à casques et à peaux de bêtes deviennent insupportables à la quatrième soirée . . . Songez qu'ils n'apparaissent jamais sans être accompagnés de leur damné "leitmotiv"; il y en a même quand ils le chantent! Ce qui ressemble à la douce folie de quelqu'un qui, vous remettant sa carte de visite, en déclamant lyriquement le contenu![39]

> Ah! my lord! How insupportable these folks wearing helmets and animal skins become by the fourth evening [*Götterdämmerung*] . . . Think of it, they never appear without being accompanied by their damned leitmotif; there are even some of them who sing it! It's like the cute madness of someone who, as he hands you his visiting card, lyrically declaims what's printed on it!

Debussy's dislike of the leitmotif is twofold: first, that the set of all its evolutions provides a form of musical continuity clumsily superimposed on the text, and probably irrelevant to it; second, that as soon as you fasten a name to the musical theme, it becomes a gross and glaring form of musical commentary on the personages—as if Hunding, when he stalked around his hut in *Die Walküre*, bore on his chest a neon sign that kept flashing the name HUNDING. The first objection pertains to the plot; the second to characterization. Debussy was following Maeterlinck's technique of deconstructing, dissolving the personages, and a name tag worked against what he was trying to accomplish. I think that Pierre Boulez had it almost right he commented on Debussy's non-leitmotif:

> Il s'agit, plutôt, d'arabesques liées aux personnages eux-mêmes sans variation autre que décorative, qui s'intègrent au contexte général sans effort.[40]

> It's instead a matter of arabesques tied to the characters themselves, without variation other than decorative, effortlessly integrated into the general context.

But the liaison between the arabesque-like themes and the characters may be a little weaker than Boulez suggests. In some sense Debussy's themes are *Verleitmotive*, misleading motifs. Just as Maeterlinck was uncomfortable with a vocabulary of symbols, Debussy was somewhat antisymbolic, too: he may well have thought that he was desymbolizing *Pelléas et Mélisande* by liberating his musical themes from names, from any intelligible semantics beyond glints and hints derived from Maeterlinck's evanescent rhetoric of feeling. Anthropometry was a sort of whole-body phrenology, in which measurements of body parts were used to define ratios that presumably gave insight into character and temperament; Debussy seems to be mocking the leitmotif system as a game that constructs icons of men and women, symbolic character shapes, through musicomathematical procedures.

The personages in *Pelléas et Mélisande* are vanishing creatures on the brink of dissolution, half-formed beings that toy with the notion of being characters in an opera. And their musical symbols are pseudomotifs that fail to constitute themselves properly and fall into signlessness.

We've already looked in some detail at Maeterlinck's strategies for attenuating and disindividuating—even in a sense abrogating—the characters in his plays. Debussy, who could have known almost nothing of Maeterlinck's theories of the drama beyond what he could infer from the plays themselves, was quite aware of the strange nullity of Pelléas, Mélisande, and the rest of the crew and tried to supply his own nullities to match. As he wrote to Chausson (probably at the beginning of 1894):

> J'ai passé des journées à la poursuite de ce "rien" dont elle est faite (Mélisande) [. . .] Maintenant c'est Arkel qui me tourmente. Celui-là, il est d'outre-tombe, et il a cette tendresse désintéressée et prophétique de ceux qui vont bientôt disparaître, et il faut dire tout cela avec do, ré, mi, fa, sol, la, si, do!! Quel métier?[41]

> I've spent some days in pursuit of this "nothing" from which she (Mélisande) is made [. . .] Now it's Arkël who torments me. That one, he's from beyond the grave, and he has the impartial and prophetic tenderness of those who are going to vanish soon, and I have to say all that with do, re, mi, fa, sol, la, ti, do!! What a job?

Mélisande is nothing, and Arkël is a sort of ectoplasm thinning into the void. Yet, as Roger Nichols and Richard Langham Smith have pointed out, Debussy himself labeled a four-measure passage at the beginning of act 1,

EXAMPLE 1. Debussy, *Pelléas et Mélisande*: first Mélisande theme, act 1, scene 3. From *Pelléas et Mélisande. Partition pour chant et piano* (Paris: A. Durand & Fils, 1907), 39.

scene 3 the "thème initial de Mélisande" (Nichols and Smith, p. 144), a theme that undergoes many vicissitudes in the course of the opera; so we have here a curious musical entity that both is and is not a leitmotif.

The little six-note phrase seen in example 1 in the middle staff of the first measure is indeed one of the opera's most salient features. It's worth noting that Debussy wasn't alone in labeling it a Mélisande theme: Paul Dukas, one of Debussy's keenest and most admiring critics, heard it the same way. In the play *Ariane et Barbe-bleue* (1899), Maeterlinck amuses himself by assigning to Bluebeard's first five wives—a spectral coven—the names of characters in his previous plays: one of them is Mélisande. In Dukas's lucid, luminous opera *Ariane et Barbe-bleue* (1907), as Sélysette announces to Ariane the name Mélisande, Debussy's *thème initial* provides a charming *carte de visite*.

I want to call particular attention to two themes in Debussy's *Pelléas et Mélisande*: one is the *thème initial de Mélisande*, but I think that the key to the opera's motivic structure lies in the other theme:

This passage shown in ex. 2 is the opera's very beginning, prefacing the scene where Golaud, lost in the forest, discovers Mélisande, lost in the forest;

EXAMPLE 2. Debussy, *Pelléas et Mélisande*: "Golaud" theme, first appearance, act 1, scene 1. From *Pelléas et Mélisande. Partition pour chant et piano* (Paris: A. Durand & Fils, 1907), 1.

the theme I mean is the one in mm. 5 and 6. It has been sometimes labeled as the Golaud theme, because it offers a striking contrast with the *thème initial de Mélisande* (also conspicuous in this prelude), and because it sometimes sounds a bit stern and, when played by horns, hunterlike; but—for reasons that will become evident—I'll refer to it as the "Golaud" theme, in quotation marks, because I feel that the name is incorrect. (For one thing, when Golaud sings his *carte de visite*, "I am Prince Golaud, the grandson of Arkël, the aged king of Allemonde," the "Golaud" theme is nowhere to be heard.) Here, in its first appearance, the theme amounts to an alternation of two chords each derived from the whole-tone scale. Later in the opera Golaud and Pelléas will grope their blind way down a subterranean path, accompanied by an up-and-down movement of a whole-tone scale, perhaps the purest expression in Western music of the directionlessness, the disorientation, the sheer absence of any possible tonic that the whole-tone scale (like any symmetrical division of the octave) entails. And right here at the beginning we have an alternation of a whole-tone chords, at once resolute-sounding and completely aimless, introducing us to a tone-domain that lacks a guiding thread, a sense of forward motion, a sense of fate—or, to say it better, that provides only a fake fatality in music, comparable to the fake fatality of Maeterlinck's text.

In example 3 we hear "Golaud" again, and then, sweetly, expressively, Mélisande, in a slightly different shape from what Debussy would label (at the beginning of scene 3) the *thème initial de Mélisande*:

Now the "Golaud" theme is more normally formed, harmonically speaking: a dominant chord in G minor, alternating with an A major thirteenth chord (if a thirteenth chord can ever be considered normal). The music seems to be refocusing, moving to a better adjusted space, a space you're less likely to get lost in. Then, for the very first time, the *thème initial de Mélisande* appears, in a manner that's equivocal—neither particularly disorienting nor particularly well oriented. The harmony isn't overly challenging: you can hear the often-repeated accompaniment figure as a B♭M^{II} arpeggio, undergirding a melody that counterasserts itself in B♭ minor. But I don't think I hear it in quite that way, and Debussy (by writing the melody with a C♯ instead of a D) doesn't spell the notes in a way that invites that interpretation. It might be better to think of the *thème initial de Mélisande*, in this guise, as a pentatonic melody—if played on a piano the melody would be all black notes—with a whole-tone accompaniment: as if both of the main themes needed to be stated first in harmonic forms at an angle to tonality.[42] But I think it's also important to note that the melody and the accompaniment alike are entirely part of the whole-tone scale, except for the single melodic note C♯. According to either analysis it's the C♯ that sticks out, since it's the one note that isn't in the whole-tone scale of the accompaniment (if you're listening on that axis) or that deviates most strongly from B♭ major (if you're listening on *that* axis). The theme is perfectly susceptible to far more orthodox harmonic forms, forms that leave the topmost note in a less glaring position: for example, the still sweeter version from the

EXAMPLE 3. Debussy, *Pelléas et Mélisande*: "Golaud" and Mélisande, act 1, scene 1. From *Pelléas et Mélisande. Partition pour chant et piano* (Paris: A. Durand & Fils, 1907), 1.

EXAMPLE 4. Debussy, "Sirènes": sirens' song. From *Nocturnes. Transcription pour deux pianos à quatre mains par Maurice Ravel* (Paris: E. Fromont, 1909), 4.

beginning of scene 3 (quoted in ex. 1) works as a compact melody supported by a B^9 chord.

There is another important theme in the opera's prelude, the one played in the very first four bars (see ex. 2): I think of it as the weather theme, because it appears when Golaud sings, "La nuit sera très noire and très froide" (The night will be very black and very cold) and because it has something of the immobile imperturbable drift of some of Debussy's cloud themes. (And yet, all the themes in *Pelléas et Mélisande* could be called weather themes.) But this theme, though we hear it often, seems to lack some of the salience of the prelude's other two themes. The persistence of these two themes (the *thème initial de Mélisande* and "Golaud") through the opera, especially in the opening acts, is astonishing, unprecedented, without a successor—except perhaps one, which I'll mention later. (At about the same time that Debussy was working on *Pelléas et Mélisande*, Jules Massenet premiered *Werther* [1892] and *Thaïs* [1894], in which the final acts manifest a similar thematic concentration, obsession.) Debussy weaves many other threads through his tapestry, some dark, some golden, such as the lovely, down-skipping theme at the beginning of act 2—he lavishes a wealth of thematic material on the opera—but the acoustic environment is created largely by the two main themes.

There is another major work by Debussy that is similarly built up from two themes—and from two themes bearing a striking similarity to these two themes: "Sirènes," the third of the *Nocturnes*. Debussy composed this piece while working on *Pelléas et Mélisande*, and it was first performed in 1901, a year before the opera. The main theme is presented in example 4.

I give it in Maurice Ravel's reduction for two pianos: in the original version, the sirens' song (the theme that begins in the third measure here, "très expressif") is sung by a wordless female chorus. Like the "Golaud" theme, the sirens' theme consists of two notes separated by a major second: indeed, the whole of "Sirènes" might be considered the apotheosis of the major second, since so much of the music is constructed around that interval. The E♯ makes for an intense sonority, since it's a tritone away from B, and B major is both the tonic and the chord that accompanies the theme, here in its first appearance. And like the "Golaud" theme, the rhythm of the sirens' song is complicated, with its ligatures connecting an eighth note to the first beat of an eighth-note triplet: the rhythm isn't urgent in the "Golaud" manner, but it's equally arresting, in a more languid way.

I think of "Sirènes" as even more oceanically alive than *La mer*. At the beginning the horns seem to make great bird-cries of desire—the sirens of antiquity weren't mermaids, but women on top and birds on the bottom—but a peculiar kind of desire, endless and insatiable, for Odysseus's ship is never going to come to their rock. The music seems to have no particular sense of beginning or end: it doesn't drive toward a cadence, it simply elaborates the big waves with little waves, underpulses, in the way that the surge of surf on a beach falls into long rhythms of tide and medium rhythms of regular wavefall and short rhythms of little splashes at the end of the regular wavefall. In the libretto that Debussy wrote for a projected opera on Poe's "The Fall of the House of Usher," Roderick Usher hears or imagines a lost bird—"Ses ailes battent comme si c'était la respiration du temps."[43] The bird's wings beat as if it were the respiration of time—and Debussy's rhythm in pieces like "Sirènes," pulse without ictus, is the sound of time's breathing.

There is one other important theme besides the song itself, seen in example 5. The chromatic figure marked *expressif* feels seductive, odalisque-like: it sounds like the music of sexual display, as if the sirens are wriggling their bodies as they sing.

"Sirènes," then, is constructed from two themes, one that is simply a complex dance across a major second, and another that is melodically intense. This is a simplified version of the recipe for *Pelléas et Mélisande* itself: the opera is constructed from a theme that is a complex dance across a major second, and another theme that is a sinuous appeal, though in a more chaste manner than that of "Sirènes."

Insofar as the "Golaud" theme is another casting of the theme of the sirens' song, it seems more appropriate to Mélisande than to Golaud. The "Golaud" theme is the motif of Mélisande as water. (Indeed, there is a sense in which all

EXAMPLE 5. Debussy, "Sirènes": snake charming. From *Nocturnes. Transcription pour deux pianos à quatre mains par Maurice Ravel* (Paris: E. Fromont, 1909), 2.

the opera's themes are folded up into Mélisande—or into that blank soul that is the soul of a child or a murderer interchangeably. This is Debussy's form of monism.) The demure, angelic Mélisande is properly represented by the *thème initial de Mélisande*; but, as we've seen, there's another way of regarding Mélisande, as a far more sexually alert being—and that version of Mélisande can be conceived along the lines of the sirens of the *Nocturnes*: the liquid Mélisande, the Mélisande of the fountain in the forest and the fountain of the blind and the grotto by the sea, the elusive Mélisande. Mélisande is Mélusine.

Maeterlinck's women are often, in one form or another, undines or naiads, images drawn on water that somehow rise into some semblance of human life. In one of Debussy's most beautiful songs, "La grotte" (1904), he sets a line by Tristan l'Hermite concerning reflections of flowers that seem like "les songes de l'eau qui sommeille." Mélisande herself is a sort of dream of the sleeping water, in the pool where, as l'Hermite puts it, Narcissus died long ago. In his early poem "Reflets," from *Serres chaudes* (1889), Maeterlinck himself seems to have remembered l'Hermite's line:

> Sous l'eau du songe qui s'élève,
> Mon âme a peur, mon âme a peur!
> Et la lune luit dans mon coeur,
> Plongé dans les sources du rêve.[44]
>
> Under the water, water gathering,
> Dream-water, my soul knows fear!
> And the moon shines in my heart,
> Plunged in the springs, dream-springs.

In *L'oiseau bleu*, a play that works as a sort of bowdlerized anthology for children of all of his favorite themes, Maeterlinck invented, as a companion to little Tyltyl, a character named Water, dressed in a costume of dripping bluish gauze, with seaweed in her hair: she enters through the tap, and, as she becomes more fully personified, she becomes disturbed that she can't leave through the same aperture. Soon afterward the Fairy tells Water that it would be nice if she didn't keep flowing all over the place; later, Tyltyl tells his crybaby sister, Mytyl, that she shouldn't weep all the time, in the way that Water does. And Water is indeed a complaining sort: at one point she groans that she's never known the least happiness. On the other hand, Water is, in her quiet, tender way, rather vocal: saying farewell, she gives some advice to the children, though her enemy Fire makes snide comments:

> *L'eau.* Aimez bien les Fontaines, écoutez les Ruisseaux . . . Je serais toujours là . . .
> *Le feu.* Elle a tout inondé! . . .
> *L'eau.* Quand vous vous assiérez, le soir, au bord des Sources . . . il y en a plus d'une ici, dans la forêt—essayez de comprendre ce qu'elles essaient de dire—Je ne peux plus—Les larmes me suffoquent et m'empêchent de parler [. . .] Souvenez-vous de moi lorsque vous verrez le carafe . . . vous me trouverez également dans le broc, dans l'arrosoir, dans la citerne et dans le robinet . . .[45]

> *Water.* Love well the Fountains, listen to the Streams . . . I will always be there . . .
> *Fire.* She's flooded everything!
> *Water.* When you sit down, in the evening, by the edge of the Springs . . . you can find more than one here, in the forest—try to understand what they're trying to tell you—I can't, any more—I'm choked with tears and I can't speak [. . .] Remember me when you see the jug . . . you'll also find me in the pitcher, in the watering-can, in the tank and in the tap . . .

I'm struck by how much Mélisande there is in all this: Mélisande enters the play through a forest fountain, almost history-less, as if she'd just recently turned into a human being; and she resists Golaud's attempts to carry her off into the human world, as if she'd prefer to deliquesce back into nonentity. "Ne me touchez pas, ou je me jette à l'eau" (Don't touch me, or I'll throw myself in the water), she warns her future husband. But, like Water, she seems already a little too big and dense to return through the tap. In this opening scene,

EXAMPLE 6. Debussy, *Pelléas et Mélisande*: sailors, act 1, scene 3. From *Pelléas et Mélisande. Partition pour chant et piano* (Paris: A. Durand & Fils, 1907), 45.

and elsewhere, she melts into tears without much provocation. Pelléas even remarks, as he takes leave of Mélisande, that his memories are like water carried in a cheesecloth bag—"tous ces souvenirs . . . c'est comme si j'emportais un peu d'eau dans un sac de mousseline." Her voice is fluent and attractive, watery: "ta voix! Elle est plus fraîche et plus franche que l'eau" (your voice! It's fresher and more open than water), Pelléas tells her. But like the voice of a brook, her voice isn't always very intelligible: "Je ne comprends non plus tout ce que je dis" (I no longer understand all I'm saying), she says as she dies, and it's not likely that others understand her riddling words very well either.

The "Golaud" motif—I'd prefer to call it the motif of water, along the lines of its cousin in "Sirènes"—is watery, *informe*, not just because of its unsteady sloshing between two chords, but for other reasons as well. The heaving of the sailors in act 1, scene 3 (ex. 6) is closely related to it.

Here the contraltos go back and forth across a major second, in dotted rhythm, just as in the "Golaud" motif, in many of its forms. Sea spray often tends, in Debussy's imagination, to gather around such melodic phrases. In Debussy's best-known essay, "L'entretien avec M. Croche," from *Monsieur Croche antidilettante*, he writes:

> Il faut chercher la discipline dans la liberté et non dans les formules d'une philosophie devenue caduque et bonne pour les faibles. N'écoutez

> les conseils de personne, sinon du vent qui passe et nous raconte l'histoire du monde.[46]

> You must seek discipline in liberty and not in the formulas of a worn-out philosophy, good only for the weak. Don't listen to the counsels of anybody, except that of the wind that in passing tells us the history of the world.

I'm not sure that Debussy has a particular musical trope that represents the counsel of the wind, though I could ask the west wind for advice, since it appears in "Ce qu'a vu le vent d'ouest" (*Préludes*, no. 1, m. 7, 1910); but I think that water has a distinct tendency to speak in a language of irregular motions across a major second.

The "Golaud" motif occasionally contracts, fascinatingly, from a major second to a minor second, as in the interlude just before the beginning of act 1, scene 2 (ex. 7). Here the chords oscillate between B major^7 and A minor. Such alternation between chords themselves a major second apart is common in the harmonization of this theme; but the minor-second melodic form is not so usual. In the later acts we sometimes hear other oscillations across a minor second.

Golaud, distraught, tries to hide his emotion from his son as he encourages the boy to spy on Pelléas and Mélisande; so he invents a wolf to explain why he seems shaken. The imaginary wolf makes this faint ululation in the depths of the orchestra (ex. 8). In retrospect, it sounds like an almost erased allusion to the Wolf's theme in Sergei Prokofiev's *Peter and the Wolf* (1936).

This sort of slow black trill is part of the normal operatic rhetoric of uneasiness. There is a similar moment in a later opera, Igor Stravinsky's *The Flood* (1962): a horn indulges in a nearly rhythmless vagrancy between adjacent semitones, B and C, as the Serpent comes to tempt Eve (ex. 9).

EXAMPLE 7. Debussy, *Pelléas et Mélisande*: "Golaud" motive in its minor-second form, act 1, scene 1. From *Pelléas et Mélisande. Partition pour chant et piano* (Paris: A. Durand & Fils, 1907), 24.

EXAMPLE 8. Debussy, *Pelléas et Mélisande*: wolf, act 3, scene 4. From *Pelléas et Mélisande. Partition pour chant et piano* (Paris: A. Durand & Fils, 1907), 173.

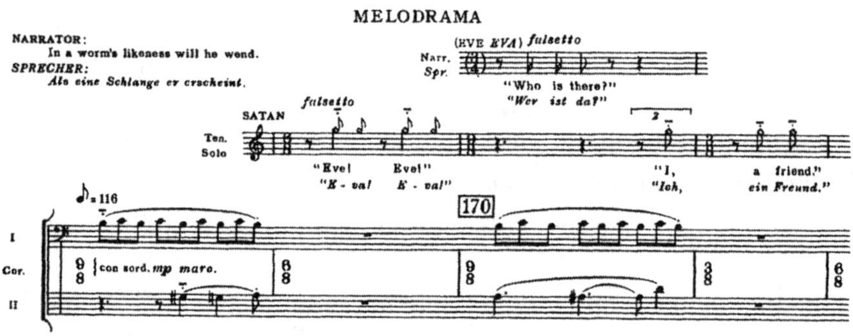

EXAMPLE 9. Stravinsky, *The Flood*: temptation of Eve. From *The Flood: A Musical Play* (London: Boosey & Hawkes, 1963), 18.

Stravinsky described his music as follows: "The Tarnhelm music for two muted horns is likely to be my first and last attempt to compose a belly dance."[47] It is the merest sketch of a belly dance, a dance for the skeleton of a belly dancer. That Stravinsky associated this little bit of music—scarcely more than an ornament—with Wagner's Tarnhelm is of interest. Now the Tarnhelm motif—the motif of Alberich's shape-shifting or invisible-making helmet in *Der Ring des Nibelungen*—appears initially as a G♯ minor chord that transforms itself into an E minor chord, recedes back to G♯ minor, tries out E minor once again, and then rises to a B chord, not marked as either minor or major (ex. 10).

It is a harmonic riddle that poses the question, how many triads contain the note B?—B is the one stable element as the motif creeps up and contracts and creeps up again. (Similarly Alberich is always Alberich, whether in the form of dragon or toad—he is going nowhere, just as the motif is going nowhere.) Stravinsky has oversimplified the Tarnhelm into the emptiest possible oscillation of two notes separated by a minor second, with a slight reinforcement (from the second horn) of the upward creep at the end of Wagner's motif.

The "Golaud" motif also operates as a kind of Tarnhelm, and indeed may have been partly inspired by Wagner's invisibility music. It is a pure isolate of instability. Golaud is of course a weak, deeply unstable man, full of bad imaginings about his wife, full of murderous frustration, and driven mad, like Othello, by the general uninterpretability of human conduct. Mélisande trickles through Golaud's hands, through Pelléas's hands, like water. Arkël, according to Debussy, is a voice from beyond the grave. One important character, Pelléas's sick father, never appears and doesn't even have a name. These wraiths are almost too translucent to cast a shadow; they are given a good deal of beautiful and touching music, but their nobodyness is given expression by the "Golaud" theme.

Instability is also a property of the castle itself, built over a chasm of whole tones, indefinite musical spaces. The scene where the castle makes itself most psychically present is the scene in the underground grotto: but there are other moments where the castle looms forth, forbidding, tenebrous:

> *Golaud.* Ne peux-tu pas te faire à la vie qu'on mène ici? Fait-il trop triste ici? Il est vrai que ce château est très vieux et très sombre . . . Il est très froid et très profond. Et tous ce qui l'habitent sont déjà vieux.[48]

EXAMPLE 10. Wagner, *Das Rheingold*: Tarnhelm, scene 3. From *Der Ring des Nibelungen. Ein Bühnenfestspiel für drei Tage und einen Vorabend* (Mainz: B. Schott's Söhne, 1899), 118 of the *Rheingold* score.

EXAMPLE 11. Debussy, *Pelléas et Mélisande*: castle, act 2, scene 2. From *Pelléas et Mélisande. Partition pour chant et piano* (Paris: A. Durand & Fils, 1907), 90.

> *Golaud.* Can't you get used to the life we lead here? Is it too sad here? It's true that this castle is very old and very dark . . . It's very cold and very deep. And all who dwell here are already old.

The brief passage shown in example 11 is one of the glories of the score: in the lowest staff, the English horn quietly, insistently traces a four-note figure that becomes a kind of soft clock, a drift of sand through an hourglass, as if the castle's stones were making a faint sound of crumbling. Maeterlinck provides other signs that the castle is falling into ruin: as Golaud and Pelléas make their way through the underground grottos, Golaud notes that the wall and columns are eaten away, and lizards live inside them—if nothing is done, one night the whole castle will be engulfed in the dead water—"tout le château s'engloutira une de ces nuits."[49] This falling asunder never occurs, but at the climax of Debussy's fragmentary opera *La chute de la maison Usher* (on which Debussy worked from about 1908) there is a moment that seems an extrapolation of the castle of Allemonde into a state of full collapse. Debussy himself considered that his Usher project had nothing to do with *Pelléas et Mélisande*; as he told an interviewer in 1910,

> Je suis très content [. . .] car non seulement l'atmosphère secrète, les sentiments, les tensions, les émotions contenus dans les nouvelles de Poe n'ont encore jamais été traduits en musique, mais aussi parce qu'on ne peut trouver contraste plus absolu qu'entre Poe et Maeterlinck.[50]

> I'm very happy [. . .] not only because the atmosphere of secrecy, the sentiments, the tensions, the emotions found in Poe's stories have never been translated into music, but also because you can't find any contrast more absolute than that between Poe and Maeterlinck.

But I think that Debussy was wrong in distinguishing so strongly between Poe and Maeterlinck. A set designer for the scene where Pelléas and Golaud grope along the walls of the grotto beneath the castle might profit from studying Poe's account of Roderick Usher's painting:

> If ever mortal painted an idea, that mortal was Roderick Usher. For me at least—in the circumstances then surrounding me—there arose out of the pure abstractions which the hypochondriac contrived to throw upon his canvass, an intensity of intolerable awe, no shadow of which felt I ever yet in the contemplation of the certainly glowing yet too concrete reveries of Fuseli.
>
> One of the phantasmagoric conceptions of my friend, partaking not so rigidly of the spirit of abstraction, may be shadowed forth, although feebly, in words. A small picture presented the interior of an immensely long and rectangular vault or tunnel, with low walls, smooth, white, and without interruption or device. Certain accessory points of the design served well to convey the idea that this excavation lay at an exceeding depth below the surface of the earth. No outlet was observed in any portion of its vast extent, and no torch, or other artificial source of light was discernible; yet a flood of intense rays rolled throughout, and bathed the whole in a ghastly and inappropriate splendor.

EXAMPLE 12. Debussy, *La chute de la maison Usher*: crack. From *La chute de la maison Usher. Drame lyrique en 1 acte et 2 scènes d'après Edgar Allan Poe. Transcription chant et piano de Juan Allende-Blin* (Paris: Société des Éditions Jobert, 1979), 40.

Maeterlinck's claustrophobias and agoraphobias are quieter than Poe's, less overwrought, but no less intense.

In *La chute de la maison Usher*, the Friend reads aloud to Roderick Usher the story of how the knight Ulrich encounters an evil hermit who turns into a fire-tongued dragon: Ulrich rushes to seize a shining bronze shield hanging on the wall.

In the reconstruction of the opera by Juan Allende-Blin (ex.12),[51] there is a maniacally repeated four-note figure that falls through major sevenths and minor seconds, from B to C to B to C. (In the reconstruction by Robert Orledge, this effect is much less striking.) It is as if the gentle structural instabilities in Arkël's very old, dark, cold, deep castle, in *Pelléas et Mé-*

lisande, had zigzagged wide open—Usher's house is falling apart before our ears. The last act of *Pelléas et Mélisande* is simply a long tapering-off, as the Doctor gives up and Golaud weeps and Mélisande unsubstantiates herself. But among the unrealized potentialities of Maeterlinck's vagrant impossible plot is a louder ending, an implosion in which the vacuum at the play's heart would take aggressive shape. In *La chute de la maison Usher*, Debussy toyed with the bang that's on the far side of all of Maeterlinck's whimpers.

The collapse of a building is a theme more resonant in opera than in prose fiction. Debussy was a keen student of early French opera: he was ravished by a performance of two acts of Rameau's 1737 opera *Castor et Pollux* (*Gil Blas*, February 2, 1903), wrote an "open letter" to "Monsieur le Chevalier C. W. Gluck" (*Gil Blas*, February 23, 1903) and even composed an "Hommage à Rameau" (the second of the *Images pour piano*, 1904–5). A remarkable number of seventeenth- and eighteenth-century French operas (by Lully, Charpentier, Gluck) end with a scene in which a huffy witch (Armide, Médée) exits on a flying chariot while her magic palace falls into ruin. Debussy had no use for dragon-drawn witches, but I think that he was deeply attracted to the idea of a building falling asunder. His older colleagues were similarly attracted: Camille Saint-Saëns' *Samson et Dalila* (1877) ends with Samson's pulling down onto his head the Temple of Dagon; and the second act of *Parsifal* (1882) ends with nightmare ferocity as Klingsor's magic castle undoes itself—you can hear in Wagner's music how the earthquake first topples the small stones at the top and then upheaves big slabs of wall.

As it happened, the composition of *Pelléas et Mélisande* was intimately bound up with *Parsifal*. On October 2, 1893, the exasperated Debussy wrote to Chausson that he was tearing up certain passages of his new opera:

> Je m'étais trop dépêché de chanter victoire pour *Pelléas et Mélisande*, car, après une nuit blanche, celle qui porte conseil, il a bien fallu m'avouer que ça n'était pas ça du tout! Ça ressemblait au duo de monsieur Un Tel, ou n'importe qui, et surtout le fantôme du vieux Klingsor, alias R. Wagner, apparaissait au détour d'une mesure. J'ai donc tout déchiré, et suis reparti à la recherche d'une petite chimie de phrases plus personnelles, et me suis efforcé d'être aussi Pelléas que Mélisande.[52]

> I was in too much a hurry to cry victory for *Pelléas et Mélisande*, for, after a sleepless night, the sort of night that brings good counsel, I've had to admit that I wasn't yet there at all! This part looked like a duet by

> Mr. So-and-so—it doesn't matter who—and above all the phantom of old Klingsor, alias R. Wagner, appeared at the curve of a measure. And so I've torn it all up, and started afresh in search of a little chemistry of more personal phrases, and have tried to be as much Pelléas as Mélisande.

There is a sense in which Debussy's opera is about magic; but there is another sense in which it's about exorcism, the dispelling of Wagner's magic in order to make room for his own. Klingsor's castle has to fall down once and for all before Arkël's castle—another rickety structure—can be built.

Debussy was haunted not only by the remarkable music that Wagner wrote for Klingsor—great nervous gasps, chromatic whirls in which the chroma varies from dark blue to black, the sound-equivalent of van Gogh's *Starry Night*—but also by the dramatic figure of Klingsor himself:

> Le plus beau caractère dans *Parsifal* appartient à Klingsor (ancien chevalier du Graal, mis à la porte du Saint-Lieu pour des opinions trop personnelles sur la chasteté). Celui-ci est merveilleux de haine rancuneuse; il sait ce que valent les hommes et pèse la solidité de leurs vœux de chasteté avec de méprisantes balances. Ce de quoi l'on peut arguer sans effort que ce magicien retors, ce vieux cheval de retour, est non seulement le seul personnage "humain," mais l'unique personnage "moral" de ce drame où se proclament les idées morales et religieuses les plus fausses; idées dont le jeune Parsifal est le chevalier héroïque et niais.[53]

> The most beautiful character in *Parsifal* belongs to Klingsor (former knight of the Grail, shoved out of the door of the Holy Place for his too singular opinions concerning chastity). He is a marvel of rancorous hatred; he knows what men are worth and weighs the solidity of their vows of chastity in the scales of his contempt. You could easily argue that this twisted magician, this old recidivist, is not only the only "human" personage, but the unique "moral" personage in this drama where the falsest moral and religious ideas are proclaimed; the young Parsifal is the heroic and nitwit knight of those ideas.

Klingsor's too singular opinion on chastity was that it would be a good idea to castrate himself in order to be immune from sexual temptation—Wagner even toyed with the idea of scoring the role for a male soprano, if Domenico Mustafa, a castrato in the Vatican choir, could be made available to sing it. Wagner's two greatest villains, Alberich and Klingsor, both renounce love in order to gain power: Klingsor manages to ruin Amfortas, the king of the knights of the Grail, by compelling the witch Kundry to seduce him. For Debussy, Klingsor was a hero of impotent despair. Debussy was far from sexually impotent, but he drove two of the women in his life to threats of suicide (his first wife actually shot herself), and I think that he may have seen himself as a sort of Klingsor, snide, spiteful, tormented and tormenting, a seducer who practiced his music-magic in a calculating, somewhat hollow manner.

Debussy, at least in certain moods, felt that his music was about emptiness: as he wrote to Pierre Louÿs on March 27, 1898,

> Les trois *Nocturnes* se sont ressentis de ma vie, et ont été pleins d'espoir, puis pleins de désespoir et ensuite, pleins de vide![54]

> The three *Nocturnes* are continuations of my felt life, and have been full of hope, then full of despair, and finally full of the void!

Each of the three *Nocturnes* trails off into nothingness: the sirens first seduce, and then turn their backs. As J. Alfred Prufrock says, I do not think that they will sing to me. If Debussy had completed his opera on the fall of the house of Usher, it would have been his finest presentation of the vacuum at the heart of things. Maybe in its unfinishedness it is a still more impressive *rien*. Maeterlinck thought that the ultimate truth of human life is that it is full of sound and fury, signifying nothing. But neither Maeterlinck nor Debussy was particularly expert in fury; an old man sitting vacantly in a vacant room, or a faint song heard from somewhere in a tower, can adequately signify nothing, too.

4. Faraway Songs

Maeterlinck was a poet before he was a playwright, and he took great care with the songs embedded in the texts of his plays. In the earliest version of *Pelléas et Mélisande*, act 3 opens with a haunting song that drifts down from the tower:

> Mes longs cheveux descendent jusqu'au seuil de la tour!
> Mes cheveux vous attendent tout le long de la tour!
> Et tout le long du jour!
> Et tout le long du jour!

Saint Daniel et Saint Michel,
Saint Michel et Saint Raphaël,
Je suis née un Dimanche!
Un Dimanche à midi!

It falls to the ground, my hair is so long!
My hair is as long as the tower is long!
Long as the day is long!
My hair waits for you!

Saint Raphael, Saint Michael,
Saint Michael and Saint Daniel,
I was born on a Sunday!
On a Sunday at noon!

Debussy was extraordinarily gifted at these ghost-songs, songs that come at you from another dimension: not only is there Madeline's song, at the beginning of the first fragment of *La chute de la maison Usher*, but also a too-little-known berceuse, "Il était une fois une fée qui avait un beau sceptre," that Debussy wrote in 1899 for René Peter's *La tragédie de la mort* (1899). The only recording Debussy ever made of music from *Pelléas et Mélisande* was a 1904 wax cylinder, in which he played a piano reduction of this (almost unaccompanied!) song, with Mary Garden, the first Mélisande, singing. The song's remarkable sense of elated remoteness comes partly from the way that the song equivocates between B minor and E minor, with the piano adding the odd comment in B major (ex. 13). The melody is limpid, effortless, but its implied harmony is hard to construe.

But Maeterlinck had second thoughts, and replaced this song with another (though he retained a bit of "Mes longs cheveux" as a spinning song for Mélisande in the preceding scene):

Les trois soeurs aveugles,
(Espérons encore).
Les trois soeurs aveugles,
Ont leurs lampes d'or.

Montent à la tour,
(Elles, vous et nous).

EXAMPLE 13. Debussy, *Pelléas et Mélisande*: "Mes longs cheveux," act 3, scene 1. From *Pelléas et Mélisande. Partition pour chant et piano* (Paris: A. Durand & Fils, 1907), 116.

Montent à la tour,
Attendent sept jours.

Ah! dit la première,
Espérons encore,
Ah! dit la première,
J'entends nos lumières.

Ah! dit la seconde,
(Elles, vous et nous).
Ah! dit la seconde,
C'est le roi qui monte.

Non, dit la plus sainte,
(Espérons encore).
Non., dit la plus sainte,
Elles se sont éteintes . . .[55]

Gabriel Fauré set this to music, oddly enough not in French, but in an English translation by Jack Mackail, for a production of the play starring Mrs. Patrick Campbell, in 1898—that is, between the composition of Debussy's opera and its first performance:

The King's three blind daughters
Sit locked in a hold.
In the darkness their lamps
Make a glimmer of gold.

Up the stair of the turret
The sisters are gone.
Seven days they wait there
And the lamps they burn on.

What hope? says the first,
And leans o'er the flame.
I hear our lamps burning.
O yet if he came!

O hope! says the second.
Was that the lamp's flare,
Or a sound of low footsteps?
The Prince on the stair!

But the holiest sister
She turns her about:
O no hope now forever—
Our lamps are gone out.[56]

This translation has the great fault of ignoring the patterned repetition of Maeterlinck's parenthetical lines, and the small fault of making too explicit the despair in the last stanza, but it nevertheless has, with its short words, the right simplicity. The sense of obstinate refrain that Mackail omitted, Fauré managed to put back, by basing the whole song on a rising five-note phrase (ex. 14), first harmonized as a simple progression (i–iv–i–VI).

Like the rising notes at the beginning of Mendelssohn's overture (1826) to *Ein Sommernachtstraum* (I–V–iv–I), it seems to say, "Once upon a time" (ex. 15); like the rising notes in the famous theme of the love duet in act 2 of *Tristan und Isolde* (composed 1857, premièred 1865), "O sink' hernieder, Nacht der Liebe" (I–vi^{7}–I$^{\sharp 5}$–i–IV^{9}), it suggests a sort of blind intimacy (ex. 16).

Eight years later, in 1906, Fauré composed *Crépuscule* and *Paradis*, to texts by Charles Lerberghe; these would become in 1910 the ninth and first songs in the sequence *La chanson d'Ève*. Both songs are based on the same five-note phrase as *Melisande's Song*—it is strange to think that the same phrase could mean hopeless yearning in a closed space, and the wide-open yearning of Eve, with all of human space and time rolling out before her. In *Crépuscule* Eve hears a mysterious cry like that of a wounded bird (ex. 17); and the five-note phrase, lovely and consoling and inevitable, seems to represent a great acquiescence in the fact of death: *Et in Arcadia ego*. The voice that cries out from the high tower, that cries out from the beginning of time, tells us that hope and hopelessness are inextricable, one.

Yet, the composer who made richest use of Maeterlinck's faraway songs was neither Debussy nor Fauré, but Dukas. *Ariane et Barbe-Bleue ou La délivrance inutile* (first published in 1899, in German translation) is like *Pelléas et Mélisande* in that a diegetic song has an important role, but in *Ariane et Barbe-Bleue* the song is not just a marginal delicacy but something deeply built into the whole dramatic structure. This is not surprising, because the

EXAMPLE 14. Fauré, *Pelléas et Mélisande*: "Melisande's Song." From *Pelléas et Mélisande* (Paris: J. Hamelle, 1937), 1.

EXAMPLE 15. Mendelssohn, *Ein Sommernachtstraum*: "Es war einmal." From *Sommernachtstraum*, four-handed piano arrangement (Leipzig: C. F. Peters, 1870), 3. This example shows the right-hand part.

EXAMPLE 16. Wagner, *Tristan und Isolde*: "O sink' hernieder," act 2, scene 2. From *Tristan und Isolde*, piano-vocal score, edited by Richard Kleinmichel (New York: Schirmer, 1906), 163.

later text was intended from the beginning as a libretto: Maeterlinck first offered it to Edvard Grieg, then to Dukas. As a libretto it is in some ways an inexpert thing: Maeterlinck arranged it so that the role of Ariane requires an elephant's stamina—she scarcely stops singing from beginning to end; the role of Bluebeard, on the other hand, is skimpy to the point of nonexistence. Still, the text has the virtue of many of the best libretti, from Striggio's libretto to Monteverdi's *L'Orfeo* (1607) on: it puts a song near the center of the action.

Dukas was almost too subtle to be an opera composer: his score is full of elegances drawn with such a fine point that they almost fail to register at all. But he had the great virtue of being able to deploy a large-scale musical dialectic, in this case a dialectic of ostentation versus shadow; and he had a tune. I mean the tune for the libretto's faraway song, "Les cinq filles d'Orlamonde":

CRÉPUSCULE

EXAMPLE 17. Fauré, *La Chanson d'Ève*: "Crépuscule." From *La Chanson d'Ève*, op. 95 (Paris: Heugel & Cie, 1910), 38.

Les cinq filles d'Orlamonde
(La fée noire est morte)
Les cinq filles d'Orlamonde
Ont cherché les portes . . .

Ont allumé leurs cinq lampes,
Ont ouvert les tours,
Ont traversé trois cents salles
Sans trouver le jour . . .

Ont ouvert un puits sonore
Descendent alors
Et sur une porte close
Trouvent une clef d'or . . .

Voient l'océan par les fentes
Ont peur de mourir

Et frappent à la porte close
Sans oser l'ouvrir . . .[57]

The five daughters of Orlamonde
(The black fairy is no more)
The five daughters of Orlamonde
They sought out the doors . . .

They lit their lamps and opened up
Their towers one by one,
They walked across three hundred halls
But did not find the sun . . .

They opened up and then went down
A deep shaft, echoey,
And found upon a door shut tight
A great golden key . . .

Afraid to death they saw the ocean
Through a narrow slit,
And knocked upon the closed door
But dared not open it . . .

Both the poem and the tune are displacements of preexisting matter.[58] Maeterlinck first published the poem in 1893, but with six daughters, not five; in some sense the libretto of *Ariane et Barbe-Bleue* is generated from this central ballad, by subtracting one member of the chorus, turning her into the protagonist, and making her vainly cajole or seduce her sister-wives into being more self-assertive. Something of this same technique for pulling an opera out of a ballad can be seen in Wagner's *Der fliegende Holländer* (composed 1841, premièred 1843).

Dukas borrowed the music for the first and third stanzas of "Les cinq filles d'Orlamonde" from a French folk song found in the third movement of Vincent d'Indy's Second Symphony (1904). But the music for the even-numbered stanzas seems largely original. Out of an unremarkable folk song, lively and lilting, with a certain rhythmic bite, Dukas managed to wring a scene of feral tremor like nothing else in the operatic canon.

Bluebeard has given Ariadne six silver keys to unlock his treasure chambers, and a seventh golden key that she is forbidden to use. Ariadne

EXAMPLE 18. Dukas, *Ariane et Barbe-Bleue*: "Les cinq filles d'Orlamonde," stanza 2, act 1. From *Ariane et Barbe-Bleue: Conte en trois actes. Poème de Maurice Maeterlinck; musique de Paul Dukas. Partition pour chant et piano réduite par l'auteur* (Paris: A. Durand & Fils, 1906), 73.

carelessly tosses aside the silver keys, since she knows that the forbidden key is the only one of interest; but her nurse picks up the discarded keys and opens the doors, finding a delirium of jewels: first amethysts, then sapphires, pearls, emeralds, rubies, at last diamonds. The nurse shrinks back from the forbidden door, but Ariadne opens it and hears a choked sound of distant chanting: it is the chorus of the wives, still alive in their shadowy vault. Dukas uses some familiar devices for creating an effect of intensifying eeriness, such as string tremoli and stepwise harmonic creep: the first stanza is in D♯ minor, the second in E minor, the third in F♯ minor, the fourth in G♯ minor. But Dukas's most striking touch is a bizarre harmonic swerve in the main phrase of the second and fourth stanzas: i–$V^{\flat 5}$–i (ex. 18).

This is true musical uncanniness, *Unheimlichkeit*: it's almost the most normal progression in music, the cadence, but the diminished fifth makes it dissolve into phantasmagoria. Olivier Messiaen once wrote of the "Chant gothique et mystérieux des filles d'Orlamonde";[59] and Dukas set up his *moderne* music-gothic with great care. The song is like one of those nineteenth-century gargoyles that Viollet-le-Duc added to Notre-Dame Cathedral.

After the song, Bluebeard appears—his only audible appearance in the opera—to make a few menacing gestures. In the second act, Ariadne tries to haul the five women out of nonentity into human life: she breaks a hole in the vault, and lets in light, and the sound of bells: the wives marvel that a real world persists beyond their tomb. And at the act's end they sing a fifth stanza of "Les cinq filles d'Orlamonde":

Les cinq filles d'Orlamonde
(La fée noire est morte)
Les cinq filles d'Orlamonde
Ont trouvé les portes! . . .[60]

The five daughters of Orlamonde
(The black fairy is no more)
The five daughters of Orlamonde
Found at last the doors! . . .

Now the shadows are dispelled: the tune is transfigured into a luminous B major, with jewellike scintillations in the accompaniment. I said earlier that scarcely any opera could match *Pelléas et Mélisande* in relying for so much of its musical effect on a single melody or two: but *Ariane et Barbe-Bleue* is in contention, because almost the entire second act can be heard as a continual retracing, refaceting, refiligreeing, of the melody of "Les cinq filles d'Orlamonde".

In the third act, Ariadne admires the charms of the five women: just as the six jewel rooms in act 1 are differentiated by color, so the wives in act 2 are differentiated by an especially splendid body part: Mélisande by her hair (when Ariadne loosens her tresses, the whole vault is lit by hair-light), Ygraine by her arms, Bellangère by her shoulders—Ariadne, in a kind of sensuous ecstasy, adorns her sister-wives with the various jewels from act 1. But the nurse announces that Bluebeard is returning: the women watch as Bluebeard's coach is set upon by the mob of peasants, who capture him, beat him, tie him up, and dump him in the castle, for the wives to treat as they will. Ariadne, exulting, unties Bluebeard, now so weak that he has become completely mute—like the Destiny of *Les fiançailles*, Bluebeard has unfated himself, turned infantile. Ariadne has liberated herself—or realized the liberation she always possessed—but she can't persuade her sister-wives to join her on her path into a bright and open world. It turns out that they prefer the dark.

It is a puzzling fable. The *New York Times* music critic (January 15, 1911), anticipating the American première, wrote that "the work is quite openly a satire on the feminist movement," if not a mere fairy tale. This seems like a strained interpretation, since Ariadne's resourcefulness, her power of will, seem so worthy of respect. Moreover, Dukas himself held a strongly pro-liberation, pro-Ariadne view of the opera:

> Personne ne veut être délivré. La délivrance coûte cher parce qu'elle est l'inconnu et que l'homme (et la femme) préférera toujours un esclavage "familier" à cette incertitude redoutable qui fait tout le poids du "fardeau de la liberté." Et puis, la vérité est qu'on ne peut délivrer personne: *il vaut mieux se délivrer soi-même*. Non seulement cela vaut mieux, *mais il n'y a que cela de possible*. Et ces dames le montrent bien (très gentiment) à cette pauvre Ariane qui l'ignorait . . . et qui croyait que le monde a soif de liberté alors qu'il n'aspire qu'au bien-être: dès qu'on a tiré ces dames de leur cave, elles lâchent leur libératrice pour leur bijoutier-bourreau (beau garçon d'ailleurs) comme il convenait! [. . .] Mais, vu du côté d'Ariane, et en laissant de côté les piètres marionnettes qui lui servent de comparses, ce refus de la liberté prend un caractère tout à fait pathétique, comme il arrive lorsqu'un être supérieur qui se croit indispensable éprouve que l'on n'a nul besoin de lui pour un dévouement héroïque, et qu'il suffit aux médiocres d'une solution médiocre.[61]

> No one wants to be liberated. Liberation costs a great deal because it is the unknown, and because men (and women) will always prefer a "familiar" slavery to the fearful uncertainty that makes up the whole weight of "the burden of liberty." After all, the truth is that no one can liberate anyone else: it is better to liberate oneself. Not only is it better, but it is the only thing possible. And these ladies demonstrate this very nicely to poor Ariadne, who didn't know it . . . and who believed that the whole world thirsts for liberty, whereas it only aspires to comfortable well-being: when these ladies were pulled out of their cave, they abandon their liberator in

> favor of their jeweler-hangman (a handsome lad, besides) as suited them! [. . .] But, seen from Ariadne's point of view, and leaving aside the paltry marionettes who act as her foils, this refusal of liberty takes on a certain pathos, as happens when a superior being who considers herself indispensable comes to understand that no one needs her heroic dedication, and that a mediocre solution suffices for mediocrities.

On the other hand, it is possible that this moral of self-liberation is reversed in the depths of the text and the depths of the music. I don't think that the opera is exactly a satire of feminism, but it's possible that Ariadne's confidence and daring and wit aren't entirely admirable, and that Bluebeard's discarded wives do well to remain in the castle's shadows.

The plot of *Ariane et Barbe-Bleue* seems a rethinking of the plot of *Les sept princesses*, written about eight years before. There the seven princesses were specular, spectral—cloudy presences made by breathing on glass, quickly gone. When the prince set out, determined to hoist these vaporous beings into flesh, he succeeded only in killing the princess he loved best. The wives in the later play are closer to entity than the princesses, but their carnality is weak and partial, glancing, a radiance of shoulder here, a sheen of lovely tresses there. The wives, like the princesses, are anamorphs, images visible only from certain angles, when you tilt the glass just right. One of Maeterlinck's earliest creative endeavors was a piece of ekphrastic fiction, *Le massacre des innocents* (1886), based on a painting by Brueghel; and to some extent Maeterlinck's whole career can be seen as a series of attempts to haul some two-dimensional image into a three-dimensional, or at least two-and-a-half-dimensional, reality. Golaud can impregnate Mélisande, but he can't make her real; she remains something less than a puppet, an Art Nouveau or Pre-Raphaelite film quivering on the air. The attempt to carnalize a ravishing image, a dream of the sleeping water, never ends well: images exist only in the imagination, as tantalizing evanescences, and always cry out, "Noli me tangere—Ne me touchez pas." She makes an effort to become a human being—she learns how to deceive, maybe even to flirt—but she dances away from any hand that tries to grasp her.

Ariadne, unlike Mélisande, is humanly beautiful: self-possessed, shrewd, even a bit brawny. It isn't easy to find another Maeterlinck heroine who resembles her: Mary Magdalene has something of her sophistication, poise, and casual vivacity, but is finally a much more anguished figure, Titianesque. Ariadne is ideal, but not imaginary: she isn't like a painted thing, or a reflection shimmering in a pool. She contrasts in every way with Bluebeard's other wives, and out of this contrast Maeterlinck generated the conflict of his play, between the actual and the virtual, the ostentatious and the recessive, the explicit and the hinted.

Bluebeard, like Ariadne, is a flagrant character, part of the world of action, not the world of art. Stern, commanding, he appears to be a tyrant—at least, the people whom he governs despise him. It is entirely in keeping that his castle features rooms full of jewels: his mode of being is deluxe gaudiness, conspicuity. But behind these highly inflected overt surfaces, he dreams—and he keeps his dreams locked away in the castle's cellar. His misfortune is that he has at last married a woman who can't be demoted to a phantasm, who insists on being his equal, even his superior. In fact, by making Bluebeard a diminished and silent presence, she has demoted *him* into a phantasmal consort for the five remaining wives: in the end, she dismisses the entire action of the drama—she leaves a place that he has entirely thinned out into sortilege and shade. But Maeterlinck is always most at home in such places—these worlds on the other side of the looking glass. Maeterlinck lived to see the triumph of Surrealism in the 1920s, and I wonder what he would have thought of plays such as Georges Neveux's *Juliette, ou La clé des songes* (published 1927, premièred 1930), in which the dreamer is given the choice of waking up or staying forever lost in his dream. *Ariane et Barbe-Bleue* prefigures this sort of theater: the sister-wives are dreams that know that they have no business in a nononeiric world, where all is vigilance and captiousness.

Dukas was sensitive to this dialectic of actual and virtual. There is a good deal of ostentation-music: abrupt murky figures for Bluebeard's threats; resolute gestures for Ariadne's firm decisions; and, most of all, the music for the jewels, all hard glitter and flash (ex. 19). The scene is a set of variations on a triumphant, rhythmically alert theme, recolored as the nurse and Ariadne proceed from amethyst to sapphire, pearl, emerald, ruby, diamond. This music of sensory overload is as far as we get toward the lavishly actual. At the opposite pole is the song "Les cinq filles d'Orlamonde," where all is reticence, trance.

Dukas experiments in reconciling these opposites. At the end of act 2 we hear the fifth stanza of "Les cinq filles d'Orlamonde," modified from minor to major and even outfitted with a bit of musical jewel-light; in act 3 Ariane decorates the wives with the jewels, as if she could bribe them, like Marguerite in Gounod's *Faust* (1859), into moving into a more meretricious world. But neither of these scenes is particularly effective: the end of act 2 is particularly disappointing, for "Les cinq filles d'Orlamonde" doesn't seem to have much intensity left after it loses its dark grace. The music seems to argue that the five daughters of Orlamonde lead a richer life as *chimères*,

EXAMPLE 19. Dukas, *Ariane et Barbe-Bleue*: jewel theme, act 1. From *Ariane et Barbe-Bleue: Conte en trois actes. Poème de Maurice Maeterlinck; musique de Paul Dukas. Partition pour chant et piano réduite par l'auteur* (Paris: A. Durand & Fils, 1906), 41.

dream figments, than they could as flesh-and-blood women. Dukas may have considered the sister-wives to be stooges and mediocrities: but he nevertheless gave them the most incomparably powerful music in the score. Maeterlinck too liked Bluebeard's castle better than the world outside it: when he bought an estate in Nice, in 1929, he named it Orlamonde. Orlamonde sounds a bit like Allemonde, the name of Arkël's kingdom in *Pelléas et Mélisande*—and Allemonde might mean "other world," *autre monde*, since *al-* is an old root for *other*, as in *allegory*, or *allotrope*, or *alien*. It is as if Maeterlinck felt happier in the far reaches of his imagination than in the free trackless plains of the Verimonde.

FOUR

Britten's Dismantlings

Les illuminations and the *War Requiem*

I.

A KITTEN STARES INTO A MIRROR; IN THE MIRROR IT SEES A lion staring back. The caption is, I is another. In the context of a kitten poster, the deranged grammar sounds like an Internet meme.

This phrase is a translation of "Je est un autre," a phrase that appears in two letters written in May 1871 by the sixteen-year-old Arthur Rimbaud—"I is somebody else." If I understand it correctly, the illustrated version should show not a kitten gazing intently at the reflection of a lion, but a reflection of a lion with nothing whatsoever in front of the mirror except a kitten-shaped hole carefully cut out with scissors. The phrase savors of annihilation—it is a formulation not too far from Iago's "I am not what I am." Rimbaud sees himself as an alter ego, but with no ego in sight—just the alter. It is true that Jacques Lacan, in his essay on aggressiveness in psychoanalysis, wrote that "Je est un autre" is not a dazzling poetical intuition, but a plain statement of psychoanalytic fact; on the other hand, Lacan thought that the ego existed more or less for the sake of keeping us sick.

Rimbaud's refusal to constitute himself as a subject is amazingly strong. In the second letter, he notes that old imbeciles have given a false signification to the *I* (*Moi*):

> Car Je est un autre. Si le cuivre s'éveille clairon, il n'y a rien de sa faute.
>
> For I is another. If brass wakes up and finds it's a bugle, it's not its fault.[1]

In the first letter, he notes

> Il s'agit d'arriver à l'inconnu par le dérèglement de *tous les sens*. . . . C'est faux de dire: Je pense: on devrait dire: On me pense.—Pardon du jeu de mots.—Je est un autre. Tant pis pour le bois qui se trouve violon, et nargue aux inconscients, qui ergotent sur ce qu'ils ignorent tout à fait!
>
> It's a matter of arriving at the unknown through the derangement of *all the senses*. . . . It's wrong to say: I think: you ought to say: Someone thinks me. . . . I is another. So much the worse for the wood that finds it's a violin.[2]

In other words, you undo your staid unpoetical self by cultivating a new sensorium: your perceptual nerves have to be wrested out of their usual channels and made to form new connections.

In founding this private *lycée* for one young poet, Rimbaud does not set himself an easy curriculum. This process of reconfiguring the sense organs and the brain has to be perpetual, because I would be just myself, not another, if I settled down in some stable shape. In his sonnet "Voyelles," Rimbaud gives a synesthetic key to linking vowel sounds with colors: A is black, E white, I red, U green, O blue; and in the section of *Une saison en enfer* called "Alchimie du verbe," Rimbaud repeats this line, with the added comment that such a key helps him to write poetry addressed to all the senses, not just to the ear. But possibly this fixed link between vowel and color tended to petrify into an arrangement of the senses, instead of a derangement of them: a thirst for derangement always entails further derangings. After he met the older poet Paul Verlaine, Rimbaud found hashish and absinthe useful in getting off the beaten track, getting out of the furrows and ruts and other predetermined paths that hinder any sort of supernatural vision; but alterity is a savage god, requiring ever stronger swerves into deliriums, and it may be no wonder that Rimbaud found it necessary to give up writing before (or very shortly after) the age of twenty-one.

In the prose poems published as *Les illuminations*, Rimbaud goes as far as he could in making the not-I or else-I speak. Even in *Une saison en enfer*, Rimbaud has a fairly steady set of identities as hyena, self-mutilator, *poète maudit*, wrangler of lice; but in *Les illuminations*, Rimbaud disperses. The universe is alive, panpsychic—jewels peer at you, and a flower tells you its name (*Aube*)—and Rimbaud scrawls on the page a diagram of its nervous system:

> J'ai tendu des cordes de clocher à clocher; des guirlandes de fenêtre à fenêtre; des chaînes d'or d'étoile à étoile, et je danse. ("Phrase")[3]

> I stretched ropes from steeple to steeple, garlands from window to window, gold chains from star to star, and I dance.[4]

> Un bizarre dessin de ponts, ceux-ci droits, ceux-là bombés, d'autres descendant ou obliquant en angles sur les premiers, et ces figures se renouvelant dans les autres circuits éclairés du canal, mais tous tellement longs et légers que les rives chargées de dômes s'abaissent et s'amoindrissent. ("Les ponts")[5]

> A bizarre pattern of bridges, some of the straight, others convex, still others, descending or veering off at angles to the first one, and these shapes multiplying in the other illuminated circuits of the canal, but all of them so long and delicate that the river-banks burdened with domes fall away and diminish.[6]

Every single thing is connected to every other single thing: the universe is thick with cross-hatches, so dense with ropes and bridges that the things connected grow small and faint from the sheer proliferation of connective tissue. But in this nervous zodiac Rimbaud himself has no fixed abode. The totality of things fiddles him like a violin or pounds him like a drum or blows him like a bugle: through the narrow aperture of Arthur Rimbaud the world forces all its music. He is less a person than a collection of instruments for transcendental expression; there is a certain passivity in this role, but a hectic passivity, for the poet finds himself assuming myriad identities as his strings are pulled taut, his valves pushed in and out, to find the exact pitch, the exact timbre, for a particular note in the universal symphony.

The presences that whittled or extruded Rimbaud into the shape of a violin or a bugle did not stop with him. Other artists have been compelled to reproduce Rimbaud's music in different instrumentations, including the composer Benjamin Britten, who set some texts from *Les illuminations* for high voice and string orchestra in 1939, and the poet John Ashbery, who translated *Les illuminations* into English in 2011.

2.

The texts in *Les illuminations* are diverse in the extreme, but it is possible to notice certain common elements. What is an illumination? Verlaine explains, in his introduction to the first publication in book form (1886), that the name *Les illuminations* is an English word meaning colored plates, and that Rimbaud intended this term as the subtitle (he does not say what title Rimbaud would have given it—Rimbaud, then a merchant trafficking in guns and gold in Abyssinia, had nothing to do with the publication). In this sense the title anticipates the prestige of the pictorial in later Modernist poetics, as in Ezra Pound's Imagism. Phanopoeia is certainly strong in some of Rimbaud's texts, but often the sheer density of nearly random detail would tend to defeat an illustrator: an abstract riot of color and confusingly intricate line might be the best way toward a visual approximation. Sometimes an illumination will read like a pre-ekphrasis of a not-yet-painted Kandinsky:

> Du détroit d'indigo aux mers d'Ossian, sur le sable rose et orange qu'a lavé le ciel vineux, viennent de monter et de se croiser des boulevards de cristal habités incontinent par de jeunes familles pauvres qui s'alimentent chez les fruitiers. Rien de riche.—La ville! ("Métropolitain")[7]

> From the indigo strait to the seas of Ossian, on the pink and orange sand bathed by the wine-colored sky, crystal boulevards rise up and intersect, immediately populated by poor families who shop for groceries at the fruit stands. Nothing posh.—The city![8]

In the swells and washes of pigment, a few humble gestures toward a representation of a city take shape.

In the absence of any clear generic precursor, we might try to infer a genre from the evidence of texts themselves. Here are some of the characteristics of the illuminations:

(a) *Opening up*. Whatever is constrained must be let loose. In "Après le déluge" (the first text in the published version, though there is no reason to think that Rimbaud assigned an order), everything flows, milk streams out, houses trickle, blood spills from Bluebeard's dwelling, from abattoirs—after the flood, nothing can stop the general surge, the *panta rhei* of things:

> —Sourds, étang,—Écume, roule sur le pont et par-dessus les bois;—draps noirs et orgues,—éclairs et tonnerre,—montez et roulez;—Eaux et tristesses, montez et relevez les Déluges.[9]

> —Well up, pond,—Foam, roll on the bridge and above the woods;—black cloths and organs,—lightning and thunder,—rise and roll;—Waters and sorrows, rise and revive the Floods.[10]

When all the world's secret springs are open, the skin loses its power to contain, and the insides of the body start to gush out:

> Devant une neige un Être de Beauté de haute taille. Des sifflements de mort et des cercles de musique sourde font monter, s'élargir et trembler comme un spectre ce corps adoré; des blessures écarlates et noires éclatent dans les chairs superbes. ("Being Beauteous")[11]

> Against snow, a tall Beautiful Being. Whistlings of death and circles of muffled music make this adored body rise, swell and tremble like a ghost; scarlet and black wounds open in the magnificent flesh.[12]

> Et, presque chaque nuit, aussitôt endormi, le pauvre frère se levait, la bouche pourrie, les yeux arrachés,—tel qu'il se rêvait!—et me tirait dans la salle en hurlant son songe de chagrin idiot. ("Vagabonds")[13]

> And, almost every night, no sooner was I asleep than the poor brother would get up, his mouth rotten, his eyes gouged out,—that was how he dreamed of himself!—and drag me into the room howling his dream of stupid sorrow.[14]

In a state of Otherness, the nightmare and the glorious dream have many common features, including physical disintegration. Admission to paradise requires exactly what admission to hell requires: mutilation of the body.

As the *I* superalienates, loses contact with any commonplace ego, there is less and less mental faculty capable of suppressing anything subterranean or extraterrestrial or intracorporeal or intrapsychic; so the earth quakes, the water rises, and the gods shimmer into being.

(b) *Copresence.* As the *I* superalienates, there is less and less mental faculty capable of discriminating or subordinating the elements of experience. So the verbal texture of an illumination may become an outspewing of glamours:

> Dans des costumes improvisés avec le goût du mauvais rêve ils jouent des complaintes, des tragédies de malandrins et de demi-dieux spirituels comme l'histoire ou les religions ne l'ont jamais été. Chinois, Hottentots, bohémiens, niais, hyènes, Molochs, vieilles démences, démons sinistres, ils mêlent les tours populaires, maternels, avec les poses et les tendresses bestiales. Ils interpréteraient des pièces nouvelles et des chansons "bonnes filles." Maîtres jongleurs, ils transforment le lieu et les personnes,

> et usent de la comédie magnétique. Les yeux flambent, le sang chante, les os s'élargissent, les larmes et des filets rouges ruissellent. Leur raillerie ou leur terreur dure une minute, ou des mois entiers.
>
> J'ai seul la clef de cette parade sauvage. ("Parade")[15]

> Wearing improvised costumes in nightmarish taste they act out ballads, tragedies of thieves and demi-gods of a spirituality hitherto unknown to history or religions. Chinese, Hottentots, Gypsies, nincompoops, hyenas, Molochs, old dementias, sinister demons, they mingle populist, maternal tricks with bestial poses and tenderness. They would perform new plays and "nice girl" songs. Expert jugglers, they transform people and places, and resort to magnetic comedy. The eyes flame, the blood sings, the bones swell, tears and trickles of red descend. Their raillery or their terror lasts a minute, or entire months.
>
> I alone know the plan of this savage sideshow.[16]

This text is a sort of freak show, but a freak show in which cheerleaders and tax accountants are just as freakish as werewolves and tattooed men. The abandonment of conscious control is remarkable. Ernest Delahaye notes that Rimbaud refers to a title of an unknown work of his, *Photographie des temps passés* (Photograph of Times Past), that may or may not pertain to what we know as *Les illuminations*. We tend to think of a camera as a machine for capturing reality, but Rimbaud may have thought of his altered, alterified intelligence as a machine for capturing a much wider field of reality than what most cameras can see. There is no criterion for distinguishing the past from the present, the fantastic from the actual: the illumination illuminates all with equably garish light.

In his *Biographia Literaria* (1817), Coleridge distinguished imagination from fancy: Imagination dissolves, dissipates, diffuses the external world in order to create a new one, whereas fancy, a much lower faculty to his way of thinking, plays with fixities and definites: it is a mode of memory emancipated from the order of time and space; while it is blended with, and modified by that empirical phenomenon of the will, which we express by the word *choice*. But equally with the ordinary memory the fancy must receive all its materials ready made from the law of association.[17]

As a sample of fancy, Coleridge gives Thomas Otway's line "Lutes, lobsters, seas of milk, and ships of amber." Otway actually wrote "Lutes, laurels, seas of milk and ships of amber"[18]—Coleridge's misremembrance of the line made it still more whimsical and arbitrary. It sounds like Lewis Carroll:

lutes and lobsters go together very much in the fashion of walruses and carpenters. And it sounds like Rimbaud. T. E. Hulme, the philosopher whose notions of a new Classicist poetry deeply influenced Pound and T. S. Eliot, considered that Coleridgean fancy, not imagination, was the sort of faculty that the new Modernist age would prize;[19] and from Rimbaud to the early Surrealists, fancy, with its rigid mechanical recombinations of the elements of experience, seems a dominant aesthetic mode. Rimbaud takes photographs of a universe emancipated from the order of time and space, from the Cartesian grid of abscissas and ordinates through which the mind makes Newtonian sense of things.

(c) *Artificiality*. In one of the May 1871 letters, Rimbaud called Charles Baudelaire the first seer, king of poets, a real god. Rimbaud was a little unhappy with Baudelaire's stingy formalities and complained that ventures into the unknown should entail new poetic forms. Baudelaire's prose poems, more than his verse, helped Rimbaud to find his way, especially the collection that Baudelaire called *Les paradis artificiels* (1860), partly inspired by Thomas de Quincey's *Confessions of an English Opium Eater* (1822). Rimbaud's own paradises, or antiparadises, are heavily artificial, and not just in the sense of being reveries contrived by hallucinogens.

Rimbaud found congenial the role of the poet as a carnival barker at some sideshow of the damned or the blessed or the inconsequential, not only in "Parade," but also in "Ornières," with

> des chars chargés d'animaux de bois doré, de mâts et de toiles bariolées, au grand galop de vingt chevaux de cirque tachetés.[20]

> parade floats covered with gilded wooden animals, masts and multicolored canvas backdrops, drawn by twenty dappled circus horses at full gallop.[21]

and in "Scènes," where

> Des scènes lyriques accompagnées de flûte et de tambour s'inclinent dans des réduits ménagés sous les plafonds, autour des salons de clubs modernes ou des salles de l'Orient ancien.[22]

> Operatic scenes accompanied by flute and drum look down from crawl spaces contrived under the ceilings, around the salons of modern clubs or audience chambers of the ancient Orient.[23]

The *illuminations* may be colored photographic plates, but I understand them more easily as the limelights in oddly shaped theaters that Rimbaud confected for his private amusement. The culmination of the self-conscious constructedness of these dreams comes in "Villes [II]":

> Ce sont des villes! C'est un peuple pour qui se sont montés ces Alleghanys et ces Libans de rêve! Des chalets de cristal et de bois qui se meuvent sur des rails et des poulies invisibles. Les vieux cratères ceints de colosses et de palmiers de cuivre rugissent mélodieusement dans les feux.[24]

> What cities they are! This is a people for whom these Alleghenies and Lebanons of dreams arose! Chalets of crystal and wood that move along invisible rails and pulleys. Ancient craters ringed by colossi and copper palm trees roar melodiously amid the flames.[25]

A visionary poet in the tradition of, say, William Blake insists that the vision pertains to some state of being more real than the world to which our sense organs give access; but Rimbaud at once credits and discredits his vision by understanding it as *hoher Leichtsinn*, some elated frivolity, an oneiropolis in which kindly volcanos provide the music.

For all of Rimbaud's famous fury of rejection, the illuminations show a certain touch of the precious:

> La cascade sonne derrière les huttes d'opéra-comique. Des girandoles prolongent, dans les vergers et les allées voisins du Méandre,—les verts et les rouges du couchant. Nymphes d'Horace coiffées au Premier Empire,—Rondes Sibériennes, Chinoises de Boucher. ("Fête d'hiver")[26]

> The waterfall echoes behind comic-opera huts. Trails of skyrockets lengthen, in orchards and garden paths along the Meander,—the greens and reds of the setting sun. Nymphs out of Horace with Directoire coiffures,—Siberian folk dances, Chinese girls painted by Boucher.[27]

This is as close as Rimbaud comes to camp, and I admire the way in which Ashbery neither minimizes nor exaggerates his timbre. The Rococo painter François Boucher created stage sets as well as the simperingly gorgeous ooh-la-la scenes with exotic bathing beauties for which he's best known—one of his aphorisms is that nature is "trop verte et mal éclairée" (too green and poorly lit). However Rimbaud may have felt about Boucher's taste, I think that he might have agreed with this opinion. The light that illuminates *Les illuminations* doesn't come from the honest sun. There is an amazing phrase at the end of "Villes [I]": "plantations prodigieuses où les gentilshommes sauvages chassent leurs chroniques sous la lumière qu'on a créée"[28] (prodigious plantations where savage gentlefolk hunt down their gossip columns by artificial light).[29]

It is fascinating to see Ashbery deploying his immense verbal resources against this untranslatable phrase, and the result is, in its way, hair-raising, but I'm not sure that "artificial light" is the best term—"the light that one has created" is certainly some sort of made light, but not necessarily the gaslight that was artificial light in Rimbaud's time. The light in the illuminations is far more artificial than can be conveyed by the term "artificial light." In his way Rimbaud is as much a *l'art pour l'art* aesthete as Théophile Gautier, though the artifactive force seems to have some origin other than the poet's conscious intelligence.

(d) *Instability of value*. The illuminations are full of highly charged words denoting value: vile, atrocious, boring, mediocre, beauteous, adored. But I often feel that if you went through the text and randomly replaced *vile* with *adored*, or *beauteous* with *atrocious*, the meaning would not be much changed. What counts is the intensity of the charge, not whether the charge is positive or negative. In the great gushing universe of total abundance, wealth abounds, misery abounds, life abounds, death abounds:

> À vendre les Corps sans prix, hors de toute race, de tout monde, de tout sexe, de toute descendance! Les richesses jaillissant à chaque démarche! Solde de diamants sans contrôle!
>
> À vendre l'anarchie pour les masses; la satisfaction irrépressible pour les amateurs supérieurs; la mort atroce pour les fidèles et les amants! ("Solde")[30]
>
> For sale: priceless Bodies, forget all limitations of race, of world, of sex, of lineage! Wealth spurts up at every step! Unsupervised sale of diamonds!
>
> For sale: anarchy for the people; irrepressible satisfaction for select connoisseurs; an atrocious death for the devout and for lovers![31]

The poet exclaims his advertisement for atrocious death with exactly as much point as his advertisement for irrepressible satisfaction.

If we carry Rimbaud's logic far enough, every illumination is also a darkening—every movement into higher being deepens our nonentity.

(e) *Instability of identity.* The personages in the illuminations keep metamorphosing into one another. The Prince in "Conte," after slaughtering his wives and his beasts, encounters a Genie of ineffable beauty who promises unspeakable love; they first die together, but then it turns out that the Prince didn't die at that time, but later, in his palace, at the end of a normal life span, and furthermore that the Genie *was* the Prince.

Still more puzzling fluctuations of being beset the *I*, the poet himself. Sometimes he sees himself as a dramatis persona in some theater of metamorphosis, such as *A Midsummer Night's Dream*:

> Au matin,—aube de juin batailleuse,—je courus aux champs, âne, claironnant et brandissant mon grief, jusqu'à ce que les Sabines de la banlieue vinrent se jeter à mon poitrail. ("Bottom")[32]

> In the morning,—a bellicose dawn in June,—I ran to the fields, a donkey, trumpeting and brandishing my grievance, until the Sabine women of the suburbs came to throw themselves at my neck.[33]

Rimbaud at first called this illumination "Métamorphoses" before settling on the Shakespearean title "Bottom": and the poet undergoes a transformation into a big blue-gray bird soaring at his lady's ceiling molding, then a big bear with violet gums, before settling on the shape of a donkey assaulted by Sabine women (whose role is reversed from their usual appearance as victims). "Sometime a horse I'll be, sometime a hound / A hog, a headless bear, sometime a fire. / And neigh, and bark, and grunt, and roar, and burn"[34]—the poet seems game to try out any zoomorph that might beguile his lady; just as, in other illuminations, the woman whom the poet pursues undergoes many kinds of shape-shifting.

Elsewhere the poet's vertigo of being seems generated less by obedience to a theatrical script than by the casual improvisations of a child's fantasy:

> Je suis le saint, en prière sur la terrasse,—comme les bêtes pacifiques paissent jusqu'à la mer de Palestine.

> Je suis le savant au fauteuil sombre. Les branches et la pluie se jettent à la croisée de la bibliothèque.

> Je suis le piéton de la grand'route par les bois nains . . .
>
> Je serais bien l'enfant abandonné sur la jetée partie à la haute mer, le petit valet suivant l'allée dont le front touche le ciel.
>
> Les sentiers sont âpres. Les monticules se couvrent de genêts. L'air est immobile. Que les oiseaux et les sources sont loin ! Ce ne peut être que la fin du monde, en avançant. ("Enfance")[35]
>
> I am the saint, at prayer on the terrance,—as meek animals graze all the way to the sea of Palestine.
>
> I am the learned scholar in the dark armchair. Branches and the rain hurl themselves at the library's casement window.
>
> I am the walker on the great highway through dwarf woods . . .
>
> I'd gladly be the abandoned child on the pier setting out for the open sea, the young farm boy in the lane, whose forehead grazes the sky.
>
> The paths are harsh. The little hills are cloaked with broom. The air is motionless. How far away the birds and the springs are! It can only be the end of the world, as you move forward.[36]

The tense structure is of interest: the poet *is* a saint and a scholar—roles somewhat distant from the identity of the historical Rimbaud—but he *would be* an abandoned child, a role that (especially if you change *abandoned* to *abandoning*) is fairly close to that of the Rimbaud who was actually writing this text. The other-*I* tends to be the easiest *I* to affirm.

But the key point of this text is that he has come to the end of the world: after you exhaust the repertoire of play identities, you leap from the cliff at Finisterre. Annihilation—annihilation of self, annihilation of world—is the secret goal of all the illuminations, and the explicit goal of some of them: this is the truth behind "Je est un autre":

> Qu'est mon néant, auprès de la stupeur qui vous attend? ("Vies")[37]
>
> What is my nothingness, compared to the amazement that awaits you?[38]

> Un rayon blanc, tombant du haut du ciel, anéantit cette comédie. ("Les ponts")[39]
>
> A white ray, falling from the top of the sky, wipes out this bit of theatricality.[40]
>
> Le pavillon en viande saignante sur la soie des mers et des fleurs arctiques; (elles n'existent pas.) ("Barbare")[41]
>
> The pennant of bloody meat against the silk of arctic seas and flowers; (they don't exist.)[42]

This last line is the refrain of "Barbare," an illumination that strikes me as the most technically advanced text that Rimbaud ever wrote: the pennant of bloody meat obsessed Samuel Beckett, an author himself expert in the construction of self-canceling artifacts—he translated it in 1934 as follows:

> Ah the banner
> the banner of meat bleeding
> on the silk of the seas and the arctic flowers
> that do not exist. ("Enueg I")[43]

In his poem "Vorgefühl" (1906), Rainer Maria Rilke compares himself to a banner that senses a storm that hasn't yet come; but Rimbaud sees (himself as?) a meat banner affixed to a cloth painted with all the gay little flowers that grow at the North Pole, the flowers missing from every bouquet. The banner (the poet?) is dripping blood; the silk cloth is fraying everywhere, unweaving itself. Rimbaud is in the midst of storm, not a storm of historical or theological tumult, but a storm of aporia, a storm of unbeing—"Live coals raining down gusts of frost," as Ashbery translates another sentence from "Barbare." *Les illuminations* is a collection of nonexistences written by nobody.

3. Pictures of Nobody

In Shakespeare's *The Tempest*, the jester Trinculo hears a tune coming from nowhere and announces that it's being played by the "picture of Nobody"—that is, Ariel, turned invisible. Shakespeare's age was oddly fascinated by pictures of nobody: around 1507 Joerg Schan published a broadsheet bearing a picture of a disreputable fellow with a winged cap whose caption reads, "Nobody is my name, I bear everybody's blame"; and in *Nobody and Somebody* (1606) appeared a woodcut of a nonchalant man whose arms and head grow directly out of his pelvis—he's Mr. Nobody because he has, well, no body. (Mr. Somebody is more or less all torso, with short stumpy legs.)

Ariel's motto is "Je est un autre." He stands at an oblique angle from the other characters in the play: he can entertain the imaginative possibility of being human, even though he knows that he is not: at the end of the play he tells Prospero that, with one look at the weeping Gonzalo, Prospero's "affections / Would become tender / . . . Mine would, sir, were I human" (act 5, scene 1, lines 18–20).[44] What does Ariel look like? In 1850 the Pre-Raphaelite painter John Everett Millais depicted him as a slender green youth borne on a sort of sedan chair made of green human-faced bats—he is leaning directly into Ferdinand's face to sing into his ear, but poor baffled Ferdinand sees nothing, because Ariel is invisible, a translucent verdancy that blends into the green of the vegetation. His sex is indeterminate—indeed, it is difficult to find in Shakespeare's dialogue any clue about Ariel's gender, though a stage direction does use a male pronoun. He is thin air, too naked to have a body, a blank paper doll that can be outfitted in any costume.

A pure isolate of theater, Ariel comprises a whole circus within himself. His greatest specialty is invisibility, a state of absence made presence, but he can command more specific improvisations of identity: he can imitate Trinculo's voice in order to provoke Stephano into beating Trinculo, and he can assume the shape of a harpy in order to cow Antonio and Sebastian. In addition to being a star mimic, singer, instrumentalist, and female impersonator, he's also a superior prop man, able to provide other characters with the costumes they need for switching their roles: Ariel assists in the Ceres masque and provides the rich apparel that enables Stephano to pretend to be a king. Ariel not only changes identity himself, he transforms everyone else too. His greatest metamorphic feat is an imaginary one, even within the confines of the play—the alchemical transmutation of Alonso: "Full fadom five thy father lies, / Of his bones are coral made: / Those are pearls that were his eyes" (act 1, scene 2, lines 397–98). This mineralization of the "dead" father is transcendentally eerie: the scene is at once ghastly and sublime, a snuff film and a lullaby. At the end of "Full fadom five," Ariel sings "Ding dong"; at the end of "Come unto these yellow sands," he sings "Bow-wow, Cock-a-diddle-dow" (act 1, scene 2, line 387): he keeps exuberating into a universe of noises. The role of Ariel is as close as anything I know in earlier literature to the mode of Rimbaud's illuminations: it isn't Ariel's fault if Prospero chops him out of a cloven pine and cuts him into the shape of a violin. Creativity is most intense when it is depersonalized, dehumanized. The illuminations are about an unstable *I* in whom a freak show is continually unfolding. Ariel's sideshows have more distinct point and intention than Rimbaud's do, but they too continually verge on nearly contentless marvels. Even Ariel's androgyny appears in the illuminations: in the belly of the son of Pan (in "Antique") there sleeps a double sex.

Ariel is without desire, except the desire to be free, unconstrained, an atom of delight hiding in a cowslip's bell or shouting wheeee! on a bat's back. In literature, wherever we find arcana treated as recombinant elements of wonder, we aren't far from Rimbaud's illuminations. But if the intent of the juggling of marvels is something other than pure play, it deviates from Rimbaud's usual scheme. The illuminations aren't love poems, nor are they expressions of emotion—they're artifacts, verbal objects, solidifications of ecstasy. They may disturb you, but they aren't meant to seduce you or to evoke particular emotions in you. To illustrate this distinction, compare the passage from "Enfance" quoted earlier (concerning the poet as saint, or savant, or abandoned child) with this passage:

> I'm all things strange and bold,
> The riderless horse,
> Snorting, stamping, stamping on the hard sea sand,
> The hero-highwayman plundering, plundering, plundering the land.
> I am King Midas with gold in his hand.
> I am the smooth world's double face,
> Mercury, Mercury, Mercury's heels
> Feathered with mischief and a god's deceit.
> The brittle blandishment of counterfeit.
> In me secrets, half-formed desires meet.
> I am the hidden life that stirs
> When the candle is out;
> Upstairs and down, the footsteps barely heard,
> The unknown gesture, the soft persistent word,
> The long sighing flight of the night-wing'd bird.

This text, like Rimbaud's, is a series of teasingly disconnected *I-am* statements, even more vagrant and fugitive than Rimbaud's. But there is a difference. This is an aria for Peter Quint in Britten's *The Turn of the Screw* (1954; libretto by Myfanwy Piper after the Henry James story): on one hand, it's a pure specimen of "Je est un autre," since Peter Quint is dead, and so any identity he posits for himself is in some sense an alter ego; on the other, the ghost is full of sexual desire, and everything he sings is designed to seduce the little boy Miles—in fact, the aria begins with a great outcry of "Miles! Miles! Miles! Miles! Miles!," all brazen melisma. The sheer urgency in his voice creates an *I*; like almost all operatic arias, this one is purposive, willful. The solution to the riddle "What am I talking about?" is a little too easy; a Rimbaud illumination is far more hermetic. The illuminations are full of Eros, and yet the only specific desire I read in them is the very desire that Shakespeare attributed to Ariel: metaphysical liberation, escape from gravity.

4.

The year 1939 was Britten's great year for spoofs. In some sense his career path resembled Picasso's: Picasso could draw like an Old Master by the age of fifteen and then, by his own admission, spent the rest of his life learning to paint like a child; Britten was composing grown-up music at the age of fourteen (*Quatre chansons françaises*), but seems to have decided, at the age of twenty-five, to see if he could find in himself the adolescent he hadn't yet been—his inner Rimbaud, one might say.

That year was also a year of exile, very tentative exile: it was the year that Britten and his lover, Peter Pears, moved from England to America. Much of the music of this year has a certain quality of release from oppression, including the oppression created by his own preternatural skill in composing. He tried his hand at silliness, by writing the cabaret song "Calypso" to a text by W. H. Auden, and by writing musical parodies, such the superbly sleazy big-band dance number *The Spider and the Fly* in his incidental music for J. B. Priestley's *Johnson over Jordan*. Priestley's play concerns a man who has just died and needs to find release from a purgatorial state by abandoning all attachments to the world of the senses; and Britten may have felt the theme of self-abandonment with some clarity.

Still more remarkable were the parodies of Wagner's *Der Ring des Nibelungen* in the music that Britten wrote a few months later for a BBC radio play, *The Sword in the Stone*, based on T. H. White's stories of the young King Arthur. Excalibur is represented by Wagner's Sword motif; and in writing bird music Britten spun off a series of goofs on the *Waldvogel* music in act 2 of *Siegfried*. Part of the joke here is that Wagner wrote his own parody of the Forest Bird motif: Siegfried cuts a reed and tries to play the birdsong back at the bird, but, incompetent oboist that he is, he succeeds only in producing horribly off-key arpeggios.

But the great achievement of 1939 was the setting of a few passages from *Les illuminations*. It would be incorrect to call these settings parodies of Wagner, but a certain Wagnerism may cling to them, a tendency to construct melodic material and even vocal lines out of triads that move in odd directions toward other triads (Wagner's Valkyrie motif, for example, consists of an arpeggiated major triad that makes a hair-raising swerve into its own mediant). Britten's *Les illuminations* is maybe the most arpeggio-intense music he ever wrote. There is a term in one the illuminations: *fanfare atroce* (from "Matinée d'ivresse"). Britten didn't set this text, but the phrase seems to sum up the aesthetic of Britten's Rimbaud music: you hear atrocious fanfares everywhere. The first number is called "Fanfares." This isn't a title Rimbaud used, and the text is a disconnected sentence that becomes the refrain of the whole piece: "J'ai seul la clef de cette parade savauge" (I alone have the key to this savage sideshow). One of Ashbery's rare miscalculations, I feel, is to translate *clef* as "plan," for Rimbaud elsewhere uses *clef* in the specific sense of musical key; in fact, in "Vies" the poet calls himself a musician who has invented something like the key of love (*la clef de l'amour*)—and the key to the parade may well be a musical key. (Also, French literature keeps appealing to Rimbaud's parade key, as when Antonin Artaud, in his 1931 essay "Sur le théâtre balinais," claims that the theater of Bali consists of "un amas de gestes rituels dont nous n'avons pas la clef"—a heap of ritual gestures to which we don't have the key.[45]) Rimbaud speaks of music everywhere in *Les illuminations*: in "Les ponts" we hear minor chords; in "Soirs historiques" a virtuoso plays an unusual instrument called the harpsichord of the meadows; in "Villes [II]" a little brigade of Rolands sound their trumpets. Rimbaud's main music here is probably brass, perhaps in honor of the brass that finds itself, through no fault of its own, forced into the shape of a bugle in the May 1871 letter.

Britten's music, however, is scored for voice and strings—there's no brass to be heard. Violins play the fanfares that seem better suited to trumpets: stringed instruments are themselves made to say "Je est un autre." In the opening measures of "Fanfares" the strings play tremoli on the notes E and F simultaneously, an effect appropriate to strings; then we hear a series of fanfares marked *quasi trombe*, pretend-trumpet, first in B♭ major, then in E major. Each fanfare is a perfectly normal triadic formation, but the juxtaposition of two keys a tritone apart is nervous-making, and the persistence of the notes E–F makes for a serious dissonance underlying the fanfares. The music feels excited and overt, as if it didn't quite understand that there was something badly wrong in its construction. In a letter to Sophie Wyss, the soprano who first performed *Les illuminations*, Britten spoke of the "exaggeratedly ecstatic mood" of one of the numbers ("Marine");[46] and exaggerated ecstasy, and ecstasy's ecstatic collapse, are the poles around which the music is organized. *Ecstasy* literally means "standing outside oneself"; and Britten is always making solid-seeming triads that turn out to be parts of unstable tonal configurations, for the pleasure of making the music stand outside the tonal system that could affirm its solidity of being.

Often the vocal line is itself shaped into fanfares. In the second number, "Villes" (based on Rimbaud's "Villes [II]"), the refrain "Ce sont des villes!" is a triumphalist gesture (initially major-scale degrees 3–1–3–5), but it keeps getting bent into odd shapes and modulating into strange keys, if modulation is the right word for key changes in such a disestablished tonal universe, in which triads keep faltering into a state of chromatic decay. This falsifying of triadic construction is everywhere. In "Antique," the first twelve measures are undergirded by completely invariant B♭ major chords, and every note of the vocal line, except one, is on scale degree 1, 3, or 5 in B♭. Then we suddenly find ourselves in C major, nearly as poised and imperturbable as the earlier B♭. And then D major—the singer is still stuck on the triad. And then E major: but at the line about the double sex of the son of Pan ("Ton coeur bat dans ce ventre où dort le double sexe"—which goes, in the Helen Rootham translation that Britten consulted and printed in the score, "Thy heart beats in that womb where sleeps Hermaphrodite"), we start oscillating between E major and D major, as if feints toward bitonality were the right way of thinking about a two-sexed being. After reaching F major, the keys start moving backwards down to the opening B♭, via E♭ major, but descent is more erratic than the ascent. The childlikeness of the first half of the setting (appropriate, in that this number is dedicated to "K. H. W. S."—Wulff Scherchen, the conductor Hermann Scherchen's nineteen-year-old son, whom Britten had known for five years) is called into question by the lascivious text and the harmonic procedures—it seems a fake tonality for a pseudochild. Twenty years later, when Britten was dealing with the fairies in *A Midsummer Night's Dream*, he would remember some of these strategies.

The climax of *Les illuminations* is "Parade." It is a march, or a dream of an unmarched march: it begins in a state of indeterminacy, a *quasi parlando* voice, little snatches of scale, gusts of rhythm, unsteady motions toward a key—it is ostensibly E♭, but A♮ is the most prominent note in the bass. Slowly, out of this aimless intrigue a rhythm starts to make itself felt, then gather confidence, a rhythm without a tune until a clear march struts forth, a most violent paradise of the enraged grimace (as the text would have it)—the march tune is in A major, contradicting, making-other, the three-flat key signature. Britten composed the melody in 1933 as an *Alla marcia* for string quartet, but in the Rimbaud context it seems phantasmagorical, like the ghost march that emerges from the rhythmicized void at the center of Debussy's *Fêtes* (1900). Marches are more typically written for brass bands than for strings, and here, as in the other numbers in *Les illuminations*, we find strings impersonating little phantom orchestras that emerge and recede and compete with one another, just as in Rimbaud's texts we find an incoherent succession of inchoate theatrical spectacles, ooze and wooden shoes and stray clues and *loup-garous*.

The circus of "Parade" is run by master jugglers, Rimbaud tells us, who "transform people and places, and resort to magnetic comedy," as Ashbery puts it.[47] Both Ashbery and Britten are comedians who try to mesmerize Rimbaud's text into *un autre*—some new channel of communication. Britten tries to match Rimbaud flamboyance for flamboyance; Ashbery, on the other hand, seems to efface himself into an achromatic medium, transmitting French syntax and idiom and punctuation into English with the sparsest possible intervention. A comparison of a phrase from "Parade" may show what I mean:

> Ils interpréteraient des pièces nouvelles et des chansons "bonnes filles."[48]
>
> They can interpret modern plays or songs of a simple naivety at will. (Rootham)
>
> They would perform new plays and "nice girl" songs. (Ashbery)[49]

Rootham intervenes in the verb tense, whereas Ashbery follows it; Rootham offers a commentary about the sorts of songs she thinks that *bonnes filles* sing, whereas Ashbery simply gives Rimbaud undiluted—though by rending *bonnes* as "nice" instead of "good," he provides a slight savor of mince, appropriately, I think. Many of Ashbery's nicest touches are in his monosyllables: by translating *rien de riche* (in "Métropolitain") as "nothing posh," for example. Of course, there are moments in *Les illuminations* where

Rimbaud's games with sound put the translator in an impossible position, as when (also in "Métropolitain"), Rimbaud writes,

> les atroces fleurs qu'on appellerait coeurs et soeurs.[50]

> the horrible flowers that might be called hearts and sisters.[51]

The rhyme is, in a prose poem, startling. I think that Ashbery made the right decision in ignoring it, but I wonder if he might have toyed with rendering *coeurs et soeurs* as, say, *hearts and tarts*. It is sometimes amazing what Ashbery's exalted simplicity can accomplish—perhaps my greatest delight in the whole book came from his effortless translation of a surpassingly strange line from "À une raison":

> Arrivée de toujours, qui t'en iras partout.[52]

> Arriving from always, you'll go away everywhere. (Ashbery)

The wonder that I feel is easy, yet ease is the cause of wonder.

5.

Rimbaud, of course, did go away everywhere. In 1876, at the age of twenty-one, Rimbaud abandoned literature for more physical adventures into the unknown: he accepted three hundred florins and enlisted as a soldier in the Dutch Colonial Army. He was sent to Indonesia, where he deserted. What little is known of his sojourn in the Far East is recounted in Jamie James's delightful book *Rimbaud in Java: The Lost Voyage*.[53]

James speculates resourcefully on the probable or possible literary sources of whatever exoticist fantasies the adolescent Rimbaud had about the East. These include William Beckford's *Vathek* (1786), in which a caliph offers to sacrifice fifty children in exchange for a talisman that will make him master of the universe, and Eugène Sue's *Le juif errant* (1844), in which is described a Javanese temple carving of an elephant-bat eating a baby. Infanticide is a standard feature of Orientalist flesh-creep and a feature of Rimbaud's *Parade* as well, insofar as Moloch is one of the star turns in the sideshow. In the Bible (Leviticus 20) God warns his people not to sacrifice their children to Moloch, and images of children thrown into the flames in front of, or into, the great bull-headed idol are common in art and literature. As for

Rimbaud, a poet who imagined himself as a boat foundering in strange seas may have seen himself as a child eaten up by uncanninesses.

The cry "Moloch" often registers strongly in a performance of Britten's *Les illuminations* (the movement called "Parade"), and Moloch, under various names, is a striking presence is Britten's music. In his church parable *The Burning Fiery Furnace* (1966), the three pious Jews at Nebuchadnezzar's court refuse to worship the Babylonian god Merodak and are tossed into a furnace for their presumption. But Moloch found his most potent musical embodiment in Britten's *War Requiem* (1962), which I understand as a kind of sequel to *Les illuminations*, in that the sound metaphors for mutilations of body and lacerations of soul that pertain in the earlier work to imaginary ecstasies are transformed, in the later one, to historical horror. In the *War Requiem* Britten is once again a lump of brass turned into a bugle, or even a cannon, but the fanfare thrusts out over a world that is actually, physically, shattered.

Britten's *War Requiem* was written for the rebuilding of Coventry Cathedral, destroyed during World War II, and the music is an attempt to rebuild the shattered conventions of religious music, called into question by war and the Holocaust. The musicologist Theodor Adorno wrote in 1949 that after Auschwitz the idea of writing a lyric poem was barbaric,[54] and Britten may have wondered whether music could take itself seriously as well. Britten wrote a great deal of straightforwardly pious Christian church music, but the *War Requiem* is a piece of Christian music that tries as much to embrace nihilism as to refute it. It is a requiem, which is the Latin word for "rest"; but the rest it offers is not simple or soothing—if rest is indeed to be found in it. By the definitions of the church, a requiem is also a mass—that is, a ritual of eucharist, in which the communicants ingest the body of Christ in the form of bread. I think, though, that Britten counterpoints against Christ's sacrifice another sacrifice: the sacrifice of human beings to the god of war. The *War Requiem* is both requiem and antirequiem, weirdly evenhanded in offering itself to Christ and to Moloch.

The text of the *War Requiem* alternates passages from the Latin mass for the dead with passages from the poetry of Wilfred Owen. Owen, born in 1893, was twenty-one when war broke out; he wrote almost everything we read in the span of one year, from August 1917 to September 1918, a period that has been compared to John Keats's production in 1819. But Keats, dead at twenty-six, lived a year longer than Owen, killed on November 4, 1918, a week before the Armistice. Both Owen's biography and his poems seem a symbol of the futility of war, and of the preciousness of what was destroyed in war.

Owen resembles Rimbaud in his rapid ascent to mastery and in his sense of the fascination of beholding a world in the act of tearing itself apart. But in Owen there is nothing of "Je est un autre": Owen has a clear, steady persona, a moralist and ironist and truth teller and compassionate witness and guilty participant. What is *entfremdet*, made strange, is less the poet than the world that the poet reports. T. S. Eliot wrote, in "Rhapsody on a Windy Night," of how the world gave up the secret of its skeleton; Edward James wrote a Surrealist poem, marvelously set to music by Francis Poulenc, called "La squelette de la mer" (The Sea's Skeleton); Rimbaud seems to annihilate himself in order to see what the commonplace mind hides from us, the bones, the stamina of things. But in order to see the world's skeleton, Owen didn't have to take hashish or to magic his own mind; he just had to lift his head out of the trenches for a moment: right before his eyes the mortar shells laid bare what ought not to be seen. So the devices that Britten used in *Les illuminations*—particularly the askew fanfares and the tritonal architecture—turned out to be suitable for the *War Requiem*. *Les illuminations* deals with the vanity of the *I*; the *War Requiem* with war's vanity, the whole world's vanity. Britten incorporates war.

Britten thought Owen "by far our greatest war poet, and one of the most original poets of this century,"[55] and Owen anticipated Britten's purposes perfectly by understanding war as a desecrated sacrifice to a mock god. In this sense the central poem is "The Parable of the Old Man and the Young," which Britten set in the Offertorium. This begins as a straightforward retelling of the Old Testament story of the sacrifice of Isaac, and the music seems straightforward too, for it continues the theme of the "Quam olim Abrahae" fugue that precedes it; soon, however, Abraham is building parapets and trenches, and sinister, militaristic themes borrowed from the setting of the Dies Irae start to intrude; for a little while, these dark reverberations are dispelled by the most conspicuous case of self-quotation in all of Britten's music, when the angel stays Abraham's knife to the words "Lay not thy hand upon the lad"—a piece of glorious euphony, complete with a halo of harp arpeggios, taken directly from Britten's canticle *Abraham and Isaac* (1952). But Abraham contemptuously ignores the deus ex machina, shrugs off the miraculous intervention in a remarkable *coup de théâtre*, and continues with the sacrifice, not just the sacrifice of Isaac: "But the old man would not so, but slew his son, / And half the seed of Europe, one by one."[56]

The most striking aspect of the Offertorium is the way in which Owen's poem creates a field of semantic force that causes us to reinterpret the sober Latin words of the liturgical text. The Offertorium begins with cool, lucid devotion: "Domine Jesu Christe, Rex gloriae." Everything about the music suggests piety and humility: Britten's technique of gathering the notes of the melody into a single complex chord—an image of time itself gathered into eternity—is a method used in such very serious works as the church parable *Curlew River* (1964). Traditionally, composers of requiems were expected to provide a fugue at the words "Quam olim Abrahae," and Britten does exactly what Palestrina and Verdi did, in admirably learned inversions, as if he were the most obedient composer of church music imaginable. But we may feel that there's something a little strange about this fugue: it has a lilt to it, a swing, unusual in church music, because the heavy accent falls on the fourth beat of a 6/8 measure—it's a clerical fugue composed from a tune suitable for a sea shanty. This melody is also borrowed from the *Abraham and Isaac* canticle, where it sounds sober, declamatory, undemotic; but in the *War Requiem* it seems, even during its fugal development, slightly impudent, almost vulgar—a quality that becomes still more prominent when the tenor and the baritone start singing Owen's "The Parable of the Old Man and the Young." At the end of this duet, when Abraham starts killing everyone in sight, the "Quam olim Abrahae" tune returns, sounding jazzy, debased; this is the sort of music that Leonard Bernstein used to characterize the tawdry exhilaration of Manhattan. The boys' choir tries to overcome the wicked perversion of "Quam olim Abrahae" by singing their "Hostias" hymn of offering sacrifice; eventually the full choir and the boys themselves resuming singing "Quam olim Abrahae," in a white, straight, devout manner—but I doubt that our ears can ever hear it as acceptably sacred again. The dubious qualities were lurking in the tune all along: the liturgical text, stressing the redemption promised to the seed of Abraham, is easily undone by the music, in which the destruction of half the seed of Europe is latent. The thing and its parody, the obverse and the reverse, confront each other, almost seem to cancel one another out. If this is rest, it's an extremely disturbing sort of rest.

Behind Owen's Abraham lie not only Lloyd George and Clemenceau and Kaiser Wilhelm, but also a kind of Antichrist. Owen's poems constitute a parody gospel of a world dominated by war. When Owen looked out over the landscape of mud, artillery, and barbed wire, he saw a moral allegory, a Christian scene, but smeared over with desecration, as if a hateful Jehovah had rewritten Christ's gospel of love into a tale of jealousy and stupid destruction. Blake took the gnostic position that the world was created by a nasty and incompetent demiurge, whom Blake called Nobodaddy or Urizen and regarded as identical with the Jehovah of the Old Testament.

Owen, as a mythologizer, had the same motor reflexes as Blake; as Owen wrote in "Soldier's Dream":

> I dreamed kind Jesus fouled the big-gun gears;
> And caused a permanent stoppage in all bolts;
> And buckled with a smile Mausers and Colts;
> And rusted bayonet with His tears.
>
> And there were no more bombs, of ours or Theirs,
> Not even an old flint-lock, nor even a pikel.
> But God was vexed, and gave all power to Michael;
> And when I woke he'd seen to our repairs.[57]

Owen did not always spare the New Testament, either: In "Le Christianisme" Owen contemplates a Virgin Mary worthy of the Great War:

> So the church Christ was hit and buried
> Under its rubbish and its rubble.
> In cellars, packed-up saints lie serried,
> Well out of hearing of our trouble.
>
> One Virgin still immaculate
> Smiles on for war to flatter her.
> She's halo'd with an old tin hat,
> But a piece of hell will batter her.[58]

At the center of Owen's imagination is a sort of eucharist of suicide, in which mankind tears itself limb from limb, blows out its own brains, not to redeem itself, but simply as an act of obedience or homage to a war that is itself a suicide worked out on a very large scale. One of his most moving poems describes just such a suicide, "S. I. W." (the abbreviation stands for self-inflicted wound):

> With him they buried the muzzle his teeth had kissed,
> And truthfully wrote the Mother, "Tim died smiling."[59]

The whole war is just a big lie we tell ourselves to rationalize suicide: as Owen famously put it, "The old Lie: *Dulce et decorum est / Pro patria mori*"[60]—it is sweet and fitting to die for the fatherland.

Owen's poetic forms are themselves perfectly adapted for the purpose of desecration. Like Emily Dickinson, a poet whom Owen resembles in several ways, Owen tends to take traditional meters and stanza forms—the hymn, the sonnet—and then to create malaise, a kind of queasiness, by taking unheard-of liberties with the old forms. Both Owen and Dickinson enjoy the dissonance produced by errors of rhyming—a dissonance that can be felt only because the stanza form is so solidly entrenched to begin with. Even when his rhyming is perfect, Owen plays with a sort of cognitive dissonance, for example by writing a sonnet in which the subject matter is entirely wrong for a sonnet: he prays, not to Christ, not to God the Father, but to a cannon; and begs the cannon not to bless, but to curse:

On Seeing a Piece of Our Heavy Artillery Brought into Action

Be slowly lifted up, thou long black arm,
Great Gun towering towards Heaven, about to curse;
Sway steep against them, and for years rehearse
Huge imprecations like a blasting charm!
Reach at that Arrogance which needs thy harm,
And beat it down before its sins grow worse.
Spend our resentment, cannon,—yea, disburse
Our gold in shapes of flame, our breaths in storm.

Yet, for men's sakes whom thy vast malison
Must wither innocent of enmity,
Be not withdrawn, dark arm, thy spoilure done,
Safe to the bosom of our prosperity.
But when thy spell be cast complete and whole,
May God curse thee, and cut thee from our soul![61]

The *War Requiem* is full of remarkable music, but nothing more remarkable than this passage: I think it gets its power from the fact that Britten, as sensitive to the conventions of musical form as Owen was to the conventions of poetical form, hears the words as an antidoxology—not "Praise God from whom all blessings flow," but a lurching and spastic liturgy, fit for the smiting god of war. It should be noted that Owen has little to say about the devil, or Satan, or witches, or any of the usual Halloween paraphernalia of evil—what is chilling about Owen's vision is not that the devil is responsible for the war, but that God is. Owen, watching the ruined battlefield, saw not a *Walpurgisnacht*, not a region of hell, but Calvary. The whole human race has become a mutilated and insignificant Christ.

Britten responded to Owen's double vision, in which good and evil waver and trade places, by writing music that's extraordinarily difficult to construe. Britten's religious music often uses perfectly conventional semantics, in which consonance stands for virtue and dissonance for vice. For example, in the radio play *King Arthur* (1937), Britten's theme for the Holy Grail is bold and scalar, possessing massive integrity, a perfect musical circle ending where it begins (Britten liked this theme and reused it in his piano concerto). And in his church parable *The Prodigal Son* (1968), as the father warns his son, "Evil lurks everywhere watching for idleness," we hear the shifty, unreliable harmonies that constitute a normal symbol for evil—the sort of music that Verdi provides when Iago tells Otello to beware jealousy, the dark, blind hydra. But in the *War Requiem*, it's hard to assign clear moral values to the themes and procedures. As we've seen, "Quam olim Abrahae" starts out as an upright liturgical fugue but soon develops worrisome aspects. And this equivocality is true of most of themes in the work.

From the time of Heinrich Biber—let alone Mozart, Cherubini, and Berlioz—Requiem masses have sometimes contained conspicuous parts for bells and brass. These instrumental part have a clear meaning: the bells represent the church bells tolling for the dead; the brass represents the *tuba mirum*, the trumpet calling all souls to the Last Judgment. Britten is always sensitive to these conventional meanings: his Dies Irae is full of brass fanfares; and, when he set his first Owen text, "Anthem for Doomed Youth"—a poem that cries out against the absence of passing bells in the battlefield ("What passing-bells for these who die as cattle? / —Only the monstrous anger of the guns. / Only the stuttering rifles' rapid rattle / Can patter out their hasty orisons"[62])—Britten provides the very bell sounds that the poet can't hear. But in addition to this pious use of brass and bells, Britten is also playing a more sinister game: he is using these extended orchestral resources to *imitate* the rifles, the artillery, the whole acoustic of war. When Owen's text speaks of the "rifles' rapid rattle," we hear nervous-making figures in the oboe, bassoon, and horn, beginning with an accented staccato. And Britten's Dies Irae sounds uncomfortably like a series of exploding mortar shells, slowly dying away into an unholy sort of peace, a landscape of dismembered bodies. The pistons of the war machine—a machine that seems to be breaking down as it chugs along—beat a strange rhythm, in 7/4 time. (Hector Berlioz anticipated this sort of lacerating meter in the "Lacrimosa" of his *Requiem*, written in 9/8 time.) The 7/4 of the *War Requiem* has choral accents on the first, third, fifth, and sixth beats; when the strings of the orchestra fill in the missing accents, on the second, fourth, and seventh beats, we seem to be listening to a sort of bebop played by a dance band in hell. I don't choose this metaphor lightly, for Britten had already written, in 1939, a scene for an actual nightclub in hell, so to speak, in his incidental music for J. B. Priestley's *Johnson over Jordan* (as I've had occasion to mention before), a pastiche of big-band music, *The Spider and the Fly*, with something of the Dies Irae rhythm. Here the band is located in *bardo*, a hallucinatory state between death and life mentioned in the *Tibetan Book of the Dead*; in Priestley's play Robert Johnson relives his life backward—and to some extent the *War Requiem* is itself a Handelian drama, an inverted *Messiah* made up of snippets of liturgy, in which sacred events are rehearsed, relived, undone.

The music of the *War Requiem* is like Joseph Jastrow's diagram, beloved by Gestalt psychologists, which can be seen as either a rabbit or a duck but never as both at the same time; there is a divine interpretation and an infernal interpretation, coexisting in the most uncomfortable way possible.

Not only the brass, but also the bells, impose some difficulty of interpretation. The meaning of the bells played in the "Anthem for Doomed Youth" section is clear enough; but what are we to make of the astonishing array of orchestral bells, antique cymbals, glockenspiel, and vibraphone at the beginning of the "Sanctus"? The musicologist Christopher Palmer was puzzled by this passage, the only one in the score, he thought, where Britten's concern "to communicate with a mass audience" in a musical language "easy to understand" gave way to "an unfamiliar linguistic element"—not part of the sonorities or the semantics of Western music, but derived from the gamelan music of Bali and Java. Like Rimbaud, Britten traveled to Java; but Britten had learned about gamelan music long before his tour of the Far East from the Canadian ethnomusicologist Colin McPhee—in fact, one of Britten's first recordings (1941) was as the second piano in McPhee's two-piano transcriptions of the wood and metal percussion orchestra, *Music of Bali* (1940). Gamelan sonority was part of Britten's musical vocabulary for unearthly beauty, as in the ballet music for Tadzio in *Death in Venice* (1973); and also his vocabulary for pacificism, as in the opera *Owen Wingrave* (1970), where the hero stares at the portraits of his military ancestors and repudiates their love of war in a great tintinnabulation aria: "In peace I have found my image, I have found myself." A bell may represent a funeral tolling; it may represent the alarm of war; but in the "Sanctus" the mingled chimes represent an extraterrestriality, a peace that passeth understanding, something beyond all semantic construction—in a sense beyond good and evil. Arnold Schoenberg, in *Moses und Aron* (1930–32), represented God's presence in the burning bush by a sensory overload, a simultaneous incomprehensible speaking and singing of twelve-tone music; and, after the tingling of seven heavens at the beginning, Britten's "Sanctus" proceeds (at the "Pleni sunt coeli") with an irregular and thrilling build-up of voices singing too many notes at the same time—at one point singing at once the notes G, G♯, B♭, C, and D (not to mention some other notes we hear in the orchestra), a musical symbol of the God beyond all binary categories, the God who is all things.

When Britten's "Sanctus" reaches the "Hosanna," we hear a mighty scalar theme in the brass, decorated with frills, in which consonant intervals are strongly emphasized. I hear this as a kind of immense steam calliope, fit for heaven's own merry-go-round. It is a perfectly circular theme, ending where it begins, like the Grail theme from *King Arthur*—and I think that, here as there, a circular theme is symbolic of goodness. The "Sanctus" proceeds from a nearly unconstruable, asemantic beginning, into something that affirms divine virtue. The ending of the *War Requiem*, the "In paradisum," is also full of circular themes, as if Britten were struggling to abandon his ambiguities in favor of a straightforward vision of rest in paradise.

But Britten does not succeed—does not actually want to succeed, I think—in creating a simple religious consolation. The beginning of the "Sanctus," with its vibraphones and bells, is as far as Britten gets into what might be called pure music—music remote from the burden of expressing human pain, remote from common semantic concerns. But not long after the Sanctus comes the setting of Owen's "Strange Meeting" in the Agnus Dei, a passage which is exactly opposite in character: instead of nearly pure music, we have almost pure speech, a long recitative for tenor and baritone above a bleak sustained G minor chord. Here the two singers represent an English soldier and German soldier, both dead, but not in paradise, simply alert in their grave, the ultimate *requies*. Britten here imagines in extremely secular terms what it feels like to be dead: deadness is a sort of deafness, for the soldiers can hear one another's intimate voices, but they can hear no music. The hollow acoustic space of Coventry Cathedral becomes, sinisterly, the hollowness of an underground pit, so deeply dug that the life of the living has shrunk to distant rumors of action:

> It seemed that out of battle I escaped
> Down some profound dull tunnel, long since scooped
> Through granites which titanic wars had groined.

Yet also there encumbered sleepers groaned,
Too fast in thought or death to be bestirred.
Then, as I probed them, one sprang up, and stared
With piteous recognition in fixed eyes,
Lifting distressful hands, as if to bless.
And by his smile, I knew that sullen hall,—
By his dead smile I knew we stood in Hell.

With a thousand pains that vision's face was grained;
Yet no blood reached there from the upper ground,
And no guns thumped, or down the flues made moan.[63]

The orchestra doodles in the margins of speech; the fanfares of the Dies Irae dwindle into the faint tracery of a single woodwind, first a clarinet, then an oboe. The requiem is in danger of un-requieming itself, losing its music altogether, until the "In paradisum" comes to conclude all in a state of musical calm.

But even the tranquility of the final bars manages to disturb, as the chorus softly sings, "Requiescant in pace. Amen." This "Amen" repeats the fundamental harmonic movement of the whole *War Requiem*, from a two-note chord (B♯ and F♯) to an F major triad. This is Britten's cadence surrogate and has been conspicuous from the opening Kyrie onward. It is a strange progression in that the opening chord consists of a bare tritone, the augmented fourth, the dissonant interval halfway between the very consonant fourth and the very consonant fifth. Indeed, the *War Requiem* seems dedicated to achieving the rehabilitation of the tritone, even the apotheosis of the tritone, as if church music had suffered from its long exclusion. Some of the mightiest passages in the *War Requiem* are achieved purely through tritonal means, most notably the "Et lux perpetua" in the Kyrie—all overlapping Cs and Fs. Here we are at the heart of Britten's semantic ambiguities, for the tritone was, according to medieval music theory, a forbidden interval, the *diabolus in musica*. What is the devil doing in the *War Requiem*? Possibly a symbol of a world in love with war. But I might make a different case: that Britten is simply confronting the same human inability to distinguish God from the devil that lies at the center of Owen's imagination of war. Owen's rhymes are often dissonant: "Strange Meeting" is a continual succession of rhymes with too little assonance (and too much consonance, in the technical sense of repeating consonant phonemes), such as *spoiled-spilled*, *wheels-wells*, *friend-frowned*, *killed-cold*. Such rhymes represented a real advance in English verse technique: W. H. Auden, for one, would use them often. I think that, in the *War Requiem*, Britten experiments with a still more striking technical possibility: that a tritone could be heard not as a dissonance, but as a consonance. After all, in a world where hatred and love are so eerily commingled, the listener is best advised to hear consonance wherever consonance can be found. What is vile is also beauteous.

Britten was a peaceful man, but his most powerful images of peace can be found at the heart of his representations of war. There is a strangely Orwellian aspect to Britten's musical imagination: War Is Peace, Freedom Is Slavery. But music is always good at saying, in a thousand gross or subtle ways, that black is white and up is down.

FIVE

Schoenberg's Shatterings

Achior. I must admit, I cannot free myself from these traps in which your words have caught me; but I am not convinced by this. I yield to your art, not to your reason. And I do not wish to desert the gods I worship and can see for a God whom I cannot even imagine.

Ozìa. If we could imagine Him, He would not be God. Who can envisage Him? He does not consist of parts, like the body; He is not distinct in concept, like our souls; He is not subject to form, like all creation; and if you assign parts, concepts, form to Him, you circumscribe Him, you mar His perfection.

METASTASIO, *La Betulia lìberata* (Mozart, K. 118)

REPRESENTATION CAN ALWAYS IMPROVE, BUT IT CAN NEVER BE exact. The only perfect act of representation would be a duplicate, a pointless copy. At the beginning of the twentieth century, it seemed that representation in art was evolving beyond all limits: Richard Strauss would soon be able to differentiate teaspoons from tablespoons by purely orchestral means; painters would make more subtly precise imitations of vision than any camera; and writers would enact the most delicate tracery of electricity through the nerves, display the passage of ideas within the brain itself, thought anterior to speech, the stream of consciousness. And yet, side by side with this impatient elaboration of images, there arose an art skeptical of mimesis, insisting on the gulf between representation and the thing represented, denying the referentiality of image and symbol. These two themes, mimesis and antimimesis, develop together and often entwine in the work of a single artist: illusion and disillusion constitute a single enchantment.

The violent quest for verisimilitude created a strain on the technical apparatus of art: when artists try to grasp something beyond their reach, they present the condition of straining, not the thing strained after. A rough law: the urge to do away with convention and technique, the urge to display something real beyond artifice, will lead to increasing preoccupation with the purely conventional and technical aspects of art; conversely, the urge to do away with representation will lead the audience to speculate endlessly about what the artwork represents—to discover a whole world in an artwork that aspires to be worldless. I will call this aesthetic seesaw the *paradox of mimesis*. This paradox can be seen most easily in the case of painting: there is a Hyperrealist school of painting, which aims for preternatural clarity in its presentation of the visual field: the straight-edge of a more naïve art is replaced by a microtome; a simple street scene, the façade of a crumbling building, is displayed with no depth of field, with no distortion of air or eye, as if it were erected in a vacuum on a moon of Jupiter and studied through a telescope.

The spectator sees the building itself, ponderable to Locke in heaven: all that is subjective has been refined away into solid slabs of light. And yet you marvel not at what's depicted—you've seen it a thousand times—but at the immense technical ingenuity, the finesse of brushstroke, the sheer knowledgeability of the artist who knows the exact outline of each piece of fruit half-hidden behind the shadows of wooden crates. Indeed, the artist seems to invite this admiration of artifice by choosing to paint such a banal subject. In theory the object is supreme and the medium has vanished into transparency; but in fact we are so enamored of the cleanness, the invisibility, of the pane of glass that we forget to look through it. The very stylelessness is an affectation of style, just as Georges Seurat's attempt, in an earlier generation, to imitate the retina's cones and rods by resolving solid color into points of pigmentation—another plausible discovery of the ultimate truth of vision—became a cliché of illustration.

Similarly, it has proved difficult to develop a wholly abstract style of painting. For several generations painters exercised every conceivable means of ridding art of representation, but for many critics representation has stubbornly inhered. When Lévi-Strauss claims that abstract painters are not abstract at all, that they seem only to paint imaginary objects,[1] I know what he means: according to past visual experience the eye interprets three blobs of paint on a fuzzy background as buoys floating on the ocean, as balloons at sunset, or as mushrooms in a meadow. No pattern is ever so far removed from the visible world that reminiscence cannot reduce it to something known from a life rich in bread mold, oil slicks, coral, icicles, plumes of rust. Wassily Kandinsky—who, despite his severe antirepresentationalism, claims that many abstract designs are beneath art and would be fit only for a necktie—writes that the painting of the future will repudiate the flatness of Cézanne and return to the presentation of three-dimensional space: and in fact many of Kandinsky's canvases show lattices or arrows ranged in orderly space, spheres swimming before and behind, obedient to the old laws of perspective: sometimes one could even build a mobile of these lucid imaginary objects that, from a certain point of view, would yield exactly the scene Kandinsky has painted. It is an art remote from nature, perhaps, but not remote from representation. The paintings of Jackson Pollock, with their tight networks of spatters that display no fixed pattern of shape and color but only the vehemence, the effort that forces the paint into its arbitrary configuration, seem as far from representation as painting can get. Yet the expressiveness that Abstract Expressionism claims for itself suggests not that representation is repudiated, but that something deeper, more point-blank than the mere forms of the visible world is being represented: interior tension, the dynamics of the brain. Anger is a striated track of paint that the sweeping fist leaves on the canvas: resignation is a slow dripping. The Pollock who says "I *am* nature" is an artist searching for the magical seizure of reality,[2] the collapse of analogy into identity—the same heresy that beguiles so many other artists of the twentieth century.

Maybe for a genuinely antirepresentational artist we should look not to Pollock but to M. C. Escher, who tries to subvert mimesis instead of abolishing it: in some of his pictures there is no single frame of reference that makes sense—space itself has grown twi-formed, monstrous. If mimesis cannot be slain, perhaps it can be tricked into committing suicide. Architectural Möbius strips and other forms of visual nonsense perform the difficult trick of making blatant the artificiality of art, the gap between what is on the canvas or page and the world of representable objects to which the image points. Merely to make a poor representation is not to prove that all representation is necessarily poor: and to incorporate bits of real objects into painting is only to extend the notion of the artist's materials, not to demonstrate that a painted stamp is incompatible with a genuine stamp. (I'm alluding to a real painting, J. D. Chalfant's *Which Is Which?* [ca. 1890], in which a postage stamp is pasted next to its exact painted copy. The challenge of the title is easily met now [the dyes on the real stamp have faded, while the copy remains bright] and doubtless was in 1890 too; but the stamp and its counterfeit, both of which are images, concord well together, gesture together toward a well-known world in which envelopes can be mailed if certain decorations appear on one corner.) Every heightening of the spectator's sense of the artificiality of art only stresses the customariness, the propriety, the naturalness of artifice; nothing is so brittle, so outrageous, that it does not belong, that we cannot clasp it to us.

T. S. Eliot argues in his dissertation that the term "a round square" is not nonsense, not a purely verbal formula, but a naming of an object, however chimerical, in the real world. It is similar with representations in painting: whatever is on the canvas may be construed as a representation of something, however bizarre or implausible or self-contradictory, in the world of visual experience. The mere appearance of the painting itself extends the world of visual experience to include what it depicts. Reference is unavoidable. The one thing no artist can paint is paint.

The history of music, much more than the history of painting, is dominated by the notion of progressive mastery of representation—in the case of music, the representation of affect, though this issue has preoccupied painters too. Nicolas Poussin, for example, tried to connect the harmony of his colors and designs with the emotional content of various Greek musical modes, such as the Phrygian mode, stern and serious; or the Ionian mode, cheerful, bacchanalian. But composers have been far more determined to understand the purpose of their art in terms of feeling representation, mood representation. Claudio Monteverdi wrote in the preface to his *Eighth Book of Madrigals* (1638) that music can depict three principal passions, *concitato* (excited), *molle* (soft), and *temperato* (restrained). The last two he found everywhere in the music of his contemporaries: but he said that had never heard a good example of the *concitato*, the music appropriate for a brave warrior in battle. Despite this omission, Monteverdi thought he could deduce or reinvent from meditation on the Pyrrhic meter and Plato's writings exactly the right *stile concitato*, which turned out to be repeated staccato sixteenth notes. So for a long time the extension of emotional representation becomes a principal justification for musical novelty, and many subsequent innovations in harmony and structure will be defended on the grounds not of irresistible musical logic, but of passion.

Most early secular instrumental music that we know of was written for dancing; music seems to evolve through the elaboration of biological rhythms, from the beat of medieval dance, the heart's iambs, to complexities of ensemble that require a metronome or conductor to keep proper time, an eighteenth-century delicacy of nerves. The temple throbbings of Beethoven seem to raise music's blood pressure more than anything that went before; and from Wagner onward no firm meter would be allowed to interfere with the representation of a tumultuous mind and body. To my ears Wagner's music is slow: even when it is frenzied, agitated, full of sixteenth notes, there is rarely the clear underlying beat that alone can make music seem rapid. Motifs that are pronouncedly rhythmic—such as, in *Der Ring des Nibelungen*, the motifs of the Nibelungs, or Hunding, or the Giants—tend to represent evil, as if rhythm were the antagonist Wagner must destroy. The passionate, lovely Wagnerian motifs are typically a long, free swelling and detumescence.

In the next generation Richard Strauss attempts, in the prelude to *Der Rosenkavalier* and in *Symphonia Domestica*, an explicit representation of orgasm. More and more of the body comes into play as music evolves after Strauss: polyrhythmic composers such as Conlon Nancarrow wrote music imitating the lack of coordination that marks the body's persistence—the way in which breathing and pulse and blinking and peristalsis seem regulated by different clocks. The last organ that music had to include for its body to be complete is the brain: and perhaps one can see, in a piece such as Györgi Ligeti's *Clocks and Clouds* (1972), with its references to the philosophy of Karl Popper, an imitation of the brain's humming rhythmlessness.

This little story of the evolution of music as a kind of physiological extension is only a prelude to a discussion of Arnold Schoenberg. Schoenberg's career extends from the 1890s until 1951, and the development of his musical thought will provide a good example of the Modernist artist's confrontation with the problem of interior representation. I think no artist ever lived with a fiercer desire to abolish all that is mediate, obstructive, stale, merely "musical," all that stands in the way of the emotion itself; expression in Schoenberg's early works is wrought to new intensity, new incisiveness, is given a clearer voice, a more fully articulated body. Sympathetic critics, such as Theodor Adorno, have praised Schoenberg for being closer to the deep truth of the Freudian id than other composers:

> The first atonal works are session notes in the sense of a psychoanalyst's session notes on a patient's dreams. In the first book published on Schoenberg,[3] Kandinsky called Schoenberg's paintings "brain acts" [*Gehirnakte*]. The scars of that revolution of expression, however, are the blots that have fixed themselves, in the music as well as on the paintings, as the messengers of the id against the composer's will—blots that disturb the surface and can no more be wiped away by subsequent correction than the traces of blood in the fairy tale.[4]

To Adorno, music until Schoenberg had created for itself a fairy-tale world, in which suffering and joy alike are transformed into pure song: but in Schoenberg's work the blood beneath has leaked through, an aspersion against and reproach of the world of illusion, to old yarns and songs in which nothing important can happen. All previous composers offer images of feeling; Schoenberg offers a direct translation of feeling into sound. A comparison of the mad scene of Gaetano Donizetti's *Lucia di Lammermoor* (1835) with Schoenberg's monodrama *Erwartung* (1909) will show what is meant. The former is the kind of operatic agony for which the myth of Philomel is the proper description: the scream resolves into gorgeous raving, dizzy falls of melody, voice and flute twined into a single acanthus: while in the latter it is not the soprano but the madness itself that sings.

In *Erwartung*, a lone woman is the only character on the stage: there is a dark wood, a clearing, a path to a house: the words she sings are disconnected phrases, an imitation of a patient's speech to his psychoanalyst. In the deep shadows, images slip and slide and will not stay still; a tree trunk seems like a dead body; a bench turns out to be the corpse of her lover—but we can't tell what of this is reality, if any, or hallucination, if any. What she sees and feels, what we in the audience hear, is only the bristling of her dementia, a prolonged moonstruckness; and the music does indeed sound like trauma made audible—one hears her feathery pulse, the ringing in her ears, the eccentric trilling of something loose and about to fall, the chirps of crickety things, the low gurgling, the leaking of blood from an artery in the brain. The woman is in such ecstasy that she is disconnected from the world; her ceaseless caressing of the corpse is almost a metaphor for her mind's desire to play upon, stimulate every physiological process, extract from the body every nuance of feeling: and the atonality, pantonality, the remoteness of the music from any conventional harmony is a reflex of her mind's self-preoccupation, its loss of society, its intense concentration upon its own processes. The absence of a tonic corresponds to the absence of conscious mental control; the forbidden intervals in the chords and melodies correspond to the naked confrontation with taboo; the emancipation of dissonance corresponds to a filling out of the full spectrum of human emotion. The woman, if she has murdered her lover, has gone mad from guilt: but her madness is not an escape into the unreal loveliness of the mad Lucia di Lammermoor, but a hellish isolation, a self-excoriation. (In an odd historical twist, Donizetti really did go insane, while Schoenberg, often accused of writing like a madman, remained canny and self-controlled.)

The title *Erwartung* seems ironic: the German word means "expectation," but, since the music provides the listener with no predictive structure, expectation becomes a free-floating anxiety. The text—by an Austrian medical student, Marie Pappenheim—was evidently a rough draft that Schoenberg decided to set without further polishing; its rawness, its unevenness, its lack of syntactical control may have seemed the literary equivalent of the encephalographically lurching music that he wanted to write.

The text's shattered, splintery diction helped him investigate form at a level of improvisation almost unprecedented in the history of the arts. Schoenberg chose a text so maimed that it seems the victim of some ghastly avant-garde surgery, too debilitated to offer any resistance to the music. The text of *Erwartung* is all ellipsis, and the music is even more elliptical in that it omits all the transitions that might soften or condone the strange successions of chords full of major sevenths, or the melodic spikes that seem to represent pathological contractions of the heart through pathological contractions of the larynx.

Marie Pappenheim was a relative of Berthe Pappenheim, the woman known to history as "Anna O.," the hysteric whom Sigmund Freud described in a famous case history. She was the patient not of Freud but of his collaborator Joseph Breuer; Freud's account of her hysteria, in *Five Lectures on Psycho-analysis*, includes the following description:

> She fell into a waking dream and saw a black snake coming towards the sick man [her dying father] from the wall to bite him. (It is most likely that there were in fact snakes in the field behind the house and that these had previously given the girl a fright; they would thus have provided the material for her hallucination.) She tried to keep the snake off, but it was as though she was paralysed. Her right arm, over the back of the chair, had gone to sleep, and had become anaesthetic and paretic; and when she looked at it the fingers turned into little snakes with death's heads (the nails).[5]

Similarly, the Woman in *Erwartung* keeps feeling, especially in scene 2, that some unknown thing from the forest is dangling down or crawling up to touch her:

> Ist das noch der Weg? . . .
> *(Bückt sich, greift mit den Händen)* Hier ist es eben . . .
> *(aufschreiend)* Was? . . . Laß los!

(Zitternd auf, versucht ihre Hand zu betrachten) Eingeklemmt? . . . Nein, es ist was gekrochen . . .
(Wild, greift sich ins Gesicht) Und hier auch . . . Wer rührt mich an?[6]

Is this still the path?
(bends down, gropes with her hands) Here it's level.
(crying out) What? . . . Let go!
(trembling, tries to look at her hand) Is my hand caught? . . . No, something crawled . . .
(wildly, grabs her face) And here too . . . Who is touching me?

The word *hysteria* comes from the Greek word for womb, and hysteria was considered a uterine disease in that repressed sexual urges, leaking out in fantastical surrogates of sexual acts, was believed to be its cause. (Breuer discontinued his treatment of Anna O. when he found her on the floor pantomiming the act of giving birth; she told Breuer that he was the father of her imaginary child.) Marie Pappenheim may have conceived the Woman of *Erwartung* as a sort of talking womb, a naked quivering organ, infinitely sensitive without much in the way of sensory apparatus except the sense of touch. Everything around her is vague and dripping and wants to violate her. Lost in the body's depths, time means nothing to the Woman: the past and the present, the real and the fantastic all coexist inextricably. The music should also give this impression: Schoenberg remarked that *Erwartung* represents "in *slow motion* everything that occurs during a single second of maximum spiritual excitement, stretching it out to half an hour."[7] It is a study of time expansion in the domain of Schoenbergian relativity. The whole thing is one short scream made interminable.

As noted earlier, in his "Beethoven" essay Wagner wrote that "the scream was the basis of every musical act." Wagner's essay is the basis of Expressionism as movement in music, since, for Wagner, expressions of rage, of misery, even of tender love, were all merely weakenings of the scream. The *Tristan* chord, then, is just a soft scream alluding to a hard scream. It was Schoenberg's gift to present the primal scream in unusually pure form.

The history of the scream is one of the good stories of Modernist music. One fine example occurs at the climax of the Adagio of Mahler's Tenth Symphony (left unfinished at his death in 1911): a huge lacerating chord that contains nine of the twelve notes of the chromatic scale. Schoenberg, too, evidently conceived of expressivity as being intense to the degree that it approximated the fullness of the chord in which all notes are sounded.

Not every musicologist agrees with Charles Rosen, who argues, following Adorno, that the "atonal" Schoenberg redefined consonance as chromatic saturation, so that the chords of *Erwartung* tend to succeed one another complementarily—a sequence of chords will contain all twelve notes of the chromatic scale.[8] It is true, however, that if you look at successive chords in *Erwartung*, the notes in one chord tend to be (sometimes) exactly those that are missing from the previous chord; so that the sequence of chords seems to be struggling to add up to the big chord that has all the notes at once. Adorno thought that this sort of complementary harmony provided an analogue to the tension and release of traditional harmony: each note, each chord, strives to lose itself in the total aggregate smash of sound. Adorno furthermore thought that this principle destroyed any sense of forward movement in time; so it makes sense that the whole opera is a single amplified second, since it isn't built on the sort of musical structure that allows for leisurely and articulate discourse. It's music that tries to abolish its own temporality.

The end is the most remarkable thing in the score, a sort of negative scream. There are no chords in *Erwartung* that actually contain all twelve notes of the chromatic scale, though such a chord does appear in Schoenberg's next opera, *Die glückliche Hand* (1912); nevertheless, *Erwartung*'s ending goes far to prove Adorno's and Rosen's idea that this sort of atonal music is always moving toward chromatic saturation:

> *(Leiser)* Es ist dunkel . . . dein Kuß wie ein Flammenzeichen in meiner Nacht . . .
> meine Lippen brennen und leuchten . . . dir entgegen . . .
> *(in Entzücken aufschreiend)* Oh, bist du da . . .
> *(irgend etwas entgegen)* ich suchte . . .
>
> *(More softly)* Your kiss is like a fiery sign in my night . . .
> My lips burn and shine . . . toward you . . .
> *(crying out in rapture)* Oh, are you there . . .
> *(toward something)* I was looking . . .

In the final bar, the runs of notes up the chromatic scale keep getting faster and faster and quieter and quieter, until they shiver away in a whisper—an effect that corresponds to the twelve-note smash chord as absence corresponds to presence. With its upward inflection, it's the apotheosis of the question mark—as if the whole system of expressive devices in music were calling itself into question. In seventeenth-century Roman oratorio there was a minor musical genre called the *vanitas*, in which both text and music urged the listener to regard everything we value in the physical world as emptiness—*vanitas vanitatum*, as the book of Ecclesiastes has it. In one such piece, the composer Giacomo Carissimi inserted odd silences, as if the vanishing of the music corresponded to a more general vanishing; Schoenberg's strange ending suggests a sudden reversion to psychic emptiness, the bursting of the mind's bubble, a general loss of function at the end of this half-hour-long instant of time.

Schoenberg seems to satirize his own public image as screamer-in-chief in an essay of 1924:

> But it should not be forgotten that the only man able to make himself noticed here will be the one found interesting by the fashion of the moment. And that varies too much to be able in itself to become the standard. Don't forget: if at present the one who knows how to scream loudest, or softest, most interestingly or most atmospherically as each pain jars him, before long it could again be the one who under no circumstance moves even a muscle.[9]

This connoisseur of screaming is a caricature of the Expressionist composer: but in what respect is it not accurate, if the resources of voice and orchestra are so bent, banged, twisted into the semblance of screams? By 1924 Schoenberg was expanding his artistic curriculum in directions well beyond the scream; but the importance of the scream to Modernist art is difficult to exaggerate. In music, this plenum of sound was the equivalent of Freud's oceanic experience, a sort of full-brain orgasm. In literature, the devil in Thomas Mann's *Doktor Faustus* (1947) offered a vision of hell as a sort of smash chord—a place where no one can hear himself singing because all sound is choked in the thick dense shouting and trilling. This novel is an imaginary biography of one Adrian Leverkühn, the inventor of the method of composing music in twelve tones. Mann was a neighbor of Adorno (and of Schoenberg) in southern California when he wrote the book, and he made Leverkühn a version of Schoenberg as one might infer or deduce him from Adorno's theories about his music.

The devil tells Leverkühn that there are two kinds of inspiration: God's, in which the composer is given a germ, the trace of an idea with which the composer must struggle, labor through many patient drafts in order to bring to fruition; and the devil's, an instantaneous presentation of the whole, a thunderclap, a fit of epilepsy in Leverkühn's syphilis-sharpened brain. No biographer has recorded any pact between the devil and the historical Arnold Schoenberg, but Schoenberg has left us a remarkable record of a similar paroxysm in his brief opera *Die glückliche Hand* (The Gifted Touch, 1912), in which the Man, a baritone representative of the modern artist and the only soloist in the piece, creates with a single casual blow of his hammer the diadem that the menacing, envious, astonished workmen could not manufacture even with much hard labor. Creation therefore is a swift and decisive flight of genius, and in fact Schoenberg said that he wrote the whole of *Erwartung* in seventeen days. But just after the Man, laughing, carelessly tosses the diadem into the gaggle of workmen—a Siegfried contemptuous of the sword that Mime with all his cunning could not forge—he is struck by a windstorm, a storm of colors, a light-crescendo extending from dull red to dirty green to dark blue-gray to violet to an intense dark red, as the spectrum intensifies through its gamut. At last a blood red is mixed with more and more orange until a climax occurs on a shade of glaring yellow, which inundates the Man's grotto from all sides at once:

> Der Mann hat dieses Crescendo des Lichts und des Sturmes so darzustellen, als ginge beides von ihm aus. Er sieht erst (beim rötlichen Licht) auf seine Hand; die sinkt dann, sichtlich ermattet, langsam; seine Augen werden aufgeregt (schmutzig-grünes Licht). Seine Aufregung wächst; die Glieder spannen sich krampfartig er streckt zitternd beide Arme von sich (Blutrot), reißt die Augen weit auf und öffnet entsetzt den Mund. Wenn das gelbe Licht da ist, muß sein Kopf so aussehen, als ob er platzen würde.

> During this crescendo of light and storm, the Man behaves as if both emanated from him. He looks first (the reddish light) at his hand; it then slowly sinks, visibly exhausted: his eyes grow excited (dirty green light). His excitement increases; his limbs clench themselves in spasms, trembling he stretches out both arms (blood red); his eyes start from his head and he opens his mouth in horror. When the yellow light comes, his head looks on the point of exploding.

This is what Leverkühn would call demonic inspiration: and Schoenberg seems to have deployed every resource of music and lighting in a sensory assault, eye and ear alike engrossed by chromatic saturation. The music for the strings insists on chord after chord distilled to maximum dissonance:

and from this harmonic pressure numerous unclear motifs for trumpet, celesta, and woodwind are continually evolved, an image in sound and light of the iridescence of glaucoma, the nimbus of migraine, brain swelling, convulsion. This moment is, I take it, the end point of Expressionism. Expression is in danger of becoming literal ex-pression, extrusion of brain tissue. The barriers between inside and outside are about to break from too much pressure; art is frustrated that it cannot go beyond the conditions of art, into the annihilation of sensuous intermediaries, into the direct insertion of electrodes, exencephaly.

In *Die glückliche Hand*, this scene of revelation provides to the Man neither joy nor a sense of accomplishment—only a nagging despair; the Woman, who seems ambiguously to represent either visionary beauty eluding his pursuit or a public hostile to his person, at last deserts him for good; and the drama ends, as it began, with a tableau of the Man eaten alive by a fantastic animal, a hyena-bat, and mocked by a chorus that reviles him for trying to find worldly fulfillment of his unworldly vision, for not contenting himself with what he can grasp, his own body, his own physical and mental pain:

> Fühlst du nur, was du berührst, deine Wunden erst an deinem Fleisch, deine Schmerzen erst an deinem Körper? Und suchst dennoch! Und quälst dich! Und bist ruhelos!

> Do you not feel what you touch, the wounds first in your flesh, the pain first in your body? And you still search for it? And torture yourself? And have no rest!

The happiest hand is the hand most content to explore immediate sensation, the environment nearby; and *Die glückliche Hand* is a parable of the artist of the early twentieth century, who embraces a simple Expressionist aesthetic, a desire to depict common pain and joy, but whose imagination leads him onward to impossible or divine expression, regions of lightning and howling that can never find satisfactory representation in art: the depiction of catastrophe itself becomes catastrophic. The Schoenberg who limits himself to the good advice of his chorus, the openhanded, finely delineating, accessible Schoenberg of *Verklärte Nacht*, the First and Fourth String Quartets, *Das Buch der hängenden Gärten* (The Book of the Hanging Gardens), or the Piano Suite, is a great and attractive composer. But it is the Schoenberg of the wilderness that is my concern here, the Schoenberg of the *Gurre-*

Lieder, the Second String Quartet, *Erwartung*, *Moses and Aron*—irrational, lavish, unbalanced works, pieces that assault the limit of expression and venture into rapture, unreliability, the unintelligibleness of God.

What gives Schoenberg's experimental pieces their peculiar savor is his intelligent recognition of the impossibility of what he attempts. It is characteristic of Schoenberg that in *Die glückliche Hand* a choral commentary is appended to the sudden kindling of the artist's inspiration, his shivering into light, in order to deride the artist for attempting to convey the unconveyable not five minutes after it is conveyed. It is an unwieldy solution for the problem that Schoenberg also will set himself in his unfinished biblical opera *Moses und Aron* (1930–32): how to perform a feat of magic, the representation of what can never be brought to earth, and simultaneously to show that the trick has failed; how to illustrate the distance between the sensuous image presented in music and that which it can never actually be an image of.

Throughout his career Schoenberg remained obsessed with the art of interior verisimilitude, the art of the blast or short-circuit, direct connection of brain to brain; but, except in *Erwartung*, there is typically some retreat from ambition or confession of failure whenever he attempts it. In *Die glückliche Hand* it is the debunking chorus. In *Pierrot lunaire* (1912) there is a song called "Gemeinheit" (Vulgarity) in which Pierrot drills a hole into the bald skull of his fellow clown Cassander; he plugs the hole with tobacco, screws in a pipestem, and smokes comfortably as Cassander's "scream rends the air." One can see the same preoccupation with opening up the brain to immediate experience, expression, as in the bursting head of *Die glückliche Hand*. (As Kafka says, "A segment has been cut out of the back of his head. The sun, and the whole world with it, peep in."[10]) But this is a minor, deformed, ironic analogue of immediate experience, the screaming of Cassander depicted only by the tiny monotone of a single note from a piccolo. Schoenberg ridicules the notion of high Expressionism here; it has sophisticated itself into a puppet show, and no spots of blood can stain the fairy tale when all the characters are made of wood. Schoenberg's last experiment with trephination is the Third String Quartet (1927), although there is a programmatic description of a doctor's hypodermic needle entering his heart, after a nearly fatal attack, in the String Trio (1946).[11] Of the Third Quartet's first movement, Schoenberg wrote:

> As a little boy I was tormented by a picture of a scene of a fairytale [called] "Das Gespensterschiff" (The Ghostship), whose captain had been nailed through the head to the topmast by his rebellious crew. I am

> sure that this was not the "program" of the first movement of the third string quartet. But it might have been, subconsciously, a very gruesome premonition which caused me to write this work, because as often as I thought about this movement, that picture came to my mind. I am afraid a psychologist might use this story as a stepping-stone for premature conclusions. Being only an illustration of the emotional background of this movement, it will not furnish enlightenment of the structure.[12]

Despite Schoenberg's discouragement, I am tempted to hear in the movement's first theme—a chattering melody in accented eighth notes—a representation of the light, incessant strokes of the crew's hammer; and in the second theme, a woeful falling motif in sustained notes, a representation of the captain's wailing. But in any case Schoenberg has used this grisly picture only to stimulate his imagination; the movement obeys the strict formality of the sonata (as Schoenberg reconceived it), and no untoward event, no cerebral accident, disrupts the neat flow of the music.

In fact, the reader of Schoenberg's essays would scarcely suspect that Schoenberg the musician ever attempted any sort of violence or electrical discharge or experimentation with the dangerously vivid. But this is perhaps not odd, for Schoenberg was accused in public of such musical insanity that it is to be expected that he would display himself as a sober, conservative, unsparing yet benign man. And yet one can find a few passages in Schoenberg's prose in which the usual self-publicity and caution and sarcasm disappear, and Schoenberg reveals the composer struck dumb before the inexpressible revelation—the same picture as that of *Die glückliche Hand*:

> In Divine Creation there were no details to be carried out later; "There was Light" at once and in its ultimate perfection. Alas, human creators, if they be granted a vision, must travel the long path between vision and accomplishment: a hard road where, driven out of Paradise, even geniuses must reap their harvest in the sweat of their brows.
>
> Alas, it is one thing to envision in a creative instant of inspiration and it is another thing to materialize one's vision by painstakingly connecting details until they fuse into a kind of organism.
>
> Alas, suppose it becomes an organism, a homunculus or a robot, and possesses some of the spontaneity of a vision: it remains yet another thing to organize this form so that it becomes a comprehensible message "to whom it may concern."[13]

This system of metaphors governs much of Schoenberg's thinking: musical structure, the succession of notes in time, is a physical body, intricate, fascinating, but ultimately of no value except insofar as it can point beyond itself to something psychic, immaterial, instantaneous, all white light. What Schoenberg wishes to convey is not the clever articulation of his golem, its obliging eagerness to haul water or dance, but instead the divine breath that animates it, as if the subject of a musical composition were neither its themes nor its development, but Inspiration itself.

In an early aphorism Schoenberg says that "the work of art is a labyrinth, at every point of which the initiate knows the entrance and exit,"[14] in which even false paths and digressions lead toward the proper goal. Again we see the same emphasis on indications—a multitude of arrows and cues pointing every which way but somehow also all pointing in the same direction. There is something gnostic in these doctrines, and, though Schoenberg is indeed a keen investigator of harmony, technique, and sound color, we should not forget that to his ear even the most delicate, subtle, uncanny combination of sound is still somewhat heavy, lumpish; he musters every technique known and invents what was not employed before, only that he may pass beyond technique, rid himself of all baggage. Schoenberg even has a certain contempt for the purely aural aspects of music—timbre, instrumentation, the blandishments of sound:

> I am much less irritated than amused by the critical remark of one Dr. X, who says that I do not care for "sound."
>
> "Sound," once a dignified quality of higher music, has deteriorated in significance since skillful workmen—orchestrators—have taken it in hand with the definite and undisguised intention of using it as a screen behind which the absence of ideas will not be noticeable. Formerly, sound had been the radiation of an intrinsic quality of ideas, powerful enough to penetrate the hull of the form.
>
> Nothing could radiate which was not light itself; and here only ideas are light.[15]

Here it seems that music and those notes that alone can convey music have little to do with each other. If the composer lacks the single-minded vision of some exterior goal toward which all the players' gestures point, then the audience hears only noise, a dead husk: the "robot" is only a heap of tin, after all, unless a spark of inspiration animates him.

Schoenberg's habitual violations and supersessions of the received rules of the art, in order to surpass "music" entirely in favor of something more electrical, are attempts to realize a music in which the hearer's primary experience is not of sound but of light; all is trivial that does not resemble the glare of the sun. No wonder such a composer would include a color organ in the score of *Die glückliche Hand* or would, in his 1938 setting of the *Kol Nidre*, require a narrator to intone the words "Let there be light!" above a single flexatone trill of such intensity that you might feel there's a whirligig inside your head, eating your eyes away.

> Let there be light! Out of space a flame burst forth. God crushed that light to atoms. Myriads of sparks are hidden in our world, but not all of us behold them.

It is the task of the composer to seek out these sparks, engage and enfold them in the casing of musical form for public display, for the enlightenment of the unrepentant.

The sound and the substance do not matter. Another who agreed with Schoenberg's philosophy was Kandinsky: and around 1912 the men felt that they were twins of a sort. Kandinsky thought that Schoenberg's music bore the closest analogy to his own aesthetic goals; as he says in *Concerning the Spiritual in Art*, Schoenberg "leads us into a realm where musical experience is a matter not of the ear but of the soul alone":

> To those who are not accustomed to it the inner beauty appears as ugliness because humanity in general inclines to the outer and knows nothing of the inner. Almost alone in severing himself from conventional beauty is the Austrian composer, Arnold Schoenberg. He says in his *Harmonielehre*: "Every combination of notes, every advance is possible, but I am beginning to feel that there are also definite rules and conditions which incline me to the use of this or that dissonance."[16]

Schoenberg's music records the very motions of the spirit, untrammeled by the usual apparatus of form and harmony: and, like Adorno after him—Adorno's favorite descriptor of Schoenberg is "seismographic," suggesting a vibrating needle registering deep tremors of affect—Kandinsky feels that a certain superficial ugliness results from extreme psychic delicacy, unconventional self-expression. Here the artist feels a certain horror at contaminating his vision with paintbrush or instrumental sound; and ugliness, external ugliness, becomes a proof of honesty, a kind of badge that proves to the world the artist's contempt for his material medium.

Kandinsky was a playwright as well as a painter—if the material medium means little or nothing, versatility comes easily—and in 1912 he sent Schoenberg the text of his newly written play *Der gelbe Klang* (The Yellow Sound), an abstract, nearly dehumanized play in which cucumbers sway on stage to the accompaniment of music full of minor seconds. Schoenberg liked the play and wrote back that artists ought to be in the business of making puzzles—if God is the ultimately incomprehensible, then the making of incomprehensible or half-comprehensible art could bring us closer to him:

> It is exactly the same as what I have striven for in my *Glückliche Hand*, only you go still further than I in the renunciation of any conscious thought, any conventional plot. That is naturally a great advantage. We must become conscious that there are puzzles around us. And we must find the courage to look these puzzles in the eye without timidly asking about "the solution." It is important that our creation of such puzzles mirror the puzzles with which we are surrounded, so that our soul may endeavor—not to solve them—but to decipher them. What we gain thereby should not be the solution, but a new method of coding or decoding. The material, worthless in itself, serves in the creation of new puzzles. For the puzzles are an image of the ungraspable. And imperfect, that is, a human image. But if we can only learn from them to consider the ungraspable as possible, we get nearer to God, because we no longer demand to understand him.[17]

Kandinsky was excited by this letter and replied immediately that behind the seeming anarchy of his paintings and dissonance of Schoenberg's music there was a higher order:

> This is what people call "anarchy," by which they understand a kind of lawlessness (since they still see only one side of the Ten Commandments) and by which they must come to understand order (in art, construction), but one which has its roots in another sphere.—Briefly stated, there is a law which is millions of kilometers distant from us, towards which we strive for thousands of years, of which we have a presentiment, which we guess, apparently see clearly, and therefore give various forms. Thus is the evolution of "God," religion, science, art.[18]

Kandinsky describes God's law as infinitely distant from the struggling artist, whose organizational principles are dim and distorted images of God's law, sensed somewhere beyond the solar system. This thought of Kandinsky's is closely related to a passage in Schoenberg's unfinished oratorio *Die Jakobsleiter* (Jacob's Ladder, 1917–22), in which the angel Gabriel says to a soul struggling toward God:

> Tritt näher du, der auf mittlerer Stufe
> ein Abbild ist und den Glanz besitzt;
> der einem Viel-Höheren ähnlich ist,
> wie dem Grundton der ferne Oberton;
> während andere, tiefere, selbst fast Grundtöne,
> ihm, wie der helle Bergkristall,
> fremder sind, als Kohle dem Diamanten!
>
> You on the middle level, step closer,
> who are a likeness and possess the radiance;
> who are similar to one Much Higher
> as the distant overtone is similar to the fundamental;
> while others, deeper, themselves almost fundamentals,
> are more foreign to him, as the bright rock crystal
> is more foreign to diamond than coal is.

Jacob's ladder is a *Tonleiter*, a scale: and God is the limit point at the top of the overtone series. But the highest overtone is like the fundamental: Schoenberg intuits a convergence between the highest and lowest—the first man is made, after all, in God's image. Coal and diamonds are both forms of carbon. Schoenberg's dissonances can be used to grasp two opposite areas of taboo, the lowest of the low, the Freudian id, as in *Erwartung*, and the highest of the high, God, as in *Die Jakobsleiter*. This is the most radical of his musical monisms.

It is fascinating to see how abruptly, after the so-called free-atonal period of 1908–13, Schoenberg reorganizes the domain of his musical investigations from the deep body and the Freudian unconscious to the crystalline spheres of the divine. In Mann's *Doktor Faustus*, Leverkühn writes an *Apocalypsis* oratorio in which the same music is used, in altered forms, to present hell and heaven—the tornado of hellish laughter and the glassy children's chorus singing the music of the spheres are mysteriously one; and this is a good insight into Schoenberg's own musical semantics. In 1912 he tended to think of a musical composition as an human body—for example, he writes that in a rondo (a composition in which a main theme is presented in the context of a pattern of symmetrical digressions) the principal theme is like blood, circulating everywhere: "Blood is present throughout, whereas eyes, arms, legs, etc., occur merely twice, so here, too, the subordinate status of the merely auxiliary organs is expressed in the form of less prolific repetition."[19] But by 1923 he mocks the followers of Richard Strauss, who compose psychological music:

> I hear that the young call their music "psychological" music. This supposedly means its effect is to be purely on the nerves. But the only changes needed for that would not be in the music, but in the nerves. One cuts them off from the rest of the personality, and henceforth the oldest and newest music alike will merely tinkle in the ears—nobody will have to think about an artist any more. That is easy enough, but I find it correspondingly difficult to think how to produce the necessary music. Imagine the X-rays it will need to use, if its own effect is to be limited to the lower half of the mind. Or, since the complete personality turns away these rays, are they supposed to stop short in monstrous disorder? What sort of parts must one write to achieve this?[20]

But Schoenberg's own *Erwartung* is, one might think, addressed to the "lower half of the mind," maybe to the lowest one-tenth. The quick of music may lie in the deep body, or in the soul caught up in divine revelation, or in some strange place that is both at once.

I think that *Erwartung* has a body, but it is not the sort of body we are used to. It is a body without arms or legs or eyes or any other symmetrical feature, because nothing is paired, nothing is repeated. What makes it hard to listen to is precisely that nothing is repeated. Schoenberg's ear became bored more easily than that of any before him. What most angers him about Debussy, about Wagner, about any composer, is excessive repetition—he even criticizes a lovely inspiration from *Tristan und Isolde* ("Befehlen liess dem Eigenholde") because the second half of the phrase is sequentially derived from the first.[21] In his own works from 1908 until the Great War he composes music of endless melody, endlessly shifting harmony, in which no note can be felt as a consequence of the notes before it, according to usual principles of consequence. (There are a few pseudo-sequences in *Erwartung*, however: when the Woman calls out "Ist hier jemand? Ist hier jemand?" [Is anyone here? Is anyone here?], the second cry repeats, inexactly, the phrase shape of the first—as if, at the one moment when a public world is in danger of obtruding on private rhapsody, Schoenberg hints at a more public, familiar kind of musical discourse.) Every bar is a new event or bears only the traces of its evolution within itself. When Mann's Leverkühn invents the aphorism—it was actually invented by Adorno—that art would like to stop being pretense and play, *Schein und Spiel*, and instead become knowledge, it is a motto appropriate to Schoenberg's atonal works, which suppress any feeling of play by the sheer novelty of gesture, perfect irregularity of form. What has no discernible rules cannot be a game.

This unpredictability is also responsible for the nervous quality of the music; what Schoenberg represents in the "body" of such a composition as *Erwartung* is chiefly a web of nerves, responding to a near-random succession of shocks and cries, which may be self-induced or may be inflicted from without, though one cannot know, since we have only the flayed skin. Thus Adorno finds a new "reality" in Schoenberg's work, the fairy tale disfigured by something welling from beneath. Schoenberg seems to cut beneath illusion, to approach his goal, his central idea, not by means of some carefully articulated structure of repetition and digression, but by some higher nakedness, some higher immediacy; *Erwartung* does not point to something beyond itself—it *is* that thing. The chromatic smear at its conclusion is a declaration of some greater existential fullness than was previously available to art. If all notes are played at once, then the composer has gone far toward making art *be*. The labyrinth is razed, exploded; one need not search for the thread that displays entrance and exit, for one is already outside, in the empty air.

Erwartung may succeed as a drama, but as magic it fails; the barrier between the artist and audience remains, and we know that the gooseflesh is on someone's skin but only vicariously on our own. Adorno has a shrewd critique of the aesthetic by which art attempts to be more real than reality: "Since the work cannot, after all, be reality, the elimination of all illusory aspects brings out all the more glaringly the illusory aspect of its existence."[22] If a demented biologist were to sew bat's wings and a goat's head onto a lizard and then teach the poor creature to flap and yowl, the chimera would not become less chimerical for being real; art can't grow so substantial, so insistent, to be such an exact representation of body or mind that it can become objective in the way that natural things are objective. Art's claim to uncontingent reality may always be doubtful; but Schoenberg's lifelong quest for the real, the setting out in music of the authentic cry, the decisive spasm of light, is no less moving for that necessary unfulfillment.

I suspect that Schoenberg tired of writing physiologically engorged, psychopathologically intense music because he felt that he had reached a barrier beyond which he could not go, and because the devices he used for conveying shock started to lose their efficacy. The tension of the music can be heightened and heightened and heightened by harmonic means, but eventually the discord begins to rest more easily on the ear, and the music starts to slacken, to lose the illusion that it is representing a mind screwed to the breaking point by terror. This is a corollary to the phenomenon Schoenberg called "the emancipation of the dissonance": the familiarization of the dissonance—the ear's acclimatizing itself to minor seconds, major sevenths, augmented fourths, the classical discords. The *diabolus in musica*, when confronted head-on, begins to smile; his horns shorten, his face grows less red, he begins a little shuffle and song. Every resource of dissonance is deployed to evoke the physical edge of horror on the audience, the slow bristling, the sudden start; yet after a while the audience begins to hear the music not as the representation of a crazy mind, but as music again, intelligible though strange sounds, descant and melody. The artifice of art, the musicality of music, according to the paradox of mimesis, will reassert itself most strongly when the art is most contorted into a means for representation. *Erwartung*, when stripped of its aesthetic, its rationale, relapses at last into the lyrical: it converges with that to which it seemed so fundamentally opposed, the mad scene of *Lucia di Lammermoor*. Each is unreally real, really unreal. Such is the monism of music.

One of Schoenberg's first desires after composing *Erwartung* was to justify it, in his *Harmonielehre* (1911); and the principal movement of his imagination for the next ten years is to turn away from psychological representation to other tactics for embodying the unnameable, the inspiration, the idea. One celebrated trial was the *Six Little Piano Pieces*, op. 19 (1911), each of which lasts about one minute; this extreme brevity shows the composer's unwillingness to tamper with, extend, play upon, or in any way develop the austere impulse behind the composition, its idea. In the case of Schoenberg's great pupil Anton Webern this utter concision of gesture became the predominant feature of his career; but Schoenberg's quickly abandoned this miniaturism. The music of the mid- to late 1910s is, with the great exception of the *Four Orchestral Songs*, op. 22 (1913–16), less decisive and accomplished than the style of the free-atonal period, 1908–13; the period is dominated by the unfinished Swedenborgian oratorio *Die Jakobsleiter*, by the interruption of World War I, by religious and artistic meditation, by performance and pedagogy.

The breakthrough, the discovery of the method of composing in twelve tones, occurred in the summer of 1921. A piece of music should be governed in every detail, except perhaps rhythm, by a single sequence of the twelve notes of the chromatic scale, called the tone row; and no note may recur until the row has completed itself. The row may be segmented and arrayed into any pattern of chords—two chords of six notes each, or three of four notes each, and so forth—but the principle of plenitude takes precedence over any principle of hierarchy, of tonic governance; chromatic saturation has been promoted from intuition into law. Melodies may be generated from any segment of the row, or by playing the row backward, or by inverting it, or by playing its inversion backward; thus, a tone row is fourfold, a magic square, like the arithmetical squares in which the numbers in every horizontal or vertical row add up to the same sum—the squares that so bemuse the young Leverkühn in Mann's *Doktor Faustus*.

This system of composition, so indifferent to any given tonality, so mathematically defensible, so equanimous, held many kinds of fascinations for Schoenberg. It offered a technique by which music could be left available to extension in time, investigation of melodic possibility, exploration at leisure of the tensions inherent in the design of intervals in the row, yet a technique that in no way distorted or compromised its *donnée*, its idea—a technique in which nothing is superfluous because every combination of sounds can be justified as a permutation of the basic row. Indeed, part of the danger of the system is that one might seem that a strict practitioner can't write bad music; the system offers a magical combination of effortless economy and effortless elaboration. And so Schoenberg repeatedly insisted that the usual virtues of imagination, clarity, tact, and structural acumen were as necessary in twelve-tone as in traditional music.

The peril that the *Six Little Piano Pieces* seemed to suggest, the fear that the quest for spiritual realism, the most severe possible presentation of the idea, would demand such brevity that music would exhaust itself in a single telling instant, contract to zero, is thus avoided by a clever tactic. Music may expand itself—Schoenberg was uneasy about the word "develop," which evidently suggests a condition in which the goal of the music is not inherent within it but imposed by force, by the composer's trickery—for minutes, hours, in which the composer's invention, as long as it obeys the one law, is free to play to his or her heart's content, to make every alteration and extravagance. Even the smallest units of a given composition contain, then, an entire realization of the composition's idea; and this omnipresence of fulfillment satisfies Schoenberg's profound desire for spiritual justification, a music Earthless, without tonic gravity, a long unfolding in outer space of something simple and supreme.

In his important essay "Composition with Twelve Tones" (1941), Schoenberg makes clear the superior claim to reality of the new music:

> *the unity of musical space demands an absolute and unitary perception.* In this space, as in Swedenborg's heaven (described in Balzac's *Seraphita*) there is no absolute down, no right or left, forward or backward. Every musical configuration, every movement of tones has to be comprehended primarily as a mutual relation of sounds, of oscillatory vibrations, appearing at different places and times. To the imaginative and creative faculty, relations in the material sphere are as independent from directions or planes as material objects are, in their sphere, to our perceptive faculties. Just as our mind always recognizes, for instance, a knife, a bottle or a watch, regardless of its position, and can reproduce it in the imagination in every possible position, even so a musical creator's mind can operate subconsciously with a row of tones, regardless of their direction, regardless of the way in which a mirror might show the mutual relations, which remain a given quality.[23]

Just as an object in three-dimensional space is independent of the coordinate system by which alone it can be apprehended—a bottle is still a bottle whether it is upside down or right side up, in Cambridge or Vladivostok or in orbit around the earth—so the tone row is independent of and inherent in its incarnations, whether its statement is in the original form or in its inversion or in its retrograde or in its retrograde inversion. In fact, there is no good reason for calling any one of the four the "straight" or "prime" version; all possible formulations and aspects of a given row are equally just, equally valid. As Adorno says, deprecating the monotony, the "magnificent failure" of the twelve-tone style, "Each entry of the row is 'the' row, just as good as the previous one, none more and none less."[24] But Adorno does not seem to understand that this evenness, this blandness of texture, is part of the explicit aesthetic of such "spiritual" music. The "body" of the music, its realization in instrumental or vocal sounds, has dwindled to transparency; since every two or four or six measures brings a new restatement of the row, the music simply presents an ever-changing succession of new avatars, each as important as the last, each as unimportant as the last, and the listener is moved to contemplate no single acoustic representation but the underlying idea, everywhere immanent, subsistent, inviolate. Twelve-tone music, therefore, is an attempt to reach the condition of light, to demonstrate the triviality of everything that is not idea. The strictness of method belies the contempt it expresses for methodology; one might say that Schoenberg deifies technique in order to abolish it.

In music of this degree of purity, of formlessness, in which all form is simply an accretion of replication, in which it is almost fair to say that all pieces of music based on the same row are the same piece of music, independent of style, seemingly independent of the composer himself, how is it possible to speak of self-expression? Webern exclaimed in 1932 about the method of composition with twelve tones that "there will no longer be any possible distinction between science and inspired creation. The further one presses forward, the greater becomes the identity of everything, and finally we have the impression of being faced by a work not of man but of Nature."[25] But if the spheres of the heavens have been given a singing voice, if Newton's laws have been trained to speak, is not individual emotion, human declamation, necessarily excluded?

> Zählt man seine Silben nach, so sind es zwölf, und alle zwölf Töne der chromatischen Skala sind ihm gegeben. . . . Es liegt zum Grunde allem, was da klingt . . . zu einer Formveranstaltung von letzter Rigorosität, die nichts Unthematisches mehr kennt, in der die Ordnung des Materials total wird. . . . Sie dient jedoch nun einem höheren Zweck, denn, o Wunder und tiefer Dämonenwitz!—vermöge der Restlosigkeit der Form eben wird die Musik als Sprache befreit. In einem gewissen, gröberen und tonmateriellen Sinn ist die Arbeit ja abgetan, ehe die Komposition nur anhebt, und diese kann sich nun völlig ungebunden ergehen, das heißt: sich dem Ausdruck überlassen. . . . Der Schöpfer . . . kann sich, in dem vororganisierten Material, hemmungslos, unbekümmert um die schon vorgegebene Konstruktion, der Subjektivität überlassen, und so ist dieses sein strengstes Werk, ein Werk äußerster Kalkulation, zugleich rein expressiv. Das zurückgehen auf Monteverdi and den Stil seiner Zeit ist eben das, was ich dir "Rekonstruktion des Ausdrucks" nannte—des Ausdrucks in seiner Erst- und Urerscheinung, des Ausdrucks als Klage.
>
> Aufgeboten werden nun alle Ausdrucksmittel jener emanzipatorischen Epoche, von denen ich die Echo-Wirkung schon nannte. . . . Man hat da den tief aufholenden Seufzer . . . die melodische Chromatik, das bange Gesamtschweigen von einem Phrasenanfang, Wiederholungen wie in jenem "Lasciatemi," die Dehnung von Silben, fallende Intervalle, absinkende Deklamation.[26]

> If you count the syllables, there are twelve, and all twelve notes of the chromatic scale are given to it. . . . It is the basis of everything you hear . . . an organization of form rigorous to the last degree, no longer admitting anything unthematic, in which the order of the material becomes total. . . . But now it serves a higher purpose; for—O wonder, O deep demonic joke!—the very all-encompassingness of the form makes possible the liberation of the music as speech. In a certain rough sense the work is done, with respect to the sound material, before the composition even begins, and this can now go on completely unconstrained: that is, it can abandon itself to expression. . . . The creator . . . can, in the preorganized material, uninhibited, untroubled by the already given structure, abandon himself to subjectivity; and so this, his strictest work, a work of the utmost calculation, is at the same time purely expressive. The return to Monteverdi and the style of his time is just what I called "the reconstruction of expression," expression in its first and primal manifestation, expression as lament.
>
> Now are summoned up all the means of expression of that emancipatory epoch, of which I have already mentioned the echo-effect. . . . We have the deep-heaved sigh . . . melodic chromaticism, the anxious general silence at the beginning of a phrase, repetitions such as in that "Lasciatemi," the stretching-out of syllables, falling intervals, drooping declamation.

But this is not a description of Schoenberg's art; it is Mann's description of Adrian Leverkühn's final masterpiece, the Faustus oratorio, from *Doktor Faustus*. This is indeed a way by which the rigidities of twelve-tone music could turn supple, rhetorical, expressive; but it is not usually Schoenberg's way. The melting, the madrigal passions of Monteverdi—the sighs, the suspensions, the chromatic intensity of his setting of Ariadne's lament ("Lasciatemi morire" [Let me die])—while technically feasible, would work against the disembodied quality, the calm luminosity, that the serial style was to some extent manufactured to convey. Behind Leverkühn's oratorio, as so often in *Doktor Faustus*, one hears the nostalgia of Mann and Adorno for a less barbaric and artificial century, a music that would naturally evolve back to nature; but for Schoenberg the natural, the physiologically expressive, is vain unless it is a realization of the supernatural. Schoenberg does not want to address his music to the nerves.

And yet Schoenberg insisted, both early and late in his career, that self-expression is the primary purpose of art; as he says in his long essay of 1948 on Mahler, the first draft of which was written in 1912, "In reality, there is only one greatest goal towards which the artist strives: *to express himself*."[27] But it is hard to see how Schoenberg plans to achieve this goal in the face of the increasingly antipsychological tendency of his music; if the acoustic vehicle of the idea does not matter very much and the idea is only an abstract redistribution of the chromatic scale, then how is the self of Arnold Schoenberg to leak into his compositions?

One solution was the composition of an opera, *Von heute auf morgen* (From Today to Tomorrow, 1928), which tells a recognizable anecdote from Schoenberg's marriage; in fact, the libretto for this little comedy of flirtation was written by Schoenberg's wife. It bears an odd similarity of intent to Richard Strauss's domestic opera *Intermezzo* (1924), in which the baritone singing the autobiographical part of the conductor wore a mask of Strauss's face onstage.

But the most ambitious solution to the problem of self-expression in the twelve-tone style is found in the work of Schoenberg's that most moves me, *Moses und Aron* (1930–32): Moses, the major role in the opera, is a speaking voice, while all the other roles are sung. Instead of the method of Leverkühn's Faustus oratorio, in which the expressiveness is made integral with the music, Schoenberg relegates his protagonist to a separate kingdom, in perpetual anguish at his own incompetence of expression, while the music goes its own way, fluent, dramatic, sensuous, vivid. In the speech of Moses—it is carefully notated *Sprechstimme*, half-sung in an imitation of a rising and falling voice, but never lyrical—we hear the usual declamatory devices of classical rhetoric, expostulation, sighing, cries of anger, sometimes uttered clearly and impressively but often thrown away in a stuttering, mumbled undertone beneath the long melodies that ignore him, rapt in their own beauty. The effect of this disjunction is completely original in musical drama; it is nothing at all like the melodrama of earlier composers, Gomatz's entrance in Mozart's *Zaide* or the duet between Leonora and Rocco in act 2 of Beethoven's *Fidelio* (not to mention full-scale melodramas, such as Georg Benda's 1779 *Pygmalion*, or Zdeněk Fibich's 1891 *Hippodamia*—operas for spoken voice), in which the orchestra intensifies the emotion of the spoken line it so tactfully interrupts. Instead the music proceeds in deliberate nonresponse to Moses's plaints and summonses, while it swells and heightens the feelings of Aron, the high priest, the Israelite orgiasts, and everyone else in the opera.

Expression, then, works in two distinct ways in *Moses und Aron*: according to the traditional operatic means, by which all affect veers into beauty (as in the florid coloratura of Aron, a Donizettian tenor) or into choral affirmations of mass power; and according to the outrageous grumbling of Moses, whose expression is often a disparagement of the whole notion of expression, a complaint over the defectiveness of his own mouth and of human speech in general.

It is true that Moses is permitted once in the opera to sing; but what he sings—"Reinige dein Denken, lös es von Wertlosem, weihe es Wahrem" (Purify your thinking, free it from worthless things, consecrate it to truth)—could be paraphrased to mean, in context, Shut up. Aron is appointed to be Moses's mouth; but Moses is so appalled by what he hears this mouth sing that he is continually waging war against it, simultaneously working to utter God's will and to retract it as soon as it is uttered, to sing and to abolish song. By his insistence on speech Moses calls attention to the artifice, the threadbareness, the conventionality of song; it is as if he were pushing over the cardboard palm tree, denying the virtue of theater, of music, of representation. This is a method by which an artist can obtain a sudden effect of the accession of reality: to incorporate into his art a built-in disillusionment, to erect a structure of artifice only so that the audience may marvel at its collapse.

No reteller of the story of Moses could dramatize Moses's reluctance more effectively than Schoenberg. The opera opens with Moses crying out to the burning bush, "Einziger, ewiger, allgegenwärtiger, unsichtbarer und unvorstellbarer Gott!" (Single, eternal, all-present, invisible, and unrepresentable God!); and the last thing Moses wants is to be the representative of the unrepresentable God. The voice of the burning bush—which Schoenberg represents by six singers and six speaking voices, intoning, sounding, and resounding in a delirium of awe, an effect of sober eeriness designed to suggest by the overlapping of speech and song a condition beyond either, an inexpressible godhead—instructs Moses to free his people, to be a model to them; but Moses's feeling of laborious inadequacy makes painful interruptions: "Ich bin alt; lass mich in Ruhe meine Schafe weiden . . . Meine Zunge ist ungelenk: ich kann denken, aber nicht reden" (I am old; let me graze my sheep in peace . . . my tongue is stiff: I can think, but not speak). The central problem of the opera is simple: the divine idea seems to demand expression, fulfillment, the righteous man as a model to his people; but that expression, when it takes place, is always partial, tainted, oversimplified, corrupt.

This is why the opera makes such a rigorous separation of Moses and Aron; Schoenberg must somehow show the discrepancy between thought and expression, dramatize the inadequacy of the dramatic method, have his music and abolish it. Moses is given a commandment he cannot obey; and, though Schoenberg insisted that the subject of his opera was religious philosophy, not an allegory of the artist,[28] artists are nevertheless in an analogous position to prophets, according to Schoenberg: they are commanded to convey their inspiration, but they can't obey the command without falsifying their idea.

Schoenberg's career is a continual tension between the construction of elaborate musical devices designed to point to the idea beyond, labyrinths that indicate entrance and exit, and an impatient desire to supersede all artifice and mediation, to burst forth in flame with the inspiration in itself; between the slow assembly of glass and tungsten into a light bulb and the direct utterance of "Fiat lux"; between Aron and Moses. According to Moses, Aron made a great error when he struck the rock with his rod instead of simply commanding the rock to give forth water (act 3, scene 1); to Moses, the use of physical mediation is a betrayal of the stark communion of man and God, the rapture of trance.

Despite his pragmatism, his demagoguery, his facility, Aron is still a figure of power; I don't think Schoenberg intends all virtue to be on Moses's side. Aron represents the principle of the validity of analogies, representations, images; his arias overflow with metaphors and ornaments, just as their musical content is a tissue of continual restatement, transposition by mirror and crab, of the basic row of the opera. Moses says at the end, when Aron is a prisoner, that, although words and images have run away from Aron, he nonetheless remains, living in his images (act 3, scene 1); and apart from this dwelling-in-images, this pictorial quality, Aron is nothing. Indeed, Aron dies when Moses tells the soldiers to release him—"Gebt ihn frei, und wenn er es vermag, so lebe er" (Set him free, and if he can, let him live)—because an image cannot survive without something to be an image of; no image can be self-sufficient. Yet while he was Moses's mouth he was impressive in his ceaseless outpouring of representations; the celebrated miracles of the story, all of which are performed by Aron in Schoenberg's version, are simply stiff, overliteral enactments of metaphors. When Aron turns Moses's rod into a snake (act 1, scene 4), it is a rhetorical device to illustrate a point and strike the gullible with awe: "In Moses Hand ein starrer Stab: das Gesetz; in meiner Hand die bewegliche Schlange: die Klugheit" (In Moses's hand a rigid rod: the law; in my hand the flexible serpent: cunning). The inconceivable God of Moses, who does not answer prayer or reward devotion or acknowledge offerings, is rejected by the Israelites; the plastic, discreet, responsive deity presented by Aron is more acceptable to them. Aron is a master of conjurer's tricks, of theater; but to Moses all this suppleness, this transformation, this instability, this metamorphosis is mere illusion, deceitful charm. Behind Aron's slick metaphors, the law—like Moses's rod, like the twelve tones of the row—was never altered in the first place, eternally defined beyond alteration. In the second of the *Six Pieces for Male Chorus* (1930), written at the same time he was working on *Moses und Aron*, Schoenberg says about the relation between law and miracle:

> Wenns so kommt, wie man es gewöhnt ist,
> ists in Ordnung: das kann man verstehn.
> Kommt es aber anders, ist es ein Wunder.
>
> Jedoch bedenke nur:
> daß es immer gleich kommt,
> das ist doch das Wunder,
> das dir unbegreiflich scheinen sollte:
> daß es ein Gesetz gibt,
> dem die Dinge so gehorchen,
> wie du deinem Herrn,
> das den Dingen so gebietet,
> wie dir dein Herr:
>
> When things go in the way we're used to,
> all's in order; we can understand that.
> But when things go otherwise, it's a miracle.
>
> Yet, just think about it:
> that things go the same way,
> *that* is the miracle
> that should seem incomprehensible:
> that there is one law,
> and all things obey,
> As you obey your lord?

This is exactly the Mosaic position: that we derive sustenance, comfort, from the cosmic rigidity of the law; the miraculous is an intolerable violation.

Yet the brilliant play and the specious analogies of Aron are necessary in the scheme of the opera. If the twelve-tone series—the abstract series prior to any sensuous realization in voice or orchestra—is like God, as David Levin and others have suggested, then the opera itself is like the golden calf:

> *Aron.* Gebilde der höchsten Phantasie, wie dankt sie dir's, dass du sie reizest zu bilden!
>
> *Moses.* Kein Bild kann dir ein Bild geben vom Unvorstellbaren.
>
> *Aron.* Shape of the highest fantasy, how it thanks you that you charm it into an image!
>
> *Moses.* No image can give you an image of the unrepresentable. (act 1, scene 2)

To some extent both Moses and Aron are right. If the primary impulse of the opera is iconoclastic, then one needs to construct the image before one can smash it. The image may be fleeting, unstable, provisional, a parody, but an artist has no other recourse; without images there can be no opera, no music, only private uncommunicable meditation. Moses's chastity of intellect is only meaningless refusal to speak, without the contrast of Aron's too-easy expressiveness. Though Aron compromises, takes satisfaction in half-truths and temporizing, he nevertheless is the avatar of imagination, of brotherly affection, of human fellow feeling. Moses, despite his hatred of the partial, is himself only a part of an ideal whole that comprises both Moses and Aron, like the quasi-Zionist Max Aruns (Moses-Aron) of Schoenberg's play *Der Biblische Weg* (The Biblical Way, 1926), who dies trying to establish a Jewish homeland in Africa but who nevertheless is simultaneously a visionary and a political organizer, the prophet and the voice. In a letter of March 25, 1933, Schoenberg says, "My Moses more resembles—of course only in outward aspect—Michelangelo's. He is not human at all."[29] Much that is valuable to Schoenberg is lacking in this horned, inhuman Moses, his stone shoulders poised to shatter from stress.

> Man hilft zur Welt dir kommen,
> Sei gesegnet!
> man gräbt ein Grab für dich,
> Ruhe sanft!
> man flickt die Wunden dir im Spital,
> Gute Bessrung!
> löscht dein Haus, zieht dich aus dem Wasser
> Fürchte nichts,

du hast selbst doch auch mit andern Mitleid!
Hilfe naht, du bist nicht allein!

We help with your birth,
Blessings on you!
we dig you a grave
Rest in peace!
in the hospital we tend your wounds,
Get well soon!
we save your burning house, pull you out of the water
Fear nothing,
You yourself have compassion for others!
Help is near, you are not alone!

This is the last of the *Six Pieces for Male Chorus*, one of the loveliest works Schoenberg ever wrote; and its humane gentleness shows the Aaronic side of the composer, his not unworthy concern for public welfare. Moses is opposed to human feeling; but a more balanced view might permit men to feel yet nevertheless to make strenuous objection to the deification of feeling.

When the dejected Israelites lose faith that Moses will return from the mountain and cry out for the slaughter of the priesthood, Aron agrees to build an idol, and they rejoice: "Juble, Israel! Götter, Bilder unsres Auges, Götter, Herren unsrer Sinne! . . . Deinen Göttern als Inhalt gabst du dein Innres, dein Lebensgefühl" (Rejoice, Israel! Gods, images for our eye, gods, lords of our senses! . . . To the gods you gave the main thing, your inner being, your feeling for life; act 2, scene 2). This is an intolerable mixing of the sensuous with the divine, a confusion that reaches its height when the seventy elders shout "Soul is sense" (act 2, scene 3); and Aron carries his ingenuity of metaphor to the point of blasphemy when he declares of the golden calf, "This image witnesses that a god lives in all things that exist. Unchangeable, like a law, is the material, the gold that you have given . . . the shape is secondary," a simile that turns the spiritual upside down and equates it with malleable gold.

The orgy that follows looses all restraint on feelings, looses a wilderness of music, so intense that you feel again how implicated music must be with the low, the carnal; the row becomes unintelligible in the incessant tumult of tiny fragments broken from it. Butchers dance with knives and toss out chunks of raw meat; rivers of wine are poured; everyone fornicates; but while the revelers exult, others simply commit suicide in a rapture of self-sacrifice.

> Menschentugend, kraftvoll, wiedererweckte:
> Ernst und Freude, Mass und Übermass,
> Frohsinn, Glück und Sehnsucht, Schwung und Ruhe, Besinnung.
> Gier, Entsagung, Geiz, Verschwendung und Habsucht,
> alles Schöne, Gute, Hässliche, Schlechte,
> Eigenlebens Zeugnis, wahrnehmbar, fühlbar.—
> Sinn schenkt Seele Sinn erst.
> Seele ist Sinn.

> Human virtue, full of power, reawakened:
> seriousness and joy, moderation and excess,
> gladness, happiness and yearning, vigor and calm, reflectiveness,
> hunger, ascetism, greed, profligacy and envy,
> everything beautiful, good, ugly, bad,
> evidence of its own existence, perceivable, touchable.
> Sense first gives sense to soul.
> Soul is sense. (act 2, scene 3).

This is the affective equivalent of chromatic saturation, a rainbow of emotion; every human desire is put into play at once. Aron had hoped that feeling, affection could somehow elevate itself to God: "Der Allmächtige verwandelt Sand in Frucht, Frucht in Gold, Gold in Wonne, Wonne in Geist" (The Almighty transforms sand into fruit, fruit into gold, gold into joy, joy into spirit) (act 1, scene 4); this is the God of Aron, a God who is himself a magician, who guarantees the efficacy of the expression of idea and the reality of miracles. In a way Aron is correct, though the golden chain by which the Almighty hauls human feeling into heaven works more complexly than he supposes.

The orgy doesn't intensify into revelation; it simply exhausts itself, falls into stupor. This is how self-expression, the loosing of emotion, must necessarily operate, for priest, orgiast, and artist alike: the expression exhausts what it expresses and leaves a condition of peace. In the list of "powerful human virtues" cited above, a certain self-canceling effect is evident; and in the free expression of lust and temperance, greed and happy satisfaction, each virtue embraces its antonym, making a double annihilation, a calm neutrality. Aron's upward aspirations collapse in utter defeat; and Moses returns from the mountain, gesticulates, and destroys the golden calf with a great shout: "Vergeh, du Abbild des Unvermögens, das Grenzenlose in ein Bild zu fassen!" (Perish, you image of the impossibility of grasping the dimensionless in an image; act 2, scene 4). I take this as the proper formula for the opera itself: *Moses und Aron* is an image of imagelessness.

When the golden calf is made to disappear, the opera is almost ready to end. In the last scene of act 2 Aron and Moses comment upon what has happened—they are already somewhat removed from action, abstracted into recitative; and Aron, in his finest moment, uses Moses's own principles to refute him, leaving him powerless to defend himself:

> *Moses.* Dein Bild verblich vor meinem Wort!
> *Aron. (sehr ruhig, aber etwas zuversichtlicher)*
> Deinem Wort waren sonst Bilder und Wunder, die du missachtest, versagt.
> Und doch war das Wunder nicht mehr als ein Bild:
> als dein Wort mein Bild zerstörte.
>
> *Moses.* Your image faded at my word!
> *Aron. (very calmly, but somewhat more confidently)*
> At your word, the images and miracles that you despised broke down.
> And yet, when your word destroyed my image,
> that miracle was nothing more than an image. (act 2, scene 5)

Moses, the purifier, cannot justify the purity of his conduct; by taking an action, by destroying the golden calf, he has rendered himself complicit with gesture, miracle, image. The abolishing of a symbol is a form of symbolic action, a piece of self-conscious theater. But a darker tangle awaits him. Aron proves that the Ten Commandments, fashioned by God on Mount Sinai, are only an image; and Moses in despair shatters the tables of the law. Moses had not understood until this moment how extensive was the collusion between God and image; and it is with something akin to horror that he looks up and sees the Israelites singing joyfully, marching in a parade toward the Promised Land, led by a pillar of cloud by day, a pillar of fire by night, themselves images, always images.

Schoenberg wrote a brief third act, a single scene showing the triumph of Moses and the death of Aron, but he could not manage to set it to music, although he attempted it sporadically for twenty years; and it is perhaps as well that the opera ends where it does, with Moses's hopes collapsing soon after Aron's, the balance of power between the major characters intact:

> *Moses.* So habe ich mir ein Bild gemacht, falsch,
> wie ein Bild nur sein kann!
> So bin ich geschlagen!
> So war alles Wahnsinn, was ich gedacht habe,
> und kann und darf nicht gesagt werden!
> O Wort, du Wort, das mir fehlt!
>
> *Moses.* So I have made for myself an image, false,
> for an image can only be false!
> So I am struck down!
> So everything was madness,
> all that I have thought,
> and cannot and must not be spoken.
> O Word, you Word, that I lack! (act 2, scene 5)

These phrases, the last phrases of the opera, are declaimed against unison violins, playing with utmost urgency first the row, then the retrograde of the row, as the row seems to fold itself up again after its prolonged involvement with the human world, its teasing and shattering into musical expression, and retreat like the law back into heaven, lingering for a final moment on its first note as Moses contemplates the silence he has uttered.

Here everything leaves off. All strategies by which one tried to grasp the inconceivable have failed, the idol is properly destroyed, and yet stray images keep proliferating, as if by their own power, more rapidly than one can abolish them. The opera ends with a paradox, a sense of profusion and inadequacy, of revelation everywhere that does not quite add up to *the* revelation. It is impossible to know what to do; the commandment against graven images was itself a graven image and has annulled itself. The mechanism of the drama can be compared to that wind-up toy, a black box out of which, when one turns the switch on, a small hand reaches to turn the switch off; Schoenberg has made a gesture that is accomplished only for the sake of its own termination—he has designed a song that intensifies silence, that dramatizes its own poverty of expression. It is still a kind of self-expression, but a kind peculiar to Modernism.

In the same essay in which Schoenberg says that self-expression is the one greatest goal for any artist, he refines the concept of self-expression in an unusual manner: "There is only one content, which all men wish to express: the longing of mankind for its future form, for an immortal soul, for dissolution into the universe—the longing of this soul for its God";[30] and later in the essay he applauds Mahler for the high spirits of his First Symphony, the resignation of his Sixth Symphony, the glorification in the Eighth Symphony of the joys of a world already nearly abandoned, the pure impersonality of his Ninth Symphony, its "objective, almost passionless statement of a beauty which becomes perceptible only to one who can dispense with animal warmth and feels at home in spiritual coolness."[31] This is self-expression as Schoenberg understands it: you divest yourself of all feeling, expend yourself like the orgiasts before the golden calf, exhaust yourself of all that you are. Self-expression is self-sacrifice. The rest is silence. It is the final trick of art to be so openhanded about its own illusions, the limitations and failures of representation, that the spectator believes that what art hints at is more real than what it palpably depicts.

I believe that in all art self-expression and self-evasion constitute a single act, and Modernist artists consciously employed this double nature for complicated effects. Several of Schoenberg's essays—such as the Mahler essay and "Opinion or Insight?"—suggest that Schoenberg deliberately intended self-expression for the sake of self-surpassing, a self-expression that is conscious atonement, a preliminary to prayer. Mann and Adorno also agree that when subjectivity is raised beyond a certain level, it becomes objective; as Beethoven expanded and defined his personality through his middle period, it at last elaborated into a transpersonal myth—"Ausgeblasenheit, Ich-Verlassenheit . . . ein neues Verhältnis, von Tode bestimmt" (deflatedness, an abandonment of the *I* . . . a new relationship, determined by death).[32] I don't know that Beethoven would have agreed that this was his intention, but it is clearly the intention of Adrian Leverkühn, the Schoenberg surrogate of Mann's novel, whose last composition passes beyond the expressiveness of madrigal to an impersonal, inhuman despair:

> Hier, finde ich, gegen das Ende, sind die äußersten Akzente der Trauer erreicht, ist die letzte Verzweiflung Ausdruck geworden, und—ich will's nicht sagen, es hieße die Zugeständnislosigkeit des Werkes, einen unheilbaren Schmerz letzen, wenn man sagen wollte, es biete bis zur letzten Note irgend einen anderen Trost, als den, der im Ausdruck selbst und im Lautwerden,—also darin liegt, daß der Kreatur für ihr Weh überhaupt eine Stimme gegeben ist. Nein, dies dunkle Tongedicht läßt bis zuletzt keine Vertröstung, Versöhnung, Verklärung zu. Aber wie, wenn

> der künstlerischen Paradoxie, daß aus der totalen Konstruktion sich der Ausdruck—der Ausdruck als Klage—gebiert, das religiöse Paradoxon entspräche, daß aus tiefster Heillosigkeit, wenn auch als leiseste Frage nur, die Hoffnung keimte? Es wäre die Hoffnung jenseits der Hoffnungslosigkeit, die Transzendenz der Verzweiflung,—nicht der Verrat an ihr, sondern das Wunder, das über den Glauben geht. Hört nur den Schluß, hört ihn mit mir: Eine Instrumentalgruppe nach der anderen tritt zurück, und was übrig bleibt, womit das Werk verklingt, ist das hohe g eines Cello, das letzte Wort, der letzte verschwebende Laut, in pianissimo-Fermate langsam vergehend. Dann ist nichts mehr,—Schweigen und Nacht. Aber der nachschwingend im Schweigen hängende Ton, der nicht mehr ist, dem nur die Seele noch nachlauscht, und der Ausklang der Trauer war, ist nicht mehr, wandelt den Sinn, steht als ein Licht in der Nacht.[33]
>
> I find here, toward the end, the most acute accents of mourning are reached, the expression of the last despair achieves is done, and—I will not say it, it would gloss over the uncompromisingness of the work, its irremediable pain, if it were said that it offers, up to its last note, any other consolation than the consolation of expression itself, its becoming-sound,—the consolation that a creature is actually given a voice for its woe. No, up to the end this dark tone-poem allows no consolation, reconciliation, transfiguration. But what if the artistic paradox—that expression is born out of total constructedness—would correspond to the religious paradox, that out of the deepest state of unsalvation, a germ of hope might emerge, even if the question is only faintly asked? It would be but a hope beyond hopelessness, the transcendence of despair—not betrayal of it, but the miracle that surpasses belief. Now listen to the end, listen with me: one group of instruments after another steps back, and what remains, as the work fades out, is the high G of a cello, the last word, the last floating-off sound, slowly dying in a pianissimo fermata. Then nothing more: silence and night. But that tone, the after-vibration hanging in the silence, the tone that is no more, the tone that only the soul can strain to hear, the tone that was the final note of mourning, is no more, changes its meaning, stands as a light in the night.

It is similar to the end of *Moses und Aron*—it is only the difference between a cello's high G and a violin's low F♯—and something of this "transcendence of despair," this oddly affirmative sense of absence, silence, night, is, I think, present in Schoenberg's work. What this sort of art can do is to make absence explicit, manifest; to show the gap between what has been done and what is not doable; to illustrate the defectiveness of our state, our knowledge of what we lack: grace. The great discouragement to nineteenth-century art was its distrust of the intellect; the great discouragement to twentieth-century art was its distrust of art. To Schoenberg, the composer was a conscious trafficker in idols, and much of the oddity, the strain, of his development arises from his need to criticize his music in the very act of writing it, to attempt by a coup de théâtre to elevate music from idolatry to prayer. The Christian artist can also be led to similar conclusions. The motto of T. S. Eliot in "East Coker," "The poetry does not matter," is amplified in his "Little Gidding":

> You are here to kneel
> Where prayer has been valid. And prayer is more
> Than an order of words, the conscious occupation
> Of the praying mind, or the sound of the voice praying.
> And what the dead had no speech for, when living,
> They can tell you, being dead: the communication
> Of the dead is tongued with fire beyond the language of the living.

This admiration for the speech of the dead, who live in a perpetual Pentecost, who communicate telepathically without any intervening material medium, can only result in disparagement of poetry, of merely human art.

But Schoenberg is not as certain as Eliot is of the incompatibility of art and prayer. In several of the works that follow *Moses und Aron* he employs its basic combination of voices, namely a speaking voice, a chorus, and an orchestra. In two of these works, *Kol Nidre* (1938) and *A Survivor from Warsaw* (1947), the sufferings of humanity—in the case of the latter, from Nazi persecution—resolve at the end into a choral setting of actual Hebrew liturgy; abjection, misery, feeling heighten themselves into the traditional and impersonal consolation of prayer. To this extent Moses's inhumanness—his Michelangelesque largeness, loftiness—is not dogmatism or apathy but transpersonalness, a state of having perfected and surpassed the sensuous, the human. He does not repudiate affection—he is in the process of going beyond it. The golden calf is destroyed to remind Aron that the phenomenal world is not everything; and divinity makes itself apparent in tablet and pillar to remind Moses that the phenomenal world is not nothing.

In Schoenberg's last work, the *Modern Psalm* (1950), he seems to find a reconciliation of these warring opposites, a manner of prayer that is faithful to both human finitude and divine starkness:

O, Du mein Gott: alle Völker preisen Dich und versichern Dich ihrer Ergebenheit.

Was aber kann es Dir bedeuten, ob ich das auch tue oder nicht?

Wer bin ich, daß ich glauben soll, mein Gebet sei eine Notwendigkeit?

Wenn ich Gott sage, weiß ich, daß ich damit von dem Einzigen, Ewigen, Allmächtigen, Allwissenden und Unvorstellbaren spreche, von dem ich mir ein Bild weder machen kann noch soll.

An den ich keinen Anspruch erheben darf oder kann, der mein heißestes Gebet erfüllen oder nicht beachten wird.

Und trotzdem bete ich, wie alles Lebende betet; trotzdem erbitte ich Gnaden und Wunder: Erfüllungen.

Trotzdem bete ich, denn ich will nicht des beseligenden Gefühls der Einigkeit, der Verbindung mit Dir verlustig werden.

[O, Du mein Gott, deine Gnade hat uns das Gebet gelassen, als eine Verbindung, eine beseligende Verbindung mit Dir. Als eine Seligkeit, die uns mehr gibt, als jede Erfüllung.]

O, my Lord, every land praises you and assures you of its devotion.

But what does it mean to you, whether or not I do it, as well?

Who am I, that I should believe that my prayer is a necessity?

If I say God, do I know that I am, by saying this, speaking of the single, eternal, all-powerful, all-knowing and unimaginable one, of whom I neither can nor should make an image.

To whom I am not permitted or able to utter a demand, who will not notice or fulfill my warmest prayer.

Yet, despite this I pray, as every living thing prays; despite this I ask for favors and miracles: fulfillment. Despite this I pray, for I don't want to lose the bliss of unity, of connection with you.

[Oh, my Lord, your grace left us prayer as a bond, a joyous bond with you. As a blessedness that gives us more than any fulfillment.]

This piece, unlike any other in Schoenberg's canon, has the sound of the opening of *Moses und Aron*: a speaker solemnly intones in the foreground while a chorus makes complicated interweavings in the dark depths; in fact, the text, with its "single, eternal, all-powerful, all-knowing and unimaginable" God, is a close echo of what Moses says at the beginning of the opera. God is no nearer to the speaker of the psalm than he was to Moses; God still pays no attention to man, does not answer prayer, remains arbitrary and inconceivable. But all has changed. Moses had asked God to relieve him of responsibility, had interrupted, objected to the divine will; but here what the speaker says is identical to what the chorus sings in the background. It is as if Moses's speaking voice had joined in perfect distinctness, perfect unanimity into the six speakers and six singers who had represented the voice of the burning bush; this device is a musical representation of the unity, the communion with God that gives more than any fulfillment. Tacit Moses has found his voice, can declaim with his old vigor; but the message he speaks is the news of his own dissolution into the godhead. With his free will he abandons his old recalcitrance, chooses to obey, to find his peace in the divine will. Like the rabbi in Isaac Bashevis Singer's story who decides to live in unceasing fasting, atonement, flagellation, a perpetual Yom Kippur, and who justifies his behavior by calling it sheer selfishness and self-indulgence in what gives him pleasure, so Schoenberg seems to find all human feeling subordinate to the pleasure of orthodoxy of devotion; his aesthetic of self-expression demands the expression of this high selfishness.

Yet the *Modern Psalm* is not a full, harmonious solution to the aesthetic problems of Schoenberg's career: he never completed the music, which breaks off at the second appearance in the text of "Despite this I pray," as if a conclusive choral allegation of actual, available grace would violate a certain tact, would make the prayer too confident of its own successful in binding man to God. In the remaining months of his life Schoenberg wrote words to several more psalms, one of which even speaks of his admiration for Jesus; but he attempted no more musical settings. Schoenberg, in his youth an agnostic Jew, had been baptized a Protestant in 1898, then returned to Judaism in 1933, *after* the composition of *Moses und Aron*; but despite the flux of his religious affiliation, the essential religiousness of his art remained the same from beginning to end.

To the art critic all religions are one religion, and the mark of religious art is the same in the work of Jew, Christian, or atheist: it is the antimimetic theme, the concentration on the disparity between the image and what it is the image of. In art, the divine is most aptly suggested by the inadequacy, the incompleteness of the work of art. The mere fact of forsaking representation implies that the locus of artistic value is somewhere other than the phenomenal world, and therefore the work of art is a looking-beyond, even an act of reverence—it doesn't matter whether you are worshiping God or just worshiping art itself. Aesthetes, however, do tend to be religious: even Oscar Wilde became a Roman Catholic on his deathbed. When art is contentless, transcendences tend to rush in to fill the gap. The aesthetic religion can embrace any god whatsoever. Auden puts it this way:

> Poems, like many of Donne's and Hopkins', which express a poet's personal feelings of religious devotion or penitence, make me uneasy. It is quite in order that a poet should write a sonnet expressing his devotion to Miss Smith because the poet, Miss Smith, and all his readers know perfectly well that, had he chanced to fall in love with Miss Jones instead, his feelings would be exactly the same. But if he writes a sonnet expressing his devotion to Christ, the important point, surely, is that his devotion is felt for Christ and not for, say, Buddha or Mahomet, and this point cannot be made in poetry; the Proper Name proves nothing.[34]

The work of art is Christian, then, not in its overt subject, but in such oblique matters as form, style, concinnity; as Auden says, "Every beautiful poem presents an analogy to the forgiveness of sins."[35]

This doctrine leaves the religious artist in an odd relation to his ostensible content; there is continual embellishment of the edges and corners of the frame, but at the center something is missing. What Lévi-Strauss says about nonrepresentational art becomes the explicit condition of the religious artist's labor: "It is a school of academic painting in which each artist strives to represent the manner in which he would execute his pictures if by chance he were to paint any."[36] Antimimetic artists, even if their aims have nothing to do with religion, even if they only wish to illustrate the uncapturability of the real and show the poverty of representation, find themselves converging with a religious approach to art. In this way a certain kind of Modernist art, art that despairs of its own achievement, finds satisfaction, kinship, with the religious art of previous centuries—Dante, J. S. Bach, George Herbert (who calls attention to his metaphors that he may say farewell to them)—while the vigorous, secular, representational art of the nineteenth century, satisfied with the accuracy of its modeling, falls into disfavor.

Artists who strive for perfect verisimilitude discover that reality eludes them, transcends their art; and this awareness of the supersensible puts them in the position in which religious artists have been all along. Maturity comes when the conditions of transcendence are accepted, deployed, made ingenious. Auden, in *The Sea and the Mirror*, has Caliban speculate on the extreme difficulty of Christian art:

> Having learnt his language, I begin to feel something of the serio-comic embarrassment of the dedicated dramatist, who, in representing to you your condition of estrangement from the truth, is doomed to fail the

> more he succeeds, for the more truthfully he paints the condition, the less clearly can he indicate the truth from which it is estranged, the brighter his revelation of the truth in its order, its justice, its joy, the fainter shows his picture of your actual condition in all its drabness and sham, and, worse still, the more sharply he defines the estrangement itself—and, ultimately, what other aim and justification has he, what else exactly *is* the artistic gift which he is forbidden to hide, if not to make you unforgettably conscious of the ungarnished offended gap between what you so questionably are and what you are commanded without any question to become, of the unqualified No that opposes your every step in any direction?—the more he must strengthen your delusion that an awareness of the gap is in itself a bridge, your interest in your imprisonment a release, so that, far from your being led by him to contrition and surrender, the regarding of your defects in his mirror, your dialogue, using his words, with yourself about yourself, becomes the one activity which never, like devouring or collecting or spending, lets you down, the one game which can be guaranteed, whatever the company, to catch on, a madness of which you can only be cured by some shock quite outside his control, an unpredictable misting over of his glass or an absurd misprint in his text.[37]

Religious artists must hope that their art will somehow sabotage itself, leading to ruin and disappointment, awareness of the awful gulf between ourselves and the authentic revelation. The image that occurs to Caliban best to express this condition is "the greatest grandest opera rendered by a very provincial touring company":

> Our performance—for Ariel and I are, you know this now, just as deeply involved as any of you—which we were obliged, all of us, to go on with and sit through right to the final dissonant chord, has been so indescribably inexcusably awful. Sweating and shivering in our moth-eaten ill-fitting stock costumes which with only a change of hat and rearrangement of safety-pins, had to do for the *landsknecht* and the Parisian art-student, bumping into, now a rippling palace, now a primeval forest full of holes, at cross purposes with the scraping bleating orchestra we could scarcely hear, for half the instruments were missing and the cottage piano which was filling-out must have stood for too many years in some damp parlour, we floundered on from fiasco to fiasco, the schmalz tenor never quite able at his big moments to get right up nor the ham bass right down, the stud

> contralto gargling through her maternal grief, the ravished coloratura trilling madly off-key and the reunited lovers half a bar apart, the knock-kneed armies shuffling limply through their bloody battles, the unearthly harvesters hysterically entangled in their honest fugato.
>
> Now it is over. No, we have not dreamt it. Here we really stand, down stage with red faces and no applause; no effect, however simple, no piece of business, however unimportant, came off; there was not a single aspect of our production, not even the huge stuffed bird of happiness, for which a kind word could, however patronizingly, be said.[38]

Yet it is at this instant, pressed by every burden of inadequacy, after the collapse of illusion into derision, that "for the first time in our lives we hear . . . the real Word." The only genuine tool of religious art is this heady disillusionment. *Moses und Aron*, with its clumsy Moses, his plain speaking voice annulling all the artifice of song, is an opera just like the subverted Donizetti of Caliban's fantasy. I know of no art before the twentieth century that makes of its own self-destruction such a calculated, impressive effect, an effect that corresponds to the sublime as implosion corresponds to explosion.

So far I have been speaking of the solemn and sacred, reverential aspects of *Moses und Aron*. But there is also a great comic opera just below the surface; and I would like to rehearse some of same elements of the score we've been studying under the aspect of spoof and parody instead of hieratic piety. Comedy and tragedy are uncomfortably interchangeable even in spoken drama: *Romeo and Juliet* and the Pyramus and Thisbe skit in *A Midsummer Night's Dream* are the same play. But in the domain of music drama this deep identity is easier to see: tragic music and comic music elide effortlessly into each other. Hugo von Hofmannsthal and Richard Strauss summed up the whole monistic aspect of opera in their *Ariadne auf Naxos* (composed 1912, premièred 1916), a mongrel opera-within-an-opera, a comedy and a tragedy performed at the same time. The most hilarious music in the score is found not in any of the commedia dell'arte zaninesses, but in the cabaletta to Ariadne's lament, "Bald aber naht ein Bote." Auden's figure of the human condition as a poorly performed tragic opera is only another way of approaching the joke that underlies every depiction of tears and prayers.

Of all the important figures in the Bible, Moses may be the most resistant to operatic treatment. There is no Moses, only a whole tribe of Moseses. In the course of his life he undergoes many shape-shifts: an abandoned child drifting down a river; a leader of a slave revolt; a guide through the wilderness; a miracle worker; a lawgiver; a literary man writing the Pentateuch; a figure of disappointment, gazing from the mountaintop at the land of milk and honey he will never be permitted to enter. It is to be expected, then, that artistic representations of Moses would be vague and contradictory.

There is a small tradition of memorable musical Moseses. For example, in Carl Philipp Emanuel Bach's oratorio *Die Israeliten in der Wüste* (1768–69), Moses is little more than a chorister promoted to soloist, the voice of his people praying to God for rescue; the main event is the miracle of the spring that suddenly flows from the rock. Bach set a text by Daniel Schiebeler, perhaps with some assistance from the redoubtable Friedrich Gottlieb Klopstock, author of *Der Messias*; and Moses as the precursor to the Messiah was the only Moses here present. A century later, in Max Bruch's oratorio *Moses* (1895), Moses's character has almost reversed: Bruch's Moses is a Jewish Wotan, thundering invective on his own people as idolators. Far from being at ease as a member of the chorus, he outshouts the whole multitude in a great antiphony, in the oratorio's one impressive passage, "Abtrünnige, kam es dahin mit euch?," at the end of part 1. Moses was always more at home in oratorio than in opera, where his lack of a dramatic sex life was a handicap; but Rossini, in *Mosè in Egitto*, perches Moses uncomfortably on top of a love story involving the Egyptian pharaoh's son and a Hebrew girl. It is always a perplexity when the lead character in an opera has no particularly intense personal relationship with the other characters; sometimes such a libretto encourages the composer to identify the lead character with the orchestra, and this is exactly what happens in *Mosè*. Moses is a faceless torso of power who summons God's revenge in the form of great orchestral interludes: the plague of darkness at the beginning, the parting of the Red Sea at the end. Rossini didn't add Moses's magnificent prayer "Dal tuo stellato soglio" until 1819; in the 1818 original, Moses had little of interest to sing—he was merely the conductor of the divine instrumentalists in the pit.

Representing Moses has been a trial for visual artists as well. They are vexed by the Vulgate's mistranslation of the Hebrew verb *qaran*, which can mean either "grow horns" or "shoot out rays"; by choosing the former definition, the translators of the Latin Bible enjoined artists to outfit Moses with a fine pair of horns on his forehead. Michelangelo knew how to sculpt Moses as an image of clenched, potent wrath, despite the horns; but Tintoretto and other painters equivocated between the two definitions of *qaran* by plunking onto Moses's head two narrow yellow triangles, an effect that gives the impression of a defective halo. Thus the traditional iconography of

Moses became entwined with the traditional iconography of fauns, satyrs, and cuckolds—and, worse, devils. Indeed Joseph Kiselewski's graceful terracotta Moses, unveiled in 1965 at Syracuse University, eventually provoked members of the Latino American Law Student Association, the Black Law Student Association, the Women's Law Caucus, the Lambda Law Student Association, and the Jewish Law Student Association to complain that he had depicted Moses as a demon.[39]

The visual Moses, then, was often at the threshold of burlesque. But Schoenberg, in *Moses und Aron*, was the first composer to imagine a musical Moses of this sort. Schoenberg's Moses doesn't sing (except for one brief optional phrase); his music-speech has pitch indications, but these pitches are gestic improvisations, not very closely related to tight unfurlings of the twelve-tone row that determines the real music in the opera. Moses is at once the opera's central force and a songless creature trying to shove and bully his way into a spectacle in which he doesn't belong; far from conducting the orchestra, as in Rossini's opera, Schoenberg's Moses is helpless in the presence of music. The origins of Moses's *Sprechstimme* lie in Humperdinck's fairy-tale opera *Königskinder* (1895–97) and in the fairy tale of nature redemption (the wild hunt of the wind) at the end of Schoenberg's *Gurre-Lieder* (1901–10): *Sprechstimme* is a kind of fairy speech. Schoenberg perfected the technique in 1912, for the peculiar cabaret show *Pierrot lunaire*; and Moses is, from one point of view, a slapstick figure, God's clown.

The traditional mask known as a Pierrot (or Petrushka) depicts a sad clown—the weeping clown who never gets the girl, who remains helpless in the face of superior force. One could understand the following exchange as part of a Pierrot skit:

> *The Burning Bush.* Take off your shoes.
> *Moses.* My tongue is stiff.

Except that this is one of the most sacred moments in the entire culture of the West. Schoenberg here promotes Pierrot's futility, his sense of inadequacy, his puzzledness, into the general buffoonery of mankind before an unfathomable God—Elohim, Adonai, Yahweh, at once singular and plural, a labyrinth of speech, a vertigo of song, an unsolvable sound knot. This is the opera's opening scene: later, Moses is stronger, more assertive and blustering, but he nevertheless remains a curiously impotent presence: in Schoenberg's rewriting of *Exodus*, the miracle worker is not Moses but Aron, who turns the rod into a snake and makes water gush from the rock. In Bertolt

Brecht's *Das Badener Lehrstück vom Einverständis* (1929), a gigantic clown complains of aches in his various limbs, and his straight men promptly saw them off, one by one; when Aron withers Moses's hand into a leprous thing, he is as much of a black comedian as anyone in Brecht. *Moses und Aron*, by this way of thinking, is a farcical quarrel between a stage magician and a schlemiel. An evil stage director could even present the shattering of the tables of the law as an act of petulance, with Moses sticking out his lower lip in a comic grimace—no one wanted these wonderful laws in the first place, and I'm taking them away [*sniff*] and going home. Maybe one reason for Schoenberg's inability to write music for the third act was his difficulty in conceiving a genuinely powerful Moses, who could demote Aron into nonentity with a wave of his hand.

Throughout the opera, Moses is a figure of heroically obsessive befuddlement. Victim of the incomprehensible command of an incomprehensible God, he imitates the divine unmeaning as best he can by speaking sentences that swallow their own tails, like the serpent of eternity: as I mentioned before, he tells the golden calf: Perish, you image of the impossibility of grasping the dimensionless in an image! But one suspects that God himself knows much finer paradoxes: Moses is only fooling around in the margins of the ineffable. For him, speech is a domain of stutters and growls and gnomic grievances; as for music, it is hard to know whether his ear can hear it at all. If Elliott Gyger is right in believing that the other characters can't hear Moses's *Sprechstimme*, then Moses is a sort of meta-operatic phantom who stalks and glowers on a level of reality on which the other characters don't exist at all: they are his hallucination and he is theirs.

Nietzsche considered that Socrates' whole philosophy was vitiated by his dislike of music—that is, until in the final days of his life, when he asked for music lessons. Thinker Moses can't sing, and may not even be able to hear correctly—he may be the first tone-deaf operatic lead. What he hears is mostly a kind of tinnitus, in the fashion of the decaying Smetana, or a kind of mute vibration, in the fashion of Beethoven, biting a stick and putting one end on the piano. Moses's *Sprechstimme* sounds like botched singing, as if Moses dimly understood that everyone else was sticking to the score, and only he was unable to follow the melody and the rhythm. And the sound of the burning bush—voiced by six singers and six speakers intricately subdivided—may represent the gibberish that a musically illiterate man hears when confronted with Modernist music. The burning bush resembles the golden calf in that it is an image of the impossibility of confining the dimensionless in an image, but Schoenberg's music, teasing, elusive, shapeless, tries to avoid any implication that the impossible might be possible after all. If it is music, it is impossible music.

In writing this scene, Schoenberg may have conceived Moses along the lines of those music critics—not necessarily hostile to Schoenberg's artistic goals, but certainly bewildered by them—who left Schoenberg's concerts scratching their heads, but with tongues far from stiff. Moses as Beckmesser. Sometimes Moses seems puzzled by music, sometimes (especially when Aron sings) he seems antagonistic to it: Moses's antecedents include the snare drum that tries, with its improvised pitchless urgencies, to overwhelm and punish the orchestra in Nielsen's Fifth Symphony (1921–22), and the baritone who puts a stop to the proceedings in Beethoven's Ninth Symphony (1824)—"O Freunde, nicht diese Töne"—though that baritone turns out to be a good deal more genial than Moses.

The high point of the first act is the opening scene, with its phonic simulation of something-beyond-music and its somewhat deaf auditor. In the rest of the first act, Schoenberg accustoms us to the shape of melodies directedly derived from the tone row: the first forty-eight notes that Aron sings, at the beginning of act 1, scene 2, comprise the row, its inversion, its retrograde, and its retrograde inversion. As the act proceeds, the row is subdivided into more and more epigrammatic and comprehensible (comprehensible, and therefore fallen) forms: at the beginning of act 1, scene 3, a girl marvels at Aron, a flame going forth to the wasteland—she sings a retrograde version of the row (R10), but repeats the first four notes three times; then a boy replies that Aron passed by like a shining cloud—he sings a retrograde inversion of the row (IR7), but also repeats the first four notes three times. In this way the first four notes of the retrograde become a striking and memorable melodic figure: we easily hear the boy as an upside-down girl. As the music descends from the realm of the divine to the realm of opera, Aaronic tenor charisma, it becomes more and more preoccupied with graspable figures and intelligible procedures, though of the sort more often found in instrumental music than in vocal.

When we come to the great orgy that occupies most of the second act, we have, for the first time in the score, music, music that anyone would understand as music. It opens with a procession of camels, asses, and horses bearing sacrificial gifts for golden calf, and a Dance of the Butchers, who are carrying long knives. Glissandi seem to imitate the panting of animals and to anticipate the lubriciousness of the upcoming revels. At the section marked "Rascher" (m. 371), Schoenberg starts up (of all things) an accompaniment figure in monotonous arpeggios of stacked fifths, one sequence

EXAMPLE 20. Schoenberg, *Moses und Aron*: xylophone. From *Moses und Aron: Oper in drei Akten, Klavierauszug von Winfried Zillig* (Mainz: B. Schott's Söhne, 1958), 210.

beginning on D, the other on C; as Gyger has commented, these figures stand out strongly because the perfect fifths are so idiomatic for the strings that the listener becomes aware of violins and violinists instead of "a subtly varying reservoir of disembodied timbres."[40]

Above these arpeggios a xylophone starts playing a catchy fragment (ex. 20) of the row (6): many of the notes from the row are omitted because they have been demoted to the accompaniment, but notes 8–10 (F–G♭–A♭) are obsessively repeated, always terminating with a repetition of the A♭ and a falling sixth (to C♭), strong on the first beat, weak on the second. The C♭ is note 11 of the row.

After the xylophone, the trumpet takes up the catchy fragment (ex. 21), and notes 8–11 (F–G♭–A♭–C♭) start to seize control of the whole texture: their rhythm (dotted eighth–sixteenth–eighth; strong eighth–weak eighth) infects figures composed of different pitches. All this is part of the introduction to the Dance of the Butchers.

The Dance of the Butchers proper begins with two fortissimo chords: the first consists of the notes D, B♭, and G; the second, of D♯, B, and F♯ (ex. 22). The first may be built from R11; the second, from IR2. The first is a G minor triad; the second, a B major triad, astonishingly abnormal in the context of this formidable opera.

This passage could have come straight out of Strauss's *Elektra* (1909)—and indeed it is possible to hear in the bellowing of the sacrificial animals and the stroke of the butcher's axe a sound not far from the crack of the axe on Agamemnon's head so often recalled in Strauss's opera. After this peremptory beginning, the dance proceeds, a fugato of trumpet figures in rhythms similar to those just described. Schoenberg provides a good deal of

EXAMPLE 21. Schoenberg, *Moses und Aron*: trumpet. From *Moses und Aron: Oper in drei Akten, Klavierauszug von Winfried Zillig* (Mainz: B. Schott's Söhne, 1958), 211.

EXAMPLE 22. Schoenberg, *Moses und Aron*: triads. From *Moses und Aron: Oper in drei Akten, Klavierauszug von Winfried Zillig* (Mainz: B. Schott's Söhne, 1958), 213.

EXAMPLE 23. Schoenberg, *Moses und Aron*: pseudo-retrograde. From *Moses und Aron: Oper in drei Akten, Klavierauszug von Winfried Zillig* (Mainz: B. Schott's Söhne, 1958), 217.

what might be called pseudo-retrograde (ex. 23), as for example at m. 446, where the rising pitches B–(A)–D♯–C are followed by the falling ones C–E♭–B♭; the phrase seems to aim for B but misses it by a half step.

Everywhere the music suggests something energetic, clumsy, crackpot, an act of blasphemy against the row. I once played this passage for my friend Robert Morris, who responded with one word: "craven."

The glissandi, the clumped vigor, the trumpet, the xylophone—all these suggest jazz, and Schoenberg may have intended it as a parody of pop music, like the ghastly stuff that comes out of the radio in Schoenberg's previous opera *Von heute auf morgen* (composed 1928, premièred 1930). But I wonder whether Schoenberg's indictment of music might be much farther-reaching.

There are passages in the grand classical tradition that have something of the sonority and constructive procedure as the Dance of the Butchers. A notable example is the hair-raising fugato in the first movement of Liszt's *Eine Faust-Symphonie* (1854), at rehearsal letter Z ("Sehr langsam"). It is made up mostly of sequences of rising augmented triads displaced over the whole gamut; but Liszt doesn't hesitate to include other sorts of triads when it suits him. Earlier examples can be found in Beethoven: the first movement of the Fifth Symphony (1808) fills up the entire phonosphere with a single figure—but that figure is much more stable than Schoenberg's; a better example is the final movement of the *Tempest* Sonata, op. 31, no. 2 (1801–2), in which the obsessive four-note figure keeps distending or contracting its intervals, reconfiguring itself, leaping around the keyboard, and yet always retaining a recognizable shape.

Schoenberg staked his career on the priority of pitch over every other musical variable. The twelve-tone system assumes that the well-tempered scale is a universal fundamental, like *pi*; and that music is a body of procedures for relating twelve different pitch classes to one another. But in Beethoven, in Liszt, and especially in Wagner and Richard Strauss, there can be found a contrary line of thought: that the rudiment of all music is the figure, the cell, the gesture; and that this figure, while composed of pitches, is not subservient to them. Often Wagner or Strauss will take a theme and completely alter its intervallic nature—and yet the theme retains its identity. In fact, in *Der Ring des Nibelungen* Wagner composed leitmotifs (Nibelungs, Hagen) so intensely rhythmic in character that you can recognize them when tapped out by a single kettledrum.

I don't know if Schoenberg quite articulated this to himself, but I see this sort of gestic music as a threat to Schoenberg's hegemony. In the Dance of the Butchers, Schoenberg uses the very compositional procedures I have just described: he retains enough of the tone row to appease his conscience, but he makes the butchers jog to continuously permuting music shapes that are remarkably independent of the intervals that compose them. In other hands (Beethoven's, or Verdi's—I'm thinking of "Dio mi potevi scagliar," from *Otello*), such music might indicate a suppleness of conception, a plasticity to altering emotional states; but in Schoenberg's hands it is merely diabolic slither.

This pandering has many ramifications. It is a concession to opera in the bad sense of the word—in Alex Rehding's words, "You want a love story? Okay, I'll give you a love story. Here, have some sex and violence." But it disparages the thing it condescends to—and it condescends not only to opera, but to the whole gestic-dramatic means of development prevalent in instrumental music. If the Dance of the Butchers constructs music from unstable cells in order to indict music constructed from unstable cells, it is proscribing a good deal of the music we hear in our concert halls. But it is possible that Schoenberg's accusations extend to everything we commonly call music. According to Schoenberg's *Harmonielehre* (1911), all music that has ever been composed and ever will be composed is sleeping inside a single note:

> The primitive ear hears the tone as irreducible, but physics recognizes it to be complex. In the meantime, however, musicians discovered that it is *capable of continuation*, i.e. that movement *is latent within it*. That problems are concealed in it, problems that clash with one another, that the tone lives and seeks to propagate itself.[41]

To think in terms of cells and gestures, independent of pitch, is to overlay an arbitrary form over the music derived from the spectral study of a note.

Furthermore, Regina Busch has called attention to a strange but important passage in *Totentanz der Prinzipien* (Death Dance of the Principles, 1915), where Schoenberg notes that bells keep ringing even after the twelfth stroke is finished:

> *One* sound! Without any differentiation. . . . We recognize that it lives; by its pallor and insipidity; by its wealth of indistinctnesses. . . . By the fact that its pallor and insipidity now resolve themselves into colours and shapes . . . it disintegrates more and more and is in motion. . . . So much and every individual thing seems important. . . . Now it sings; each one sings something different, thinks that he sings the same, and really in one direction it sounds in unison; (in amazement) in another polyphonic. In a third and fourth it sounds different again; but that cannot be expressed.[42]

It is as if silence, or a reverberation impinging on silence, can slowly gather its vaguenesses together, clasp itself into *tönend bewegte Form*, form made of moving sounds; and this sound shape can appear as one note or as a complicated composition, according to where the listener stands with respect to it. A single note is always in the act of becoming all sounds; a complex web of sound is always in the act of refining itself down to a single note. The infinitely varied and the ultimately simple are two faces of the same thing. Therefore the God of *Moses und Aron* expresses his monotheistic character by whispering and shouting and singing all the notes at once—white noise has all frequencies, just as white light has all colors.

Music, then, is a motion that expresses a stasis. There is something deeply Parmenidean in Schoenberg's musical makeup: Parmenides taught that the world is an unchanging whole, and change is only an illusion created by the defects in our sensory organs; Parmenides' pupil Zeno tried to confirm this belief through his celebrated paradoxes: the arrow shot by the archer never leaves the bow, because in a single instant it could travel no distance at all, and, since time is nothing but a heap of instants, the sum of a sequence of zeroes must remain zero. Schoenberg's music is astonishingly complicated, dense in event, but it keeps alluding to a transcendental plainness. In the end, perhaps all music is contaminated and compromised by its very audibility, its motility, its lack of changelessness; perhaps unheard melodies are not only sweeter, but the only music worth attending to.

Schoenberg was fond of music that leaves off on nothingness: the accelerating vanish of the shiver at the end of *Erwartung*, the soprano voices that climb to the threshold of hearing in *Herzgewächse* (1911) and at the end of the *Jakobsleiter* fragment (1917–22). In the last-named work, the angel Gabriel says, in a passage I quoted before, a passage that seems to me near the heart of Schoenberg's philosophy of music:

> You on the middle level, step closer,
> who are a likeness and possess the radiance;
> who are similar to one Much Higher
> as the distant overtone is similar to the fundamental;
> while others, deeper, themselves almost fundamentals,
> are more foreign to him, as the bright rock crystal
> is more foreign to diamond than coal is.

In a perspective drawing there is always a vanishing point exactly opposite the eye, toward which all parallel lines toe in; and Schoenberg seems to have conceived music similarly, as an art in which all sounds point upward toward some single sound far above the threshold of hearing. *Moses und Aron* begins with God-music, an audible omnipresence, passing human understanding; it ends with a single prolonged F♯, as if all music had folded itself back up into that single note in which all music is latent. This is God's other face, the unitary simplicity on the far side of all complexity, the grace that comes (in Heinrich von Kleist's phrase) when we eat a second time from the fruit of the tree of knowledge.

But *Moses und Aron* is a work of art, not a theological tract, and the ending is trickier than it first seems. What drives Moses to despair is the sight of his people following an image: not the golden calf, but the pillar of cloud by day, the pillar of fire by night. To oppose magic is one thing when the magician is your oily brother Aron; another thing entirely when God himself stoops to miracle. The happy populace marches behind the pillars to repetitive, clunky music with a high rhythmic profile, a dumbed-down version of the procedures we heard in the Dance of the Butchers. (We heard this same music at the end of act 1: it's as if, after all the sex and glitz and suicide, after the production of the Ten Commandments, after the destruction of the Ten Commandments, nothing has happened at all.) Moses feels himself an unwitting accomplice in God's own incentives to idolatry.

The last few bars are among the most widely admired of Schoenberg's achievements, partly because of the overwhelming beauty of the unison melody, partly because Moses and the orchestra seem no longer at odds with one another: the strings play the last seven notes of the row (IR4), but get the row wrong by reversing the B and the C♯, as if the row were

EXAMPLE 24. Schoenberg, *Moses und Aron*: end of act 2. From *Moses und Aron: Oper in drei Akten, Klavierauszug von Winfried Zillig* (Mainz: B. Schott's Söhne, 1958), 300.

acquiescing in the general error of the human condition, allowing itself to *express* Moses's despair instead of representing a glassy mathematical transcendence in which Moses could play no part (ex. 24). In every way the music, like God himself, seems to be trying to accommodate human frailty.

I spoke earlier of the *Sprechstimme* of *Pierrot lunaire* as a kind of clown-speech, but that wasn't quite right: the performer doesn't represent Pierrot himself—she recites little poems *about* Pierrot's antics and impersonates Pierrot from a great distance. If the parallel with *Moses und Aron* is exact, Moses is not himself the clown, but a narrator telling us about the behavior of a superior clown, namely God. Schoenberg was not a frivolous man, but there are some odd features to his theology. The only work of Schoenberg's that closely resembles (texturally speaking) *Moses und Aron* is his very last composition, the unfinished *Moderner Psalm* (1950): a speaker intones a prayer over orchestral and choral accompaniment, thanking God for not paying any attention to his prayers; the pleasure lies in the praying itself, not in the expectation of blessing. A deaf God who amuses us (amuses himself?) with inventing rules and then making exceptions to them, who dazzles us and ignores us, who craves our love and yet craves nothing—such is the clown God, the clown Schoenberg.

SIX

Stravinsky's Nightingales

WHAT IS STRAVINSKY'S MUSIC ABOUT? THERE ARE SEVERAL ways of answering that question. The critic can say that a piece of Stravinsky's is about how rhythm governs the tension between certain melodic intervals. Stravinsky had no objection to this approach. But the critic always wants to say more, and then immediately gets into trouble.

Music criticism, like the criticism of painting and of literature, consists of the struggle to remove an object from the world in which it takes place (the Amsterdam Concertgebouw, the Louvre, the shelf of my library) and deposit it somewhere else. I might deposit a musical composition on a mathematical grid to study pitches and meters; or I might deposit it amid similar musical compositions to note its deviations from some theoretical norm. But if I feel tempted to deposit it outside, in the world of experience, and to relate its intelligible sounds to birdcalls, whistles, thunders, automobile traffic, shouts, I have, according to Stravinsky, committed a hostile act.

Stravinsky went to great pains to deny that music had any significant relation to the outer world—or to the inner one. In his first major statement of aesthetics, in 1936, he wrote the most often quoted sentence of his life:

> For I consider that music is, by its very nature, essentially powerless to *express* anything at all, whether a feeling, an attitude of mind, a psychological mood, a phenomenon of nature, etc. . . . *Expression* has never been an inherent property of music. . . . If, as is nearly always the case, music appears to express something, this is only an illusion and not a reality. It is simply an additional attribute which, by tacit and inveterate agreement, we have lent it, thrust upon it, as a label, a convention.[1]

If there is an expressive aspect to music, that aspect has simply been tied to the helpless notes, like a tin can to a dog's tail. We fasten the expressiveness to the piece of music and then pull it up and admire it as if it were a new discovery. In later life Stravinsky tried to clarify this remark:

> The over-publicized bit about expression (or non-expression) was simply a way of saying that music is supra-personal and super-real and as such beyond verbal meanings and verbal descriptions. . . . It was offhand and annoyingly incomplete, but even the stupider critics could have seen that it did not deny musical expressivity, but only the validity of a type of verbal statement about musical expressivity. I stand by the remark, incidentally, though today I would put it the other way around: music expresses itself.[2]

This formula, however, does nothing to improve the available critical apparatus. The critic has only his vocabulary, which he knows to be crude and inept when confronting the nonverbal, and yet which he hopes can clasp something of the music it reaches toward. But if music is suprapersonal and superreal, it inhabits its own crystalline sphere beyond the range of verbal apprehension, an object that can never be hauled down into the critic's homely universe of discourse. Stravinsky simply laughs at the critic who thinks that Liszt's *Nuages gris* was caused by gray clouds;[3] indeed, "The one true comment on a piece of music is another piece of music."[4] It is easy to accept that no essay could take the place of *The Rite of Spring*; and yet, it is doubtful that language is wholly useless for criticizing music. If it were, Stravinsky himself wasted many an hour at this vain job.

Despite all this certitude about music's immiscibility with the natural world and with discourse, a study of Stravinsky's remarks shows a surprising amount of leakage. Whether or not Liszt had ever observed a gray cloud before writing *Nuages gris*, Stravinsky knew of an occasion when he himself wrote a piece of music in direct response to an outer stimulus: the second of his *Three Pieces for String Quartet* (1915), developed from the "jerky, spastic movement" of a clown called Little Tich.[5] Similarly, though Stravinsky hated imitative effects, hated the notion of music as illustrator or mood creator or handmaid to some other art, he nevertheless pointed out a few bits of mimesis among his own compositions: for instance, a passage in his *Symphony of Psalms* where triplets for horn and piano suggest Elijah's chariot ascending to heaven.[6] At least momentarily, music can find itself embedded in a larger, lower world, and without too much contamination from the verbal, pictorial, and human company in which it finds itself.

But it is also possible that music can be "about" something in much more global ways. In 1966 Stravinsky was eighty-four years old, and he found himself too weak to compose; he spent much of his time listening to Beethoven on the phonograph. In youth and middle age, Stravinsky had on occasion found bashing Beethoven a pleasant pastime; but at the end of his life he found himself engaged in an increasingly intimate and rewarding study of his music. And he wanted to find a kind of meaning in the music, although he could state it only in a gingerly fashion:

> Does a world of the Beethoven quartets exist outside of music, then, and is it possible to discover a reflective system between the language structure of the music and the structure of the phenomenal world? No, to the first, but to the second, well, yes, perhaps, eventually. . . . My . . . belief is that the quartets are a charter of human rights. . . . A high concept of freedom is embodied in the quartets, both beyond and including what Beethoven himself meant when he wrote to Prince Galitzin that his music could "help suffering mankind."[7]

Here Stravinsky did not retreat from his insistence on the autonomy of the musical act—it is not contingent on or expressive of something outside itself. But, by positing a "reflective system" between music and the world of experience, he liberated music from the narcissism that threatened it when it could express only itself, when it seemed to disdain contact with the mire of organic life. Beethoven's quartets may not be free; they may not be an expression of freedom; but there is something about their cobbling together that is analogous to what freedom is in human life. Stravinsky was never moved by the choral finale to Beethoven's Ninth Symphony, which he thought a hopelessly banal tune affixed to Schiller's mighty ode of liberation and brotherhood; but the late quartets, with their sophisticated upheaval of sonata form, seemed a mirror image of political freedom. Music, then, can be "about" freedom, not by setting a text urging men to be free, but through its own internal constitutive processes.

There are few other examples from Stravinsky's published writings of reflections between music and the phenomenal world. Indeed, he seemed to believe that music criticism did not yet exist but might someday exist, "well, yes, perhaps, eventually." And, although he busied himself a little with music criticism, he did not write formal essays—he only threw out speculations, usually in the course of dialogues with Robert Craft. There is scarcely a single word of Stravinsky's that can be attributed to him with perfect confidence, except in his letters—otherwise his published works are hybrids or fakes. Among his chief literary coworkers were Alexis Roland-Manuel (the author of "Stravinsky's *Poetics of Music*"), Walter Nouvel (the coauthor, at least, of *An Autobiography*), and Robert Craft. (So reticent was Stravinsky about unmediated appearance on paper that he would occasionally sign his letters with Craft's name, even though he wrote them himself.) Therefore his criticism, like Socrates', is a record of a mind in flight, never pausing to chisel an argument into final form. He did not close, tighten, or fully define his discourse. As he himself said, referring to the grammatical form of his name in Russian, I am an adjective, not a noun.[8]

If Beethoven's music is "about" freedom, what is Stravinsky's "about"? I am tempted to say "enslavement," so much did he insist on the strictness and rigidity of his processes of composition, on the exactitude of metronome markings, on *secco* textures and inflexible rhythms. But there is another, I think better, argument to be made.

In old age Stravinsky frequently found himself defending his decision to become a serial (or twelve-tone) composer—that is, to write music not in major or minor keys based on a fundamental note, but in a system where each of the twelve notes of the chromatic scale has equal importance, and the melodies and chords are derived from an ordered sequence of the twelve notes of the chromatic scale (a tone row). Many listeners found his serial music discordant or disorienting, dry, distant, wholly different from the opulent popular successes of his early period, such as *The Firebird*. Stravinsky thought that those who disliked serial music for its harsh, mathematical character made a serious error in thinking that the old, major-minor tonal system (on which is based everything from "Jingle Bells" to Wagner's *Götterdämmerung*) is somehow "natural":

> Yesterday's non-starter [the man who resists serial music] . . . opposed the substitution of an "arbitrary order" (those Draconian twelve-tone laws!) for a "natural gravitational system," as if both the arbitrary and the natural were not equally artificial and composed.[9]

This, I think, is what Stravinsky's music is "about": the deep equivalence of the natural and the artificial. At the center of his dramatic imagination is the desire to juxtapose in a single work two competing systems—one of which seems natural, tasteful, approved alike by man and God, the other of which seems artificial, abhorrent, devilish—and to subvert these distinctions as best he can. This is Stravinsky's brand of musical monism.

A certain anxiety about the unnaturalness of nature is an old theme in nineteenth-century art. Kleist, in his dialogue essay "On the Puppet Theater" (1810), had one of his characters claim that every ballerina tries in vain to imitate the perfect grace of marionettes, whose limbs, moved by a system of counterweighted pendulums, trace a precision of gesture impossible for mere human flesh to achieve. Kleist even drew a comparison between the puppet and the god:

> "But just as the intersection of two lines from the same side of a point, after passing through the infinite, finds itself suddenly again on the other side; or, as the image of the concave mirror, after having gone off into the infinite, suddenly stands right before us again, so grace returns again after knowledge, as it were, has gone through the world of the infinite, in that it appears best in that human bodily structure which has no consciousness at all, or has an infinite consciousness—that is, in the mechanical puppet, or in the God."
>
> "Therefore," I said, somewhat confused, "we would have to eat again of the tree of knowledge to fall back into the state of innocence?"
>
> "To be sure," he replied. "That's the last chapter of the history of the world."[10]

This state of envy for the inorganic would grow more common as the century progressed. E. T. A. Hoffmann, the German writer of fantastic tales, found his best shock effects in the confusions between dead images and living organisms—shadows and mirror reflections that embody human souls, paintings that come to life, the toy nutcracker that springs up to do battle with a mouse. Among the most resonant of his tales was "Der Sandmann" (1817), in which a man, looking through a distorting lens, falls in love with a life-sized mechanical woman, the "daughter" of one of his professors; he meets her at her coming-out party, where the precision of her dancing puts other dancers to shame, and her singing is "like the sound of a glass bell, clear and almost piercing":

> Surreptitiously, he took Coppola's glass from his pocket and looked at her. Oh! Then he perceived the yearning glance with which she looked

> at him, and he saw how every note achieved absolute purity in the loving glance that scorched him. Her skillful roulades appeared to him to be the heavenly exaltations of a soul transfigured by love; and, finally, when the cadenza was concluded, the long trill echoed shrilly through the hall and he felt as if he were suddenly embraced by burning arms. No longer able to contain himself, rapture and pain mingling with him, he cried, "Olympia!"[11]

After much wooing and long humiliation, this romantical fellow learns that his darling is not human. Both before and after this revelation, however, he is subject to fits and dreams, during which Clara—his hometown, organic sweetheart, a sensible girl—seems to look like an automaton; the wall of separation between person and thing is unstable, shifting.

What is interesting, for our purposes, is that the "expressiveness" of Olympia's aria is of exactly the style that Stravinsky reported in *An Autobiography*: the exultation of her cry, evidence of a "mind transfigured by love," is simply superadded by the listener; her song is pure music, objective and soulless. Hoffmann was a professional composer and music critic as well as a short-story writer, and some suspicion of the unreality of romantic expressivity seems to have dwelt in this most romantic of tale tellers. Elsewhere, too, Hoffmann considered the dangerousness of expression; for instance, his story "Rath Krespel" tells of an invalid soprano forbidden to sing, but whose need to express herself is so urgent that she sings herself to death. In a strange way Hoffmann seems to recommend apathy, the life of the automaton; though he may also have felt some sympathy with those university boys at the end of "Der Sandmann" who look for small errors in the singing and dancing of their girlfriends, endearing imperfections that prove them made of flesh and blood.

The prestige of Hoffmann's tales among musicians and artists has always been great. "Der Sandmann" was the basis of Léo Delibes's ballet *Coppélia* (1870), of one act (and "Rath Krespel" the basis of another) of Jacques Offenbach's *Les contes d'Hoffmann* (1881), and of an episode in Federico Fellini's film *Casanova* (1976). "Der Sandmann," like Kleist's essay, is disturbing because it suggests the morbidity of the ideal. Plato taught that ideal forms are beyond our life, unsusceptible to the taint of dirt, knowable only through copies; but, by the nineteenth century, as the art of modeling grew more cunning, certain contrivances of metal, wood, paint, or glass seemed capable of embodying the ideal directly, imperishably, as if we could hope to embrace not a woman but Woman itself. Olympia, the ideally beautiful doll, is a goddess reduced to a puppet and a parody—the penultimate chapter of the world's history.

"Der Sandmann" helped to teach the world that the highest sort of art might inhabit a dubious limbo between life and death. In the ballet, particularly, the boundary line became uncertain. Two of the greatest ballets of the nineteenth century are *Coppélia* and Adolphe Adam's *Giselle* (1841): one is the story of a dancer who pretends to be the faultless machine with whom her sweetheart has fallen in love; the other is the story of a man compelled by the spirits of unmarried maidens—the Wilis—to dance himself to death. The first tells of a dead thing that lifts itself into a semblance of life, and of a woman who substitutes herself for the surrogate; the second tells of a live dancer transported into such rapture of movement that he dies. The dancer, then, dances on the knife's edge between life and death, looking from one side like ecstatic flesh, on the other side like a machine or a corpse. At the peak of the dance, the perfection of nature and the perfection of unnature converge, seem ready to trade places, as in the image in the concave mirror of Kleist's simile.

Stravinsky achieved international fame as a composer of ballet, with *The Firebird* (1910), *Petrushka* (1911), and *The Rite of Spring* (1913). In later life he expressed surprise that he could have made a career in ballet, in an era when ballet seemed slightly fatuous and outmoded; but the genre of dance suited his favorite themes perfectly. The plot of *The Firebird* never much attracted Stravinsky;[12] but the two later ballets were perfectly designed to show off the Giselle-Coppélia theme, the line of contact between human being and eidolon or corpse.

> *Petrushka* began its existence not as a ballet but as a kind of piano concerto:
>
> My first idea was to compose a *Konzertstück*, a sort of combat between the piano and the orchestra. . . . In that first version I saw a man in evening dress, with long hair, the musician or poet of romantic tradition. He placed several heteroclite objects on the keyboard and rolled them up and down. At this the orchestra exploded with the most vehement protestations—hammer blows, in fact.[13]

Here we have objects that speak by rolling on the piano keys, and a hammer in the orchestra that replies. (In the finished ballet, this effect is most clearly heard near the beginning of the Second Tableau—the first music Stravinsky wrote for the score—in which a piano cadenza, all black keys in the left hand, all white keys in the right hand, introduces an orchestral caterwaul representing Petrushka's curses. This cadenza gives a credible imitation of a bowling ball studded with nails rolling around the keyboard.) The character of Petrushka, the puppet given life by the Charlatan, is one of these talking objects promoted into the role of doll. Petrushka, that "droll, ugly, sentimental, shifting personage,"[14] is paradoxically the most human creature in the entire ballet. Stravinsky seems able to attribute pathos, dejection, jealousy, and wit more easily to an object than to a man. Things have passions, while the real people at the carnival behave obtusely, coarsely.

The ballet tells the story of Petrushka, the Ballerina, and the Moor, three puppets whom the Charlatan invests with life so that their dances may amuse the visitors at the Shrovetide fair. Petrushka falls in love with the Ballerina, who only scorns his deformity; she prefers the attentions of the Moor. Petrushka, mad with jealousy, interrupts the two lovers; the Moor runs after him and kills him with his scimitar. The crowd is horrified—until the Charlatan shows them that Petrushka is only a doll filled with sawdust. But on the rooftop Petrushka's spirit appears, waving his arms, mocking, threatening.

The music of *Petrushka* depends on the contrasts among three different clusters of characters: (1) the crowd, rambunctious, loud, stomping, earthy, often accompanied by music derived from folk themes; (2) the Ballerina and the Moor, whose music is simple, repetitive, "balletic" in a dim, Minkus-like, rehearsal-piano style; and (3) Petrushka himself, by turns furious, grumpy, abrupt, his emotions portrayed with the full resources of modern expressive dissonance, a style flexible in rhythm and harmony. The two classes of puppet music show two different strategies for escaping from the aesthetic of Expressionism: Petrushka's music parodies expression, while the Ballerina remains purely inexpressive, a stick figure moving (in the Danse de la Ballerine) stiffly, metronomically, to inflectionless cornet arpeggios—she is an object, and deserves "objective" music.

Toward the beginning of *Petrushka* a music box plays a little tune; melodies appropriate to music boxes are common throughout the ballet. The spell that breathes life into the puppets is a flute melody, played by the Charlatan, called the Tour de Passe-passe, a section that Debussy commended for its "sonorous magic";[15] the panpipe-like melody zooms up and down and up and down in eccentric triads. It is a sort of snake-charmer tune; its mechanical nature may hint that the wooden puppets brought to life will in fact remain wood, tapping their feet to the Charlatan's bidding.

Stravinsky wrote that he imagined the Charlatan as "a character out of Hoffmann . . . the flute music, too, is Weber-like, or Hoffmann-like."[16] Now, in Offenbach's *Les contes d'Hoffmann*, the aria of the doll Olympia is a piece of flutelike coloratura, in which one hears all too literally the tension on the mainspring of her wind-up voice box. Stravinsky has converted Hoffmann's mechanical doll from a figure of fun into a figure of power. *Petrushka* is "Der Sandmann" told from the doll's point of view, a fable about insensitive human beings unable to appreciate the energy and precision of a puppet. At the end Petrushka derides not only the crowd at the carnival, but us, the spectators of the ballet, as well:

> Petroushka's ghost, as I conceived the story, is the real Petroushka, and his appearance at the end makes the Petroushka of the preceding play a mere doll. His gesture is not one of triumph or protest, as is often said, but a nose-thumbing addressed to the audience.[17]

The most vital spirits are those that incarnate themselves in things. *Petrushka* is a ballet about abstract forces, forces that never descend into human beings but that may electrify objects temporarily. It is (at least in retrospect) a parable about the objectivity of music, for music pertains not to the passions of men, but to something suprapersonal, superreal—the human subject is carved up into a ghost and a doll. It is Stravinsky's first attempt to create a theatre of speaking, singing, dancing objects, to realize on stage his vision of an objective music cut free from the slush of expression. The only expressive "subject" in the ballet is filled with sawdust, and he twists his pliant limbs in an impudent semblance of emotion.

Two trumpets play the music that accompanies this nose-thumbing: they wander off into different, extremely remote keys—C major and F♯ major—and, oblivious of the clash, keep playing. (The superimposition of these two keys is Petrushka's harmonic signature throughout the ballet.) This striking effect suggests how far afield from the conventions of common, affable musical discourse Stravinsky is willing to go: Petrushka, like the music itself, ends by inhabiting a different world, at right angles to the world of the spectators at the carnival.

It was Stravinsky's peculiar gift that he could write stage pieces that represent simultaneously the extreme concreteness and the extreme abstraction of music, as he understood it. The end of *Petrushka* dismisses the whole fable; if Stravinsky had specified that the ghost of Petrushka was deriding the fairgoers from the planet Pluto, he could not have produced a greater impression of remoteness and unearthliness. (The equivalent moment in Schoenberg's work occurred in 1908, in his Second Quartet, when a soprano sings—just before the music abandons any semblance of a key signature—"I feel air from another planet.") The ballet unballetizes itself, turns back into abstract music. What began as a *Konzertstück* for piano ends as exactly that.

In many places in his writings, Stravinsky affirmed the essentially abstract character of music: for instance, he claimed that musique concrète—music made of arranged noises rather than sounds produced by musical instruments—fails because it violates the "transcendent (or 'abstract' or 'self-contained') nature of music."[18] And yet, Stravinsky regarded musical compositions as objects and spoke of composing as a craft akin to the construction of a chair. Even musical intervals were, in a sense, things:

> After working late one night I retired to bed still troubled by an interval. I dreamed about this interval. It had become an elastic substance stretching exactly between the two notes I had composed, but underneath these notes at either end was an egg, a large testicular egg. The eggs were gelatinous to the touch (I touched them). . . . I woke up knowing that my interval was right.[19]

The fables that most attracted Stravinsky were those that let him express the inexpressiveness of music—its abstraction from human passions—and the objectivity of music—its constitution of its own world of things. Therefore he liked puppets, liked machines, liked musical-instrument stage props (such as the Goat's *guzla* in *Renard*, the devil's violin in *The Soldier's Tale*, or, in *Orpheus*, the lyre that lives on even after Orpheus's death). The stage pieces continually work to stifle, suppress the human subject, as if musical instruments and tangible note intervals, dangling down in their own private space, were glad to be rid of those who played them.

After *Petrushka*, Stravinsky's next important work was *The Rite of Spring*. Here, it seems, we are as far as possible from the mechanical or the doll-like: the action of this ballet takes place in pagan Russia and shows the awakening of the earth from winter, the ceremonial games and conjurings of spring, and at last the sacrifice of a virgin to the nature god. One might argue that Stravinsky's music, instead of being inexpressive, is in fact all-expressive: in its ferocity, its driving rhythms, it seeks to embody the trembling, the heaving, the spurting, the huge sexuality of nature itself. As the original libretto itself says, the ballet is not a story but a surge.[20]

And yet, *The Rite of Spring* is, in its way, as distant from finite human expression as *Petrushka* is. It represents a convergence of the all-expressive with the nonexpressive, a coincidence of opposites. Human subjects dwindle, disappear before the nature-fury that animates them.

Most of the documents that survive from the inception of *The Rite of Spring* suggest that all its collaborators were aware of the ballet's antihuman tendencies. The libretto was written by Stravinsky and Nicolas Roerich (who also designed the set); an early letter by Roerich shows that he planned to dress the men "in bearskins, to show that the bear was man's ancestor."[21] This suggests that the subject of the ballet consisted of men so primitive that they were themselves half bear, and it would have been only one step to a spectacle (like Stravinsky's *Renard*) in which the actors were themselves animals. Vaclav Nijinsky, the ballet's choreographer, said in an interview in 1913—the year of the première—that "it is really the soul of nature expressed by movement to music. It is the life of the stones and the trees. There are no human beings in it."[22] And Stravinsky himself, in an essay published in *Montjoie!* (1913)—the text of which is even more dubious than most Stravinsky texts—offered, or may have offered, these comments:

> I have tried to express in this Prelude the fear of nature before the arising of beauty, a sacred terror at the midday sun . . . some adolescent boys appear with a very old woman, whose age and even whose century is unknown, who knows the secrets of nature. . . . She runs, bent over the earth, half-woman, half-beast . . . the adolescent girls come from the river. . . . They are not entirely formed beings; their sex is single and double. . . . The Elect [the sacrificial virgin] is she whom the Spring is to consecrate, and who will give back to Spring the force that youth has taken from it. . . . The annual cycle of forces which are born again, and which fall again into the bosom of nature, is accomplished in its essential rhythms.[23]

The Rite of Spring, then, concerns the human race before it has become human, before sexual differentiation, when it is still only a provisional manifestation of nature. Men and women arise laboriously out of the earth, lumpish and only half formed, and at last subside back into it. Petrushka, like any doll, is posthuman, an artifact derived from human shape; *The Rite of Spring* depicts the prehuman. It is strange that Stravinsky despised Walt Disney's cartoon of this ballet, in *Fantasia* (1940)—Stravinsky called it an "unresisting imbecility"[24]—for by making the action a minuet of dinosaurs and volcanos Disney succeeded in eliminating the human presences that were always to some extent an embarrassment to the spectacle.

The Rite of Spring represents another version of the assault on subjectivity that is part of Stravinsky's program for objectifying music. We know that the origin of the ballet was a vision of death:

> One day, when I was finishing the last pages of *L'Oiseau de Feu* in St. Petersburg, I had a fleeting vision which came to me as a complete surprise . . . I saw in imagination a solemn pagan rite: sage elders, seated in a circle, watched a young girl dance herself to death.[25]

If *Petrushka* is a new *Coppélia*, *The Rite of Spring* is a new *Giselle*. (*The Soldier's Tale* also contains a *Giselle* episode, in which the soldier plays on his violin a tune that compels the devil to dance until he collapses in exhaustion.) Dancing is an act that pertains to death, or at least to energies that are beyond the merely human. Not only the girl of the sacrifice but all the characters of the ballet are effaced, dehumanized, by the obliterating music of Stravinsky's score. The original scenario has proved difficult to choreograph: most of the memorable realizations depart from it radically, such as Paul Taylor's cheeky setting of the two-piano version or Oliver Hermann's Santeria-themed "silent film to the music of Stravinsky"); and Stravinsky himself came to prefer to hear it in the concert hall, rather than the theater. At the première, the most famous fiasco in the history of music, Nijinsky told the dancers to pay no attention to the conductor or to the music and instead to coordinate their gestures according to a cadence that he counted out backstage; but the dancers were unable to follow even this simplified beat.[26] The drumbeats and brass chords pound the human agents back into clay; no subject can sustain itself before that onslaught of force.

The Rite of Spring is the climax of nature expression, but it also has hints of the unnatural. When T. S. Eliot heard it in 1921 he wrote that the music seemed to "transform the rhythm of the steppes into the scream of the motor-horn, the rattle of machinery, the grind of wheels, the beating of iron and steel, the roar of the underground railway, and the other barbaric noises of modern life."[27] Similarly, Jean Cocteau called the Dance of the Chosen One "a mad, naive dance, dance of an insect, of a doe fascinated by a boa, of a factory blowing up."[28] It is easy for any hearer, I think, to transpose the scene of the libretto, a bare spring landscape depopulated except for some small, bearlike men, into another scene entirely: a bare urban landscape populated entirely by the machines of heavy industry. The posthuman vista is latent in the music; and I would enjoy seeing a production of the ballet that took its staging from Eliot's comment.

However, the most unnatural reimagining of *The Rite of Spring* comes not from Eliot but from Thomas Pynchon, in his novel *V.* (1963). This is the story of a woman, V., of many identities, the agent of every political catastrophe of the twentieth century and also the spirit of artistic Modernism. At every stage of her sinister career she substitutes prostheses for various limbs (a glass eye with a little clock in it, an ivory foot with the veins in intaglio instead of bas-relief), so that as she ages she becomes increasingly beautiful and inorganic—she is a Clara determined to become Olympia by cultivating soullessness. The year 1913—the year of the première of *The Rite of Spring*—finds her in Paris as a lesbian fetishist in love with a ballerina, Mélanie, from a company clearly modeled on Diaghilev's Ballets Russes. V. devotes herself to increasingly dangerous objectifications of herself and her ballerina lover; her only desire is to turn them both into things:

> It was a variation on . . . the Tristan-and-Iseult theme . . . "the act of love and the act of death are one." Dead at last, they would be one with the inanimate universe and with each other. Love-play until then thus becomes an impersonation of the inanimate, a transvestism not between sexes but between quick and dead; human and fetish.[29]

Mélanie is to dance the lead role in a new ballet called *The Rape of the Chinese Virgins*, in which she plays a virgin tortured to death defending her purity against the invading Mongols. All the other female parts are taken by dancing automata built by a German engineer. At the end at the ballet, she is to be impaled by the Mongols; but at the première she neglects to put on the protective chastity belt into which the tip of the pole is to fit, so that she is really killed on stage. (It is possible that Pynchon got the impalement theme from Emmanuel Chabrier's 1877 operetta *L'étoile*, in which a gorgeous impalement device figures in the act 1 finale.)

Pynchon's revised *Rite of Spring* skillfully adds the *Coppélia* theme to the *Giselle* theme of Stravinsky's original: the dancers are demoted to wind-up toys, except for the heroine, who yearns to join them in inanimation. I think that Pynchon was right to understand that *The Rite of Spring*, like other works by Stravinsky, treats the sexuality of objects, the erotics of death. Recent scholarship has distinguished, in interesting ways, the fetish from the idol:

> [Idolatry] preserves a residual consciousness that what is worshipped is only represented by, not embodied in, the idol; fetishism is a step further down the ladder in that it worships things as and for themselves.[30]

In the fetish we have an extremely primitive religion as well as a decadent sexuality—the convergence of the sophisticated and the prehistoric.

Stravinsky's investment of an object world with human passion—more-than-human passion—leads properly to Pynchon's substitution of automata for human dancers. The world of Stravinsky's music is a domain of supersaturated objects, where human affections have been translated, transubstantiated, into something alien:

> If a movement in a ballet should happen to be a visualization of the words "I Love You," then this reference to the actual world would play the same role in the dance that a guitar would play in a Picasso still-life: something of the real world is caught as pretext or clothing for the inherent abstraction. . . . Even in older ballets like *Giselle*, descriptiveness has been removed . . . to a level of objectivity and pure art-play.[31]

In *Giselle*, the deathliness of art is an explicit theme; Stravinsky, however, goes much further than Adam in denaturing the ballet. Stravinsky's ballets posit things, but things stripped of their thingliness, their context of human use, and degraded to abstract forms. "I Love You" exists still, but without an "I," or a "You," or "Love." If one were to imagine a striptease in which a woman took off her arms and legs and replaced them with decorous plastic, Stravinsky's music would make a good accompaniment.

Stravinsky's playing at the unsettled border between the natural and the unnatural can be seen most clearly in his short opera *The Nightingale*. The first act was written in 1909, before *The Firebird*; acts 2 and 3 were written in 1913–14, after *The Rite of Spring*. Here the automaton that briefly, uneasily came to life in *Petrushka*, that dwelt in *The Rite of Spring* only metaphorically, through the piston chuggings and traffic thunders of the music, has stepped forth and declared war on a live creature. The machine seems to be defeated; but it turns out, as we will see, that it is surprisingly difficult to tell the victor apart from the vanquished.

The libretto was written by Stravinsky and his friend Stepan Mitusov and is based on the famous Hans Christian Andersen fairy tale. Before

Andersen's fable there was a tradition of contests between birds and artisans: for example, Richard Crashaw's poem "Music's Duel" (1646), itself a translation of a neo-Latin poem, tells of a song fight between a nightingale and a lutenist in which the nightingale so exhausts itself in melody that it at last collapses, dead, upon the lute—art becomes nature's grave. But Andersen, a kind of Luddite of the imagination, contrives his story so that artifice proves unconsoling, deathly, while the real bird soothes and delights, brings the sick emperor back to life.

Stravinsky's opera is divided between the early style of act 1 and the advanced style of acts 2 and 3. Act 1 is pastoral, canorous. It begins with a tranquil Fisherman's Song (used to frame the beginnings and ends of all three acts); then some courtiers appear with a cook-girl, who is to guide them to the haunts of a nightingale—rumors of the beauty of the nightingale's song have reached the court. But the courtiers are not used to the outdoors, and when they hear a frog croak they think it is a nightingale and praise its lovely song (earlier they made the same mistake about the mooing of a cow). The cook-girl corrects the courtiers and eventually directs them to the nightingale. They persuade the reluctant nightingale to return with them to the court.

In act 2 we see a great pageant for the entrance of the emperor of China. So unnatural is the court that little bells are tied to every flower. Some of the courtiers are disappointed that the nightingale is a small gray bird, nothing magnificent or shining or diamondlike. The nightingale sings an audition aria; the emperor weeps at the beauty and offers the bird a reward. But the Japanese ambassadors come bearing the gift of a mechanical nightingale; they wind it up, and it sings a toy tune and captures everyone's fancy. The real nightingale flies away unobserved, and the emperor grants the automaton a privileged position on his nightstand.

The somber third act takes place many years later, in the emperor's bedroom. Specters taunt him with memories of the past; Death sits by his bedside. The real nightingale flies in the window and starts to sing; Death so enjoys the song that she offers to let the emperor live if the nightingale will continue the music. After a while Death disappears, and the emperor falls asleep; the courtiers, in the midst of a funeral march, mourn the emperor whom they think dead, but he appears before them in full regalia, bathed in light.

This plot line is a substitution comedy, like Delibes's *Coppélia*: Stravinsky swiftly switches from the real to the artificial and back again. Clearly the effect of the opera depends on the contrast between nature and the world of the court:

> As there is no action until the second act, I told myself that it would not be unreasonable if the music of the Prologue [that is, act 1] bore a somewhat different character from that of the rest. And, indeed, the forest, with its nightingale, the pure soul of the child who falls in love with its song . . . all this gentle poetry of Hans Andersen's could not be expressed in the same way as the baroque luxury of the Chinese Court, with its bizarre etiquette, its palace fetes, its thousands of little bells and lanterns, and the grotesque humming of the mechanical Japanese nightingale . . . in short, all this exotic fantasy obviously demanded a different musical idiom.[32]

Actually, Stravinsky thought of making the bizarrerie of the court even more extravagant than it is in the finished opera. Alexandre Benois, the stage designer, applauded (with some reservations) Stravinsky's idea of having the emperor carried in on a palanquin, then inserted like a doll into his throne.[33] And Stravinsky wanted the act 2 prelude to be accompanied by "Chinese shadows . . . like a magic lantern."[34] If the opera had gone further in this direction, the Chinese court would have been reduced to a puppet show or mere slide projection. As it is, when the Japanese ambassadors present the artificial nightingale to the court, they are only bringing a machine to another machine.

How does the music of the real nightingale differ from that of the mechanical? The old-fashioned means of differentiation might have been to assign diatonic music to the real bird and chromatic music to the unnatural being. Stravinsky, however, did just the opposite: the real nightingale sings swaying chromatic runs ending in swoons and droops. And the automaton (represented mostly by an oboe, but with a few cheeps from piccolo and celesta) sings crisp, clear seconds and thirds, symmetrical figures rapidly stitched up and down the staff.

The real nightingale is expressive in exactly the way that Stravinsky deprecates elsewhere—melancholy mood music, humid music that all too slavishly illustrates the text, which tells of wet gardens shivering in the tears of a moonlit night. The mechanical nightingale sings thing-music, clean and objective, like the Tour de Passe-passe in *Petrushka*. And when the mechanical nightingale's song is over, the orchestra continues and intensifies the sense of mechanism: the emperor and his retinue leave the court, accompanied by the most powerful music in the score, a largo maestoso march at once machine driven and barbarous—a music box fit for Genghis Khan. The real nightingale's music is at once flashy and slightly sodden, colorful in a bleary, Rimsky-Korsakov sort of way, while the mechanical nightingale's music sounds like the dry, learned Stravinsky of the years to come. *The Nightingale* erects a theater of automata in order to show how smeared and faded the old operatic expressivity of the bird sounds by contrast.

It is not certain that, in 1913, Stravinsky thought of his opera as a parable about the objectivity of music; but that is what his subsequent development has made it become. In later life Stravinsky said of Mozart's *The Magic Flute* (1791) that

> the intentional meaning of the opera, the triumph of Life over Death, is reversed at times in the depths of the music; in the brave little parade of Music through the gates of Death, for example, the flute charms the Keeper into a stay of execution, but the piece is a funeral march, nonetheless.[35]

I think this is just what has happened in *The Nightingale*: the triumph of nature over art, described in the libretto, is reversed in the depths of the music. (In fact, the exchange of "brave little parade" and "funeral march" takes place exactly as Stravinsky describes in *The Magic Flute*.) The emperor and his court were all dead to begin with, and life never seemed anything but an irrelevant intrusion; nature is the thick domain where nightingales and cows and frogs all sound approximately alike.

And yet, from another point of view, the real nightingale is not much different from the mechanical. The real bird represents subjectivity, expressiveness, but a cool, detached subjectivity, a subjectivity in the absence of a subject. The bird sings of human passion but itself feels no pang; its song is a critique or epitome of musical expression, rather than expression per se. If a society of dolls listened to erudite explanations of human melancholy, those dolls might imagine that the song of the real nightingale expressed sadness; but if that aria were transposed to, say, a Verdi opera, it would sound like the most frigid coloratura exercise, little different from the toy tootling of the artificial bird. The mechanical nightingale has only the briefest role in *The Nightingale*, and yet it is the opera's true hero: the action is seen from its point of view. The insertable emperor, the pink-and-black magic-lantern décor, the act 2 Prelude that sounded to Stravinsky like the ringing of a telephone,[36] all suggest a machine's fantasy of human life.

In a letter written when he sent the opera to the printer, Stravinsky remarked, "I composed *The Nightingale* in the period of my infatuation with birds (at any rate, when I was at my bird-best)";[37] but Stravinsky was never other than at his bird-best. Birds were a lifelong obsession, from his first success, *The Firebird*, to his last original work, *The Owl and the Pussy-Cat* (1966). The song of a bird takes place at the juncture of nature and art, and therefore is the ideal medium to test their relation.

Can a bird's song be considered music? In *Poetics of Music*, Stravinsky (or Roland-Manuel, following a suggestion of Stravinsky's) said no:

> I shall take the most banal example: that of the pleasure we experience on hearing the murmur of the breeze in the trees, the rippling of a brook, the song of a bird. All this pleases us, diverts us, delights us. We may even say: "What lovely music!" . . . These natural sounds suggest music to us, but are not yet themselves music. . . . They are promises of music; it takes a human being to keep them.[38]

Very rarely did Stravinsky write a direct imitation of a bird's song: for example, in the soprano cuckoo calls in "When Dasies Pied"—that "word of feare, / Unpleasing to a married eare" in the last of the *Three Songs from William Shakespeare* (1953). The cuckoo sings in falling minor thirds, just as in real life, or, at least, as in Beethoven and Berlioz. (It may be significant that here Stravinsky recalled a birdsong that inspires dread, not an exclamation of "What lovely music!") But generally Stravinsky deplored composers like Messiaen whose music was closely based on birdsong or other sounds of nature, as he explained in an interview:

> *C[ommentary Magazine].* Do you agree with Messiaen that "Nature" (he writes it in upper-case)—its sounds, colours, forms, rhythms—is the composer's supreme resource?
>
> *I.S.* . . . I do not deny the legitimacy of Messiaen's imitations, of course, or the fertility, to him, of "natural" resources. What I do say is that no matter how faithful, these imitations are necessarily expressed in, cannot escape being contained by, the harmony, rhythm, instrumental colour, and (especially in Messiaen's case) volume of the contemporary musical language.
>
> *C.* Do you think of "art" and "nature" as two realities, Mr. Stravinsky, and is there any act of transformation of the one in the other?
>
> *I.S.* There are any number of realities. . . . For me, music is reality, as I have said before, and like Baudelaire, but unlike Messiaen, "*J'aime mieux une boîte à musique qu'un rossignol.*" As for transformation, I do not admit the idea . . . Obviously the phenomenal world is refractable in music, or

> represented in it. The point is simply that I don't understand the mirroring (or the transforming) chemistry.[39]

"I prefer a music box to a nightingale"—*there* is the subversive motto of Stravinsky's first opera, everywhere contradicting the moral of Andersen's fairy tale. Stravinsky's "real" nightingale and his artificial nightingale alike are music boxes, equally remote in tenor from the liquid siftings of actual nightingales audible in forests. (The bird is not native to the Americas, but many of us know its song from the field recording used in Respighi's *The Pines of Rome*, 1916.) The subject of *The Nightingale* seems to be the transformation of nature into art; but in fact the "natural" act 1 is as artificial as the "artificial" acts 2 and 3. There is transformation, but not from nature to art, only from one system of artifice to another. Nowhere does a breath of fresh air intrude into the music. The opera is a further demonstration of the fact that in music, no natural system can exist, no means of embracing or imitating nature can exist. As Cocteau said in *Le coq et l'arlequin* (1918), one of the bibles of neoclassicism in music, the nightingale sings badly.

Long after *The Nightingale*, the relation of bird to machine exercised power in Stravinsky's imagination. In the 1910s Ravel was one of Stravinsky's closest friends, and it cannot have been by chance that Ravel outfitted a room of his house, in which he wanted Stravinsky to stay, with a mechanical nightingale.[40] When Stravinsky moved to Hollywood, California, he noted with horror that among the appurtenances of the mortuary parlors were "Japanese electronic canaries"[41]—perhaps a modern producer of *The Nightingale* could move the setting to Forest Lawn cemetery with little detriment to the opera's theme. Near the end of Stravinsky's life he received as a Christmas present a canary "whose finest *fioriture* seem to be mating responses to our electric juice-squeezer."[42] The real canary's wooing of the machine is a fine pendant to the action of Stravinsky's opera: not only does Stravinsky prefer the music box to the nightingale, but, so to speak, the nightingale itself prefers the music box. We know that Stravinsky's favorite pet bird was a parrot—but a silent parrot, as if music constituted itself in nature's absence of sound.

In Yeats's "Sailing to Byzantium" (1927), the poet envies the state of a bird made out of gold:

> Once out of nature I shall never take
> My bodily form from any natural thing,
> But such a form as Grecian goldsmiths make

Of hammered gold and gold enamelling
To keep a drowsy Emperor awake;
Or set upon a golden bough to sing
To lords and ladies of Byzantium
Of what is past, or passing, or to come.

Yeats, like Stravinsky, was attracted to Andersen's fairy tale; and, like Stravinsky, he revised it into an ambiguous parable of the superiority of art to nature. It is possible that Stravinsky on some level felt the same wish: to *be* a mechanical bird, to identify himself with the metronome and be rid of the inaccuracies of flesh.

"I prefer a music box to a nightingale" also came to mean "I prefer a player piano to a piano player." Beginning in 1914 Stravinsky became fascinated with the pianola—indeed, when he was old, he marveled at the amount of time he had spent transcribing his works for piano rolls. The pianola seemed to offer many advantages over other means by which music could attain acoustic realization: (1) it eliminated human interpretation, so that no middleman interfered with the composer's plan;[43] (2) it offered technical resources beyond a human pianist's wildest dreams—Stravinsky told the poet Mayakovsky that he intended to compose twenty-two-hand piano music;[44] (3) its incapacity for nuances of tempo seemed right for the hard, objective music that he wanted to write;[45] (4) it seemed to be the instrument most characteristic of the modern age—"Bach wrote for the clavier because it was the instrument of his time. . . . Why, then, should I not write for the mechanical piano?"[46] In 1922 Stravinsky decided to make his studio in the factory where the Pleyel company made pianolas[47]—thus managing to live inside a music box, where he devised piano-roll perforations to his heart's delight.

Though he wrote an "Etude for Pianola" and many pianola transcriptions, the great result of his study was *The Wedding* (*Les Noces*, 1914–23). This astonishing piece, an assault of nonsense syllables, snatches of conversation, fragments of ritual, is an enactment, or Cubist reconstruction, of a Russian peasant wedding, but, despite the Christian saints whose names are invoked, it might be Neolithic, or Australopithecine, so backward-looking is its range of auditory allusion. We watch as the tresses of the bride are bound and the hair of the groom is slicked down with oil; the bride and groom are led to each other; the nuptial bed is warmed by a man and a woman chosen from among the guests. All the action is accompanied by chatter, out of which emerges a whoop or intelligible phrase: we hear pet names, silly games (the guests prattle about strawberries that bow and talk sweetly to each other and then remind themselves that these berries are only figures of speech for the bride and groom), much calling upon saints, much doting on the wine and the "nine kinds of beer," some veiled sexual talk. But the speeches suggest cultural complexities, not psychological ones, and the guests seem as overt and predictable as animals or dolls. The singers are not to be thought of as dramatis personae:

> As a collection of clichés and quotations of typical wedding sayings it [*The Wedding*] might be compared to one of those scenes in *Ulysses* in which the reader seems to be overhearing scraps of conversation without the connecting thread of discourse. . . . Individual roles do not exist in *Les Noces*, but only solo voices that impersonate now one type of character and now another. . . . the fiancé's words are sung by a tenor in the grooming scene, but by a bass at the end. . . . Even the proper names in the text such as Palagai or Saveliushka belong to no one in particular. They were chosen for their sound, their syllables, and their Russian typicality.[48]

It is a Derridian opera—the auditory equivalent of the strips of newsprint that Picasso glued to some of his canvases. The speeches lack even the faintest authority of a speaker and continually degenerate into rhythmic babble; the names of the "characters" are anonyms. Richard Taruskin has noted that, in the first of the *Three Japanese Lyrics* (1913), "the verbal and musical stresses . . . cancel one another out, leaving a dynamically uninflected, stressless line, the musical equivalent of the flat surface of Japanese paintings and prints."[49] In *The Wedding*, the pictorial effect is different: the musical stresses do not efface the verbal ones, but squash them together into a giant word balloon, a collage in which the texts of the understrips are barely visible through the translucent overstrips.

Stravinsky liked the "non-personal" conception of the première: "The choreography was expressed in blocks and masses; individual personalities did not, could not, emerge. . . . [It was] a stylization not unlike Kabuki theatre."[50] I would think it was a stylization quite unlike Kabuki theater. Stravinsky's actors were not determinate, single-thrusting, like the Japanese actors who bear their fixed identities incised on their masks or makeup; they were instead molecules unconsciously agglomerating into forceful motion. If *The Wedding* is Kabuki-like, it is Kabuki smashed into a thousand pieces that gradually reassemble before our eyes: the action is irresistible, though the actors are negligible; underneath the shouts, the exclamations, the isolated speeches a firm rhythm establishes itself and sweeps all else away.

The orchestra at the première of *The Wedding* consisted of four pianos and a battery of percussion—that is, an all-percussion orchestra, since Stravinsky regarded the piano as entirely percussive in character.[51] The orchestration of the piece vexed the composer: as early as 1917, Stravinsky had written a nearly complete score with a somewhat more traditional instrumentation, and by 1919 he had written a version of the first two of the four tableaux in which there was a prominent part for a pianola. Stravinsky abandoned this version because it was too difficult to synchronize the mechanical piano with the live instrumentalists; but anyone who has heard Robert Craft's fascinating recording (in 1974) of the 1919 score—made tangy by a cimbalom's plink and a harmonium's drone, as well as by a pianola—might think that it is potentially the most impressive of the three versions of the score.

As in *The Rite of Spring*, we see that, in Stravinsky's imagination, sexuality is intimate with the machine; the peak of the organic and the peak of the inorganic are one and the same. In Fellini's *Casanova* the hero likes to pace his sexual thrusts to the beat of a wind-up mechanical bird; and a similar sense of sexual biophysics seems to be part of Stravinsky's nature. *The Wedding* ends at the verge of a remarkable, completely unstageable spectacle: a wedding night in which mannequins copulate to the pounding of a player piano. In the same year as the pianola version of *The Wedding*, Stravinsky considered a commission to write music for a puppet-play based on the Homeric "Battle of the Frogs and Mice";[52] and it is certain that the idea of a fully denatured theater was much on his mind. Some years after, when he began his career as a concert performer, he had a hallucination in the midst of playing his piano concerto: "I was suddenly obsessed by the idea that the audience was a collection of dolls in a huge panopticon."[53] That is the logical endpoint of Stravinsky's fantasy: a theater of faceless and nameless puppets, impelled by the rhythm of mechanical instruments, in front of an audience of dolls.

The Wedding was among the first of many vocal works by Stravinsky to do violence to language. Not only did Stravinsky wish to destroy the expressive character of sounds, he also wished to destroy the semantic character of words. Often in *The Wedding* the human voice is itself used as a percussive instrument, chugging out *ah*s and *oo*s in thick, fast panting. The basic unit of Stravinskyan vocal music is the not the word, but the syllable—or, even less than the syllable, the phoneme.[54] The composer did what he could to frustrate the ear's desire to bind these bits of sound into meaningful propositions.

Some of the vocabulary of Stravinsky's texts consists of nonwords—an easy way to empty language of significance. The text of *The Wedding*, and of several other works of this period, comes from two anthologies of Russian folk verse. Stravinsky preferred the most nonsensical poems. In *The Wedding*, there is a word, *lushenki*, that "is a rhyming word, in fact, the diminutive of a rhyming word; it has no 'sense.'"[55] In a short suite of Russian songs called *Pribaoutki* (1914)—the title refers to a verse form similar to a limerick—there appears a counting-game song, like the English "eeny, meeny, miny, mo."[56] Clearly Stravinsky wanted words for color, for quantitative value, for impulse, for a logical pattern. Taruskin has said of the third of the *Pribaoutki*: "It is not about a colonel, not about a quail. It is about the letter *P* and . . . rhythmic groups that all end in the vowel *A*."[57] No composer ever demanded language to be more docile, and no composer was ever more suspicious of any insubordination of meaning in the texts he employed.

But what is disquieting about Stravinsky's vocal compositions is not that he set nonsense texts but that he seemed to regard all texts (once incorporated into a musical composition) as nonsense. It is as if sense and music were profoundly incompatible. Music is eerily indifferent to the meaning of the texts it uses: "The words even of the Ninth Symphony [of Beethoven] can be reduced to nonsense without affecting the music."[58]

According to Stravinsky, every composer approaches a poem intending to tear it to pieces, to purge it of meaning—or at least not minding if that is the result. The text of *The Wedding* had the great advantage that it was flayed to ribbons even before it was set to music; but Stravinsky never hesitated to perform radical surgery even on far more august words. Speaking of the final bars in the second and third movements of his *Symphony of Psalms* (1930), Stravinsky said: "I really do tire of people pointing out that *Dominum* is one word and that the meaning is obscured the way I respirate it."[59] But if a composer spreads "Do [*breath*] Mi Num" over great distances, he can expect people to wonder why the name of the Lord has been disarticulated into solmization syllables. Perhaps Stravinsky felt that he could improve the sanctity of his music to the extent that he could drain the words of their holiness.

When, after *The Wedding* and the comic-operatic scene *Mavra* (1922), Stravinsky decided that Russian was no longer an acceptable medium for an international composer, he set out in search of a new language. The most attractive languages, he discovered, were those that no one spoke:

> [In Genoa] I happened to find in a bookseller's a volume by Joergensen on St. Francis of Assisi . . . the familiar speech of the saint was Provençal, but . . . on solemn occasions, such as prayer, he used French. I have always considered that a special language, and not that of current converse, was required for subjects touching on the sublime.[60]

This was the origin of Stravinsky's decision to write his opera-oratorio *Oedipus Rex* (1927) using a text in Latin. He set about obtaining it by asking Cocteau, who was eager to collaborate, to write a brief version, in French, of Sophocles' Greek tragedy, and then by finding a Latinist (Jean Daniélou) to translate Cocteau's French into Latin. Certain modern poets liked to create texts thick with overtones by piling one translation on top of another: Ezra Pound, for instance, wrote "Canto I" by translating into English a passage from a Renaissance Latin translation of Homer's *Odyssey* in order to impart a special depth to the language. But the text of Stravinsky's *Oedipus Rex* uses similar means to exactly the opposite goal: each stage of its development is an evacuating, a thinning of meaning, a loss of authorial responsibility. The text is so corrupted that it becomes sublime. Stravinsky confessed that he did not know what certain passages meant and disliked some passages that he did understand:

> [One] line mentions a "witness to the murder, who steps out from the shadows," and I have always wondered who that interesting character might be. . . . But the final "*on t'aimait* [we loved you]" is the most offensive phrase of all, for it is a journalist's caption and a blot of sentimentality . . . [concerning the phrase *omniscius pastor*, all-knowing shepherd:] *Why* the shepherd should be omniscient I do not know.[61]

We have, then, a version of the Oedipus story told by an ignorant, snooty, and sentimental narrator, where the musical accompaniment is (by Stravinsky's admission) a *Merzbild* of Folies Bergère tunes, Wagnerian seventh chords, florid Handelian arias, and dramatic intensification devices out of Verdi.[62] (The Dada collagist Kurt Schwitters liked to attach the nonsense syllable *Merz* in front of words—so a *Merzbild* is a nonsense image.) As for the actors, Stravinsky considered many means for degrading them, too. He thought first of a performance entirely by puppets, à la Gordon Craig, or of an Oedipus masked like an Oriental sun god[63]—as if *Oedipus Rex* were a divertissement performed for the enjoyment of the Japanese ambassadors in *The Nightingale*. Then he thought of having the singers holding up scrolls as they sang their parts,[64] as if we were witnessing not a performance but a rehearsal of a performance from the fifth century BCE. Then he thought of having each actor stand behind his own private curtain, whence he would step out before singing[65]—thereby fracturing the stage into an ensemble of tiny stages, each inhabited by its own soliloquist. At last, for the première, Cocteau designed for Oedipus a mask with pop-out eyes[66]—the Mr. Potato Head approach to Greek tragedy. The general result of these changes is to murder Sophocles' play—to disable the action and petrify the actors, to present a dead spectacle in a dead tongue. Stravinsky aspired to make of *Oedipus Rex* a "waxworks."[67]

Why? Stravinsky was not frivolous by temperament and had no desire to write a burlesque. If he demeaned the dignity of the actors, the narrator, and even the musicians, it was because he wanted to represent onstage something from which the actors, the narrator, and the musicians might distract:

> I consider this static representation a more vital way to focus the tragedy not on Oedipus himself and the other individuals, but on the "fatal development" that, for me, is the meaning of the play. . . . My audience is not indifferent to the fate of the person, but I think it far more concerned with the person of the fate. . . . The stage figures are more dramatically isolated and helpless precisely because they are plastically mute. . . . Crossroads are not personal but geometrical, and the geometry of tragedy, the inevitable intersecting of lines, is what concerned me.[68]

Just as, in *The Rite of Spring*, the individuals were effaced so that the energy within them might leap forth, so in *Oedipus Rex* the dramatis personae are made to shrink into a musicomathematical notation of fate's vectors. We see not "Oedipus" but a showy tenor who keeps singing "Ego clarissimus Oedipus" (I, most illustrious Oedipus), overinsisting on the character's name but not persuading us that he has assumed the character's identity. We hear the *fioriture* that, in a Handel opera, would be expressive of pride; but here they sound like a bad singer's rote performance of Handel. Temporarily Fate takes the role of Creon, or Oedipus, or Jocasta—or, as Shepherd and Messenger, sings a duet with itself; but there are no individuals, only a grand objectivity that briefly falls into an illusion of various subjects.

Oedipus Rex is a kind of machine that erects characters, pushes them forth, and at last annihilates them—an iron maiden, a rack for the dismemberment of puppets.

Cocteau's stingy, skeletal, "unmusical" (by Cocteau's own admission) text greatly assisted Stravinsky's assault against dramatic character. A normal dramatist, adapting Greek tragedy to a puppet stage, would take out the verbal flourishes and strip the play to bare action; Cocteau, however, emptied the play of action and left only a few withered flowers of rhetoric. Nearly the most common word in the text is *dicere*—everyone "says," or "answers," or "reports," or "speaks," or "refuses to speak," or "tells true," or "tells false"—no one "does." Only one character is actually named the Messenger; but in fact everyone except Oedipus is a message conveyor or a message frustrator. Creon's aria begins, "Respondit deus" (The god answers) as he reports the oracle's message—the plague will only end when Laius's murderer is found; the chorus then mutters, "Deus dixit, dixit, dixit" (The god said, said, said). Then Tiresias enters; his aria begins, "Dicere non possum" (I cannot say), and he refuses to speak until Oedipus accuses him of the murder of Laius—at last Oedipus's taunt forces him to utter ("Dicam" [I shall speak]) the terrible truth, that the king's murderer is himself a king. This rhythm of speech giving and speech withholding continues through the opera—in act 2 Jocasta tries to block messages, to discredit them, while the Messenger and the Shepherd try to utter what they know.

László Somfai has called attention to Stravinsky's habit of setting to music the peripheral elements of texts—such as (in *Threni*, 1958) titles and chapter numbers—as part of a strategy of depersonifying music.[69] Somfai also points to Stravinsky's calculated reversal of the audience's expectation (in the second part of *A Sermon, a Narrative, and a Prayer*, 1962) when the tenor, who "plays" the role of the martyr Stephen, at last sings the phrase "he fell asleep"—as if Stephen suddenly became the narrator of his own death. *Oedipus Rex* is, similarly, a depersonified opera, an opera of speeches in quotation marks. The only words that signify are the gods' words; the characters in the opera are only playback devices (or erasing devices) for speeches that are not their own. Somfai notes that in *Abraham and Isaac* (1964)—a setting of the original Hebrew text—the most salient musical phrase accompanies the oft-repeated word "Vayomer" (he said); and the continual emphasis in *Oedipus Rex* on "dic," "dixit," "dicere," "dico," and so forth anticipates this device. The fact of speaking seems of greater interest to Stravinsky than the content of what is spoken. Speech does not belong to anyone in particular but inhabits a huge, anonymous space.

Stravinsky's chief device for anonymizing the text consists of bizarrely varied repetition. For example, the chorus will hear a word from an aria—itself only a quotation—and requote it over and over again, draining it of whatever relation it once had to a particular speaker. Often these repetitions, whether choral or solo, will keep changing in meter: an obvious instance occurs when the chorus hears Jocasta sing of the crossroads (*trivium*) where Laius was murdered and hollowly repeats "trivium," first as a dactyl, then as an anapest. One perceptive critic, Mathias Hansen, has made a catalog of the compulsive reaccentuations of key phrases in the opera. Hansen seems partly to accept Somfai's belief that by this meter play Stravinsky intended to intensify the meaning of these words, but he also argues that "through the alteration of stress there comes about, proceeding from the alteration of the musical accenting, an alienation [*Verfremdung*] of the verbal message."[70] Hansen also remarks, discussing Creon's aria, that the articulation of the musical form has no relation to the divisions of the text, and that this incongruity is one of Stravinsky's techniques for achieving an effect of distancing.[71]

This seems to me the correct road to interpretation; and one might go down it still further. Hansen's model for Stravinsky's dramatic art seems to be the practice of Brecht: the audience is not encouraged to identify itself with the characters, but to contemplate the message objectively; indeed, Hansen applauds Stravinsky for creating an "effective corrective" to the "misuse of myth and history as an apology or at least a veiling of bourgeois reality . . . a religious-regressive defense of master-and-servant relations."[72] I see *Oedipus Rex* as a work engaged in a far broader attack, an attack on language itself. A modern audience, hearing the word "trivium" over and over again, may meditate on the significance of "crossroads"; or it may think of the most available homophone in all European languages, "trivial." I think this textual debasement was part of Stravinsky's intention.

Stravinsky was not a Latinist, but as a well-educated man he knew that Latin poetry is strictly governed by the quantity of syllables: long syllables must be pronounced twice as long as short syllables. Indeed he thought that Latin prosody determined the music: "All of my 'ideas' for *Oedipus Rex* were in one sense derived from what I call the versification."[73] The queasy shifts of syllabic length from one repetition to the next (*TRI-vi-um, tri-vi-UM*, just after Jocasta's aria at the beginning of act 2) seem to imply that neither the chorus nor the actors quite know the language that they speak: they keep searching for a meter but not finding it, for the meter lies beneath them, in the music, unavailable to speech. The incongruity between language and music is no mere device for estranging an audience, for hindering empathy; it suggests how little relation is possible between the basic structure of music and that of language. The inner drama lies in the pounding pulse of the music, and the speakers try as best they can to accommodate their ugly, deliberately inept language to it. Sometimes (as in "Delie, exspectamus") the chorus seems partly to succeed in aligning itself with fate's underpulse; but even in that powerful utterance the speech is squeezed onto a musical grid in 9/8 and 6/8 time, alluding to a classical dactylic meter (though expressed accentually, not quantitatively) to which the singers, bound to Daniélou's choppy Latin prose, can never properly conform.

This chorus is a serious parody of a Greek chorus. But most of the arias illustrate a more violent struggle against the musical meter. Oedipus himself, the main actor in the play, never reaches even the slightest accommodation with the music until his final phrase. When he shouts, when he curses, when he preens himself as a coloratura tenor—when he insists on his private *melos*—he is impeding the drama. The aimless vocalisms proclaim that the character is a liar. At one point he even steps out of the music entirely and declaims, to no particular pitch, "Stipendarius es, Tiresia!" (You are a mercenary, Tiresias!)—as if he disdained to take further part in the opera. But when, in his last words, he resigns himself to the subsistent rhythm, he advances the drama. There are many moments in the opera when truth—which is here a property only of music, never of words—is represented by some extremely simple, insistent musical device: for example, when the Shepherd and the Messenger deliver the horrifying message that Oedipus was not the son of Polybus, an emphatic C major scale descends in the bass. And when Oedipus understands everything, his self-abandonment is represented by his resignation to a plain B minor triad, "Lux facta est" (light breaks). The words of Cocteau's text exist only to illustrate the collapse of rhetoric, the priority of music over speech.

There are other impediments to audience comprehension besides the choice of language and the continual misaccenting. Much of the text is obscured by the peculiarities of the vocal line—without the narrator, feeble and foolish as he is, even an audience of Latin scholars might have difficulty in following the "action." In Jocasta's great aria, for instance, she keeps intoning, in her very lowest register, "o ra cu la o ra cu la o ra cu la" with such evenness of pulse that the line might as well be "la la la la la la la la la la la." She is far too oracular to be understood. The burden of her message is "Oracles are liars," but in the general mess of the text the oracle seems no more true or false than any other proposition. As is usual in Stravinsky's mature vocal music, the words are in danger of separating into a heap of syllables:

> Much to the contrary of the traditional concept, which submits music to the psychological expressiveness or to the dramatic significance of the word, in my *Oedipus Rex* the word is pure material, functioning musically like a block of marble or stone in a work of sculpture or architecture.[74]

> What a joy it is to compose music to a language of convention, almost of ritual, the very nature of which imposes a lofty dignity! One no longer feels dominated by the phrase, the literal meaning. . . . The text thus becomes purely phonetic material for the composer.[75]

Just as the actors are reduced to puppets, or human surrogates for puppets, so the words are demoted to things: bits of marble or stone, ground up into the concrete from which the music is built.

The advantage of a dead language is that it does not resist further decomposition. Modern languages have sinew, tensile strength; but Latin has such advanced rigor mortis that it could shatter into syllables without much effort. Stravinsky found that Latin was even better than nonsense, in that its decline into meaninglessness, pure sonority, was exciting. To kill words was more exhilarating than to find dead syllables. Stravinsky thought of vocal composition as a struggle for dominance between the composer and the librettist, as we can see in a note he gave to Roland-Manuel to help with the writing of *Poetics of Music*:

> The musician can approach the words that he puts to music in two ways. First, the word can be treated as sonorous material of expression itself. . . . Second, the word can determine the meaning of the music, [in which case] it is left meaningless without the word. The second approach is the passive one. The active approach is that of the musician who employs the word as sonorous material *only*, taking no account of its literal significance.[76]

Oedipus Rex shows signs of a fight for authority between Sophocles and Stravinsky, in which Sophocles' words are mangled by condensation, mistranslation, and contorted musical setting so that the drama behind the words, the drama obscured by the words, might be elucidated.

Obviously, however, Stravinsky could not spend the rest of his career setting texts in bastardized Latin. Over the course of his career, he wrote pieces in French, English, Russian, Latin, Slavonic ("Ave Maria," 1934), Hebrew (*Abraham and Isaac*), Italian (his reworking of the Pergolesi songs in *Pulcinella*, 1919), and even German—not long before his death, he orchestrated two songs by Hugo Wolf (1968)—as if, by continually changing languages, he need not commit himself to any language in particular. But of all these languages, the abrupt, blustery, crabbed, curious Latin of *Oedipus Rex* seemed the most suitable to his strange requirements—nowhere else is his vocal music quite so daring, so sure of its asemantic, instrumentalized character.

But there are hints, in this interview in the *New York Review of Books*, that he craved a language even more objective, even narrower in its width of denotation, than the pop Latin of Cocteau and Daniélou:

> *N.Y.R.* What did you mean . . . when you declared your disbelief in words? Is it a question of their inexactness?
>
> *I.S.* They are not so much inexact as metaphorical; not so much another form of notation as an irrelevant and unedifying form. Sometimes I feel like those old men Gulliver encounters in the *Voyage to Laputa*, who have renounced language and who try to converse by means of objects themselves. A composer is always in that position: he has no verbal control over his music.[77]

Here Stravinsky complained of the inadequacy of words to comment on music; but there is evidence that he also would have liked to have available for use in musical composition some language akin to the bag of objects that the philosophers of Swift's Academy of Lagado haul on their backs—a thing-language. In 1953 Boston University proposed to commission Stravinsky and Dylan Thomas to write an opera, and both parties were eager:

> "His" opera was to be about the rediscovery of our planet following an atomic misadventure. There would be a re-creation of language, only the new one would have no abstractions; there would be only people, objects, and words. He promised to avoid poetic indulgences: "No conceits, I'll knock them all on the head."[78]

Thomas died before they could begin; but this opera about the destruction and reinvention of language would have made explicit a theme latent in many of Stravinsky's works. This pared-down tongue, incapable of any speech act except the starkest reference, would have been a metaphor for the general demotion of words to sound concretions.

Stravinsky began *An Autobiography* with an odd account of his earliest memory of sound:

> I can see it now. An enormous peasant seated on the stump of a tree. . . . He was dumb, but he had a way of clicking his tongue very noisily . . . he would begin to sing. This song was composed of two syllables, the only ones he could pronounce. They were devoid of any meaning, but he made them alternate with incredible dexterity in a very rapid tempo. He used to accompany this clucking in the following way: pressing the palm of his right hand under his left armpit, he would work his left arm . . . he extracted a succession of sounds . . . which might be euphemistically described as resounding kisses.[79]

It is as if the world begins, and the world ends, to the tune of clucks and farts. There is the only real language; all else is literary artifice. Stravinsky once said that, as a composer, he took very literally the Bible verse "In the beginning was the word";[80] but that aboriginal word is more like an imbecile's rude noise, or like the half-language of a ruined earth, than like a theologian's subtle formulations of the Logos.

Sometimes Stravinsky's vocal music simply sinks into a sublanguage of clucks—most notably in his barnyard fable *Renard* (1915), where the Cock goes "Chuck-chuck-chuck-a-dah," and the animal musicians imitate musical instruments: "Plinc, plinc," "zoum! zoum! patazoum!" But often Stravinsky set modern-language texts of a much more highfalutin kind, as in *Perséphone* (1934); Stravinsky thought that André Gide's libretto consisted of *vers de caramel*, but the composer did little to unsugar the melodrama. It seems that Stravinsky wished to demonstrate the sad incompetence of modern speech, its slackness and artificiality. Lacking true concreteness, lacking any firmness of reference, modern languages must be made to display their eviscerated state.

And yet, Stravinsky loved words precisely because they failed to mean anything much. Nonsense, tongue clicks, advanced literary discourse have this in common: they fail to mean:

> Doubtless you recall the discussion in the *Cratylus*, Socrates refereeing at first, then refuting Hermogenes' argument that names are not attached to things by nature but are conventions of the users? Well, so far as my *art*

> is concerned I am on the side of Hermogenes, even though he is opposed by modern philology, which holds that names possess "echoic" value and that word conventions are anything but arbitrary. . . . Derivations in nature are not the artist's affair, nature being only another convention to him.[81]

Word and thing are unrelated—or, to put it another way, a word is a thing essentially alien to that other thing that claims to be its referent in the world of experience. Language, therefore, is music. It is music deficient in pitch and infirm in rhythm, but music nonetheless. All the distortions in Stravinsky's vocal lines—syllabic misemphases, melismata, dissection of words—can be justified: for if language is an arbitrary system, there is no reason not to refit its acoustic matter into another arbitrary system, invented by Stravinsky for a certain composition. By exerting extraordinary stress on language, Stravinsky proved its plasticity, its detachability from the world of its reference.

In 1944 the American composer-conductor Nathaniel Schilkret (who conducted the first recording of Gershwin's *An American in Paris*) commissioned Stravinsky, Schoenberg, and five others to write a movement each for a suite based on the book of Genesis. Stravinsky wrote a brief cantata, *Babel* (1945)—his first use of an English text. I know of no other version of the story which so rejoices in the confounding of human language: the music that accompanies the building of the tower is smooth, quiet, with little profile; but the music that accompanies the destruction of speech is kinetic, propulsive—the dismemberment of speech is every bit as exciting as the dismemberment of Orpheus in Stravinsky's ballet of 1948. Later, Stravinsky wrote that he liked hearing his works performed untranslated, in the various original languages of their composition: "Musically speaking, Babel is a blessing."[82] The fall of the tower of Babel is a Fortunate Fall: for in the scattering of the tongues language lost its canonical relation to nature, became suitable for song: "Music is a non-analogous system—or several non-analogous systems: it is more of a Babel than a universal language."[83] Therefore *Babel*, like *Apollo*, is a parable about the origin of music. It is the Old Testament account of the creation of the unnatural.

Once the inconvenient illusion of meaning has been dispelled, a word can be taken for what it really is: a suggestion of rhythm. Stravinsky dismissed semantics as an idle exercise in besmudging sounds with a pollen of signification; but he believed that prosody was a serious discipline. In Eden, Adam fastened names to things; in Babylon, God unfastened the names and gave them rhythmic force.

His concern with prosody was lifelong. In 1914 Stravinsky decided to compose music for a passage from a book of humorous and nonsensical Russian verse called *Koz'ma Prutkov*; this project never came to fruition, but some sketches survive, with examples in musical notation of trochaics, dactyls, and anapests[84] In *Oedipus Rex*, Stravinsky said, he based his music on prosodic rhythms, though this refers only to the musical underpulse—for Stravinsky paid, as we have seen, no attention to the scansion of the Latin text he was in fact setting to music. Indeed, his habit of ignoring the tonic accent sometimes came to embarrass him: for instance, by stressing the first syllable of *cecidi* in "ego senem cecidi," Stravinsky made his phrase mean (meaninglessly) "I fell the old man," instead of "I killed the old man."[85] But this did not so distress the composer that he bothered to change the music.

Why should a composer obsessed with prosody disregard the actual prosodic values of the words before him? He seems to have felt that any given word makes a botch of its own rhythm, just as it makes a botch of its meaning. Beneath a verbal phrase, there is a push, a division, an inflection; but if the syllables must be finagled to make explicit this subsistent rhythm, Stravinsky did not object to finagling them. Stravinsky admired the famous phonograph record of Yeats reading his verse:

> Yeats pauses at the end of each line, he dwells a precise time on and in between each word—
>
> one could as easily notate his verses in musical rhythm as scan them in poetic metres.[86]

Stravinsky was quite correct—perhaps he did not know that, in collaboration with Florence Farr, Yeats had in fact converted some of his poems to musical notation, to be chanted to a psaltery. But Yeats's strange, neoquantitative reading style—he pretended that English syllables, like Latin, must be either half notes or quarter notes—was as much a willful imposition of scansion as any passage of *Oedipus Rex*. Prosody exists at the place where music and poetry join together, where they display their pure arbitrariness unimpeded by expression, or meaning, or even particular sounds: the daDAdaDA without da or DA.

The study of prosody informed Stravinsky's instrumental compositions as well as his vocal ones. His first important work after *Oedipus Rex* was the ballet *Apollo* (1928), which begins with the birth of Apollo and offers a pageant of the Muses, displaying their arts to the newborn god:

> The real subject of *Apollo* . . . is versification, which implies something arbitrary and artificial to most people, though to me art is arbitrary and must be artificial. The basic rhythmic patterns are iambic, and the individual dances may be thought of as variations of the reversible dotted-rhythm iamb idea. . . . I cannot say whether the idea of the Alexandrines, that supremely arbitrary set of prosodic rules, was pre-compositional or not.[87]

Apollo is a sort of poem without words, a delicate filigree of intersecting meters, as if the pattern of macrons and breves written out above some lines of verse were looped over a musical staff. The action of the ballet is a rehearsal of an aesthetic equation—Calliope + Polyhymnia = Terpsichore:

> Calliope, receiving the stylus and tablets from Apollo, personifies poetry and its rhythm; Polyhymnia, finger on lips, represents mime. . . . Finally, Terpsichore, combining in herself both the rhythm of poetry and the eloquence of gesture, reveals dancing to the world.[88]

Oedipus Rex is loud classicism; *Apollo* is hushed classicism. The opera is propelled by the tension between the words, which try to assert their own meters, their own meanings, and the music, which insists far more emphatically on its own immitigable rhythms. The ballet, however, is poised, elegant, still; nothing contradicts the iambs proposed by the unanimous strings.

Behind *Oedipus Rex* is Sophocles. Behind *Apollo* is the seventeenth-century French poet Boileau, one of whose couplets is used as an epigraph to the "Variation of Calliope":

> *Que toujours dans vos vers le sens, coupant les mots,*
> *Suspende l'hémistiche, en marque le repos.*
>
> (*L'art poétique*, 1:105–6)

Boileau was not the greatest poet of his time, but he was the greatest legislator of poets—he sought to give order and symmetry, propriety, to verse. In the quoted couplet Boileau asked poets to devise alexandrines that fall sensibly into two equal six-syllable half lines. Stravinsky designed the "Variation of Calliope" to be a musical exposition of this motto.[89] The score of *Apollo* is a meditation on the theme of making up rules—indefensible rules, unnatural rules, arbitrary rules, but rules without which art is impossible.

Apollo is born, not in a sunburst or a clang of the spheres, but quietly, a little god in the costume of Boileau or Alexander Pope, with a powdered wig.

Stravinsky's concept of mute prosody, poetry with a finger on its lips, extended beyond *Apollo*. His Duo Concertant for violin and piano (1934) was composed as a "musical parallel to the old pastoral poetry";[90] among its movements are two Eglogues and a Dithyrambe. And twenty years after *Apollo*, Stravinsky wrote another classical ballet, *Orpheus* (1948), in which the theme of music-by-rule alters into the theme of rule-by-music, for Orpheus's lyre can tame savage beasts, can make trees pull their roots out of the ground and walk. *Orpheus*, however, is a far more anguished ballet than its predecessor: by introducing a human being into the divine vibrations of musical action, Stravinsky introduces desperation, ecstasy, madness, all that Apollo blissfully ignored. The dismemberment of Orpheus—the climax of the ballet—shows yet again that human subjects and their expressive clamor cannot sustain themselves in the ether of music. Just as Oedipus's words had to be disarticulated, just as Petrushka's sawdust had to be knocked out of him, so Orpheus's crazy pain must be liquidated into the calm plinks of a harp:

> Lost in his immeasurable grief, he scorns the Bacchantes, the jealous Thracian women, and in a frenzy they tear him to pieces. Orpheus is no more, but his song lives. Apollo appears radiant in sunlight, the god raises the lyre of Orpheus, lifting his deathless song to the eternal sky.[91]

Boileau triumphs, and Dionysus, the god of expression,[92] is defeated. After *Oedipus Rex*, Stravinsky's music was mostly depopulated, disengaged, inward-turned, serenely investigating the principles of its own composition. But with *Orpheus* that unkillable phantom the human subject returns to disturb the prosody of the music—a revenant that foreshadows the drama of the greatest project of Stravinsky's life, *The Rake's Progress*.

The Rake's Progress (1951) is the only work of Stravinsky's that provides a full evening's entertainment—it is more than twice as long as any other of his compositions. Whereas most of Stravinsky's other vocal stage works are hybrids—opera-ballet (*The Wedding*, *The Nightingale*), or opera-oratorio (*Oedipus Rex*), or opera-melodrama (*Perséphone*)—*The Rake's Progress* is an old-fashioned eighteenth-century "number" opera, divided into arias, duets, and recitative. It is a conventional work. But, to Stravinsky, music *is* convention—there is no nature to which music can hope to appeal. The theme of *The Rake's Progress* is conventionality, for its hero is confounded by his attempts to be spontaneous, free, governed by nature rather than by rule.

In 1947 Stravinsky saw an exhibition in Chicago of the celebrated series of eight paintings (better known as etchings) by William Hogarth titled *A Rake's Progress* (1733), in which a young man inherits his father's estate and seduces a town girl, learns good manners, roisters about with whores, is arrested for debt (the town girl ransoms him with her savings), marries an ugly rich woman (the town girl, their child in her arms, is excluded from the ceremony), loses a second fortune in a gaming house, is sent to prison for debt, and is at last committed to the madhouse, where the town girl continues to visit him. Hogarth's rake is a pale, inert figure surrounded everywhere by grotesques, gargoyles, who at last tear him asunder—the narrative must have seemed to Stravinsky partly parallel to the theme of the ballet that he was writing, *Orpheus*. When Stravinsky asked his friend Aldous Huxley to recommend a librettist, Huxley mentioned Auden, who, upon inquiry, was eager to collaborate. I wonder whether Stravinsky or Auden ever noticed that, in the fine print on a long scroll on the second of the *Rake's Progress* images, Hogarth listed a gift to an Italian opera singer, namely a gold snuff box decorated with an image of Orpheus.

Auden came from New York to California to work on the scenario as a guest at Stravinsky's home; the poet amazed the composer with his erudition, his technical facility in verse, his poor personal hygiene, and his odd beliefs, such as in the telepathic powers of cats.[93] Soon they expanded Hogarth's slender outline into a plot (their original scenario has been printed, with some errors).[94] Hogarth's story has no conflict except that provided by the contrast between the town girl's restraint and fidelity opposing the rake's licentiousness; but Auden and Stravinsky outfitted the tale with a whistling villain (who eventually became the jolliest, most major-mode devil in the operatic literature) to conduct the hero to his ruin.

Most of the newly devised scenes show the hero pushing at the limits of the human condition. Hogarth's rake had fairly pedestrian desires—a little excitement, a little wealth, a little whoring, a respectable marriage; but Stravinsky and Auden's hero, Tom Rakewell, dreams of restoring mankind to paradise by means of a machine that extracts gold from seawater (in the finished opera, a machine that turns stones into bread). Tom Rakewell is metaphysically ambitious in a way impossible for Hogarth's rake; behind Tom is Adonis, Adam, the Everyman of the old morality play, a whole assortment of Modernist archetypes, just as the flaccid characters of Eliot's *The Waste Land* are held upright by the mythological beings to whom they allude. It has often been noted that *The Rake's Progress*, like Stravinsky's *The Soldier's Tale* (1918), is a retelling of the Faust legend—indeed, Eliot thought that the libretto failed in its attempt to combine Hogarth's narrative with the traditional pact with the devil.[95] But it is specifically a Faust story on the model of Goethe's, for Tom Rakewell, like Faust, is a creature of unlimited desire, tottering on a confused path to the verge of ultimate things.

Stravinsky knew almost nothing about Auden before inviting him to write a libretto. He was amazingly lucky, for it happened that Auden shared many of Stravinsky's opinions about the virtues of the conventional and about the relation between nature and art. In his essay "Making, Knowing, and Judging," Auden offered a brief test to determine whether a man's assumptions about art were compatible with his own:

> "Do you like, and by like I mean really like . . .
> (1) Long lists of proper names such as the Old Testament genealogies or the Catalogue of ships in the *Iliad*?
> (2) Riddles and all other ways of not calling a spade a spade?
> (3) Complicated verse forms of great technical difficulty . . . ?
> (4) Conscious theatrical exaggeration, pieces of Baroque flattery . . . ?"[96]

To anyone who answered yes to all four, who delighted in language's unmeaning self-delight, Auden felt sympathetic. It is a test that Stravinsky could have passed effortlessly. Auden, like Goethe, thought that art is art because it is not nature, and relegated art to its own private sphere of operation, what he called the secondary world.

Auden's attitude toward the primary world—nature—was uneasy. He was an avid student of biology, psychology, and (from children's guides) physics; and he generally saw nature as inhuman, unpleasant, difficult to apprehend, ruled by impersonal forces such as gravitation, sexual desire, and evolutionary survival urges. Opposed to this species of nature is spirit:

> *The Two Real Worlds*
> (1) The Natural World of the Dynamo, the world of masses, identical relations and recurrent events, describable, not in words but in terms of numbers, or rather, in algebraic terms. . . .
> (2) The Historical World of the Virgin, the world of faces, analogical relations and singular events, describable only in terms of speech.[97]

In this essay, "The Virgin and the Dynamo," Auden went on to posit two chimerical worlds, one caused by the false attempt to personalize the dynamo, to pretend that masses have faces, as if the force of gravity might be swayed by fervent prayer, and the other caused by the false attempt to depersonalize the Virgin, to treat human beings as statistical abstractions, the pawns of impulse, in the manner of Zola. This dialectic of nature and spirit was an attempt to discover how a Christian might do justice both to his soul—unique and personal—and to his body—material and animal, subject to biophysical laws.

But Auden had an aesthetic dialectic as well as a Christian dialectic. Here we have not nature versus spirit, but nature versus art. Here nature is not so much a physicist's abstraction of vectors colliding on a three-dimensional grid, but a kind of chaos, sloppy and wet, unintelligible, weedy, a landscape without a gardener. Art, on the other hand, is exactly the opposite: spruce and spiffy, in fact a bit too neat, for the privet is always perfectly cut and in the end the good guy always gets the girl.

Auden thought, correctly, that his greatest work was *The Sea and the Mirror* (1944), which is his fullest statement of the relation of nature to art. It is a commentary on Shakespeare's *The Tempest*, in which Auden resurrects the dramatis personae and requires each one to comment, in his or her own voice, on the action of the play. The subtlest of the commentators is, surprisingly, Caliban, who gives a long speech in the most florid, baroque, Henry Jamesish prose. Caliban claims that Shakespeare spoiled his play by introducing into it a personification of nature, Caliban himself—for lumpish, unlovely nature is the one thing that resists all of the transforming magic of art, the brute guest at the cocktail party of the Muses. In fact, nature and art are hopeless opposites:

> You yourself [Shakespeare], we seem to remember, have spoken of the conjured spectacle as "a mirror held up to nature," a phrase misleading in its aphoristic sweep but indicative at least of one aspect of the relation between the real and the imagined, their mutual reversal of value, for isn't the essential artistic strangeness to which your citation of the sinisterly blessed image would point just this: that on the far side of the mirror the general will to compose, to form at all costs a felicitous pattern becomes the *necessary cause* of any particular effort to live or act or love or triumph or vary, instead of being as, in so far as it emerges at all, it is on this side, their *accidental effect*?[98]

Nature is chaos struggling toward order; art is a backward image of nature, for art begins in order, in intendedness, and struggles to diversify itself into a semblance of the richness and variety of nature.

Caliban goes on to show the horrors of strictly unnatural art and of strictly artless nature. If Ariel, the artistic imagination, becomes the dominant force in a man's being, that man will live in an endless dream, where fantastic images form and teem and vanish without any standard of reality or truth. But to a man in whom Caliban predominates, a man without imagination, nature reveals itself to be a wasteland of extinct volcanos, an airless lava plateau—a scientist's caricature of the physical world. Ariel's feeling for the ideal is needed to soften the asperity of nature; and Caliban's sense of fact is needed to anchor, secure, and validate the imagination's intuitions.

These two dialectics—the virgin and the dynamo, and Ariel and Caliban—govern the progress of Tom Rakewell. Though Stravinsky helped with the construction of the scenario and Auden's friend Chester Kallman wrote much of the libretto—including some of its best scenes—there is nothing in *The Rake's Progress* that falls outside the orbit of Auden's intellectual world. Anne Trulove, the opera's heroine (Hogarth's town girl moved into the country and made chaste) is the virgin of Auden's dialectic, a respecter of the soul's uniqueness, a Marylike intercessor for Tom's salvation; whereas Tom, the nature child, embodies the values of the dynamo. By another analysis, as we shall see, Tom is Caliban, while Nick Shadow, the devil, is a sinister Ariel, provoking outlandish images of bliss.

Some critics have seen the opera, at least in part, as warm, subjective, psychological, "human and haunting," and to that extent a repudiation of the heartless objective music of Stravinsky's earlier days.[99] I hope to show the opposite: that while the libretto, like the libretto of *The Nightingale*, seems to illustrate the victory of the human over the inhuman, the opera as a whole celebrates system and inflexible rule.

The characters of the opera are colder than they appear at first. As far as Auden was concerned, there are two types of drama: objective drama (the detestable kind), in which the playwright carries a camera and tape recorder to study human behavior at a far remove; and subjective drama (the good kind), in which the playwright illuminates the human ego exercising its freedom by making choices:

> If I try . . . to project my subjective experience of life in dramatic form the play will be of the allegorical type like Everyman. The hero will be the volitional ego that chooses, and the other characters, either states of the self, pleasant and unpleasant, good and bad, for or against which the hero's choices are made, or counselors, like reason and conscience, which attempt to influence his choices.[100]

The Rake's Progress is clearly a "subjective" drama; but it is subjectivity objectified, picked apart, projected into a battery of allegorical figments. Pathos is diminished, in the absence of any independent agent except the hero. In Auden's view, almost every interesting story is secretly a *psychomachia*, a battle of internal forces within a single soul. Thus he described Don Quixote and Sancho Panza as the twin aspects of a single being, one a mad improver of life and the other a lax bland realist; similarly twinned are Don Giovanni and Leporello, Lear and his Fool, Tamino and Papageno (in Mozart's *The Magic Flute*), Bertie Wooster and Jeeves. (All these are discussed in the essay "Balaam and His Ass.")

But the most important pair of master and servant, for our purposes, is Goethe's Faust-Mephistopheles. Auden would have them played by "identical twins,"[101] for they are alike in that each is fundamentally a nonentity:

> the story of Faust is precisely the story of a man who refuses to be anyone and only wishes to be someone else . . . Mephisto . . . [is] the manifestation of possibility without actuality.[102]

> In our age . . . Our real, because permanent, idolatry is an idolatry of possibility. And in such an age the Devil appears in the form of Mephisto, in the form, that is, of an actor. The point about an actor is that he has no name of his own, for his name is Legion. One might say that our age recognized its nature on the day when Henry Irving was knighted.[103]

The Rake's Progress was Auden's contribution to the literature of nonpersons. Neither its hero nor its villain is anything but a pregnant zero, a creature shapeless with unreal potentialities. Stravinsky had long worked toward a theater of inexpressiveness; and at last he had a libretto crammed with histrionic opportunities, but populated only with generic, brand X human beings, characters who secretly lack identity. *Petrushka* treated puppets; *The Nightingale* treated machines; *The Rake's Progress* treats actors, toying with roles, conniving at the crowd.

Act 1, scene 1. The opera opens in cool pastoral, at the garden of Trulove's house. Anne and Tom sing a duet about Aphrodite, who will "with a kiss restore the Age of Gold." The duet becomes a trio as the prudent Trulove worries whether Tom can keep his vows to his daughter Anne—*vow* is one of the crucial words of the opera, for behavior that is constrained, circumscribed by vows differs from the radically free behavior that Tom will cultivate; the vow is convention, freedom is its opposite. Trulove has found Tom a job in a countinghouse, but Tom declines—in a soliloquy-aria, Tom scoffs at steady employment:

> Since it is not by merit
> We rise or we fall,
> But the favour of Fortune
> That governs us all,
> Why should I labour
> For what in the end
> She will give me for nothing
> If she be my friend? . . .
> My life lies before me.
> The world is so wide:
> Come, wishes, be horses;
> This beggar shall ride.
> [*recit.*] I wish I had money.

Tom trusts heaven's "predestination" to determine his fate. One of Hogarth's paintings is called *The Gaming House*; and while there is no gaming house in the opera (the official gambling scene takes place in a graveyard), nevertheless the whole world is, to Tom, a kind of casino. Despite Tom's pious talk of predestination, trusting in luck is, to Auden, a rejection of God: in his poem "Casino" (1936) Auden speaks of games of roulette as a kind of atheist's love feast, "a rite of disbelief." Here Tom reveals his allegiance to the dynamo: he abdicates responsibility for himself, lets his life be determined by mass and force.

"Come, wishes, be horses," is a common sentiment in Auden's poetry. Auden distinguishes wishes from desires—a desire is capable of being gratified, while a wish is not: "A desire for a Cadillac which may be real for a prosperous American businessman would be fantastic for a Chinese peasant."[104] To wish—in the way that a Chinese peasant wishes for a Cadillac—is to fill oneself with self-hatred, because, as Auden explains, when the peasant asks himself why he does not have a Cadillac, the only answer is: Because I am I. The wisher ultimately wishes to be someone else. Tom's nonentity, like Faust's, springs from this fascination with alternate selves.

"I wish I had money" is Nick's cue to enter—he will provide the illusory identities Tom hankers for. This whole scene, from the love duet about Aphrodite to the appearance of Nick, is an expansion of a song that Auden wrote in 1941:

Aphrodite's garden is
  A haunted region;
For the very signs whereby
Lovers register their vow,
  With a look, with a sigh,
Summon to their meetings One
  Whose name is Legion.[105]

Here Legion goes by the name of Nick Shadow, who claims to be the servant of a recently deceased uncle of Tom's—an uncle Tom never knew he had—who has left his fortune to his nephew. Nick urges Tom to leave the country estate and go to London to take care of business:

A thriving fortune has its roots of care:
Attorneys crouched like gardeners to pay,
Bowers of paper only seals repair . . .
Tom. Well, then if Fortune sow
A crop that wax and pen must cultivate,
Let's fly to husbandry . . .

The world of London banking is a mock pastoral, growing endless reams of paper instead of fruit and foliage. This is the first appearance in the opera of the surrogate theme, the substitution of the unnatural for the natural—a theme that will have astonishing developments in act 2. As Tom says farewell to Anne and her father, Nick steps out of character—he must show that he is not the devil, only an actor—to announce to the audience: "The Progress of a Rake begins!"

Act 1, scene 2. We are in Mother Goose's brothel. A chorus of Whores and Roaring Boys sings (in the words of the original scenario) of "the Love of War and the War of Love."[106] Instead of inaugurating an Age of Gold, Aphrodite has joined forces with her husband, Ares—not her lover, Adonis; in London, sex is intimate with casual destruction. In his elegy on Freud, Auden speaks of "anarchic Aphrodite,"[107] and it is clear that the corrupt institutions of the city are not so much unnatural as themselves derived from nature—pastoral, in a sick way. Who is more natural than Aphrodite, even when her name is Mother Goose?

Nature. NOW WHY DID I CHOOSE
TO PLAY MOTHER GOOSE?

FOR MAN MY HERO IS A RAKE!
YES SENIOR POET, YOU SAW THAT & MORE:
SAW NATURE AS HIS PASSION AND TOO OFT HIS WHORE.[108]

In the late 1970s, the ghost of Auden (who died in 1973) attended a séance at James Merrill's Ouija board and remembered with pleasure the night of the première of *The Rake's Progress*; Nature also came to the party to note that she had played the role of Mother Goose in the opera. Merrill, following supernatural instruction, put a record of the brothel scene on his phonograph so that the assembled spirits could enjoy Stravinsky's music. I invite the reader of this essay to do the same, as we return to the spectacle before us.

Nick introduces Tom to Mother Goose, whom he calls the "Lady Bishop of the game." The game, of course, is chess; like Lewis Carroll's *Through the Looking-Glass*, *The Rake's Progress* is itself a kind of chess game, where abstract figures are moved jerkily, predictably, according to rule, across a neutral field of action. Stravinsky's usual way of tackling a new assignment was to look for models; and the chief model he chose for this opera was the Mozart–da Ponte *Così fan tutte* (All Women Do It, 1790), a performance of which Stravinsky saw in 1948.[109] *Così fan tutte* is an opera about two soldiers so proud of the fidelity of their fiancées, so eager to prove it to a skeptical friend, that they disguise themselves as Albanians—and each tries to seduce the other's fiancée. To their horror, both succeed, after a little struggling; but in the end the soldiers marry their original girlfriends, with fewer unrealistic expectations about the nature of love. There are some musical resemblances between Mozart's opera and Stravinsky's,[110] but the most important resemblance is in the machine-tooled rigidity of the plot: either of these "heartless" operas could be staged on a chessboard, for the characters are not individuals but mathematical counters pushed through pretty symmetries of attraction and repulsion. Both operas offer strong distinctions between sexual love and the other kind: sexual love is inherently frivolous, omniform, seeking new objects, while the other kind, the love determined by vows, is stable. *The Rake's Progress* is of the eighteenth century in its niceness of categories, its plotting of its hero's progress on a grid of discriminations.

Mother Goose and Nick propound to Tom the catechism of the dynamo:

Nick. What is thy duty to thyself?
Tom. To shut my ears to prude and preacher

And follow Nature as my teacher. . . .
Mother Goose. What is Pleasure then?
Tom. The idol of all dreams, the same
Whatever shape it wear or name;
Whom flirts imagine as a hat,
Old maids believe to be a cat. . . .
Nick. One final question. Love is?
Tom. Love, Love!
That precious word is like a fiery coal;
It burns my lips, strikes terror to my soul.

Here, as in the first scene, we see Tom's contempt for rules, precepts, all that restrains the free life of impulse—though, as Tom will discover, the man who chooses to be nature's pupil is less free than he may imagine. Tom's definition of pleasure is amusing because hat and cat seem to be such silly sources of gratification; but in fact this speech touches on one of the opera's more serious, even frightening themes, the arbitrariness of the object of desire.

We want the object of our desire to be attainable, and we want it to be dignified, culturally acceptable; but alas, we crave all sorts of inappropriate and bizarre things:

Love requires an Object,
But this varies so much,
Almost, I imagine,
  Anything will do:
When I was a child, I
Loved a pumping-engine,
Thought it every bit as
  Beautiful as you.[111]

This stanza from "Heavy Date" (1939)—maybe Auden's nastiest poem—contains a message as remarkable as anything a poet ever wrote to his beloved. No one can keep his desire steadily focused: the objects of desire slip and slide grotesquely, tend to drift outside the human and the animate into broken-down industrial machines, as well as cat and hat. This is why love needs to be bound by vows: desire is too unreliable for a single night's entertainment, let alone a lifetime of companionship. Eros and Philia have nothing to do with each other, and, according to Auden, it is an error of Western civilization to pretend otherwise. "Love" is the precious word that burns Tom's lips, for he cannot find any way to integrate the virgin, the realm of the sacred, into the secular and erotic world of the brothel. Auden's partner Chester Kallman—who wrote the words of this scene—may have been thinking of Eliot's *Little Gidding*, the last of the *Four Quartets* (1942):

> Love is the unfamiliar Name
> Behind the hands that wove
> The intolerable shirt of flame
> Which human power cannot remove.[112]

Stravinsky set this to music too, in a stark four-part chorus called "Anthem" (1962).

In the brothel, a cuckoo clock strikes one, and Tom, love-chastened, rises to leave; but Nick turns the hands back to midnight—Nick will also show himself the keeper of the opera's metronome in the graveyard scene, when he interrupts the midnight chime, gives Tom a little extra time to sweat before carrying off his soul to hell. Tom sings to the Whores a song about the betrayal of love, about the weeping lover who "renews the vows he did not keep"—the Whores are saddened, moved, and offer to console him in their arms. This scene is congruent with that part of the ballet *Orpheus* in which Orpheus plays his lyre so affectingly that Hades permits him to take his dead wife back to earth—but, of course, in the Hades of the brothel, Tom is simply invited to join the damned in their damnation. Mother Goose claims Tom as her prize for the night, and the Whores and Roaring Boys serenade them to the gayest, most lighthearted and rollicking tune in the opera:

> The sun is bright, the grass is green.
> Lanterloo, lanterloo!
> The King is courting his young Queen.
> Lanterloo, lanterloo, lanterloo, my lady.
> *Women.* . . . They go a-riding. Whom do they meet?
> *Men.* Three scarecrows and a pair of feet.
> What will she do when they sit at table?
> *Women.* Eat as much as she is able.
> What will they do when they lie in bed? . . .
> *Men.* Draw his sword and chop off her head.

Stravinsky said of these verses (written by Auden), "I wonder whether any poet since the Elizabethans has made a composer such a beautiful gift of words for music."[113] But the beautiful words have some sinister suggestions. Beneath the bright excitement of Stravinsky's pseudo-Elizabethan melody, sexual love is shown to be gluttony and murder—*dying* in a sense beyond the Elizabethan one. In act 2, Tom will, in a manner of speaking, decide to marry a scarecrow—the sexual instinct seems naturally to lead to the pursuit of hollow images, ever more famishing.

In the first two scenes of act 1, we have traveled from pastoral to mock pastoral; the mock pastoral seems to have a real pastoral inside it ("The sun is bright, the grass is green"), yet inside this winter's dream of spring there is only more desolation. This scene ends with Nick's summary: "Dreams may lie, / But dream. For when you wake, you die." But Tom will never wake. Tom's hunger for illusory objects implicates him in fantasy more and more, and his only escape will be to the madhouse, to the endless dream role of Adonis. There can be no exit into nature from the competing artifices that constitute the opera.

Act 1, scene 3. This brief scene consists entirely of Anne's big aria. She wonders why Tom has failed to write, and hopes that love, and the night, and the moon can provide some sort of connective tissue between the two lovers:

> Guide me, O moon, chastely when I depart,
> And warmly be the same
> He watches without grief or shame;
> It cannot, cannot be thou art
> A colder moon upon a colder heart.

These lines (by Auden) show how hard it is properly to delineate the boundary between virgin and dynamo. Virginal Anne wants to personalize the landscape, to imbue the moon with a vague pathos, a slight warmth; but she fears that, instead, the dynamo will infect human hearts with its own inanimation. In Auden's "Nocturne" (1951), the poet looks at the moon full of rapt wonder and wishes to address the moon as "Mother, Virgin, Muse" but finds that he knows too much astronomy to credit the personification:

> The Goddess, clearly, has to go,
> Whose majesty is but the mask
> That hides a faceless dynamo[114]

As in the opera, the subjective tenderness is a lie and must be rejected. Stravinsky's music cleverly imitates the chill of "a colder moon upon a colder heart"; of course, Stravinsky was a specialist in musical refrigeration. He once spoke of using rhythmic means to freeze the drama of Oedipus into music;[115] and the freezing of *The Rake's Progress* was no difficult feat.

Anne's aria (like the final aria of her namesake, Donna Anna in Mozart's *Don Giovanni*, 1787) ends in a great show-off cabaletta:

> Love cannot falter,
> Cannot desert;
> Though it be shunned
> Or be forgotten,
> Though it be hurt,
> If Love be love
> It will not alter.

Stravinsky makes a joke at Anne's expense by having her sing rapid runs on the first syllable of *alter*—love may not alter, but the word *alter* goes through spasm after spasm of altering. Berlioz wrote in his memoirs that he would gladly shed his own blood if he could erase the end of Donna Anna's aria, for the roulades destroyed the sentiment, the feeling of injury, that Mozart so carefully depicted in the aria's first section. Stravinsky, however, delights in demoting Anne from a figure of pathos to nothing more than an agile soprano.

Act 2, scene 1. We are back in London, where Tom is eating breakfast. The act opens with an aria of disgust:

> Vary the song, O London, change!
> Disband your notes and let them range;
> Let rumour scream, let folly purr,
> Let tone desert the flatterer.
> Let Harmony no more obey
> The strident choristers of prey;
> Yet all your music cannot fill
> The gap that in my heart—is still.
> *[recit.]* O Nature, green unnatural mother,
> how I have followed where you led.
> Is it for this I left the country?
> No ploughman is more a slave to sun,
> moon, and season
> than a gentleman to the clock of fashion.

This is a prayer for chaos. The previous act ended with the hope for the changeless; this one begins with the opposite request. Tom is sick of false concord, sick of hypocrisy—he wants ugliness to sound ugly. (Stravinsky's music is not ugly, but it is unsettled, slightly queasy: fragments of melodies fail to assemble into complete lines, the harmony gropes for a firm bass, and the vocal ornaments seem to be embellishing nothing in particular—a pile of Styrofoam angels and popcorn balls without a Christmas tree in sight.) Hoping to find freedom by moving to London, Tom has instead discovered himself snared by another system, another set of rigid rules—and he is willing to go to extreme measures to extricate himself from systems.

"O Nature, green unnatural mother," though written by Kallman, is an adaptation of a line of Auden's, a line that might serve as the motto of Stravinsky's career: "Nature by nature in unnature ends." This appears in "In Sickness and in Health" (1947), a poem that deserves more than casual attention, because, in a sense, *The Rake's Progress* is a gigantic expansion of this rich lyric. It is an epithalamium, a marriage poem, ostensibly dedicated to two acquaintances of Auden's but in fact, according to Humphrey Carpenter, a covert celebration of the vows that Auden and Kallman swore to each other.[116] It falls neatly into two parts, sickness and health, or the dynamo and the virgin.

The sickness section is a meditation on the precariousness of love. Love tends to decay—love is instinct with chaos. Auden looks to opera for his models of the perversions of love:

> Nature by nature in unnature ends:
> Echoing each other like two waterfalls,
>   Tristan, Isolde, the great friends,
> Make passion out of passion's obstacles,
> Deliciously postponing their delight,
> Prolong frustration till it lasts all night,
> Then perish lest Brangaene's worldly cry
> Should sober their cerebral ecstasy.
>
> But, dying, conjure up their opposite,
> Don Juan, so terrified of death he hears
>   Each moment recommending it
> And knows no argument to counter theirs:
> Trapped in their vile affections, he must find
> Angels to keep him chaste; a helpless, blind

Unhappy spook, he haunts the urinals,
Existing solely by their miracles.[117]

Auden thought that the complementary myths of Don Giovanni and Tristan were "diseases of the Christian imagination."[118] Each myth shows how love grows twisted, incoherent, if it lacks a telos—a finite, intelligible object of affection. Love is confounded by an infusion of the infinite: Tristan's boundless love for Isolde reduces all the rest of the universe to zero, while Don Giovanni is in love not with a woman but with his list, an infinite series of conquests—"Don Giovanni's pleasure in seducing women is not sensual but arithmetical."[119] Stravinsky remembered that, when Auden first visited him to work on their opera, Auden talked about Tristan and Isolde[120]—and I imagine that Auden's favorite theories on the viciousness of absolute love were discussed during the original formulation of the scenario.

Stravinsky studied the score of *Don Giovanni*, as well as that of the subsequent opera by Mozart and da Ponte, *Così fan tutte*, while he worked on his own; and, though Tom Rakewell is not quite so promiscuous, his affections are every bit as energetically vagrant as those of Don Giovanni. *The Rake's Progress* is a kind of sequel to *Don Giovanni*: the libertine has at last exhausted sexual delight (during the intermission between acts 1 and 2), reached the end of the endless list, and so decides that he must seek novel stimulation through strange, strange paths.

The sickness section of "In Sickness and in Health" goes on to show that perverse sexual love is the cause of all wars—the Roaring Boys of *The Rake's Progress* were right in thinking that a good smash-up lies at the end of whoring. The health section of "In Sickness and in Health" suggests the only possible cure for the disease of love, the only way to confine love to a single coherent shape: the vow:

All chance, all love, all logic, you and I,
  Exist by grace of the Absurd,
And without conscious artifice we die:
So, lest we manufacture in our flesh
The lie of our divinity afresh,
Describe round our chaotic malice now,
The arbitrary circle of a vow.[121]

Anne Trulove offers Tom a means of self-definition, self-circumscription, personhood, instead of the continual refinement of sensation that Tom has sought. Distention of being, shapelessness and self-hatred, fall upon Tom in the absence of Anne's control. The arbitrary vow offers relief from the natural and the unnatural alike.

Long before writing "In Sickness and in Health" Auden explored the relationship between the natural and the unnatural. In a journal of 1929, Auden wrote that the unnatural is the goal of the human race:

> The progress of man seems to be in a direction away from nature. The development of consciousness may be compared with the breaking away of the child from the Oedipus relation. Just as one must be weaned from one's mother, one must be weaned from the Earth Mother (Unconscious?). . . . Man is a product of the refined disintegration of nature by time.[122]

Once Auden became a Christian, he found that he could not value the unnatural—the sophisticated, the hyperconscious—any more than the natural. He continued, however, to posit a continuum between the two, even a convergence of opposites; that is why nature naturally ends in unnature. When Caliban in *The Sea and the Mirror* is made to speak like Henry James's own Henry James, it is because nature can utter only inarticulate grunts and moans—a wholly unnatural tongue is the only way of calling attention to this central languagelessness. As Stravinsky said, nature is only a convention, just like any other.

Tom Rakewell too cultivates the unnatural life: he eats "curious viands" and drinks the "precious wines" of Oporto and Provence until he chokes on them. It is precisely because he is Caliban, a nature worshipper, that he declines into such abstraction from nature; he slides wildly from one end of the continuum to the other. Aphrodite, the goddess of nature, has goaded Tom into an increasingly chaotic, stylized, studied, denatured way of life—fine port instead of fruit juice. Only Anne holds out the promise of escape. Tom ought to choose between two systems: either a regulated life based on appetite (Aphrodite) or a regulated life based on a vow of love (Anne). But instead, at the behest of the devil he tries to deny both sets of rules, both artifices, and espouse the life of radical freedom.

At the end of his aria "Vary the song," Tom exclaims, "I wish I were happy." After hearing a similar whine in act 1—"I wish I had money"—Nick provided money; now he will provide some pseudo-happiness. He shows Tom a portrait of—of all people on the face of the earth—a "gorgon," a hideous circus performer, Baba the Turk, and advises Tom to marry her. Tom is aghast, but Nick explains his reasoning. He says that men are unhappy because they are unfree:

> Why? Because the giddy multitude are driven
> by the unpredictable Must of their pleasures
> and the sober few are bound by the inflexible
> Ought of their duty, between which slaveries
> there is nothing to choose.
> Would you be happy? Then learn to act freely.
> Would you be free? Then learn to ignore
> Those twin tyrants of appetite and conscience.

To marry Baba the Turk is to escape from the grid, to embrace the unpredictable.

The introduction of Baba is the crucial element in the plot of *The Rake's Progress*. In the original scenario, Tom was to marry an ugly duchess—exactly as in Hogarth—not a circus freak; and it would be interesting to know how Auden and Kallman came to the notion of a *mariage gratuit*. The great master of the theme of gratuitous action was André Gide, whose *Les caves du Vatican* (1914) tells the story of a sophisticated nature child who murders a stranger simply to prove himself free and capable of anything. A gratuitous act is a hole in the causal chain, an irruption of chaos, as Nick explains in an aria:

> For he alone is free
> Who chooses what to will, and wills
> His choice as destiny.
> No eye his future can foretell,
> No law his past explain
> Whom neither Passion may compel
> Nor Reason can restrain.

This speech is a paraphrase of Gabriel's annunciation to the Virgin Mary in Auden's Christmas oratorio *For the Time Being* (1942):

> Since Adam, being free to choose,
> Chose to imagine he was free
> To choose his own necessity,
> Lost in his freedom, man pursues
> The shadow of his images.[123]

Nick's offer of Baba the Turk is a type of the fall of man. The useless exercise of freedom ruined Adam—and, just as Gabriel predicts, Tom Rakewell, lost in freedom, will pursue the most farfetched images, provided by Nick Shadow.

Stravinsky's music betrays the impossibility of freedom: most of the aria advances calmly, steadily, predictably, though Nick keeps declining to sing the cadence proffered by the orchestra; in the middle, when Nick starts his chiasmus between freedom and choice, there is a sudden outburst of whistles (fossils of the whistling villain of the original scenario) in the orchestra, as if the music had at last escaped from its own pulse; but in fact the whistling figures are stiffly symmetrical, as law-determined as anything else. In Arrigo Boito's 1868 opera *Mefistofele*, Mephistopheles does a lot of whistling to show his contempt for the human comedy.

After the aria, Nick and Tom look at each other and gradually break out in loud laughter. The scene ends with a lively duet in which Tom thinks how scandalous his marriage will be: "My tale shall be told / Both by young and by old." He is already starting to see himself as a character in a drama—he can conceive human identity only as an arbitrary role, easily shed, a prelude to his complete self-oblivion in act 3, scene 3, where he is all tale, no man.

Act 2, scene 2. Anne stands uncertainly outside Tom's house. She sings an aria of resolution to screw up her courage:

> Hear thou or not, merciful Heaven,
> ease thou or not my way;
> A love that is sworn before Thee
> can plunder Hell of its prey.

Here, as elsewhere in the opera, she sounds like one of those noble, ineffectual, not-too-interesting Mozart characters, such as Don Ottavio in *Don Giovanni*. She is puzzled by the numerous strangely shaped packages that servants are carrying into Tom's house. A sedan chair enters, and Tom steps out; he dismisses her eager greetings and tells her to leave vicious London, where "virtue is a day coquette"—real virtue has no place in it, indeed is a kind of threat to the general regulation of vice, just as love burned a hole during the catechism of pleasure in act 1, scene 2. Despite his protestations of unworthiness, Anne keeps insisting on his return—until a heavily veiled woman thrusts her head through the sedan chair window and starts to reprove Tom for his poor etiquette. It is Baba the Turk, Tom's new wife; Anne's hopes are crushed. Tom, Anne, and Baba sing a trio, actually a sort of duet plus one, for Baba's impatient interjections are in a different acoustic world from the close, interechoing harmonies of Anne and Tom:

Anne. Could it then have been known	*Tom.* It is done.
When spring was love, and love took all our ken,	I turn away, yet should I turn again,
That I and I alone	The arbour would be gone
Upon that forsworn ground	And on the frozen ground
Should see love dead?	The birds lie dead.

Baba is ceremonious, extraverted, while Tom and Anne turn inward to their private pastoral, a January eclogue. Like the Lanterloo chorus in the brothel scene, this duet suggests the nullity at the opera's heart. The pastoral is the most artificial of the modes through which nature can be represented—a landscape of decorous vegetables and toy sheep; and here it has been still further emptied of nature, until it contains little besides dead birds.

At the end of the trio Anne flees, and Tom helps Baba out of the sedan chair; as they advance with majestic lentor to Tom's house, Baba receives the cheers of her many admirers. At the threshold she turns to the crowd and throws open her veil to reveal a full black beard. The scene ends.

Baba's hermaphroditic nature has always been vexatious. In 1948 Stravinsky's lawyer, one Aaron Sapiro, urged him not to compose the opera, because it would make him an accessory to the "homosexual joke of Baba the Turk"[124]—no fool he. Stravinsky was obviously willing to take that risk, but why did Auden and Kallman introduce a bearded lady into the action?

There is some literary precedent for Baba. In Poulenc's opera *Les mamelles de Tirésias* (The Dugs of Tiresias, 1947), with a libretto by Apollinaire, the heroine, Thérèse, is a feminist fed up with her husband: she decides to become a man by removing her breasts from her blouse and popping them like balloons, then completes her transformation into Tiresias by growing a beard before our eyes. Death, too, is purely conventional: murdered characters can come back to life at the librettist's convenience. Both Baba and Thérèse are characters that have cut themselves free from the inconveniences of fact—for them, male and female and life and death are reversible jackets, simply matters of fashion.

And yet, Baba is not entirely Dada. Insofar as she introduces an undertone (in some productions the role is sung by a countertenor) of submerged homosexuality into the opera, Baba derives some of her force from

Auden's theories about homosexuality. Auden thought that homosexuality was more ritualized, stylized, magical than heterosexuality;[125] and if the progress of the human race is a steady advance into the unnatural, as he said when he was young, it is also a movement toward the homosexual. Earlier I quoted two stanzas from "In Sickness and in Health" concerning Tristan and Don Giovanni, emblems of unnatural love; and in Auden's mythology both are homosexual: "The Tristan and Isolde one actually meets are a Lesbian couple, the Don Juan a pederast."[126] As Tom Rakewell's tastes keep sophisticating away from the organic, a bearded lady starts to become the proper object of his affection.

Auden's fullest published account of the nature of homosexuality occurs in his essay on J. R. Ackerley, "Papa Was a Wise Old Sly-Boots." Ackerley was an editor, man of letters, and troubled homosexual, who slept with disappointing young working-class men but who achieved lasting happiness—Auden calls it a "miracle"[127]—through the love of an Alsatian bitch named Tulip. We have already seen the instability of the object of desire, how it may seek such extravagances as pumping engines; and in Ackerley's case the object of desire mutated completely outside the human, to a dog. Tulip must have seemed a more loyal and satisfying companion than Baba the Turk; but in both cases we see the exorbitance of desire, its tendency to exhaust heaven and earth and still to crave something beyond.

In Auden's view, Don Giovanni, despite his frenzy to hug every woman (or boy) alive, is secretly a man who wants nothing at all:

> The man who refuses to be the servant of any *telos* can [not be represented in a drama]. He can sing his rapture of freedom and indifference, but after that there is nothing for him to do but be quiet. In a drama he can only be represented indirectly as a man with a *telos*, indeed a monomania, but of such a kind that it is clear that it is an arbitrary choice; nothing in his nature imposes it on him or biases him toward it. Such is Don Giovanni.[128]

Such also is Tom Rakewell. Auden takes the fact that Don Giovanni does not care whether his conquests are rich or poor or ugly or beautiful as a sign of the arbitrariness of his affection. Baba the Turk is a personification of arbitrariness; Auden does not have to show Tom engaging in multiple seductions precisely because Baba is all of Don Giovanni's conquests rolled into one. Tom seems to have unlimited desires, but in fact he is no one and desires nothing. Baba is simply Nothing, made embraceable.

Act 2, scene 3. This begins with a sample of Tom's married life, breakfast with Baba:

> As I was saying, both brothers wore moustaches,
> But Sir John was taller; they gave me the musical glasses.
> That was in Vienna, no, it must have been in Milan
> Because of the donkeys. Vienna was the Chinese fan
> —or was it the bottle of water from the River Jordan?
> I'm certain at least it was Vienna and Lord Gordon. . . .
> You're not eating, my love. Count Moldau gave me the gnome,
> And Prince Oblowsky the little statues of the Twelve Apostles,
> Which I like best of all my treasures except my fossils.
> Which reminds me I must tell Bridget never to touch the mummies,
> I'll dust them myself. She can do the waxwork dummies.
> Of course, I like my birds, too, especially my Greak Auk.

This is a patter song, but strangely shrill and emphatic—Gilbert and Sullivan in hell. In fact, the whole musical atmosphere has been shifting during act 2. The music of act 1 had something of the settled character of a textbook of old musical forms—or, more exactly, approximations to and witty evasions of old musical forms. Perhaps in imitation of Alban Berg, Stravinsky decorated his published score with form labels (not just Aria and Recitative, but Cavatina, Cabaletta, Duet-Finale, and so forth). But in this scene the music is more modish; some of the music that Stravinsky wrote for Baba sounds a little like Poulenc—busy, breezy, chattery, full of false gestures, as if the emotional suggestions were to be put in quotation marks. Baba's breathless barrage of detached sixteenth notes has an almost inhuman speed—it is machine-music; and Baba is herself (to borrow the title of a Paul Klee painting) a twittering machine. Tom has married the robot that was the last and greatest of Casanova's loves in Fellini's film.

Baba is the mechanical bird of *The Nightingale* promoted into the semblance of human shape. The singing contest of the earlier opera appears intact in *The Rake's Progress*, for Anne Trulove is a reincarnation of the "real" nightingale, mooning over the countryside and embodying an ideal of warmth and purity of expression. Once again a hero is asked to choose between the real and the mechanical; once again we see the jealousy, the intimacy that exists between them.

Why would Stravinsky conceive Baba as a sort of wind-up toy? In many ways, Baba signifies something exactly opposite to a machine: she embodies randomness, freedom—she is an object of desire chosen by a cast of dice, herself in love with the miscellaneous. But it is hard to make a convincing musical representation of disorder, and I think that Stravinsky had good reason to treat Baba as he did.

Several times Stravinsky faced the problem of trying to find the shape of shapelessness, to make something artistic out of the random. In his card-game ballet "in three deals," *Jeu de cartes* (1937), "the Joker [the principal dancer] is a bonus, an element of chance and an escape from . . . combinations";[129] but the music that characterizes the Joker offers no particular contrast to the (not strikingly good) music of the rest of the ballet. In the television operacule *The Flood* (1962), Stravinsky (like Haydn in *The Creation*, 1798) wanted to write a prelude to represent chaos, but found the task puzzling:

> How, please, does one represent chaos in music? I took certain elements, intervals, and chords made up of fourths. My "material of Chaos" is limited, however, and I couldn't make my Chaos last very long.[130]

Baba is the joker in the card game of *The Rake's Progress*, and the chaos in its version of the fall of man—and Stravinsky found a better way of realizing her character than in the other two cases. Stravinsky (especially if he had written the opera in the 1960s) might have wondered for a moment whether to have her sing something like aleatory music, music in which the notes are determined by random processes—throwing dice, notating the pattern of raisins in a fruitcake or birds on telephone wires. But Stravinsky hated this sort of music. Among the milder of his many denunciations of aleatory music is:

> What I cannot follow are the manic-depressive fluctuations from total control to no control, from the serialization of all elements to chance.[131]

Here is a clue about the musical formation of Baba: Stravinsky has rebounded from no control (what Baba represents) to total control. Just as Auden leaped from goallessness to an arbitrary goal in inventing her, so Stravinsky leaped from the stochastic to the all-determined in writing the proper music for her. Like Offenbach's Olympia in *Les contes d'Hoffmann*,

Baba sings music that sounds at times like a singer's vocal exercises, lalálalalálalalá.

Unlike Olympia's aria (which speaks of little but pretty birds singing prettily in the trees), Baba's songs have a wide field of reference—from the River Jordan to the North Pole. She is a collector of knickknacks from all over the world, and she likes to talk about them, admire them. She is surrounded by things, emphatically dead things: fossils, mummies, waxwork dummies—the triumph here is the great auk, which manages not only to be flightless and stuffed but extinct. They seem to infect her with their thingliness, make her seem even more frantically inert than before. As she babbles on—her very name suggests Babel—she seems puzzled by Tom's boredom; she cannot understand any human emotion except the lust for objects, the lust to become an object.

Soon Baba grows angry at Tom, and, assuming that he is distracted by thoughts of Anne, she storms about, smashing objects—objects alone are her means of emotional relief. As she starts exercising her chest register on the first syllable of "never," Tom rises suddenly, seizes his wig (in the original scenario a tea cozy), and plops it down on her head; she stops in mid-note, freezes, and remains for the rest of the scene in this strange mock rigor mortis. The gorgon is herself turned to stone. She has become a backward Petrushka, cast by magic into the form of a doll.

Tom falls asleep after this "murder"; and Nick enters, wheeling in with him a "fantastic baroque machine." He puts a loaf of bread in one compartment and a piece of broken china into the machine's hopper, and by turning a wheel he makes the loaf fall out of a chute. It is the most obvious sort of fraud. This pantomime of wheeling and cranking is accompanied by nonchalant piccolo whistles.

Since this scene began we have watched two "transformations": a woman has been turned to stone, and a stone has been turned into bread. Of course, each is only a parody of a transformation: Baba is still Baba, and the stone is still a stone. Perhaps the character of *The Rake's Progress* is clearer in this scene than anywhere else: musically and dramatically it is an opera of nontransformations.

A history of opera could be written on the theme of metamorphosis. In eighteenth-century opera, metamorphosis is conducted mostly through stage machinery, not through music; even in a forward-looking opera such as Gluck's *Armide* (1777), the great finale, during which demons raze Armide's palace and the sorceress flies away in a rage, is accompanied by a pleasant racket in the orchestra—but it is brief and fairly static, a representation of the horror aroused by the transformation, not of the transformation itself. One of the great achievements of nineteenth-century opera was the invention of persuasive musical representations of change: in Wagner's *Parsifal* (1882), for example, the second act ends with the spectacle of a magic castle falling into dust; but the musical figure that represents the collapse is not simply stated and repeated, à la Gluck, but spun out over many bars, moving lower and lower in pitch, as bits of rubble bounce in lower and lower arcs, a nightmare of ruin.

In *The Rake's Progress*, we have music that declines the privilege of metamorphosis. As Paul Griffiths notes in his helpful book on the opera, "Stravinsky does not modulate but rather slips from one key into another."[132] *The Rake's Progress* is formally jagged, like Matisse's scissor-cut stars and waves glued onto a background, instead of the imperceptible graduation of tone in oil painting. Stravinsky juxtaposes keys in such a way as to leave them unrelated to each other, instead of painstakingly demonstrating the relation. I believe that Stravinsky's theory of nature is behind this practice: for Wagnerian metamorphosis assumes that an artificial form must be slowly, carefully undone, transformed into its natural form—a given leitmotif can be tricked up in a thousand pretty ways, but each variant is measurably deviant from an original; Stravinskyan nonmetamorphosis, on the other hand, assumes that one form, or figure, or key, or system of organizing musical ideas, is no more natural or just than any other. What sets Stravinsky apart from eighteenth- and nineteenth-century opera composers is that Auden and Kallman's text calls for mock metamorphoses, not real ones; the plot and the music agree.

While Nick demonstrates his hoax to the audience, Tom dreams; and when Tom awakes he tells Nick his dream, of a marvelous machine that can make "earth become an Eden of goodwill." Nick whips the dust cover off the contraption: there it is. Here Nick asserts his character as a corrupt Ariel: he stands for false imagination, a faculty that will mire Tom more and more deeply in flimsy unrealities. In this appeal to fantastic ambition, Nick is also the well-known Satan of Genesis, as Auden's plot outline shows:

Bordel	—Le plaisir [Pleasure].
Baba	—L'acte gratuit [The gratuitous act].
La Machine	—Il désire devenir Dieu [He wishes to become God].[133]

As Tom, the mock god, plans his recapture of Paradise, he takes a giant step into unnature—accompanied by a sprung, spangled, bearded Eve. In a duet,

Tom, "très exalté," exclaims over his wondrous machine, while Nick invites the audience to buy shares in the company that will market it: "There's no fantastic lie / You cannot make men swallow if you try."

Act 3, scene 1. In this, the auction scene, instead of the heaven on earth predicted in the last scene, we open with cries of "Ruin, Disaster, Shame." The bubble of speculation has burst: duchesses have committed suicide, orphans scavenge in the street, and all the goods of bankrupt Tom are to be auctioned. Anne is looking for Tom, but no one knows where to find him. The babblers come to order as Sellem, the auctioneer, mounts his dais. Sellem makes large claims about the existential value of auctions:

> Truly there is a divine balance in Nature:
> a thousand lose that a thousand may gain;
> and you who are the fortunate are not so
> only in yourselves, but also in being Nature's
> missionaries. You are her instruments for the
> restoration of that order we all so worship,
> and it is granted to, ah! so few of us to
> serve.

Like the roulette wheel in Auden's "Casino," the auction is an instrument for one of the sacred rites of the dynamo: the random redistribution of objects. Nature is a zero-sum game, and Sellem is the priest who celebrates the equation of profit and loss. In act 2 we ventured into the far reaches of the unnatural; in act 3 many sorts of artifices and illusions will be scattered, dispelled, as nature's equilibrium is restored once again. In the Stravinsky canon, Sellem's role is that of Namer, like the square-dance caller in *The Flood* who enumerates the animals in Noah's ark; to the heap of vendable objects—as disconnected, as lacking in syntax, as those in the bags toted around by the mute pedants of Swift's Lagado—Sellem provides a corresponding heap of words.

Sellem is overcome by a strange glee in the performance of his rite: amid exclamations of "La!" and "Hmmm!" and "Poof!" he sells a mounted fish and a Roman bust—each item leading to surge of arithmetical excitement in the crowd as bids are shouted. It is an illustration of the dynamo's essentially numerical nature. For his third item, Sellem walks up to the covered Baba:

> An unknown object draws us, draws us near.
> A cake? An organ? Golden Apple Tree? . . .

Oracle? Pillar? Octopus? Who'll see?
Be brave! Perhaps an angel will appear.
La! come bid.
Hmmm! come buy.
Aha! The it.

Baba is the algebraic *x*, an all-purpose thing, a representation of the mutability of the object of desire. She seems about to decompose into a whole hardware store or museum basement. When Sellem calls her "the it," it may be an allusion to one of Auden's favorite books, Georg Groddeck's *Das Buch vom Es* (The Book of the It, 1923), which describes an impersonal evolutionary force (the It), a drive that directs the growth of all life on earth through its confused attempts to realize itself. Auden identified the It with Aphrodite, the sexual instinct; and Sellem's strange comment may therefore be a clue about the unity of Baba and Aphrodite, unnature and nature. It is as if, at the end of the evolution of life on our planet, Aphrodite grew a beard and a mainspring.

After Baba is sold, Sellem snatches Tom's wig from her head; this ends her suspended animation, and she resumes singing "never" at the exact point where she left off in act 2, scene 3. Like the murdered characters in *Les mamelles de Tirésias*, Baba can come back to life at any time; she is a piece of nonsense, beyond the usual constraints of life. She does not understand that time has passed and thinks that thieves are trying to loot her apartment.

Outside the voices of Nick and Tom are heard singing a street-vendor's chant: "Old wives for sale!" Clearly dispossession has not dampened their spirits, and Baba too soon reconciles herself to the loss of her gnomes and apostles and mummies and all the rest. Anne enters, and the crowd settles down to watch what it hopes will be a still more interesting event than the auction: the confrontation between Baba and Anne. But instead of recriminations, Baba offers Anne some unexpected advice: go find Tom, for he still loves you. In act 3 there are a great many reversions from the unnatural to the natural, but this is perhaps the most surprising of all: Baba evolves from a thing into a person. Under Anne's—the virgin's—benevolent gaze, even the dynamo can grow kind, develop a human face. Sellem wondered whether an angel might lie underneath Baba's dust cover; and for a moment it seems that he was right.

As Baba imperiously announces her imminent return to the stage, Tom and Nick are again heard singing outside the window:

If boys had wings and girls had stings
And gold fell from the sky,

If new-laid eggs wore wooden legs
I should not laugh or cry.

Anne recognizes Tom's voice and runs after him. This sour, careless rhyme shows how far the rake has progressed into disillusionment since we saw him in act 2, scene 3, about to market his stone-transformer, his machine to get gold from the sky. Preposterous dreams will trouble Tom no longer—he will not laugh or cry. Nick, in the next scene, will no longer be Ariel, the conjurer of fantasies, but instead the punishing destroyer of fantasy.

Act 3, scene 2. The prelude to this, the graveyard scene, was the first music Stravinsky wrote for the opera, and it is perhaps the most frigid music he ever wrote—the temperature is well below the chilliest moment of act 3 of Puccini's *La bohème* (1896), or of Vivaldi's "Winter" Concerto (1725), or of the winter masque in Purcell's *King Arthur* (1691). Nick and Tom are alone. A year and a day (the stated period of the contract) have passed, and Nick claims his wage: Tom's soul. Instead of the infinite fancies of act 2, Tom in act 3 is in a domain of strict terms and precise obligations. Nick points to the open grave that awaits Tom and takes several objects out of his bag: a knife, a rope, a bottle of poison, a gun. Tom's options, once amazingly wide-ranging, have contracted to these: a choice of means for suicide. Nick's bag contains an even less attractive assortment of objects than Baba's apartmentful of knickknacks. In act 2 Tom married a thing; now he is himself in danger of being reified.

As the ninth chime sounds on the approach to fatal midnight, Nick agrees to stop time and play a card game for Tom's soul: if Tom can guess the three cards Nick pulls out, he will be saved. For the first card, Tom guesses the queen of hearts—a symbol of Anne. That is correct. For the second card, Tom is stymied:

Tom. . . . how throw the die
To win my soul back for myself?
Nick. Was Fortune not your mistress once?
Be fair.
Give her at least the second chance to bare
The hand of Shadow.
(The spade suddenly falls forward with a great crash.)
Tom. (startled, cursing) The deuce!
(He looks at what fell.) She lights the shades
And shows the two of spades.

Nick asks whether fortune has been Tom's mistress. She has indeed, in act 2, in the person of Baba, the random object of desire; but in this scene Tom's mistress is not fortune but love, Anne Trulove. It is love that leads Tom to rationalize, to find design in random events—such as a spade's sudden tumble. A card game, even more than a chess game, is a pure exercise in mathematical fortuity, an investigation of the patterns of disordered things—that is why Lewis Carroll wrote *Alice's Adventures in Wonderland* (1865), his playing-card fable, before *Through the Looking-Glass* (1871). Up to now Tom has flirted with disorder, perhaps even slept with her; but now he is trying to align his wishes, his hope of survival, with some principle of order. Following his appetites has led Tom further and further into the waste land, until he is now at the brink of the grave; his last hope is to find some other system on which to base his life.

Of course that guess is correct, too. For the last card, Nick decides to play a trick: he slips the discarded queen of hearts back into the pack and selects it as the final test. With mounting horror, Tom sees the track of cloven hooves, feels damnation near. But at the last minute he hears Anne singing a phrase from her aria in act 2, scene 2:

> A love
> That is sworn before Thee can plunder
> Hell of its prey.

This phrase is sung with no bar lines, as if it were absolute, a pure cantillation outside the meter of the rest of the opera. Here Anne offers Tom a real telos, a finite, intelligible goal for his affection—in great contrast to the chimeras that drove him on throughout the first two acts. Tom guesses the queen of hearts once again and is saved. Nick's contract was not the only one Tom agreed to; his vows to Anne also constituted a contract, much violated but still in force. In "In Sickness and in Health," the arbitrary vow of love can "show the whirlwind how to be an arm,"[134] can rescue from chaos and constitute a firm image of self and other. Similarly Anne's vow can force the distended Tom back into human shape.

Tom is saved, but his sins enable Nick to punish him by taking away his reason. Nick sinks into the grave intended for Tom:

> I burn! I burn! I freeze! In shame I hear
> My famished legions roar;

> My own delay cost me my prey
> And damns me all the more.

This great cry is accompanied by the most ferocious music in the score, as if sledgehammers were driving Nick into the ground—the rhythmic force is somewhat similar to that of certain Verdi arias, such as "Eri tu" in *Un ballo in maschera* (1859). For the first time we see (or, more exactly, hear) Nick for what he is: Satan—the music is worthy of his majesty. *The Rake's Progress* is an opera full of secrets and disguises, but not metamorphoses: Nick and Anne and Baba and the rest have an underlying allegorical significance, from which only slight deviations are permissible. The function of the music is to keep steady focus on the value of each figure: clearly to denominate Nick as ace of spades, Anne as queen of hearts, Baba as the joker.

The scene ends with mad Tom smiling in the dawn, transfigured: "Adonis is my name." His reversion to nature is now complete, for he is both a fertility god and a natural in the Elizabethan sense of the word—an idiot. He has explored all of unnature and turned upside down in the concave mirror once again. He is hauled off to the lunatic asylum.

Act 3, scene 3. In this, the madhouse scene, Bedlam is populated with figures directly from Hogarth: a crippled soldier, a man with a telescope, a blind man with a broken fiddle—this last madman appealed to Stravinsky from the beginning and suggests the ruin of music, the falling-into-discord that Tom requested at the beginning of act 2, scene 2.[135] Tom answers to no name but Adonis and insists that his fellow madmen are also "heroic shades":

> Anoint your limbs with oil,
> put on your wedding garments . . .
> Venus, queen of Love, will visit
> her unworthy Adonis.
> *Madmen.* Madmen's words are all untrue;
> She will never come to you.
> *Tom.* She gave me her promise.
> *Madmen.* Madness cancels every vow

But vows are stronger than the madmen suppose. To some extent the madmen are willing to participate in Tom's fantasy—for example, they refer to their keeper as Minos, the judge of dead souls. But for the most part the madmen understand that Bedlam is a realm where there are no identities, mythological or social or otherwise:

Down in Hell as up in Heaven
No hands are in marriage given,
Nor is honour or degree
Known in our society.
Banker, beggar, whore and wit
In a common darkness sit.

This chorus is an adaptation of Auden's "Domesday Song" (1941):

Jumbled in one common box
Of their dark stupidity,
Orchid, swan, and Caesar lie[136]

Most of Tom's career has been a cultivation of nonbeing, a striving after the random; and Bedlam is the logical culmination, a chamber of clouds, a heat sink of identity, a condition of complete freedom.

Anne comes, and Tom invites his Venus to mount her throne. Anne is not Aphrodite but the heavenly Venus, Urania—also the Muse of astronomy, as the madman's telescope might hint. Tom confesses to her that he has been caught "in a foolish dream," and has "hunted shadows," and he asks her forgiveness. The shadows that he renounces include not only Nick Shadow but all the false Venuses—Mother Goose (sexual indulgence), Baba (gratuitous action), Fortune—that had lured him into the waste land. In the midst of despair comes grace—Auden was a Kierkegaardian, and *The Rake's Progress* is, among many other things, a parable of fear and trembling. Anne in the madhouse operates as a clandestine Holy Spirit. Auden liked to scandalize less adventurous Christians by announcing that heavenly grace was arbitrary—and that too is illustrated in the opera's magnificent celebration of the Arbitrary.

Anne has succeeded in making a heaven of hell: "Rejoice, beloved: in these fields of Elysium / Space cannot alter, nor time our love abate." The rake's progress is at last coming to a halt—his progress never was much more than the frantic illusion of change. As Anne and Tom embrace, they assume the same posture they had in act 1, scene 1, as if the opera had never happened at all, as if Baba and Nick and all the rest were indeed nothing but foolish dreams. Within the arbitrary circle of a vow, Anne and Tom are immune from phantoms.

Tom is weary and asks Venus to sing him to sleep. Anne responds with the twentieth century's most ravishing lullaby:

> Orchards greenly grace
> That undisturbèd place,
> The weary soul recalling
> To slumber and to dream,
> While many a stream
> Falls, falls, falls,
> Descanting on a child-like theme.
> *Madmen.* O sacred music of the spheres!

She sings of the Islands of the Blest, and of the Peaceable Kingdom, where the lion and the lamb are friends. Her vision of pastoral resembles some of the more frigid pastorals seen in the earlier acts; but the touches of the sacred, of a child's picture-book of heaven, place it on a different plane of artifice. The speaking landscape is Auden's favorite image of paradise—indeed, he once wrote that the first sign to Adam and Eve of the fall of man was that "the stream was dumb with whom they'd always planned."[137] Here that stream is revoiced. At the end of *The Sea and the Mirror*, Caliban tells us that Shakespeare included him deliberately in order to spoil the beauty of his play, and, furthermore, that a Christian poet should always try to botch his best effects, to include in his work a shock of disillusion—for in the unbridgeable gap between ideal and real, the vision of grace, the prefigurement of heaven, must constitute itself. *The Rake's Progress* has insisted on its illusory character in many ways—through the asides to the audience, through the presentation of absurd, unassimilable, indigestible characters like Baba; the opera discredits itself from beginning to end. And amid the general collapse, Anne's lullaby hints at a revelation beyond fiction.

Anne can do no more for Tom, so she leaves; as her father says, "the tale is ended." Tom awakes, finds her missing, and calls on Achilles, Helen, Eurydice, Orpheus, Persephone—the madmen—to show where they have hidden her. But she is gone.

> *Tom.* My heart breaks.
> I feel the chill of death's approaching wing.
> Orpheus, strike from thy lyre

a swanlike music,
and weep, ye nymphs and shepherds
of these Stygian fields,
weep for Adonis, the beautiful, the young;
weep for Adonis whom Venus loved.

And he dies. The summoning of Orpheus may have awakened in Stravinsky a memory of the aria "Possente spirto" from Monteverdi's *L'Orfeo* (1607)—the aria in which Orpheus tries to charm implacable Charon into letting him enter Hades—for Stravinsky's vocal line is nearly as florid and expertly mournful as Monteverdi's. Much of the character of this final declamation comes from a musical device, a rapid quavering up and down the interval of a half step, which we hear at "Stygian fields," "the beautiful, the young," and "Venus loved"—as if Tom's voice were breaking with emotion and he had to end each phrase with a catch in his throat. Similar figures have been heard elsewhere in this scene: during Tom's and Anne's duet, we hear the same quick flickers all through "Rejoice, beloved: in these fields of Elysium / Space cannot alter, nor time our love abate."

Elsewhere in Stravinsky's late works, we find crucial lines decorated with this same figure: for example, in the second of his *Three Songs from William Shakespeare* (1953), the whole song is a continual tissue of these half-step shakes:

Full fadom five thy Father lies,
Of his bones are Corrall made:
Those are pearles that were his eies,
Nothing of him that doth fade,
But doth suffer a Sea-change
Into something rich and strange.

Stravinsky himself called attention to his use of a different but related figure: in his "Elegy for J.F.K." (1964)—his only setting of an Auden text besides *The Rake's Progress*—Stravinsky used (at the line "The heavens are silent") a rising and falling whole tone, slightly slower and wider than the figure I have been speaking of. He called this two-note chain "a recurring stutter in my musical speech from as long ago as *Les Noces*."[138] Not long afterward Stravinsky wrote "Introitus: T. S. Eliot in Memoriam" (1965), in which "the music of 'et perpetua' is a quotation of my setting of Auden's line 'The Heavens are silent.'"[139]

Why should the same, or similar, music be used to describe the timelessness of Elysium, the sea change of King Alonso into coral and pearls, and the deaths of John F. Kennedy, Tom Rakewell, and T. S. Eliot? I think it is the figure that Stravinsky uses to mean immortality. On one hand, it is the quake of a man overcome with feeling; on the other hand, it is simply a blank oscillation of pitch, without direction, without any particular impulse of melody or harmony or rhythm—change so pointless that it embodies unchangingness. It lies at the place where the expressive touches the inexpressive, where bone starts to turn into coral, where life is at the edge of death. (Christopher Hogwood has pointed out that, strangely enough, Handel has an immortality motif, also a rising and falling whole-tone phrase, used in *Messiah*, 1742, and *Acis and Galatea*, 1718.) Stravinsky's music cannot illustrate metamorphosis because it constitutes itself in a boundary region where there is no distinction to be made between nature and artifice, eye and pearl, expression and its opposite.

Many of Stravinsky's works end with what Stravinsky called an apotheosis: a passage of solemn repetitions of a short phrase, slowly intensifying and dissolving. To such music, in *Apollo*, the god assumes his godhead; in *Orpheus*, the lyre lives on though the hero dies. *The Rake's Progress* does not have a declared apotheosis, but the madhouse scene ends with a lament for Adonis, a sternly lugubrious chorus that takes the place of an apotheosis. Tom is deified, though in a less happy manner than Apollo. Both the apotheosis and the immortality figure are means by which Stravinsky's music declares its essentially static nature. Often in his later years he commented on this quality of standing still: "My later music is . . . static and objective."[140] I think this is why Stravinsky wanted to write an opera in which all the action is imaginary, all the expression histrionic: he needed a plot that stood still.

Epilogue. This brief conclusion, like the graveyard scene, is an adaptation of an idea prominent in *Don Giovanni*. The characters, wigless and beardless, comment on their own theatricality and offer little fragments of moral advice:

> *Anne.* Not every rake is rescued
> At the last by Love and Beauty;
> Not every man is given an Anne
> To take the place of Duty. . . .
> *Tom.* Beware, young men who fancy
> You are Virgil or Julius Caesar,

Lest when you wake
You be only a rake. . . .
All. . . . For idle hands
And hearts and minds
The Devil finds
A work to do.

Anne's message is a version of one of Auden's favorite endings, that of Brecht's *Die Dreigroschenoper* (1928), where a messenger rides up to the gallows as the thief Macheath is about to hang and announces that the queen has spared his life and given him a castle and a lot of money; and Mrs. Peachum notes how good life would be if messengers always appeared in such fashion. In other words, the fable is deceptive. Tom tells us, on the other hand, to take the fable seriously. Not every critic has thought that Auden intended us to take the final proverb—that the devil finds work for idle hands—as the true moral of the opera. But it is an opera that shows how mankind is corrupted either by infinite goals (to be Virgil or Julius Caesar, to restore paradise) or by the absence of goals (idleness)—so perhaps the moral is surprisingly just.

In the course of this chapter we have seen many convergences of opposites: nightingale and machine, chaos and total control, nature and artifice. Robert Craft writes that, in the late 1930s, when Stravinsky was preparing notes to help Roland-Manuel write *Poetics of Music*, Stravinsky read Nicholas of Cusa and became interested in the notion of *coincidentia oppositorum*.[141] Nicholas was a fifteenth-century German prelate whose best-known treatise is called *De Possest* (Of Can-Is, or On Actualized-Possibility). Stravinsky probably took note of this passage:

> And when we attempted to see Him beyond being and not-being, we were unable to understand how He could be visible. For He is beyond everything simple and everything composite, beyond everything singular and everything plural, beyond every limit and all unlimitedness; He is completely everywhere and not at all anywhere; He is of every form and of no form, alike; He is completely ineffable; in all things He is all things, in nothing He is nothing. . . . He is encountered—unlike any other existing thing—ignorantly or unintelligibly, in a shadow or in darkness or unknowingly. . . . [He is encountered] as a thing in which opposites coincide (e.g., motion and rest, together)—not as two but as above duality

or otherness. This vision occurs in darkness, where the hidden God is concealed from the eyes of all the wise.[142]

Human thought is bound by dichotomies; but God refuses to be limited by such divisions. Elsewhere Nicholas offered the following exercise for imagining God: consider a child's top; the faster it spins, the stabler it becomes; if it were spinning infinitely fast, it would be at rest. God is at the coinciding point of motion and rest.

If God were to be embodied in music, how could it be done? Stravinsky was a pious man and wrote a number of liturgical settings and psalms; and I think that *The Rake's Progress* is also about God. Through the coincidence of opposites, he made oblique reference to the hidden God of Nicholas of Cusa, ineffable, dwelling in darkness. Indeed, Stravinsky contemplated a coincidence of opposites that would have horrified Nicholas: the coincidence of God and the devil. We read among his working notes to *The Flood*: "God's music is sometimes reminiscent of Shadow's music in *The Rake*, which should prove, if proof were needed, that musical identities are purely circumstantial."[143] Similarly (indeed to my ear more noticeably), the hen-scratching tune of Nick's first speech, "Fair lady, gracious gentlemen," is a faster version of the main melody of the second movement of the *Symphony in Three Movements* (1946), a piece written to illustrate Bernadette's vision of the Virgin Mary for Franz Werfel's film *Song of Bernadette*.

Stravinsky liked these consternating reversals because they showed the arbitrariness of the link between music and its meaning or reference; but he also may have enjoyed them because, by intensifying music's ineffability, they provided an intuition of the divine, beyond human conceptions of good and evil. *The Rake's Progress* has little in common with the other great opera of the century, Schoenberg's *Moses und Aron* (1932); and yet it is possible to believe that each gropes after an expression of the inexpressible, an image of what cannot be confined to an image. The inexpressive and the inexpressible may turn out to be one and the same—another monism. Yeats once spoke of a friend who dreamed of God in the form of a slug, as if what is "beyond comprehension is mirrored in the least organized forms of life."[144] But Stravinsky, like Kleist, preferred to represent God by means of even lower forms, by nonsense syllables and painted dolls.

EPILOGUE

IS MUSIC LIKE SPOKEN LANGUAGE OR UNLIKE IT? FOR CENTURIES music theorists have tried to understand music as a language, an art with its own rhetoric. In his 1739 treatise *Der vollkommene Capellmeister*, Johann Mattheson argued that the art of musical composition is classical rhetoric transposed into a language of tones, cleanly organized into *inventio*, *dispositio* (articulation of the invented idea into parts), *decoratio*, and *pronuntiato* (delivery)—Mattheson even plays with forensic models of musical rhetoric, in which a composition is divided into *exordium*, *narratio* (statement of facts), *divisio* (forecast of main points in the speaker's favor), *confirmatio*, *confutatio* (rebuttal), and *peroratio*. Mattheson and other musical rhetoricians, such as Kircher, also provided tables of figures of speech complete with examples, so that the reader can ponder the musical equivalent of (say) anaphora, exclamation, ellipsis, and pleonasm. There are times when I listen to music that I indeed hear it as rhetoric: I have certainly never read an essay that concludes more irrefutably than Bruckner's Fourth Symphony.

And it is possible that music is like spoken language in its small, subtle details as well as in its overall shape. Speech inflections can be imitated quite effectively by orchestral instruments, as when Strauss, in *Ein Heldenleben* (1899), instructs the violinist who plays the role of the hero's wife to phrase in a "heuchlerisch schmachtend" (hypocritically languishing) manner; or when Britten, in a piece called "Bacchus at Whose Orgies Is Heard the Noise of Gaggling Women's Tattling Tongues and Shouting Out of Boys"—the fourth of the *Six Metamorphoses after Ovid* (1951)—asks a solo oboist to tattle and shout a language that the listener has never been taught and yet understands quite clearly.

Yet, it may be that music is most like speech when it is least like music. Strauss, Britten, Marc-Antoine Charpentier, and many other composers have written music that sounds like talking, but mostly as special stunts, marked as speechlike through the absence of poised cantilena and other features that mark music as "musical." And the old rhetoricians of music tend to search for figures of speech in odd or puzzling passages, difficult to construe as pure music, and therefore inviting the critic to look for meaning in out-of-the-way places, such as tables of tropes in spoken or written language.

In the twentieth century there was a revolt against the notion that music was a kind of language: Stravinsky, with his famous comment that music expresses nothing, was the leading rebel. In the world of Modernism, music at once sought to rival language in semantic precision and also sought to deny any semantic character whatsoever. It is my belief that the final monism of the music of this age is the collapse of the distinction between language and languagelessness. Any music drama can be understood as a kind of dialectic: we have studied many dialectics in this book, such as chastity and sexuality, terror and pity, eloquence and stammering, virgin and dynamo. But Modernist music drama can never disregard the other possibility: that all music is just pure wordless sound, even if a singer tries to fasten a text to its tail—sound shorn of any possibility of dialectic, indeed of meaning. We speak of "abstract art," but any painting, whether by Kandinsky or by Raphael, can be regarded as abstract or concrete, just as the critic chooses—"abstract" and "concrete" are not properties of art, but points of view available to the critic. Similarly, no musical composition is either semantic or asemantic—the terms represent points of view through which a composition can be scrutinized. The composers I have studied are, I believe, among the first to have understood that, while musical meaning can be intensified almost without limit, musical meaning is always precarious, and the savoring of that precariousness, that preciousness, is a necessary moment in the evolution of music drama.

ACKNOWLEDGMENTS

DAN ALBRIGHT'S PREVIOUS TWO BOOKS WERE DEDICATED TO me, but he did not have time to dedicate this one, or to write acknowledgments. I know that he appreciated the help and support of all who contributed to this book, especially Alexander Rehding, who wrote the foreword. I would like to dedicate it, on his behalf, to all those of you who called, visited, and worked to honor his memory after his too-soon, too-sudden death.

Marta S. Rivera Monclova

A portion of chapter 5, "Schoenberg's Shatterings," first appeared as "Butchering Moses," *Opera Quarterly* 23, no. 4 (2007): 441–54. *Opera Quarterly* is published by Oxford University Press. This text also appeared as Chapter 6 in *Music Speaks: On the Language of Opera, Dance, and Song* (University of Rochester Press, 2009), 94–104.

Chapter 6, "Stravinsky's Nightingales," first appeared as *Stravinsky: The Music Box and the Nightingale* (London: Gordon & Breach, 1989), now out of print.

NOTES

Chapter One

1. T. S. Eliot, *Knowledge and Experience in the Philosophy of F. H. Bradley* (New York: Farrar, Straus, & Giroux, 1964), 195.

2. As Jacques Derrida puts it: "One could reconsider all the pairs of opposites on which philosophy is constructed and on which our discourse lives, not in order to see opposition erase itself but to see what indicates that each of the terms must appear as . . . the other different and deferred." Derrida, *Margins of Philosophy*, trans. Alan Bass (Chicago: University of Chicago Press, 1982), 17.

Chapter Two

1. The *Ring*, comprising *Das Rheingold, Die Walküre, Siegfried*, and *Götterdämmerung*, was first performed as a cycle in 1876. On destruction, see, for example, Wagner's letter to August Röckel, January 25–26, 1854.

2. Plato, *Cratylus*, trans. Benjamin Jowett, 432d.

3. Letter of May 30, 1846, in *Richard Wagner Sämtliche Briefe*, ed. Gertrud Strobel and Werner Wolf (Leipzig: VEB Deutscher Verlag für Musik, 1970), 2:511.

4. *Richard Wagner: Gesammelte Schriften und Dichtungen* (Leipzig: C. F. W. Siegel's Musikalienhandlung, 1907), 5:179, 181.

5. The essay is reprinted in the original French in Margaret Miner, *Resonant Gaps: Between Baudelaire and Wagner* (Athens: University of Georgia Press, 1995), 167–96.

6. Richard Wagner, *Oper und Drama* (Leipzig: J. J. Weber, 1852), 48.

7. Wagner, *Oper und Drama*, 111.

8. In the periodical *Gil Blas*, June 1, 1903, collected in Debussy, *Monsieur Croche et autres écrits*, ed. François Lesure (Paris: Gallimard, 1987), 180.

9. Richard Wagner, *Eine Mitteilung an meine Freunde: Erklärung an das Publikum* (Berlin: Hofenberg, 2015), 90.

10. Richard Wagner, *Mein Leben* (München: F. Bruckmann, 1911), 604.

11. *Gesammelte Schriften und Dichtungen von Richard Wagner* (Leipzig: E. W. Fritsch, 1872), 6:379.

12. Entry of October 23, 1870, in Cosima Wagner, *Die Tagebücher*, ed. Martin Gregor-Dellin and Dietrich Mack (München: R. Piper, 1976), 1:302.

13. Entry of December 8, 1880, in C. Wagner, *Die Tagebücher*, 1:635.

14. Richard Wagner, *Die Wibelungen: Weltgeschichte aus der Sage* (Leipzig: Verlag von Otto Wigand, 1850), 9–13.

15. Wagner, *Die Wibelungen*, 26.

16. Wagner, *Die Wibelungen*, 25.

17. Wagner, *Die Wibelungen*, 34.

18. Richard Wagner, *Mein Leben* (Munich: List Verlag, 1976), 511–12.

19. Letter of May 31, 1852, in *Briefe*, 4:385, May 31, 1852.

20. Theodor Adorno, *Philosophy of Modern Music*, trans. Anne G. Mitchell and Wesley V. Blomster (New York: Seabury, 1973), 51.

21. Wagner, *Die Wibelungen*, 54–55.

22. Richard Wagner, *Sämtliche Schriften und Dichtungen*, 16 vols. (Leipzig, 1909–16), 10:268.

23. *Briefwechsel zwischen Wagner und Liszt*, ed. Erich Kloss (Leipzig: Breitkopf & Härtel, 1919), 2:41.

24. Entry of April 7, 1873, in C. Wagner, *Tagebücher*, 1:667, April 7, 1873.

25. Richard Wagner, *Jesus von Nazareth: Ein dichterischer Entwurf aus dem Jahre 1848* (Leipzig: Breitkopf & Härtel, 1887), 26–27.

26. Wagner, *Jesus von Nazareth*, 47.

27. Wagner, *Oper und Drama*, 63–64.

28. Wagner, *Oper und Drama*, 59.

29. Wagner, *Oper und Drama*, 99.

30. Entry of June 30, 1872, in C. Wagner, *Tagebücher*, 1:541.

31. Samuel Taylor Coleridge, *The Friend* (London: Routledge & Kegan Paul, 1969), 1:94.

32. *Briefwechsel zwischen Wagner und Liszt*, 2:42.

33. *Richard Wagner: Gesammelte Schriften und Dichtungen*, 5:177–78.

34. See Anthony Winterbourne, *A Pagan Spoiled: Sex and Character in Wagner's "Parsifal"* (Madison, NJ: Fairleigh Dickinson University Press, 2003), 64.

35. *Tagebücher* 2:1002, September 14, 1882.

36. *Richard Wagner an Mathilde Wesendonck: Tagebuchblätter und Brief, 1853–1871* (Berlin: Alexander Dunker Verlag, 1910), 243.

37. Richard Wagner, *Lettres à Judith Gautier* (Paris: Gallimard, 1964), 66.

38. Entry of September 20, 1881, in C. Wagner, *Tagebücher*, 2:796, September 20, 1881.

39. Thomas Mann, *Schopenhauer* (Stockholm: Bermann-Fischer Verlag, 1938), 26.

40. *Briefwechsel zwischen Wagner und Liszt*, 2:42.

41. Richard Wagner, "Beethoven," in *Gesammelte Schriften und Dichtungen von Richard Wagner* (Leipzig: E. W. Fritsch, 1888), 9:69.

42. *Richard Wagner an Mathilde Wesendonck*, 57, 79.

43. Friedrich Nietzsche, *Die Geburt der Tragödie aus dem Geiste der Musik* (Leipzig: E. W. Fritsch, 1872), 121.

44. *Richard Wagner an Mathilde Wesendonck*, 260.

45. *Richard Wagner: Gesammelte Schriften und Dichtungen*, 5:177.

46. See *The Diary of Richard Wagner: The Brown Book, 1865–1882*, ed. Joachim Bergfeld, trans. G. Bird (Cambridge: Cambridge University Press, 1980), 56.

47. Entry of June 27, 1880, in C. Wagner, *Tagebücher*, 2:556.

48. Wagner, *Mein Leben*, 523.

Chapter Three

1. Claude Debussy, *Pelléas et Mélisande: An Opera in Five Acts with French and English Texts; Vocal Score* (Boca Raton, FL: The Well-Tempered Press, n.d.), 67–69; cf. Maeterlinck, *Théâtre, Vol. 2* (Brussels: Paul Lacomblez, 1908), 27–28.

2. From Maeterlinck's preface to *Pélléas and Mélisande, Alladine and Palomides, Home*, trans. Richard Hovey (New York: Stone & Kimball, 1911). Available from Project Gutenberg, http://www.gutenberg.org/files/13329/13329-8.txt.

3. Maeterlinck, *Théâtre, Vol. 2*, 102–3.

4. Samuel Beckett, *Endgame: A Play in One Act, followed by "Act Without Words," a Mime for One Player* (United Kingdom: Grove Press, 1958).

5. Maeterlinck, *Théâtre, Vol. 2*, 183.

6. Maurice Maeterlinck, *Le trésor des humbles* (Paris: Société du Mercure de France, 1904), 182–84, 187.

7. Maurice Maeterlinck, *L'autre monde, ou Le cadran stellaire* (New York: Éditions de la Maison Française, 1942), 201.

8. Gertrude Stein, *Everybody's Autobiography* (Cambridge, MA: Exact Change, 1993), 292.

9. Maeterlinck, *Le temple enseveli* (Paris: Bibliothèque-Charpentier, 1908), 112–13.

10. Maeterlinck, *Le temple enseveli*,128–29.

11. Maeterlinck, *Le temple enseveli*, 158–59. See also Maurice Maeterlinck, *Théâtre, Vol 1* (Brussels: Paul Lacomblez, 1908), xiv.

12. Maeterlinck, *Le temple enseveli*, 126.

13. Maeterlinck, *Le temple enseveli*, 165–66.

14. Maeterlinck, *Joyzelle* (Paris: Librairie Charpentier & Fasquelle, 1903), 10.

15. Maeterlinck, *Théâtre, Vol. 1*, iv.

16. Maeterlinck, *L'autre monde* (1942), 43.

17. Maeterlinck, *L'autre monde* (1942), 96.

18. Maeterlinck, *La vie des abeilles* (Paris: Bibliothèque-Charpentier, 1905), 273.

19. Maeterlinck, *Théâtre, Vol. 1*, v.

20. Friedrich Nietzsche, *Jenseits von Gut und Böse* (1886; Hamburg: Diplomica Verlag, 2016), 81.

21. Maeterlinck, *Théâtre, Vol. 2*, 122–23.

22. Maeterlinck, *La vie des abeilles*, 130.

23. Vladimir Nabokov, *Strong Opinions* (New York: McGraw-Hill, 1973), 172.

24. W. H. Auden, *Collected Poems*, ed. Edward Mendelson (New York: Random House, 1976), 340.

25. Maurice Maeterlinck, *Les fiançailles: Féerie en cinq actes et onze tableaux* (Paris: Fasquelles, 1922), 36.

26. Maeterlinck, *Les fiançailles*, 177.

27. Maeterlinck, *Le temple enseveli*, 131.

28. Maeterlinck, *Théâtre, Vol. 2*, 85–86.

29. Maeterlinck, *Théâtre, Vol. 3* (Brussels: Paul Lacomblez, 1908), 43–44.

30. Maeterlinck, *Le trésor des humbles*, 68–69, 74.

31. Maeterlinck, *Le trésor des humbles*, 33.

32. Oscar Wilde, "The Decay of Lying" (1889), in *Complete Works* (London: Collins, 1973), 975.

33. Maurice Maeterlinck, *Avant le grand silence* (Paris: Bibliothèque-Charpentier, 1934), 29–34.

34. Maeterlinck, *Joyzelle*, 91.

35. A. Hoéré, "Entretiens inédits d'Ernest Guiraud et de Claude Debussy notés par Maurice Emmanuel (1889–1890)," in *Inédits sur Claude Debussy* (Paris: Les Publications techniques, Galerie Charpentier), 28–29.

36. Roger Nichols and Richard Langham Smith, *Claude Debussy: "Pelléas et Mélisande"* (Cambridge: Cambridge University Press, 1989), 184–85.

37. Letter to Guiraud, September 1890, in Hoérée, *Inédits sur Debussy*, 33, cited in Nichols and Smith, *Claude Debussy: "Pelléas et Mélisande,"* 193.

38. *La revue blanche*, May 15, 1901, in Claude Debussy, *Monsieur Croche et autres écrits*, ed. François Lesure (Paris: Gallimard, 1987), 41–42.

39. *Gil Blas*, June 1, 1903; Debussy, *Monsieur Croche et autres écrits*, 180.

40. Pierre Boulez, *Points de repère*, vol. 2, *Regards sur autrui*, ed. Jean-Jacques Nattiez and Sophie Galaise, Collection Musique/passé/present (Paris: Bourgois, 2005), 134.

41. Claude Debussy, "Deux lettres de Debussy à Ernest Chausson," *Revue musicale* 3, no. 7 (May 1, 1926): 87–88 (183–84).

42. This is also how Nichols and Smith hear it: see *Claude Debussy: Pelléas et Mélisande*, 91.

43. Claude Debussy, *La chute de la maison Usher*, vocal and piano transcription by Juan Allende-Blin (Paris: Société des Éditions Jobert, 1979), 29.

44. Maurice Maeterlinck, *Hothouses: Poems 1889*, trans. Richard Howard (Princeton, NJ: Princeton University Press, 2003), 64.

45. Maurice Maeterlinck, *L'oiseau bleu* (Paris: Librarie Charpentier & Fasquelle, 1912), 246.

46. *La revue blanche*, July 1, 1901, in *Monsieur Croche et autres écrits*, 52–53.

47. Igor Stravinsky and Robert Craft, *Dialogues* (Berkeley and Los Angeles: University of California Press, 1982), 75.

48. Claude Debussy, *Pelléas et Mélisande: An Opera in Five Acts with French and English Texts: Vocal Score*, 90–91; cf. Maeterlinck, *Théatre, Vol. 2*, 33–34.

49. Maeterlinck, *Théâtre, Vol. 2*, 56.

50. Debussy, *Monsieur Croche et autres écrits*, 310.

51. Score, 29.

52. *Claude Debussy: Lettres, 1884–1918*, ed. François Lesure (Paris: Hermann, 1980), 55.

53. *Gil Blas*, April 6, 1903, in Debussy, *Monsieur Croche et autres écrits*, 143–44.

54. Debussy, *Lettres*, 90.

55. Maeterlinck, *Théâtre, Vol. 2*, 48.

56. This is cited from *Melisande's Song of "Pelleas et Melisande"* (Paris: J. Hamelle, n.d.), from which the following score quotation is also taken.

57. Maeterlinck, *Théâtre, Vol. 3*, 144–45.

58. A full account of these displacements can be found in Anya Suschitzky's illuminating and profound article "*Ariane et Barbe-Bleue*: Dukas, the Light and the Well," *Cambridge Opera Journal* 9, no. 2 (July 1997): 150ff.

59. Olivier Messiaen, "Ariane et Barbe-Bleue," in "Paul Dukas," special issue of *La revue musicale* (May–June 1936): 84.

60. Maeterlinck, *Théâtre, Vol. 3*, 164.

61. Paul Dukas, *Les écrits de Paul Dukas sur la musique* (Paris: Société d'Éditions françaises & internationales, 1948), 623.

Chapter Four

1. Arthur Rimbaud, *Collected Poems*, ed. Oliver Bernard (New York: Penguin, 1962), 9.

2. Rimbaud, *Collected Poems*, 7.

3. Rimbaud, *Collected Poems*, 253.

4. Arthur Rimbaud, *Illuminations*, trans. John Ashbery (New York: Norton, 2011), 65.

5. Rimbaud, *Collected Poems*, 256.

6. Rimbaud, *Illuminations*, trans. Ashbery, 73.

7. Rimbaud, *Collected Poems*, 274.

8. Rimbaud, *Illuminations*, trans. Ashbery, 115.

9. Rimbaud, *Collected Poems*, 234.

10. Rimbaud, *Illuminations*, trans. Ashbery, 21.

11. Rimbaud, *Collected Poems*, 244.

12. Rimbaud, *Illuminations*, trans. Ashbery, 43.

13. Rimbaud, *Collected Poems*, 261.

14. Rimbaud, *Illuminations*, trans. Ashbery, 83.

15. Rimbaud, *Collected Poems*, 243.

16. Rimbaud, *Illuminations*, trans. Ashbery, 37, 39.

17. Samuel Taylor Coleridge, *Biographia Literaria*, vol. 1 (London: Rest Fenner, 1817), 296.

18. Thomas Otway, *Venice Preserv'd* (1682), 5:369.

19. T. E. Hulme, "Romanticism and Classicism" (1911–12), in *Speculations: Essays on Humanism and the Philosophy of Art*, ed. Herbert Read (New York: Harcourt, Brace, 1924), 113–40.

20. Rimbaud, *Collected Poems*, 258.

21. Rimbaud, *Illuminations*, trans. Ashbery, 77.

22. Rimbaud, *Collected Poems*, 278–79.

23. Rimbaud, *Illuminations*, trans. Ashbery, 141.

24. Rimbaud, *Collected Poems*, 259–60.

25. Rimbaud, *Illuminations*, trans. Ashbery, 79.

26. Rimbaud, *Collected Poems*, 272.

27. Rimbaud, *Illuminations*, trans. Ashbery, 111.

28. Rimbaud, *Collected Poems*, 262–64.

29. Rimbaud, *Illuminations*, trans. Ashbery, 91.

30. Rimbaud, *Collected Poems*, 295–98.

31. Rimbaud, *Illuminations*, trans. Ashbery, 123.

32. Rimbaud, *Collected Poems*, 283.

33. Rimbaud, *Illuminations*, trans. Ashbery, 149.

34. William Shakespeare, *A Midsummer Night's Dream*, in *The Riverside Shakespeare* (Boston: Houghton Mifflin, 1974), act 3, scene 1. All Shakespeare quotations are from this edition.

35. Rimbaud, *Collected Poems*, 235–39.

36. Rimbaud, *Illuminations*, trans. Ashbery, 27, 29.

37. Rimbaud, *Collected Poems*, 245–46.

38. Rimbaud, *Illuminations*, trans. Ashbery, 45.

39. Rimbaud, *Collected Poems*, 255.

40. Rimbaud, *Illuminations*, trans. Ashbery, 73.

41. Rimbaud, *Collected Poems*, 275–76.

42. Rimbaud, *Illuminations*, trans. Ashbery, 119.

43. Samuel Beckett, *Collected Poems in English and French* (New York: Grove, 1977), 12.

44. William Shakespeare, *The Riverside Shakespeare* (Boston: Houghton Mifflin, 1974).

45. Antonin Artaud, "Sur le théâtre balinais," in *Le théâtre et son double* (Paris: Gallimard, 1938), 86.

46. Benjamin Britten, *Letters from a Life*, vol. 2, *1939–1945* (London: Faber & Faber, 2011), Letter 215.

47. Rimbaud, *Illuminations*, trans. Ashbery, 39.

48. Rimbaud, *Collected Poems*, 242.

49. Rimbaud, *Illuminations*, trans. Ashbery, 39.

50. Rimbaud, *Collected Poems*, 274.

51. Rimbaud, *Illuminations*, trans. Ashbery, 115, 117.

52. Rimbaud, *Collected Poems*, 274.

53. Jamie James, *Rimbaud in Java: The Lost Voyage* (Singapore: Éditions Didier Millet, 2011).

54. Theodor Adorno, *Kulturkritik und Gesellschaft* (Frankfurt: Suhrkamp, 1977), 30.

55. *Britten on Music*, ed. Paul Francis Kildea (Oxford: Oxford University Press, 2003), 63.

56. Wilfred Owen, "The Parable of the Old Man and the Young," in *The Collected Poems of Wilfred Owen*, ed. with an introduction and notes by C. Day Lewis (New York: New Directions, 1965), 43.

57. Wilfred Owen, "A Soldier's Dream," in *Collected Poems*, 84.

58. Wilfred Owen, "Le Christianisme," in *Collected Poems*, 83.

59. Wilfred Owen, "S.I.W.," in *Collected Poems*, 74–75.

60. Wilfred Owen, "Dulce et Decorum Est," in *Collected Poems*, 55–56.

61. Wilfred Owen, "Sonnet," in *Collected Poems*, 85.

62. Wilfred Owen, "Anthem for Doomed Youth," in *Collected Poems*, 44–45.

63. Wilfred Owen, "Strange Meeting," in *Collected Poems*, 35–36.

Chapter Five

1. Claude Lévi-Strauss, *The Savage Mind* (1962; Chicago: University of Chicago Press, 1986), 29–30.

2. *New Yorker*, May 6, 1967, 162.

3. Namely *Arnold Schönberg* (1912), ed. Alban Berg et al., reprinted in *Arnold Schoenberg, Wassily Kandinsky: Letters, Pictures and Documents*, trans. John C. Crawford (London: Faber & Faber, 1986), 125.

4. Theodor Adorno, *Philosophie der neuen Musik* (Frankfurt: Europäische Verlagsanstalt, 1966), 43.

5. Peter Gay, ed., *The Freud Reader* (New York: W. W. Norton, 1995), 75.

6. This, and all subsequent quotations from Schoenberg's libretti, are from the website of the Arnold Schoenberg Center, https://www.schoenberg.at/index.php/de/schoenberg/kompositionen.

7. Arnold Schoenberg, *Style and Idea*, ed. Leonard Stein, trans. Leo Black (Berkeley and Los Angeles: University of California Press, 1984), 105.

8. Charles Rosen, *Arnold Schoenberg* (New York: Viking, 1975), 43.

9. Schoenberg, *Style and Idea*, 254.

10. *The Diaries of Franz Kafka: 1914–1923*, ed. Max Brod, trans. Martin Greenberg (New York: Schocken, 1974), 192.

11. Willi Reich, *Schoenberg: A Critical Biography* (London: Longman, 1971), 219.

12. *Schoenberg Berg Webern: The String Quartets: A Documentary Study*, ed. Ursula v. Rauchhaupt, notes to compact disc DG 2720 029, 52.

13. Schoenberg, *Style and Idea*, 215.

14. Theodor Adorno, *Philosophy of Modern Music*, trans. Anne G. Mitchell and Wesley V. Blomster (New York: Seabury Press, 1977), 114.

15. Schoenberg, *Style and Idea*, 240.

16. Wassily Kandinsky, *Concerning the Spiritual in Art*, trans. M. T. H. Sadler (New York: Dover, 1977), 16–17.

17. *Arnold Schoenberg, Wassily Kandinsky: Letters, Pictures and Documents*, 54–55.

18. *Arnold Schoenberg, Wassily Kandinsky*, 57.

19. Schoenberg, *Style and Idea*, 266.

20. Schoenberg, *Style and Idea*, 138.

21. Schoenberg, *Style and Idea*, 129.

22. Adorno, *Philosophie der neuen Musik*, 71.

23. Schoenberg, *Style and Idea*, 223.

24. Adorno, *Philosophie der neuen Musik*, 96.

25. Willi Reich, *Schoenberg: A Critical Biography*, 135.

26. Thomas Mann, *Doktor Faustus* (Frankfurt am Main: Fischer Taschenbuch Verlag, 1973), 487–88.

27. Schoenberg, *Style and Idea*, 454.

28. Arnold Schoenberg, *Letters*, ed. Erwin Stein, trans. Eithne Wilkins and Ernst Kaiser (Berkeley: University of California Press, 1987), 288.

29. Schoenberg, *Letters*, 172.

30. Schoenberg, *Style and Idea*, 464.

31. Schoenberg, *Style and Idea*, 470.

32. Mann, *Doktor Faustus*, 55.

33. Mann, *Doktor Faustus*, 490.

34. W. H. Auden, *The Dyer's Hand* (New York: Random House, 1962), 458.

35. Auden, *The Dyer's Hand*, 71.

36. Lévi-Strauss, *The Savage Mind*, 30.

37. W. H. Auden, *Collected Longer Poems* (New York: Random House, 1966), 247–48.

38. Auden, *Collected Longer Poems*, 248–49.

39. For a photograph of Kiselewski's Moses, see https://www.kiselewskisculpture.com/1960s.

40. Elliott Gyger, personal communication.

41. Arnold Schoenberg, *Theory of Harmony*, trans. Roy E. Carter (Berkeley and Los Angeles: University of California Press, 1983), 313.

42. *Texte* (1926), trans. Michael Graubart, 25, cited by Regina Busch in "On the Horizontal and Vertical Presentation of Musical Ideas and on Musical Space (I)," *Tempo: A Quarterly Review of Modern Music* 154 (1985): 2–10.

Chapter Six

1. Igor Stravinsky, *An Autobiography* (New York: W. W. Norton, 1962), 53–54. This is an anonymous translation of *Chroniques de ma vie* (1934).

2. Igor Stravinsky and Robert Craft, *Expositions and Developments* (Berkeley and Los Angeles: University of California Press, 1981), 101.

3. Igor Stravinsky and Robert Craft, *Conversations with Igor Stravinsky* (Berkeley and Los Angeles: University of California Press, 1980), 19.

4. Stravinsky and Craft, *Dialogues*, 63.

5. Igor Stravinsky and Robert Craft, *Memories and Commentaries* (Berkeley and Los Angeles: University of California Press, 1981), 95.

6. Stravinsky and Craft, *Dialogues*, 46.

7. Igor Stravinsky and Robert Craft, *Themes and Conclusions* (Berkeley and Los Angeles: University of California Press, 1982), 147.

8. Stravinsky and Craft, *Themes and Conclusions*, 32.

9. Stravinsky and Craft, *Themes and Conclusions*, 92.

10. "Essay on the Puppet Theater," trans. Eugene Jolas, *Partisan Review* 14 (1947): 57–62.

11. "The Sandman," in *Tales of E. T. A. Hoffmann*, ed. and trans. Leonard J. Kent and Elizabeth C. Knight, illust. Jacob Landau (Chicago: University of Chicago Press, 1969), 1:158.

12. Stravinsky and Craft, *Expositions and Developments*, 128.

13. Vera Stravinsky and Robert Craft, *Stravinsky in Pictures and Documents* (New York: Simon & Schuster, 1978), 66.

14. V. Stravinsky and Craft, *Stravinsky in Pictures and Documents*, 67.

15. Stravinsky and Craft, *Conversations*, 48.

16. Stravinsky and Craft, *Memories and Commentaries*, 33–34.

17. Stravinsky and Craft, *Memories and Commentaries*, 34.

18. Stravinsky and Craft, *Themes and Conclusions*, 188.
19. Stravinsky and Craft, *Conversations*, 17–18.
20. V. Stravinsky and Craft, *Stravinsky in Pictures and Documents*, 75.
21. V. Stravinsky and Craft, *Stravinsky in Pictures and Documents*, 77.
22. V. Stravinsky and Craft, *Stravinsky in Pictures and Documents*, 95.
23. V. Stravinsky and Craft, *Stravinsky in Pictures and Documents*, 525.
24. Stravinsky and Craft, *Expositions and Developments*, 146.
25. Stravinsky, *An Autobiography*, 31.
26. Stravinsky and Craft, *Expositions and Developments*, 143.
27. "London Letter," *The Dial*, September 1921.
28. Minna Lederman, ed., *Stravinsky in the Theatre* (New York: Da Capo Press, 1975), 18.
29. Thomas Pynchon, *V.* (New York: Bantam Books, 1968), 385.
30. David Simpson, *Fetishism and Imagination* (Baltimore, MD: Johns Hopkins University Press, 1982), 13.
31. V. Stravinsky and Craft, *Stravinsky in Pictures and Documents*, 358.
32. Stravinsky, *An Autobiography*, 51.
33. V. Stravinsky and Craft, *Stravinsky in Pictures and Documents*, 116.
34. V. Stravinsky and Craft, *Stravinsky in Pictures and Documents*, 118.
35. Stravinsky and Craft, *Themes and Conclusions*, 148.
36. Stravinsky and Craft, *Expositions and Developments*, 30.
37. Igor Stravinsky, *Selected Correspondence*, vol. 2, ed. Robert Craft (New York: Knopf, 1984).
38. Igor Stravinsky, *Poetics of Music in Six Lessons*, preface George A. Seferis, trans. Arthur Knodel (Cambridge, MA: Harvard University Press, 1970), 23.
39. Stravinsky and Craft, *Dialogues*, 69–70.
40. Stravinsky and Craft, *Conversations*, 66.
41. Stravinsky and Craft, *Themes and Conclusions*, 117.
42. Stravinsky and Craft, *Themes and Conclusions*, 131.
43. Stravinsky, *An Autobiography*, 101.
44. V. Stravinsky and Craft, *Stravinsky in Pictures and Documents*, 213.
45. Stravinsky and Craft, *Expositions and Developments*, 70.
46. V. Stravinsky and Craft, *Stravinsky in Pictures and Documents*, 622.
47. V. Stravinsky and Craft, *Stravinsky in Pictures and Documents*, 213.
48. Stravinsky and Craft, *Expositions and Developments*, 115.
49. Richard Taruskin, *Stravinsky and the Russian Traditions: A Biography of the Works through "Mavra,"* vol. 1 (Berkeley and Los Angeles: University of California Press, 1996), 840.
50. Stravinsky and Craft, *Expositions and Developments*, 117.
51. V. Stravinsky and Craft, *Stravinsky in Pictures and Documents*, 122.
52. V. Stravinsky and Craft, *Stravinsky in Pictures and Documents*, 186.
53. Stravinsky and Craft, *Expositions and Developments*, 47.
54. Stravinsky and Craft, *Expositions and Developments*, 121.
55. Stravinsky and Craft, *Expositions and Developments*, 116.
56. Stravinsky and Craft, *Expositions and Developments*, 121.
57. Taruskin, *Stravinsky and the Russian Traditions* 2:1224.

58. Stravinsky and Craft, *Themes and Conclusions*, 290.
59. Stravinsky and Craft, *Dialogues*, 46.
60. Stravinsky, *An Autobiography*, 125.
61. Stravinsky and Craft, *Dialogues*, 30–31.
62. Stravinsky and Craft, *Dialogues*, 27.
63. Stravinsky and Craft, *Dialogues*, 24.
64. Stravinsky and Craft, *Dialogues*, 23.
65. Stravinsky and Craft, *Dialogues*, 23.
66. V. Stravinsky and Craft, *Stravinsky in Pictures and Documents*, p. 418.
67. Stravinsky and Craft, *Dialogues*, 24.
68. Stravinsky and Craft, *Dialogues*, 24.
69. László Somfai, "Sprache, Wort und Phonem im vokalen Spätwerk Strawinskys," from R. Stephan, ed., *Über Musik und Sprache* (Mainz: Schott, 1974), 34.
70. "'. . . Stille anonyme Formeln einer entlegenen Zeit . . .': Analytische Bemerkungen zu Vertonungsprinzipien Igor Strawinskys im 'Ödipus Rex,'" in *Arbeitsheft 35: Musikalische Analyse in der Diskussion: Gespräche, Analysen, Dokumentation*, ed. Mathias Hansen (Berlin: Akademie der Künste der Deutschen Demokratischen Republik, 1982), 61.
71. "'. . . Stille anonyme Formeln einer entlegenen Zeit . . . ,'" 54.
72. "'. . . Stille anonyme Formeln einer entlegenen Zeit . . . ,'" 62.
73. Stravinsky and Craft, *Dialogues*, 28.
74. V. Stravinsky and Craft, *Stravinsky in Pictures and Documents*, 205.
75. Stravinsky, *An Autobiography*, 128.
76. Stravinsky, *Selected Correspondence*, 2:508.
77. Stravinsky and Craft, *Dialogues*, 62.
78. Stravinsky and Craft, *Conversations*, 78.
79. Stravinsky, *An Autobiography*, 3–4.
80. Stravinsky and Craft, *Dialogues*, 22.
81. Stravinsky and Craft, *Themes and Conclusions*, 88–89.
82. Stravinsky and Craft, *Conversations*, 35.
83. Stravinsky and Craft, *Themes and Conclusions*, 146.
84. V. Stravinsky and Craft, *Stravinsky in Pictures and Documents*, 133.
85. Stravinsky and Craft, *Memories and Commentaries*, 150.
86. Stravinsky and Craft, *Conversations*, 120.
87. Stravinsky and Craft, *Dialogues*, 33.
88. Stravinsky, *An Autobiography*, 134.
89. Stravinsky and Craft, *Dialogues*, 33.
90. Stravinsky, *An Autobiography*, 171.
91. V. Stravinsky and Craft, *Stravinsky in Pictures and Documents*, 381.
92. Stravinsky, *An Autobiography*, 100.
93. Stravinsky and Craft, *Memories and Commentaries*, 157.
94. Stravinsky and Craft, *Memories and Commentaries*, 167–76.
95. V. Stravinsky and Craft, *Stravinsky in Pictures and Documents*, 540.
96. W. H. Auden, *The Dyer's Hand and Other Essays* (New York: Random House, 1962), 47–48.

97. Auden, *The Dyer's Hand*, 61.

98. W. H. Auden, *Collected Poems*, ed. Edward Mendelson (New York: Random House, 1976), 330.

99. Gabriel Josipovici, in Paul Griffiths, *Igor Stravinsky: The Rake's Progress* (Cambridge: Cambridge University Press, 1982), 73.

100. Auden, *The Dyer's Hand*, 172.

101. Auden, *The Dyer's Hand*, 116.

102. Auden, *The Dyer's Hand*, 115.

103. Auden, *The Dyer's Hand*, 118.

104. Auden, *The Dyer's Hand*, 338.

105. Auden, *Collected Poems*, 214.

106. Stravinsky and Craft, *Memories and Commentaries*, 168.

107. Auden, *Collected Poems*, 218.

108. James Merrill, *The Changing Light at Sandover* (New York: Atheneum, 1983), 485.

109. V. Stravinsky and Craft, *Stravinsky in Pictures and Documents*, 72.

110. Griffiths, *Igor Stravinsky*, 96; see also a review by David Hamilton in *Opus*, October 1985, 25.

111. Auden, *Collected Poems*, 207.

112. T. S. Eliot, *Collected Poems, 1909–1962* (New York: Harcourt Brace, 1963), 207.

113. Stravinsky and Craft, *Themes and Conclusions*, 77.

114. Auden, *Collected Poems*, 446.

115. Stravinsky and Craft, *Dialogues*, 29.

116. Humphrey Carpenter, *W. H. Auden: A Biography* (Boston: Houghton Mifflin, 1981), 263, 313.

117. Auden, *Collected Poems*, 247.

118. W. H. Auden, *Forewords and Afterwords* (New York: Random House, 1973), 25.

119. Auden, *The Dyer's Hand*, 119.

120. Stravinsky and Craft, *Memories and Commentaries*, 157.

121. Auden, *Collected Poems*, 248.

122. W. H. Auden, *The English Auden: Poems, Essays, and Dramatic Writings, 1927–1939*, ed. Edward Mendelson (New York: Random House, 1977), 298.

123. Auden, *Collected Poems*, 279.

124. V. Stravinsky and Craft, *Stravinsky in Pictures and Documents*, 648.

125. Auden, *Forewords and Afterwords*, 453.

126. Auden, *Forewords and Afterwords*, 25.

127. Auden, *Forewords and Afterwords*, 453.

128. Auden, *The Dyer's Hand*, 118–19.

129. Stravinsky and Craft, *Themes and Conclusions*, 45.

130. Stravinsky and Craft, *Expositions and Developments*, 124.

131. Stravinsky and Craft, *Themes and Conclusions*, 33.

132. Griffiths, *Igor Stravinsky*, 99.

133. Stravinsky and Craft, *Memories and Commentaries*, 161.

134. Auden, *Collected Poems*, 248.

135. Stravinsky and Craft, *Memories and Commentaries*, 155.

136. Auden, *Collected Poems*, 213.

137. Auden, *Collected Poems*, 150.

138. Stravinsky and Craft, *Themes and Conclusions*, 61.

139. Stravinsky and Craft, *Themes and Conclusions*, 66.

140. Stravinsky and Craft, *Dialogues*, 24.

141. Stravinsky, *Selected Correspondence* 2:503.

142. *De Possest* 74, in Jasper Hopkins, *A Concise Introduction to the Philosophy of Nicholas of Cusa* (Minneapolis: University of Minnesota Press, 1978), 151, 153.

143. Stravinsky and Craft, *Dialogues*, 73.

144. W. B. Yeats, *A Vision* (New York: Macmillan, 1956), 284.

INDEX

Page numbers in italics refer to figures.